THE PRINCETON REVIEW

STUDENT ACCESS
GUIDE TO

THE
BEST
MEDICAL
SCHOOLS

1996 Edition

Books in The Princeton Review Series

Cracking the ACT
Cracking the ACT with Sample Tests on Computer Disk
Cracking the GED
Cracking the GMAT
Cracking the GMAT with Sample Tests on Computer Disk
Cracking the GRE
Cracking the GRE with Sample Tests on Computer Disk
Cracking the GRE Psychology Subject Test
Cracking the LSAT
Cracking the LSAT with Sample Tests on Computer Disk
Cracking the MCAT
Cracking the MCAT with Sample Tests on Computer Disk
Cracking the SAT and PSAT
Cracking the SAT and PSAT with Sample Tests on Computer Disk
Cracking the SAT II: Biology Subject Test
Cracking the SAT II: Chemistry Subject Test
Cracking the SAT II: English Subject Tests
Cracking the SAT II: French Subject Test
Cracking the SAT II: History Subject Tests
Cracking the SAT II: Math Subject Tests
Cracking the SAT II: Physics Subject Test
Cracking the SAT II: Spanish Subject Test
Cracking the TOEFL with Audiocassette

SAT Math Workout
SAT Verbal Workout

Don't Be a Chump!
How to Survive Without Your Parents' Money
Trashproof Resumes

Grammar Smart
Math Smart
Reading Smart
Study Smart
Word Smart: Building an Educated Vocabulary
Word Smart II: How to Build a More Educated Vocabulary
Writing Smart

Grammar Smart Junior
Math Smart Junior
Word Smart Junior
Writing Smart Junior

Student Access Guide to America's Top Internships
Student Access Guide to College Admissions
Student Access Guide to the Best Business Schools
Student Access Guide to the Best Law Schools
Student Access Guide to the Best Medical Schools
Student Access Guide to the Best 309 Colleges
Student Access Guide to Paying for College
Student Access Guide to Visiting College Campuses
Student Access Guide: The Big Book of Colleges
Student Access Guide: The Internship Bible

Also available on cassette from Living Language

Grammar Smart
Word Smart
Word Smart II

THE **PRINCETON** REVIEW

STUDENT ACCESS
GUIDE TO

THE
BEST
MEDICAL
SCHOOLS

By Andrea Nagy

Random House, Inc.
New York 1995

1996 Edition

ISSN 1067-2176
ISBN 0-679-76149-7

Manufactured in the United States of America on acid-free paper

9 8 7 6 5 4 3 2

Revised Edition

FOREWORD

For the past ten years, The Princeton Review has offered preparatory courses and tutoring for standardized tests like the SAT, MCAT, LSAT, GRE, and GMAT. Over 60,000 students took our courses last year, and hundreds of thousands have bought our books. At the center of our approach is helping students tear away the shroud of mystery that has surrounded these entrance exams for so many years. We show them how the tests are structured, what they're designed to measure, who writes them—and how to use all this knowledge to their advantage. Students pay to take these exams, after all. And The Princeton Review has long been an advocate of a student's right to be an informed consumer.

Students are also the consumers of education. Before investing in a graduate or undergraduate degree, they have both a right and an obligation to gather as much information as they can. Much of this information can be provided by the schools themselves. However, we believe it's also important to consult fellow students. It was for this reason that The Princeton Review decided to create its Student Access series of guides to graduate and undergraduate programs. These books include *Student Access Guide to the Best 309 Colleges, Student Access Guide to the Best Business Schools, Student Access Guide to the Best Law Schools,* and *Student Access Guide to the Best Medical Schools.*

Our approach with these guides was to provide not only basic admissions, demographic, and financial data, but to go to the students themselves at each school and ask for their evaluations of their programs. We accomplished this by visiting each campus and asking students to answer multiple-choice questions on subjects ranging from the school's academics to the quality of life. We asked them to tell us what other schools they had applied to. Finally, we asked students for their comments. We wanted you to hear from as many of your potential future classmates and colleagues as possible, to get a real sense of how satisfied they were with their choices.

Our efforts on undergraduate, law, and business schools campuses were highly successful. We spoke with over 70,000 students and were able to provide readers with valuable information on the programs we covered. Our efforts to survey U.S.

medical schools, on the other hand, brought us markedly different results. Of the 126 medical schools certified by the Association of American Medical Colleges (AAMC), only two-thirds allowed us to speak with their students. We would like to thank those schools for helping us bring you much of the information in this book. Their participation gave us both broad and specific data that will be invaluable to anyone considering going into the medical field. The entries in this book for each of these schools contains a "Student Life" section, which summarizes the results of our student survey at that school.

When we asked the schools that didn't participate in our project the reason for their reluctance to allow us to set up a table or stand outside their buildings for a couple of hours one day, many schools offered no explanation. Some told us that filling out our (one-page, multiple-choice) questionnaire would be unduly burdensome to their students. Most, however, cited an AAMC memorandum, sent to all accredited medical schools, that specifically mentioned our project and advised that the AAMC did not endorse the project and that all our requests for information should be directed to the AAMC itself. We were curious about this memo, so we decided to get a copy for ourselves.

The memo expressed concern "about the burden of completing the questionnaires, the disposition and interpretation of the information once it was provided, and the possible effect the reporting burden would have on the completion of AAMC-related surveys" and advised the schools that they "should feel no obligation to complete these surveys." (The Princeton Review wasn't the only organization mentioned in the memo, by the way; we were paired with a stridently right-wing anti-abortion group that had been mailing literature to students.)

We're disappointed that we couldn't provide you with student data from those schools that used this memo as a basis for refusing our request for information. On the other hand, this memo, and the reaction medical schools had to it, did bring up some interesting issues. First, are these medical schools hiding something? We couldn't figure it out. Maybe you can. But it would seem the medical profession is already mysterious enough to most people. Obscuring the facts surrounding the training of future physicians only creates further mistrust in an era in which doctors' practices are increasingly scrutinized and criticized.

Second, the AAMC is the *de facto* governing body of American medical schools. Medical School Admissions Requirements, published annually by the AAMC, was—until this book was published—the only book of its kind. Based on their reaction to our book research, it would seem that the AAMC is very interested in maintaining its monopoly on information about medical school. We at The Princeton Review think you should be privy to what current students have to say about their programs, their teachers, and their schools in general—especially since visiting a bunch of campuses in person is difficult for most students. That's why we created *The Best Medical Schools*—to provide the next best thing to questioning students yourself.

Despite the obstacles, we have given you the best medical school guide available. *The Student Access Guide to the Best Medical Schools* provides information that can be found in no other publication. We hope you find it a useful tool, and wish you good luck as you pursue your career in medicine!

If you have any questions, comments, or suggestions, please e-mail your insights to us over the Internet at Books@review.com. We appreciate your input and want to make our books as useful to you as they can be.

ACKNOWLEDGMENTS

To the editors, researchers, pagemakers, and friends who asked, "When the hell are you going to finish that book?"—I can finally reply, with immeasurable relief, "IT'S DONE!" But I would never have finished without the tireless efforts and good nature of my editor and friend, Cynthia Brantley, and her assistant, the ever-cheerful, fabulous Lee Elliott. My undying gratitude goes to both of them for knowing when to prod, when to lay off, and—when all else failed—when to send presents.

Much credit also goes to Marcia Lerner for her rewrites, pep talks, and, most of all, her patience when we were all going crazy and needed her most. I hope to someday be able to thank her face-to-face. Thanks also to Chris Kensler, for his copyediting expertise.

Special thanks also must go to the thousands of med students and scores of admissions officers who supplied the information in this book and to the people who made sense out of all their responses: Andrew Dunn, Bruce McAmis, Joseph Keith, Bruno Butler, Joe Pelletier and Thane Thomsen. Julian Ham, Maria Quinlan, Meher Khambata and the rest of the Student Access pagemaking crew should get credit for working their magic to make these pages look so good.

The financial aid chapter could never have been done without the help of the fine folks at the Loyola and Northwestern financial aid offices. And to a certain person in Houston who asked to remain nameless until he was accepted into med school—I could never have completed the Texas profiles without your help, and I know you will someday be a fine doctor and scientist.

Thanks to Alicia, John, Mark, Bruce, and Steve for giving me the chance to do this project. Jae, Rick, and the rest of the folks in the Chicago office have my undying gratitude for doing research, and, more importantly, just being great friends. And thanks to Nedda, my partner in procrastination, for keeping me sane.

To Phil and the rest of my family and friends—without your love and support I'd never have been able to get through the deadlines, late nights, and general havoc this book wrought. And, finally, to Gram, whose journey through this life ended the same day I typed the final words of this book, thanks for everything.

How to Use This Book

How This Book Is Organized

The information for each school listed in this book is broken down into five sections of text (a short overview, followed by four sections on academics, student life, admissions, and financial aid, respectively). Also, at the end of each school listing is a column of admissions statistics, financial facts, hits and misses lists, and graphs.

Here's what you will find in the various sections of each school listing:

Overview

A brief description of how the school is generally characterized. Here also may appear statements concerning the school's self-perception, including comments we solicited directly from the school's medical students.

Academics

Concerned mostly with curriculum and academic facilities, this section, whenever possible, also contains comments from students on how they feel about their teachers, their classes, and the program in general.

Student Life

At every medical school we were permitted to survey, we asked the students to tell us what life is like both on campus and off. Competitiveness, safety, and cost of living are just some of the issues dealt with in this section. Here is where you will find students reflecting on their life in medical school.

Admissions

What the school is looking for in its prospective students. Also listed in this section are special programs for members of under-represented minorities, as well as a brief description of the school's transfer policy.

Financial Aid

What kind of resources does the school offer to ease the financial burden of medical school? This section will tell you.

Admissions Facts

The shaded column of statistics and graphs at the end of each school listing contains the following information:

■ *Demographics*

Percent of men, percent of women, and percent of minorities of the class entering in 1993.

■ *Deadline & Notification Dates*

AMCAS: Whether or not the school participates in The American Medical College Application Service.

Regular Application: The date by which all application materials must be received by the school.

Regular Notification: The date by which prospective students will be notified of the school's decision concerning admission.

Early Decision Application: The deadline for submission of application materials under the Early Decision plan.

Early Decision Notification: The date by which prospective students who have applied under the Early Decision plan will be notified of the school's decision.

■ *# of Applicants*

Graphically illustrates the total number of people who applied to the school in 1993, along with the number of state residents and the number of non-residents who applied.

■ *# of Applicants Interviewed*

Graphically illustrates the number of people who interviewed at the school in 1993. Also broken down in terms of state residency.

■ *# of Students Matriculating*

Graphically represents the number of people who applied who actually entered the school as first year medical students in 1993. The figures for in-state and out-of-state tell you the number of residents and non-residents, respectively, who matriculated, in relation to the number of residents and non-residents who applied.

First Year Statistics

■ *Average GPA*

Overall undergraduate grade point average of the students who matriculated in 1993. Wherever possible, this figure is broken down to reflect the grade point average of these students in science courses and non-science courses, respectively.

■ *Average MCAT*

Average MCAT scores of the students who matriculated in 1993, broken down into the following areas: Biology, Verbal, Physical Science, and Essay.

Financial Facts

■ *Tuition and Fees*

Most recent yearly tuition figures available for both state residents and non-residents, as well as estimated yearly costs of both on-campus and off-campus housing when available.

■ *Financial Aid*

Percentage of medical students at the school receiving some sort of financial aid; whether the school offers scholarships based on merit.

■ *Hits and Misses*

A listing of both the school's strong points and weak points, the strong points falling in the 'hits' column and the weak points falling in the 'misses' column. These lists are based solely on students' opinions of their schools and appear only with the schools we were allowed to survey.

■*Tuition Overview*

Relates the school's tuition for both residents and non-residents (where applicable) to the average tuition figures for all the medical schools in the nation.

CONTENTS

THE **PRINCETON** REVIEW

STUDENT ACCESS
GUIDE TO

THE
BEST
MEDICAL
SCHOOLS

1996 Edition

CHAPTER ONE

Applying to Medical School

From the mid 1980s to the early 1990s, the number of med school applications hit an all time low. Although no one is sure exactly why this happened, some speculate that would-be doctors gave up their dreams of healing for the get-rich-quick lure of Wall Street. But now, with investment bankers in the news for doing time instead of deals, med school applications are once again on the rise and now approach the peak levels of the early 1980s. What this means to you, as a potential med school applicant, is that a traditionally competitive admissions process is going to be even more selective. But don't lose heart. Even though about half of each year's applicants don't find a place in any of the med schools in this book, half do. And if you have good undergraduate grades and decent MCAT scores, have taken courses that show you can hack med school work, choose wisely the schools you apply to, and take the time to make sure that your applications show how great a candidate you really are, your chances of getting in should be much better than fifty percent. So relax and get ready to work. The first thing you need to know is how the admissions process works.

What Can You Expect?

The Admissions Process in a Nutshell

Most U.S. medical schools use a common application process that is administered by AMCAS, a division of the American Association of Medical Schools. Currently, only a handful of the 126 U.S. medical schools don't use the AMCAS application, so chances are good that at least one school you apply to will require it. You can obtain an AMCAS application from your premedical advisor, or call AMCAS at (202) 828-0600 to request one. AMCAS recommends that while you're waiting for the application, you begin retrieving and compiling the data necessary to complete your application. After you've requested your AMCAS application, you should also send for unofficial transcripts from any undergraduate institutions where you took classes. Inspect the transcripts carefully to make sure they don't contain any errors since you'll have to send official (straight from the school) copies to AMCAS when you submit your application. Official transcripts may be sent to AMCAS before you send the remainder of the application, but no transcripts will be accepted before March 15.

The AMCAS application provides medical schools with enough information to make an initial screening; it includes a modified undergraduate transcript, science and overall GPAs, MCAT scores, information about extracurricular activities, and a short personal comment. You may submit your completed application, with the appropriate fee, no earlier than June 15. The final deadline depends on which schools you apply to, but can be as early as the beginning of October or as late as mid-January. Regardless of these deadlines, however, admissions officers recommend you submit your application as early as possible. Early decision applicants must have all materials to AMCAS by August 1. Procrastinators take note: AMCAS is serious about its deadlines; if an application is late, you'll get it back.

Schools that participate in AMCAS generally use the AMCAS application to make a preliminary screening of candidates; those that don't participate usually have an initial application of their own. On the basis of the screening of the first application, the Committee will either reject you or send you a supplementary application. The supplementary application asks for more detailed information and usually requires you to write essays, some of which will ask you why you've chosen the medical field. Be prepared to answer this question throughout the application process because it comes up over and over on applications and in interviews. Receiving a supplementary application is a good sign, but don't become overconfident if you receive one. Some schools send supplementary applications to all candidates, and the rumor among recent applicants is that many underqualified students are asked to submit these applications so that additional fees may be collected.

When you receive a supplementary application, complete and return it immediately. Many schools have a rolling admissions policy in which admissions committees consider and make a decision on each application as it comes in. In this process, admission stops once enough qualified applicants are accepted and matriculated, so it is in your best interest to apply as early as possible. Schools that don't have a rolling admissions policy set a deadline by which date all materials, including recommendations, must be received. Don't be late—like AMCAS, most schools will return any application that arrives after the deadline.

After the admissions committee reviews your supplementary application, they will do one of three things: reject you, invite you to the campus for an interview, or hold your application until after the first round of interviews. Final decisions are usually made after the interview. Again, there are three possible outcomes: you can be rejected, accepted, or put on a wait list.

At this point, getting into med school can seem to take as much effort as staying in. By the time you're finished with the process, you will have spent nearly a year and hundreds, even thousands, of dollars applying to med school. Because of the cost, both in time and money, it's not a process you want to repeat. How can you make sure you do it right the first time? We asked current med students and admissions officers what advice they would give to a prospective applicant. What did they tell us? Make sure you know what you're looking for in a med school and make sure you know what med schools are looking for in you.

What Are You Looking for in a Med School?

You've made the decision to apply to med school, but what kind of med school is right for you? Although it's tempting to choose a school solely on the basis of its reputation, you should keep in mind that any ranking system is subjective and may not take into consideration the characteristics you're looking for in a school. For this reason, we've avoided rating the schools included in this book and have, instead, focused on what med students say they like and dislike about their schools. Although impressions about individual schools can be found later in this book, following is an overview of some of the factors students say you might want to consider in deciding which schools to apply to.

Reputation

The obvious goal of an applicant to medical school is to get into the most prestigious institution to which he or she can be accepted. But the students we surveyed warn that a school's reputation—often based on quantitative factors like the amount of research funding or the percentage of accepted applicants—may not tell you what you need to know about a school. For instance, if you're interested in primary care, you won't necessarily be happy at a med school that's a leader in research but gives you little patient contact in the first two years. On the other hand, if you're interested in becoming an academic physician or a biomedical investigator, a school whose mission is to educate family practitioners may leave you pining for the lab. To find out which schools best match your interests, read the profiles in this book, order school catalogues, get in touch with med students, talk to physicians, and pick the brains of your premed advisor and professors.

Curricula

Until relatively recently, med school curricula were structured according to a formula adopted in the early part of this century: the first two years were dominated by large, teacher-directed lectures that focused on the sciences basic to medicine, and the second two years were devoted to clinical experiences—exposure to patients, primarily in hospital settings. Since the mid 1980s, however, curricula have been in a state of flux. In response to criticism that traditional curricula result in an unnatural schism between the scientific and clinical aspects of medicine and that lectures and other teacher-directed learning formats stress rote memorization over real understanding, med schools have begun to change the way they train physicians.

Traditional lectures are giving way to small-group, problem-based learning strategies, and patient contact, formerly reserved for the last two, clinical years, is beginning as early as the first week of med school. Although nearly all of the med schools in this book have made changes in their programs in the past several years, some are further along in their reforms than others. Some schools now augment lectures with small discussion sections while others offer pathways that are almost entirely student-directed. By now, you know your learning style. If you're comfortable guiding your own education and feel constricted by too much structure, a more modern, flexible curriculum is for you. If, on the other hand, you thrive on structure and work better in a less personalized environment, you may want to consider med schools with a more traditional curriculum. It is worth noting, however, that curricula which give students the opportunity to work in small groups and which expose students to patients early in their med school careers were most popular with the students we surveyed.

Location

No matter how hard you intend to study, there is life outside the lab. A school's location can seriously affect the kind of lifestyle you'll be able to have. Before you set your heart on a school because of an innovative curriculum or a top-notch research program, make sure you can live with your choice for at least four years. For example, if you're leaning toward Columbia, but have never lived in a big city, you'll need to spend some time in New York before you make your final decision. On the other hand, if you're a die-hard urbanite who doesn't enjoy the great outdoors, Dartmouth is probably not the place for you.

Size

Size can also play an important role in how you'll feel about a school. Very small and very large schools have their advantages and disadvantages. Popular among students from small schools are the personal contacts students have with their professors and the close bonds they form with their fellow students. Students at large schools are enthusiastic about the number of opportunities they have to participate in academic and extracurricular activities. On the negative side, some small-school students dislike the "clubby" atmosphere the size engenders, while their large-school counterparts complain that they sometimes feel like numbers in large lecture classes.

Diversity

Even though white males still represent the largest proportion of U.S. med students, times are changing. Most schools are committed to enrolling a student body that more accurately represents the makeup of society than did med school classes of the past. At this time, most special recruiting efforts are directed at women and members of minorities traditionally underrepresented in medicine, specifically African Americans, mainland Puerto Ricans, Mexican Americans, and Native Americans.

Efforts to increase the number of female med students are paying off. At several schools, women are in the majority, and, at many others, genders are nearly balanced. But the picture isn't completely rosy. According to the students we surveyed, sexism is alive and well in our nation's med schools. As you will see in the next chapter, differences in the treatment of men and women surface as early as during the admissions interviews, where our respondents report that women are more likely than men to be asked about personal relationships and plans to have families. Unfortunately, things don't seem to improve much once women are admitted. When we asked whether women are afforded equal treatment by students and faculty, we found that answers varied greatly between the sexes. Regardless of the school, men were generally consistent in saying that treatment was equitable; in contrast, women's ratings were all over the map. The graph on the next page illustrates the results.

Equal Treatment GPA

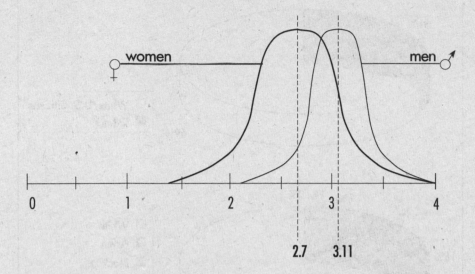

While perceptions of equal or unequal treatment are subjective, our results clearly show that men and women have different ideas of what is really going on in med school classrooms. Although it is difficult to say which schools are doing the best job of fighting gender discrimination, our female respondents recommend that applicants look for evidence of support for women in medicine from a school's faculty, administration, and student body. Examples of such support are mentor programs in which female students are paired with practicing female physicians, research efforts directed at women's health issues, and a strong representation of women in senior faculty and administrative positions.

Although women are becoming more adequately represented in U.S. med schools, members of certain minorities are not. The percentage of African Americans, mainland Puerto Ricans, Mexican Americans, and Native Americans in med school doesn't come close to representing the proportion of members of those groups in society.

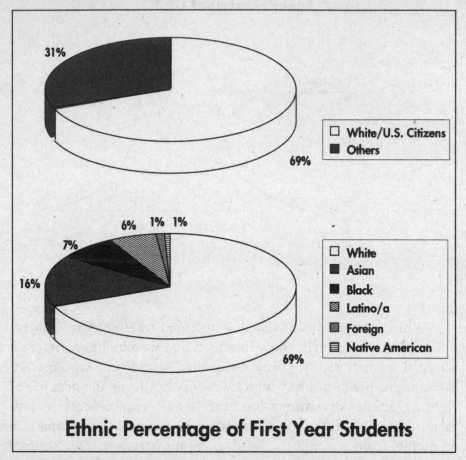

Ethnic Percentage of First Year Students

To be fair, this problem doesn't start in med school; these groups are equally underrepresented in the nation's colleges. For this reason, some schools' recruiting efforts include outreach programs designed to develop grammar school and high school-aged students' interest in medicine. For older students, many schools have special summer programs to help minority students make the transition from college to med school. Information about such programs, and other special services schools provide can be found in individual schools' profiles later in this book.

What Are Admissions Committees Looking for in You?

We asked admissions officers to tell us what they felt were the most important criteria in their admissions decisions. Responses for individual schools can be found later in this book, but following is a list of the factors officials most often mentioned.

Undergraduate Coursework

In the past, if you wanted to go to med school you almost had to be a science major, and college advisors encouraged undergrads to concentrate on typical "premed" fields like biology, chemistry, and physics. Today, you have more choice. Most med schools encourage students to pursue a broad, liberal arts education and place more emphasis on the breadth and depth of coursework than the area of study. Still, admissions committees need to know that you can handle the rigors of science-intensive med school coursework and maintain certain minimum requirements. Although mandatory courses vary somewhat from school to school, the basic requirements at most schools are as follows:

Biology or Zoology	1 year with lab
Inorganic Chemistry	1 year with lab
Organic Chemistry	1 year with lab
Physics	1 year with lab
English	1 year

A number of schools also require coursework in calculus or college level math, behavioral science, the humanities, and computers. Some more competitive schools require advanced level science courses, especially for students who meet basic requirements through high school advanced placement credits.

Grade Point Average

Most of the admissions officers we surveyed placed GPA at or near the top of their rankings of selection factors. In assessing your GPA, admissions committees look at two different values: your science GPA and your overall GPA. While the science GPA has traditionally been the more important of the two, the movement toward recruiting a more well-rounded student body has added to the weight of the nonscience GPA. In general, successful applicants have very high GPAs, and your cumulative average is likely to have a large impact on where you are admitted. For the 1991–92 school year, the mean GPA of accepted students was 3.42 (out of 4.0), and 46.2 percent had a GPA of 3.5 or above. Only 2.1 percent of accepted students had a GPA of 2.5 or under. Most students who are admitted with substandard GPAs are chosen because admissions committees recognize either mitigating factors that adversely affected the GPA (such as an educationally disadvantaged background) or significant and progressive improvement of grades in the upper-class years. Medical schools can also be swayed by an exceptional performance on the MCAT.

The Medical College Admissions Test (MCAT)

The Medical College Admissions Test (MCAT) is a multiple-choice, standardized exam that is required by all but a few med schools. The test was revamped in 1991 in response to criticism that while it measured the science knowledge necessary to be a successful medical student, it failed to assess the verbal and problem-solving skills essential to becoming a good physician. To answer this perceived need, the writers of the test incorporated broader-range reading passages and essays into the exam. It was hoped that the new MCAT would therefore measure not only proficiency in the basic sciences, but also the more general prob-lem-solving, critical thinking, and communication skills devel-oped in humanities curricula. Whether the MCAT actually serves this—or any other—purpose is open for debate. No matter what your opinion, though, there can be no question that your score can affect where you go to school; nearly all of the admissions officers we surveyed placed the MCAT among the top three selection factors.

The MCAT is given twice a year: once in April and once in September. Nearly all medical schools suggest that you take the MCAT in the spring of the year you apply, and almost all schools require the new format test. The MCAT consists of four timed sections, administered over a period of more than seven hours. The new MCAT is structured as follows:

The MCAT			
Section	**Questions**	**Time**	**Score**
Verbal Reasoning	65	85 minutes	1–15
Physical Sciences	77	100 minutes	1–15
Essay Writing	2	60 minutes	J–T
Biological Sciences	77	100 minutes	1–15

All four sections of the MCAT are scored. The two essays, graded together, are assigned a letter grade of J (lowest) to T (highest). The Physical Sciences, Biological Sciences, and Verbal Reasoning sections are each scored on a scale of 1 (lowest) to 15 (highest). Depending on their degree of selectivity, med schools consider a score of between 8 and 10 on each of the numerically graded sections to be "superior." Mean MCAT scores are listed for most schools in their individual profiles later in this book.

Letters of Recommendation

Letters of recommendation from your premed advisor or from several of your undergraduate professors are required at most schools. According to admissions officers, these letters play an important role in giving the members of the selection committee their first glimpse of you as something other than a file full of numbers. Because these recommendations are so vital, it is in your best interest to choose professors who know you very well to write them. Remember, the object is to present you in a way that makes the committee want to invite you to an interview. You can help your recommenders write letters that accomplish this aim by providing them with information about your interests, accomplishments, and goals.

Exposure to the Medical Field and Community Service

Since med schools are increasing their efforts to reinstate the patient as the top priority of the physician, admissions officers say it's important to show a genuine commitment to helping and serving others. Volunteer efforts that are linked with your interest in medicine are especially compelling, because they show that you have tested out your interest in medicine through real experience. If you can, explore a number of medical settings. Volunteering at a hospital provides a good introduction to working with ill patients, but it doesn't represent the whole story. Other settings like nursing homes, rehabilitation centers, and clinics for the homeless give you more diverse experiences and, if you're lucky enough to land an interview, give you more exposure to a variety of health care issues that might come up.

Extracurricular Activities

Because of the rigors of med school, admissions committees look for students who are able to motivate and discipline themselves to learn and to balance academic pursuits with their personal lives. Extracurricular activities, especially those in which you have a leadership role, are a good place to demonstrate your dedication and commitment to things in which you are involved.

Personal Characteristics

Motivation, the ability to communicate effectively, maturity, empathy, intellectual curiosity, and a commitment to lifelong learning are personal qualities that many admissions officers cite as important in a future physician. Although these qualities aren't easy to convey, they come through in essays, extracurricular activities, recommendations, and interviews.

State of Residence

Of the 126 med schools, 74 are public and 52 are private. Because they receive funding from their states, all public and some private schools give preference in admissions to applicants from within their state. If you're interested in applying to a school from out of state, be aware of special admissions restrictions that may apply to you. Some schools require that you apply early decision, while others prohibit you from doing so. And several schools accept only state residents. In order to avoid being one of the hundreds of careless people who apply as nonresidents to schools that don't accept *anyone* from out of state, check the school's policy before sending in your application. This information can be found in the Admissions section of each school's profile later in this book.

The Interview

Med school interviews are *much* more important than undergraduate interviews. In fact, on-site interviews are required at nearly every school and most of the admissions officers we surveyed place them among the top three selection factors. These meetings, usually conducted by admissions officials, faculty members, community physicians, or med students give the admissions committee the opportunity to find out more about you and give you the opportunity to find out more about the school. Because your chances for admission usually skyrocket once you're invited to an interview, we've devoted an entire chapter to the subject. In Chapter Three, you'll find out what the students we surveyed think you should know about their interviews and what kind of questions they were asked. Get ready, you may be surprised by what they have to say.

CHAPTER TWO

Financing Medical School

How Much Is All of This Going to Cost?

There's no doubt that med school is expensive. For the 1992–93 school year, the average first-year tuition at private medical schools was $21,869. The average at public schools was $8,331 for in-state students and $18,147 for out-of-state students. When planning for the cost of attending medical school, however, tuition is only part of the picture. You must also pay for books, equipment, housing, utilities, food, insurance, transportation, and miscellaneous costs. All of these expenses add up quickly; depending on where you attend school, they may equal or exceed the price of tuition.

The cost of a medical education is daunting, but, once in practice, physicians are among the most highly paid professionals. Currently, the average physician earns over $160,000 annually. While it will be years before today's first-year students make that kind of money, they can assume the financial burden of their education with the confidence that they will one day make enough money to justify the investment.

And How Can I Pay for It?

Since the medical student of today will be the well-paid physician of tomorrow, medical schools expect the student and her family to be responsible for the cost of her education. Except in cases in which a student has exceptional financial resources, it is essential to rely on outside sources of financial assistance to pay the bill.

Financial Aid Programs

There are two general types of financial assistance: **loans** and **scholarships**. **Loans** must be repaid, and have varying interest rates, deferment options, and repayment periods. Many loans will be available to you only if you have documented need, but some funds are available regardless of your financial situation. Most medical students borrow heavily, relying on the potential of a generous salary once they begin practice. For students graduating in 1992, the average debt was over $50,000 and, by all indications, that amount will continue to increase. **Scholarships**, or grants, are gifts that you don't need to repay. They can be awarded on the basis of any of three factors—financial need, outstanding academic merit, or a promise of future service—or a combination of those factors.

Loans

Anyone with good credit, regardless of financial need, can borrow enough money to finance a medical education. If you have financial need, you will most probably be eligible for some types of financial aid if you meet the following basic qualifications.

- You are a U.S. citizen or a permanent U.S. resident.

- If you are a male 18 years of age or older, you are registered for Selective Service or you have documentation proving that you are not required to register.

- You are not in default on student loans obtained prior to applying to medical school.

- You have a good credit history.

If you have financial resources that disqualify you for some types of aid, but meet the above requirements, you are still eligible for assistance, but the loans for which you are qualified usually have higher interest rates, offer less favorable repayment schedules, and often require that interest payments be made during school.

There are four basic types of loans: federal, state, private, and institutional. Following is a description of each loan type.

- *Federal:* Federal loan programs are funded by the federal government. The amount available each year is based on the national budget and is affected by the priorities of the executive and legislative branches of the government. Federal loan resources have been declining for the last several years, and the downward trend will probably continue. Even so, federal loans, particularly the Stafford Loan, are usually the "first resort" for borrowers. Most federal loans are need-based, but some higher-interest loans are available to a student or his family regardless of financial circumstance.

- *State:* Students who are residents of the state in which they attend medical school may be eligible for state loan programs. Like federal loan funding, state funding has been decreasing. Eligibility is usually based on need and may be further tied to specific segments of the population (e.g., minority or disadvantaged students or students who are interested in practicing family medicine in underserved areas of the state). Individual schools can provide you with information about state loan programs.

- *Private:* Private loans are funded by contributions from foundations, corporations, and associations. A number of private loans are targeted to aid particular segments of the population (e.g., minority or disadvantaged students, women, or students who are interested in practicing family medicine in underserved areas of the state). You may have to do a good deal of investigation to identify all of the private loans for which you might qualify. The best place to begin your search is in public, undergraduate, and med school libraries. There are also a number of commercial financial aid search services available, but beware—financial aid officers warn that search services sometimes charge hefty fees for information that, in the majority of cases, students can obtain themselves.

- *Institutional:* The amount of loan money available and the method by which it is disbursed varies greatly from one school to another. Private schools, especially those that are older and more established, tend to have larger endowments and, therefore, can offer more assistance. To find out about the resources available at a particular school, refer to its catalogue or contact its financial aid office.

We have compiled a table of the most commonly used loan programs. Included in this table is information about the characteristics of each loan. For your convenience, following is a definition of each category.

- *Name:* The full name of the loan and the acronym, if applicable, by which it is most commonly known.

- *Source:* Information about who funds and who administers each loan.

- *Eligibility:* Some loans are need-based. Others are open to people regardless of their financial situation. A few federal and private schools require that a student fit a specific demographic profile. Additionally, some federal loans require that students register for the Selective Service and that they not be in default on previous student loans.

- *Maximum Allocation:* There is a maximum amount of money you can borrow from any one program, so many medical students find it necessary to borrow from more than one source. Most loans have both maximum yearly and aggregate loan amounts. Amounts you borrowed from the same loan program for your college education are deducted from the aggregate amount you can borrow in medical school.

- *Repayment and Deferral Options:* Important considerations in structuring your educational debt are how long you have to pay back loans and whether principal and/or interest may be deferred until you have completed your education. This column provides information about the repayment period and deferral options for each loan. It is important to remember that, no matter what the source of a loan, the responsibility for keeping track of loan activity is yours.

- *Interest Rate:* This column provides information about the current interest rate of the loan. Fixed-rate loans use the same interest rate throughout the life of the loan. Variable-rate loans base their interest rate on established financial values, usually 91-day Treasury Bills (T-Bills) or the prime lending rate. Since these rates fluctuate greatly, you should check with a bank to find out the exact interest rate.

- *Pros:* Listed in this category are factors that make this an attractive loan source. Attractive features include long repayment terms, deferral policies that waive both interest and principal throughout medical school and all or part of residency training, and low, fixed-rate interest.

- *Cons:* Listed in this category are factors that make a particular loan unattractive. Such features include short repayment times, limited deferral options, or variable, high-interest rates.

TABLE OF LOANS

NAME OF LOAN	SOURCE	ELIGIBILITY	MAXIMUM ALLOCATION
Federal Stafford Student Loan (SSL, formerly GSL)	Federal, administered by participating lender	Demonstrated financial need; selective service registration; not in default on any previous student loan	$8500/year with maximum aggregate of $65,500. Aggregate includes undergraduate loans made under the same program and undergraduate and graduate loans made under the Unsubsidized Stafford Student Loan program.
Unsubsidized Stafford Student Loan	Federal, administered by participating lender	Not need based; selective service registration; not in default on any previous student loan	$8,500/year with maximum aggregate of $65,500. Aggregate includes undergraduate loans made under the same program and undergraduate and graduate loans made under the need-based Federal Stafford Loan program.
Health Education Assistance Loan (HEAL)	Federal, administered by participating lender	Demonstrated financial need	$20,000/year, with aggregate of $80,000. Yearly maximum cannot exceed total financial need minus any other loans.
Federal Supplemental Loan for Students (SLS)	Federal, administered by participating lender	Not need based, but must first apply for Federal Stafford Student Loan.	$10,000/year, with aggregate of $73,000. Aggregate includes undergraduate loans.
Health Professions Student Loan/Primary Care Loan (HPSL)	Federal, administered by school	Exceptional financial need; interest in primary care.	Tuition plus $2500 stipend
Perkins Loan (formerly NDSL)	Federal, administered by school	Demonstrated financial need; selective service registration; not in default on student loans.	Aggregate of $18,000. Aggregate amount includes undergraduate loans.
Alternative Loan Program (ALP)	AAMC, administered under MEDLOANS division of AAMC	Not need based	$20,000/year, $80,000 aggregate

PAYMENT AND DEFERRAL OPTIONS	INTEREST RATE	PROS	CONS
10 years to repay. Begin repayment 6 months after graduation. Forbearance possible for up to three years of residency training.	Variable, based on 91 day T-Bill plus 3.1%; current cap is 9%	Most common medical school loan. Interest is waived during school. Once you get a loan, any subsequent loans are made at the same rate.	None
10 years to repay. Principal is deferred while in school, but interest accrues immediately. Begin repayment 6 months after graduation. Forbearance possible for up to three years of residency training.	Variable, based on 91 day T-Bill plus 3.1%; current cap is 9%	Not need based. Same interest rates as Federal Stafford. Once you get a loan, any subsequent loans are made at the same rate.	Interest accrues immediately and is capitalized if deferred.
10 to 25 years to repay. Principal is deferred while in school and residency, but interest accrues immediately.	Variable, 91 day T-Bill + 3.0%	High maximum allocation	Often called a "loan of last resort" for first and second year students. High interest rate. Interest accrues immediately upon disbursement, and is compounded during residency.
10 years to repay. Interest accrues immediately.	Variable, 52 week T-Bill + 3.1%. Capped at 11%.	High aggregate amount	High interest rate. Interest accrues while in school and capitalizes if deferred.
10 years to repay, beginning one year after graduation. Deferrable during residency and under special circumstances.	Fixed, 5%	Low interest rate	Very limited funding.
10 years to repay. Begin repayment 9 months after graduation. Can be deferred for 2 years during residency.	Fixed, 5%	Low interest rate	Low maximum allocation; primarily restricted to first and second year students.
10-25 years to repay. Can be deferred for one year after residency.	Variable, based on 91 day T-Bill plus 3%.	High maximum allocation; not need based.	High interest rate. Interest accrues upon disbursement and is compounded during residency. Not federally insured.

Grants and Scholarships

Some grant, or gift, money comes with no strings attached; these are nonobligatory scholarships. While such scholarships may be available on the basis of outstanding academic merit alone, others are based on a combination of merit and need. In fact, all federal, nonobligatory scholarships are based on need and may also require that you fit a particular demographic profile. Scholarship amounts vary, and they are administered by the same groups as loans: federal and state governments, private foundations, and institutions. For more information about state and institutional scholarships, contact the financial aid offices at some of the schools to which you are going to apply. The private scholarship opportunities available to you depend on such diverse factors as your ethnic identity, your socioeconomic background, and your field of interest. You can find out about private scholarship or grant opportunities at your public or university library.

Obligatory Scholarships

Some federal scholarships are available to students who agree to serve at the Public Health Service, at the Veterans Administration, or in the Armed Forces. These scholarships provide full tuition, some or all expenses, and a monthly stipend. Service-based scholarships which are not based on need, all carry an obligation to serve at least one year for every year of support. The advantage— a "free" medical education—is obvious, but this is not an option to take lightly. Time spent in residency does not count toward your service debt, so you may be out of medical school for seven to twelve years before you're free of your obligation. Some states and counties also have some service-based scholarship programs or tuition remission programs available. Despite their lengthy obligations, service-based scholarships are in high demand. To increase your chances of obtaining one, apply as early as possible. Ask the financial aid offices of schools in which you are interested whom to contact locally for more information.

Following is a list of common federally and privately sponsored scholarship programs.

TABLE OF GRANTS

NAME OF GRANT	SOURCE	ELIGIBILITY	SERVICE OF OBLIGATION	AMOUNT OF GRANT
National Health Service Corps (NHSC)	Federal	Need-based; former EFN recipients and students with interest in primary care are preferred	Four year contract. Years spent in residency does not count toward fulfilling obligation.	Maximum amount is full tuition and fees plus stipend
Veterans Administration Health Professions	Federal, Veterans Administration	None	One year at the VA for every year of support.	Full tuition and fees, stipend
Financial Assistance for Disadvantaged Health Professions Students (DHP)	Federal, administered through school	Exceptional financial need and/or disadvantaged background	None	Varies
National Medical Fellowship Scholarship (NMF)	Private	First or second year underrepresented minority, female, rural or disadvantaged background with documented financial need	None	Varies
Exceptional Financial Need Health Professions Scholarship (EFN) Financial Aid for Disadvantaged Health Professionals	Federal, administered through school	Exceptional financial need and/or disadvantaged background	None	Varies
Armed Forces Health Professions Scholarship	US Army, US Navy, and US Air Force	Able to serve in military; age restrictions	One year for every year of support. Years spent in residency do not count toward fulfilling obligation.	Full tuition, "reasonable" fees, and stipend. Student becomes officer in service branch upon matriculation and receives all benefits of rank.

THE FINANCIAL AID PROCESS

Preparing to Apply

Many students miss out on assistance for which they are eligible by making some basic, avoidable mistakes. Top financial aid officers supplied the following common errors and their suggestions to avoid them.

- *Missing Deadlines and Keeping Poor Records:* Like your applications for admission, your financial aid applications should be submitted as early as possible. To make sure that you have the data required by the financial aid office, file your income tax forms early and encourage your parents (even if you are an independent student) to do the same. Photocopy all forms that you submit and note the date you send them. Make a financial aid file of these forms and any material related to the decisions of the financial aid committees of the schools you apply to. Keep careful track of deadlines—if you miss them, you miss out on the opportunity for most aid.

- *Submitting Information to the Wrong Needs Analysis Service:* There are three different needs analysis services (ACT, CSS, and GAPSFAS). Each medical school uses one of these services to determine how much financial assistance their prospective students require. Many applicants assume that, because they have submitted information to one of the services for one school, they have done everything they need to do for all the schools they are considering. This assumption can have serious repercussions. Until the proper service completes the needs analysis, the financial aid office cannot package your financial aid. To avoid making this mistake, check with the financial aid offices of all the schools to which you apply to see which service they use, and submit the proper materials to the appropriate service. More detailed information on the needs analysis services and their function can be found under "Calculating Your Contribution."

- *Having a Poor Credit History:* People are often unpleasantly surprised when they see their credit histories. Even relatively minor financial problems, like making a couple of late payments on loans or credit cards, can lower your credit rating. Also, credit bureaus sometimes make mistakes, causing negative, but false, information to show up on your record. Since a bad credit history will make you ineligible for many, if not all, loan programs, it is a good idea to check your credit history before you apply for financial aid. Since it usually takes several weeks to obtain a copy of your history, you should order one well in advance of the time you will begin to submit your applications. There is usually a fee for this, but it's worth the few dollars to check to make sure it is accurate.

- *Defaulting on Undergraduate Student Loans:* If you haven't been keeping up with your student loan payments, you will have a very hard time qualifying for loans, especially those funded by the federal government. Clear up any problems with prior student loans well before applying for additional assistance. If you are still in school, and have not yet begun repaying your loans, talk to your undergraduate financial aid officer to clarify repayment and deferral options on your loans. Remember also that the burden of keeping track of your loan activity is on you, and that, once you begin attending medical school, you must keep the lenders apprised of your whereabouts.

Applying for Aid

Students who seek financial aid must go through additional steps in the admissions process to find out whether or not they qualify for assistance. Schools' policies may vary somewhat, but they all follow the same general lines. To determine whether or not you qualify for aid, and if you do, how much aid you need, schools must first determine how much it will cost for you to attend, and then how much of that cost you and your family can bear.

How Schools Determine Their Cost

Each medical school prepares a student budget that includes the expenses associated with being a first-year medical student. Included in this budget are items such as tuition and fees, books, equipment, housing, utilities, food, insurance, transportation, and personal expenses. To figure out how much assistance you will need to pay this cost, schools must determine the amount that you and your family can reasonably contribute.

Calculating Your Contribution

To determine how much you and your family can contribute, medical schools use one of three federally approved needs analysis services: GAPSFAS (Graduate and Professional School Financial Aid Service), CSS (College Scholarship Service), or ACT (American College Testing). All of these services require you to submit an FAF (Financial Aid Form) or FFS (Family Financial Survey), tax information, and other relevant financial data. You should submit the needs analysis information as soon after January 1 as possible. To make sure you have all the required information, you should file your previous year's income tax returns early. Since some federal loan programs and some institutions require parental information even from independent or married students, your parents should also file their income tax forms as early as possible.

In 1993 an additional step was introduced to the process. All students who wish to be considered for federally funded loans must submit the Free Application for Federal Student Financial Aid (FAFSA). You can get a FAFSA from the financial aid office of the schools to which you apply. Again, you should submit this form as soon after January 1 as possible to maximize your chances of getting the financial aid for which you are eligible.

On the basis of the information you give them, GAPSFAS, CSS, or ACT calculates your financial need by subtracting your expected personal and family contribution from the total student budget furnished by the school. If expenses are higher than the estimated contribution, you show financial need.

Your Tentative Financial Aid Package

Once the existence and amount of need has been determined, the financial aid office of each school you apply to puts together a tentative financial aid package to meet that need. The package can include loans, scholarships, grants, or a combination of these elements.

Accepting Your Financial Aid Package

Once you matriculate at a school, the financial aid office will put together your actual financial aid package. At this point, you should take a close look at what you are offered. In most cases, loans will make up a portion of the package. Remember, loans must be repaid—with interest—and the amount of this debt will affect your lifestyle far beyond medical school and residency. For instance, if you borrow a large sum of money for medical school, you may have trouble later obtaining a loan for a large purchase like a car or a house. It is not required that you accept all the aid you are offered, so it is in your best interests to borrow only what you need to meet your expenses.

Medical schools formulate their student budgets by using average expenses for everything except tuition. By making some adjustments to your lifestyle, it is usually possible to undercut this budget, and therefore decrease the amount of money you borrow. Following are some strategies recommended by financial aid professionals to reduce debt.

CUTTING COSTS

Living Expenses

Living with roommates or in a smaller apartment lowers rent and utility expenses. Food costs can be cut by brown-bagging, dining out less often, and shopping wisely.

Books and Equipment

Buy good-quality used textbooks and equipment whenever possible. Selling books and equipment you no longer need will raise extra cash.

Transportation

Automobile loan payments, insurance premiums, licensing fees, fuel, and maintenance really add up. Evaluate your need for a car before taking one to medical school. If you attend school in a place where public transportation is available, or where you can bike or walk to school, leave the car behind. If you must have a car, you can save by raising insurance deductibles and carpooling with fellow students.

Insurance

Most medical schools require that you carry medical and, in some cases, disability insurance. Before you buy into the school's plan, check your existing coverage. If your parents still claim you as a dependent, or if you have a spouse whose medical benefits extend to you, you may already have adequate coverage.

Other Expenses

Millions of Americans find themselves in financial straits each year because of revolving credit. Medical students are no exception. If you find that you have trouble avoiding the temptation of pulling out the plastic for purchases you can't afford, cut up your cards. Remember, if you can't afford to pay for something with cash or a check, you probably can't afford to charge it, either. To keep discretionary expenses from getting out of hand, set up a detailed budget and stick to it. If you've never used a budget before and need help, there are many computer software programs that help you set up a budget, track expenses, and give you reports on how you're doing.

A Final Word:
Your Financial Aid Rights and Responsiblities

Your Rights

- You have the right to expect that the financial aid office will assist you in obtaining financial aid and information about financial aid opportunities.

- No financial aid award that would give information about your or your family's financial profile will be publicized.

- You have the right to accept or decline all or part of the aid offered.

- You have the right to appeal your financial aid package if your financial aid picture changes for the worse. (This does not necessarily mean, however, that the amount of aid will increase.)

- You have the right to examine your financial aid file at any time.

- You are entitled to treatment that does not discriminate on the basis of race, creed, age, handicap, gender, or national origin.

Your Responsibilities

- You are responsible for meeting the expenses related to attending medical school.

- Your are responsible for reading and understanding the conditions and terms of all of the elements in your financial aid package.

- You are responsible for submitting financial aid applications on time.

- You are responsible for obtaining and filling out financial aid forms and supplying accurate and complete information on these forms.

- You are responsible for reporting to your financial aid office any outside scholarships or loans that may affect your amount of need.

- You are responsible for using loan funds to pay tuition.

- You are responsible for repaying all loans.

- You are responsible for notifying all lenders of all changes of address during and after medical school.

- You are responsible for keeping accurate and complete records of all financial aid applications and transactions.

CHAPTER THREE

The Interview

Separating the Merely Qualified from the Truly Worthy

Be proud if you're invited to an interview. You've made it through two initial screenings, one before and one after the supplemental application. Usually, this means that the Admissions Committee thinks you're qualified to attend their school. Unfortunately, they also invite a lot of other qualified people, and they don't have space to admit all of you. The object is to convince everyone who interviews you that the school would be a better place with you in it. Easy to say, a little harder to do.

Since almost everyone has heard horror stories about some-one else's interview, most people start to worry about the interview before they even submit their applications. Try to relax. A good interview begins with good preparation. You can start by becoming familiar with the interview process.

Who Conducts Interviews?

Different schools have different policies about who conducts the actual interview. In general, schools have a Medical Selection Committee made up of professional admissions or student affairs people and faculty members. Often, especially in more progressive schools, upper level med students also participate. At some schools, you'll have a couple of separate, one-on-one interviews; at others, you'll be interviewed by a panel. You may be the only applicant in front of a panel (this really seems like an inquisition) or you may be joined by other candidates.

At many schools, the person or people you speak with become your advocates in the final selection process. When all the interviews in a certain time period are finished and the Selection Committee meets, these people share their observations about you and sometimes recommend a particular action. The final decision, of course, is up to the entire committee.

What Can I Expect?

Since med schools are trying to revise their curricula to make medical education more people-focused, you can assume that the interview process will also reflect this change. Eventually. For the time being, though, a number of schools still design the process to see how well you function under stress.

Stress interviews can take a lot of different forms, but their main characteristic is that the interviewer puts you in a position where he or she can observe how you act—and how you speak—under pressure. Proponents of stress interviews argue that they get you to drop your carefully studied "med school interview facade" and reveal what you're really like. Typical tactics include asking questions about sensitive or controversial topics, delving into extremely personal matters, rattling off a series of game-show-like trivia questions, or showing disapproval—through challenging remarks or negative body language—at almost everything you say.

The way to handle this type of interview is to try to relax and try not to get defensive or confused. Remember, it is generally not what you say that stress interviewers are interested in, but how you say it. Keep your composure, take your time, and, when things get too uncomfortable, try to guide the interviewer back onto a subject with which you feel secure.

Before you get too worked up over the stress interview, you should be aware of two things. First, students we surveyed who reported being flabbergasted by an aggressive interviewer were often accepted at that school anyway. So don't place too much importance on a bad experience. They expect you to be stressed, and you probably didn't do nearly as badly as you think. Second, and more important, most interviews aren't like this. People don't often talk about their good experiences, but there are plenty of them.

How Should I Act?

The golden rule for interviews is "Be Yourself." Interviewers have been through all of this before, and they're pretty good at spotting people who are putting on an act or reading from a mental script. Remember, what they're trying to find out from this interview is what kind of person you are and how you relate to others. Up until now, you've been only a few sheets of paper, a bunch of numbers, and a—probably horrible—photograph. Now's the time to show them your stuff.

Be Prepared: While there is no way to prepare yourself for every question you may be asked (and, as you'll see, some of the questions may be bizarre), you should be ready to answer questions about your motivation to become a physician, your academic background, your extracurricular and leisure activities, your job or research experience, and your views on medical problems and ethical issues. Later in this chapter is a sampling of questions that current medical students were asked in their interviews. Some of them are typical; others are truly strange. As you get ready to interview, try to answer some of these questions to yourself, and then to a friend, parent, or professor. In addition, you may want to audio- or videotape mock interviews to see how you sound and look. When you choose a guinea pig to be your surrogate interviewer, select someone who will be honest with you about the strengths and weaknesses of your responses. Don't try to memorize answers word for word; canned responses, no matter how valid, are stiff and unconvincing (just look at a tape of a presidential debate). Come up with general responses and, where appropriate, cite facts to support your opinions and conclusions.

Approach with Confidence: Like dogs, interviewers seem to smell fear. The tone of your interview is often set in the first few seconds, so approach with confidence. Greet your interviewer with a firm handshake and look her in the eye. During the interview, be positive. Think of it as a pleasant conversation with someone you'd like to get to know better. A good interview is a dialogue, where there is considerable "give and take." Unless your interviewer brings them up, avoid controversial or emotionally charged subjects like abortion. If you're asked your views, state them and move on.

Take Your Time: In the course of your interviews, you will be asked scores of questions, some on issues you haven't given a great deal of thought to. Your interviewers don't expect you have a ready answer for every one of these questions, but they do expect you to come up with a coherent, well-thought-out response. Many applicants are afraid that, if they hesitate, it will seem that they are unprepared. Not so. A good physician doesn't rush to a conclusion without considering the facts; rather, she thinks through a problem before she decides how to act. If a question catches you off guard, take a second to think it through. If it seems ambiguous, don't be afraid to ask for clarification. If you don't know, admit it and ask the interviewer to share the answer. By taking the time to make sure that your response is well conceived and well spoken, you will impress the interviewers as thoughtful and articulate—two characteristics essential in a good doctor.

Ask Questions: Although the interview is the time for medical schools to find out about you, it is also an excellent opportunity for you to find out more about the school. Before you go to an interview, make sure that you've studied the school's information packet and are ready to ask intelligent questions about the program. Do a search at your undergraduate or public library to see if the school has been in the news and, if so, for what. Unless you are a great actor, ask questions only about those things you are truly interested in; you don't want to look like you're sucking up.

Be on Time: Make sure that you get detailed directions before you make the trip, and arrive with enough time to park and find the office. If you are invited to interview at several schools in the same geographic region, you might save on travel costs and time by making an interview "circuit," visiting several schools on the same trip. This can mean that you have several interviews in the same week, or even the same day. Give yourself as much time as possible at each, so that you have time to make the transition, both physically and mentally, from one school to the next. If you can, try to get to each campus early enough to walk around, talk to students, and formulate questions that are specific to the school.

Dress for Success: Like it or not, looks count. No matter what your usual mode of dress, you should dress conservatively and professionally for your interviews. For men, this means a suit, or a blazer and nice slacks (and, of course, a tie); for women, a suit, blazer and skirt or dress slacks, or a business-style dress is appropriate. Regardless of your gender, keep an eye to detail; even the most beautiful suit looks shabby if your shoes are scuffed and worn, and the effect of a great-looking blazer is ruined by a ragged backpack. Polish your shoes, invest in a nice portfolio or case for your papers, and by all means, iron your clothes. If you are generally somewhat less than conservative in your dress, you may want to tone it down: men, replace the big hoop earring with a stud; women, take off the gold glitter polish and paint on clear. After all, you don't want to be asked, as one of the respondents to our survey was, "Why are you dressed the way you are? Why did you come here looking the way you do?"

Conduct Yourself Professionally: Admissions committees can see from your application that you are smart, accomplished, and highly regarded by your professors. The interview is an opportunity for them to gauge things that are not so easily conveyed on paper. Medical schools are looking for students with maturity, empathy, and superior interpersonal skills. All of these things come through in the interview. In a group setting, where the committee talks with more than one candidate at a time, you will be observed not only when you answer a question, but also when your fellow applicants are speaking. Keep alert, and show interest. After all, you never know what you may learn that you can use in your next interview.

Follow up with a Thank-You: In most cases, you won't be told whether or not you are admitted on the day of the interview; it may be a week, or in some cases a month or more. A timely thank-you note will put you back in the forefront of your interviewer's mind. As soon as you are finished with the interview, while all the details are fresh in your mind, write a thank-you to all the people who interviewed you. Make it personal, but keep it short.

What Are They Going to Ask?

While the following list of questions is by no means exhaustive, it is a good sampling of questions that were asked in real interviews in the recent past. When we first decided to ask current med students what they were asked in their interviews, we had no idea how strange—and it some cases disturbing—some of their responses were going to be. Get ready, because, while some of the questions are pretty standard, others are truly bizarre.

So You Want to Be a Doctor?

Some of the students we surveyed were unprepared for questions like those that follow, thinking them so mundane that they wouldn't be asked. From our research, however, we can say with confidence that if you're granted even one interview, you're almost sure to be asked several questions about your motivation and suitability for medical school.

- Why do you want to be a doctor?

- The future of medicine looks bleak. Why do you want to go into it?

- What articles have you read recently that relate to the reasons you want to become a doctor?

- What do you see yourself doing with a medical degree?

- Were you influenced by relatives to pursue a career in medicine?

- How do you know you want to be a doctor if your parents aren't doctors?

- How will you be a better doctor than your [FAMILY MEMBER]?

- Why do you want to attend [NAME OF SCHOOL]?

- Why should we accept you?

- How are your accomplishments better than those of the other candidates in this interview?

- Evaluate yourself based on the required evaluation of the interviewer.

- Why on earth did they give you an interview?

- Do you think you are motivated enough for medical school?

- Would you give up a body part to gain entrance to medical school?

- *When* you don't get into medical school, what will you do?

- What would you do if Saddam Hussein took over our country and wouldn't allow women in medical school?

- What career path would you follow if all the medical schools closed today?

- You've taken an odd, nontraditional path to get here. Why are you interested in medicine?

- What disadvantages do you see in being an older student?

- Can you afford to come here?

- How will you finance your medical education?

- Describe what you believe to be the financial rewards of medicine.

- If doctors were paid as much as teachers, would you still want to be a doctor?

- Come on, don't you see yourself driving a Mercedes convertible in ten years?

- Doctors have the power to give or take life. How do you feel about "playing God"?

- Why didn't you become a veterinarian?

Tell Me a Little Bit about Yourself...

Selection committees use the interview as an opportunity to find out what makes you tick. Prepare yourself for personal questions about your character traits, your coping mechanisms, and your life experiences. You may also be asked to comment on your interpersonal relationships.

- What is your worst quality?

- If you could change anything about yourself, what would it be?

- Are you aggressive?

- What makes you a fun person?

- Do you have a good sense of humor? Tell me the funniest joke you ever heard.

- What makes you angry?

- What makes you sad?

- What scares you?

- Do you like sick people?

- Are you afraid of death?

- What are you ashamed of?

- What are you the most proud of?

- One of the people who wrote a letter of recommendation for you described you as [ADJECTIVE]. Do you agree with that description?

- Was there a time in your life when you had tremendous responsibility?

- What is the wackiest thing you've ever done?

- What was the biggest mistake you ever made?

- What is the worst thing that has happened to you in the past four years?

- Tell me something you wanted to achieve but did not, or something you've failed at. How did you cope with failure?

- What role has stress played in your life?

- How could you prove to me that you can perform well under stress?

- What do you do to alleviate stress?

- What support structure do you have in [TOWN IN WHICH SCHOOL IS LOCATED]?

- Tell me about your family.

- Tell me about your mom.

- What does your father do for a living?

- What does your brother do for a living?

- What role do you play in your family dynamic?

- How is your relationship with your parents?

- What is the physical health of your parents, and how would you handle an illness of theirs while attending school?

- Who is the person in the world to whom you are closest?

- Describe your best friend.

- What does your closest friend think about your relationship with him or her?

- Give one word that a friend would use to describe you.

It's all Academic

Grades, MCAT scores, and courses are fair game for the inquisitive interviewer. You may be asked to explain your performance in a course or to tell what you learned. A hint: to be better prepared for questions of this type, get a copy of your transcript and take a look at it. Look for things that might cause an interviewer to ask a question. Lower than normal grades stick out, as do courses with funny names (like *Poets Who Sing*).

- What do you think of the GPA as a valid method of categorizing students?

- Why were your first-year grades so bad?

- Why do you have so many C grades on your transcript?

- Explain your low math grade.

- Why are your grades high compared to your MCAT scores?

- Do you realize that your MCAT scores aren't anything special?

- Tell me about your research.

- Have you taken any humanities classes and what papers did you write in them?

- What did you learn in [NAME OF COURSE]? (It's worth noting that some people were asked about normal courses like *Philosophy 101* and others were asked about bizarre courses like

The Art of Murder, Fairy Tales, and *Play, Games, Toys, and Sports*.)

- Who was the author of your biochemistry textbook?

Extra, Extra, Read all about It!

Whatever your extracurricular activities and work experiences, you will likely be asked how they relate to your commitment to and preparedness for studying medicine. Think about your extracurricular experiences and what you learned about yourself, the medical field, and/or working with people as a result of participating in these activities. If you've been out of school for a while and have worked extensively in another field, be ready for questions about why you decided to change fields. Scientific or medical research experience is a plus, but can be a real liability if you're not able to discuss it in detail.

- What are your hobbies?

- How does your hobby relate to being a doctor?

- Have you taught yourself to do anything, and if so, what?

- How has working as a [NAME OF JOB] made you a better candidate for medical school?

- What volunteer work contributed to your commitment to become a doctor?

- What did you do with your job earnings?

Medical Issues and Ethics: Where Do You Stand?

Most students were asked at least one question about a medical issue or about an ethical dilemma that was related to medicine. In general, there is no wrong answer to these questions. You should know the terminology (for example, what is the difference between euthanasia and euthenics?), and be aware of some pros and cons for each of these issues. Since the health care crisis and attendant problems in reforming the health care delivery system have been grabbing headlines, you should be prepared to discuss the issue intelligently. No one expects you to be an expert on this or any other issue, but you should do some research before your interviews. Don't be surprised if an interviewer challenges your view on an issue; usually, he or she is trying to see how well you support your argument.

- What is the greatest problem facing medicine today?

- What do you consider the most important thing medicine has done for mankind?

- What do you think will be the most significant scientific breakthrough in the next ten years?

- If you could find a cure for AIDS or for cancer, which would you choose and why?

- If you were Surgeon General, what is the first thing you would do?

- If you were the Health Commissioner of [A LARGE CITY], what would you do?

- What is preventative medicine?

- What is the biggest problem family practitioners face?

- What are your views on euthanasia?

- What do you think about euthenics (not euthanasia)?

- What would you do about the alcoholism problem in this country?

- What do you think about condoms being distributed in high schools?

- What are your views on mandatory HIV testing for doctors and patients?

- Current AIDS education programs aren't working; what should we do?

- Why will organ rationing be the problem of the future in medicine?

- If brain transplants were possible, what would be your opinion of them?

- Should people have the right to sell their own organs?

- Do you think it's ethical to take the life of a fetus for a cell line to save the life of a sibling with cancer?

- Should we spend so much time and effort trying to keep premature infants alive?

- Should retarded people be sterilized without their consent?

- If a cure were invented for aging, what repercussions would it have on society in general and the medical profession in particular?

- How do you feel about animal research?

- What is the proper treatment of laboratory rats?

- What role should politics play in medicine?

- Is health care a right or a privilege?

- What is your opinion of socialized medicine?

- How would you organize health care in an ideal world?

- Discuss the health care system of Australia.

- What do you think should be done about patients who can't pay for treatment?

- What is the difference between Medicare and Medicaid?

- What is your opinion of HMOs and PPOs?

- How will you react to the death of your first patient?

- Who would you go to if your mom needed surgery: a surgeon with good hands and a bland personality or a surgeon with not as good hands with a great personality?

- If your father was dying of cancer and you were an attending resident, how would you break the news?

- How would you tell your best friend's wife (who is your patient) that she has cancer? What would you do if she then refused to tell her family?

- Pretend to tell me a loved one of mine has died.

- You have to amputate one of the legs of an eight-year-old child. How would you tell him?

- Would you give a transfusion to a child whose parents were Jehovah's Witnesses?

- If a Hindu, for example, comes in and refuses surgery on the basis of religion, and the surgery is his only hope, what would you do? Also, what if the patient is this man's child?

- Would you refer a terminal patient to a "suicide doctor?"

- If you diagnosed a patient with a terminal illness as having only two months to live and the family and the patient wanted to end the turmoil ("pull the plug"), would you allow it or strongly disagree?

- What would you do if you came upon a bleeding child on the side of the road?

- What would you do if you had a female patient who was trying to conceive, and your colleague had that patient's husband and the husband was HIV positive?

- If one of your colleagues refused to treat a patient with AIDS, how would you address that person?

- How would you react if a fellow medical student had AIDS and entered surgery with you?

- Would you perform a hair transplant on an AIDS patient?

- Would you let a surgeon with AIDS operate on you?

- Would you treat a white supremacist, and should physicians be forced to treat such a patient?

- If you made a mistake as a physician, how would you handle it?

To Choose, or Not to Choose

Abortion is not only a hot political topic, it also seems to be a hot topic for interviews. Some schools are affiliated with hospitals where abortions are performed; some are not. Don't try to guess if the interviewer is hoping you will espouse a particular position; honesty seems the best policy on this issue. If you are asked about your willingness to perform an abortion (as a large number of those we surveyed were), you may want to mention that it is not only your conscience, but also the rules of the hospital or laws of the land that you must consider.

- What should a physician's role be in the politics of abortion?

- What are your views on abortion?

- What would you do as a physician if you were asked to do something contrary to your stand on abortion?

- Would you perform an abortion for a teenager, and would you tell her parents?

- How do you justify being a Catholic and going to an institution that allows abortion?

- If you wouldn't perform an abortion because of your religious beliefs, but you would refer a patient to another physician who *would* perform an abortion, are you not just as guilty in God's eyes?

Have You Heard the News?

Good doctors are aware of, and involved in, the world around them. You may be asked about current events, even things completely unrelated to medicine. The questions that follow are only examples; in most cases, these events are no longer current. To prepare for questions like these, keep up with what's happening. If you get most of your news from the TV or radio, start reading newspapers and news magazines for more in-depth coverage.

- Who is the U.S. secretary of state?

- What do you think about the current situation in Yugoslavia?

- What do you think about the current social climate in Mozambique?

- What do you think about the political situation in Iraq and surrounding countries?

- What is your opinion on the confirmation hearings of Clarence Thomas?

- Why did Margaret Thatcher resign?

- Do you think the Israelis beat up on the Palestinians?

Philosophy 101

From the serious to the silly, questions interviewers ask can make you stop and think. (And, for some of these questions, one of the things you might think is, "What does this have to do with med school?")

- What are the top five priorities of society?

- What is your purpose for living?

- How do you resolve the apparent dichotomy between the cruelty and suffering in the world and your belief in a loving God?

- Do you see any parallels between medicine and the priesthood?

- Do you feel Catholics are morally superior?

- What is Zen Buddhism?

- Explain Hinduism.

- Are you a racist?

- Do you have trouble working with black people?

- Do you believe that racism still exists?

- How do you feel about affirmative action?

- Would you move to Canada to avoid serving active duty during a military conflict abroad?

- What is your view on censorship in the arts?

- What would you do if you saw a classmate cheating on a test?

- Do you believe in drug legalization?

- Do you believe that volunteerism could help eliminate greed from society's social structure?

- Is altruism ever pure, without some kind of motive?

- Do you believe in life after death?

- What is your opinion about natural law ethics?

- Explain the mind-body problem.

- Are you a vertical or horizontal thinker?

- If you could be any cell in the human body, what would you be?

- If you were to build a human being, what would you include and exclude?

- Define *hope*.

Tried and True

Some questions sound more like pickup lines than med school interview questions. While none of those surveyed was asked, "What is your sign?" there were plenty of old favorites that you may as well be prepared for.

- Are you a person who thinks a glass is half empty or half full?

- If you could go back in history and meet anyone, who would it be and why?

- If you could talk to someone from the future, what would you ask him?

- If a genie were able to grant you three wishes, what would they be?

- If you were stranded on a desert island, what five books would you want?

- If your house was burning down, and you could save only one thing, what would it be?

- If you could be any vegetable, what would you be?

- If you could be any kind of fruit, what would you be?

- If you could be any kind of animal, what would you be?

- If you could be any inanimate object, what would you be?

- If you could be any cartoon character, who would it be?

- What is your favorite color?

- What was the last book you read and how did it influence your life?

- What was the last good movie you saw?

- Tell me what you see when you look in the mirror.

- What was the most embarrassing moment in your life?

- Who is your hero?

- If you could invite three role models to dinner, who would they be and why, and what would you serve them?

- When you die, what would you like your tombstone to read?

I'll Take *Potpourri* for $500, Alex

The students we surveyed were asked some trivia worthy of Final Jeopardy. The bad news is that, because of the very nature of these questions, you can't prepare for them. The good news is that a simple "I don't know" seemed to satisfy the interviewers. For bonus points, ask for the answer, or, as one student did, tell them you'll check and get back to them. He did, and subsequently he got in.

- What is the largest lobbyist group in the U.S.?

- Which state first had women's suffrage?

- What language did Abraham (of the Bible) speak?

- When did Iraq become an independent nation?

- How many numbers that contain 9 are there between 1 and 100?

- What is the capital of Vietnam?

- When and how was Pakistan formed?

- Who won the 1969 World Series?

- Name a seven-letter word with three *u*'s in it.

- What is the difference between European and American eighteenth-century poetry?

- Why was the Civil War fought?

- What is the origin of the name "Cincinnati"?

- What do the *e*'s in e.e. cummings's name stand for?

- When and why was the March of Dimes founded?

- When did Istanbul become Istanbul?

- Name the four non–Arabic-speaking countries in the Middle East.

- What was Thomas Aquinas famous for?

- Who was the architect who built the Great Wall of China?

- Where was Millard Filmore born?

- Give a brief history of the Jesuit order.

- Define the Apollonian and the Dionysian as they figure in the philosophy of Nietzsche.

- Who was the head of NATO during World War II?

- What size tippets do you use on your fly lines with a 14X fly?

A Corollary: I'll Take *Science & Medicine* for $1,000, Alex

A few interviewees were asked trivia that actually related to science and medicine. For the most part, they knew the answers. When they didn't, and the question was obscure, it didn't seem to hurt their chances for getting in. Your undergraduate coursework and MCAT review should be preparation enough for a lot of these questions.

- What was the first industrialized country to practice socialized medicine? The second?

- How much does the U.S. spend each year on medical care?

- How does a lightbulb work?

- What would be the physiological effects of performing the high jump in Mexico City?

- Why don't fish die in winter?

- Why does ice float on the top of water?

- How do you make a protein?

- So, what is Alzheimer's disease anyway?

- Where is your hamstring region?

- Tell me what you know about DNA.

- What is the Grignard Reaction?

- What is Poisson's equation?

- Describe protein structure.

- What is PKU?

Anita Who?

Despite the media attention focused on the issues of gender discrimination and sexual harassment, medical school interviewers are still asking questions that, if they were asked in a job interview, would be deemed inappropriate or illegal. The students who told us they'd been asked these questions (and there were lots of them, mostly female) expressed emotions from confusion to outrage. Still, most admitted to being intimidated that they would be rejected if they did anything but reply calmly, and therefore they answered honestly and without additional comment. How you handle a question like this is up to you. At this point, you too might feel that there is too much at stake to make waves, but, on the other hand, it is certainly within your rights to ask how the question is relevant or even to politely decline to answer.

- How did you get such a high score in math?
  I've never seen such a high score from a woman!

- Do you know that you have extraordinarily good looks?

- Why is a pretty young girl like you wasting her time and money applying to med school?

- Why do you want to be a doctor rather than a nurse?

- Will you faint if I take you into surgery?

- Would you feel uncomfortable being alone with a male patient?

- How did taking a nude art class make you feel?

- What would your ideal date be?

- Do you find it hard to find educated black men to date?

- What was the strangest sexual position you have ever employed?

- Who do you think the best model is in this year's *Sports Illustrated* swimsuit issue?

- How frequently do you masturbate?

- Are you gay?

- Why don't you like men?

- Do you have a boyfriend?

- How does your boyfriend feel about your going to medical school?

- Would having a boyfriend affect your decision in choosing a medical school and career?

- Are you prepared to handle possibly losing your boyfriend over the stress and distance?

- Are you married?

- What kind of person would you like to marry?

- Do you plan to marry while in medical school?

- Why aren't you married?

- How will you deal with being married while in medical school?

- What does your husband do?

- Why did you get divorced?

- Do you plan to remarry?

- Do you expect to have a family? If so, why are you applying to medical school?

- If you become pregnant, what will you do?

- Have you ever gotten a girl pregnant?

- How do you plan to manage a family and a career? After all, you are a woman.

- How would you raise your children if you were a doctor?

- What would you do if you were sexually harassed at any time during school, residency, or your career?

- Are you prepared for the sexual discrimination you are most likely to face as a student, resident, intern, and so on?

Expect the Unexpected

Although most of the questions fall into one of the previous categories, some of the questions are just plain off the wall. Some of the following questions were logical from the perspective of the candidates' background, so be prepared to answer questions about the leisure activities you listed on your application or the experiences you related in your essays. Other questions came straight out of left field. These are unlikely to be repeated, but they give you an idea of the kind of things interviewers ask to catch you off balance. If you're asked a question like this, take your time and think it through. If all else fails, remember, it's better to say "I don't know" than to try to "baffle 'em with bull." As one of those surveyed said after an unsuccessful attempt at bluffing, "It doesn't work, they've heard it all before."

- Why didn't you bring me a doughnut?

- What would you do if I dropped unconscious right now?

- What would you do if you ran me [the interviewer] over as you left the campus?

- What would you say if you smashed your finger with a hammer?

- How tall are you?

- How did you get your hair to do that?

- Is that your natural hair color?

- What bar or dance club did you get that hand stamp from?

- Where did you buy your suit?

- Why are you dressed the way you are? Why did you come here looking the way you do?

- What's that stain on your sleeve?

- Can you sing the blues?

- Do you think that anyone can become a singer?

- Do you know how to play an instrument?

- How do you play your guitar and harmonica at the same time?

- Who is your favorite classical music composer?

- What's your favorite Beatles album?

- Do you like MC Hammer?

- Do you like Axl Rose?

- What is your favorite college football team?

- What do you think the chances are that the [TEAM NAME] will make the playoffs?

- Why are the majority of NBA players black?

- How much can you bench press?

- If you're accepted, will you play on our softball team?

- What was your opinion of the rich, yuppie Greek students on your undergraduate campus?

- How much do you drink?

- Have you ever cheated?

- Have you ever tried an illegal substance?

- Have you ever stolen a car?

- What kind of car do you drive?

- What is your opinion of Charlie Brown?

- Do you prefer the old *Star Trek* or the new one?

- Why didn't you take Latin?

- Do you dream in Chinese or English?

- Do you know how to surf?

- Are you most like Madonna, Margaret Thatcher, or Mother Theresa, and why?

- What is your favorite card game?

- Do you play bingo?

- Does your mother know where you are?

CHAPTER FOUR

The Best Medical Schools

University of Alabama School of Medicine

Admissions, VH 100, Medical Student Services, Birmingham, AL 35294
(205) 934-2330

OVERVIEW

School officials describe U of A as a school "on the move." Indeed, its clinical and research reputations continue to improve, applications have increased, and MCAT scores and GPAs are up for this year's entering class. But some of the those we surveyed feel that the school needs to slow its growth and take care of some housekeeping. First- and second-year students would like to see more clinical correlations in the basic science years and earlier, more extensive hands-on contact with patients. Still, students at U of A say they are pleased with their overall med school experience, citing a caring faculty, outstanding clinical facilities, and a solid track record in research as the school's main draws.

ACADEMICS

The curriculum style at U of A is traditional, with the first two years devoted to the basic sciences and the last two spent doing clinical clerkships. One recent innovation at U of A is a requisite four-week rotation in rural medicine, a requirement that fits well with the school's commitment to serving the health care needs of the state.

Beyond the traditional lectures and labs, U of A employs some small group learning in the basic science years. Students laud the "very caring faculty" and are relatively enthusiastic about the quality of teaching and the accessibility of their professors. They do cite some shortcomings, however. Complains one student, "In the classroom, lectures are sometimes given by individuals who do not even have a working English vocabulary, let alone a mastery of the English language. Few lecturers appear to be concerned about getting their material across to the students in a way that is clearly understandable." Others report that first-year lectures are "too crowded."

Considering the traditional basic science/clinical split, it comes as little surprise that students are only moderately satisfied with the amount of clinical exposure they have in the first year. Students do say, however, that opportunities for early hands-on experience are available through extracurricular organizations, such as the Family Practice Club.

Students are enthusiastic about the quality of the labs used in the basic science years, but are slightly less excited about the classroom and library facilities. Without exception, students rate the school's clinical teaching facilities as outstanding.

Grading/Promotion Policies: A through F for regular courses, P/F for electives. Passing grades on the USMLE Parts I and II are required for promotion and graduation.

Additional Degree Programs: U of A offers combined BS/MD and MD/Ph.D. programs.

STUDENT LIFE

Students rank their classmates as very competitive and say that much of their out-of-class time is spent studying. The heavy workload and the number of classroom hours leaves all but the most organized students little time to get involved with the large variety of school and community activities. Some students aren't too happy about this: "This school is very busy trying to make a name for itself. However, little attention is given to the students' quality of life. Our time is monopolized by busy work."

Students are satisfied with Birmingham, but give lukewarm reviews to the campus. Although U of A offers several different styles of on-campus housing at the Birmingham location, students give university housing very low marks. They were quite pleased with available off-campus housing.

ADMISSIONS

Preference in the selection process is given to residents of Alabama, but out-of-state students are welcome to apply. Only exceptionally well-qualified nonresidents should submit applications, however. The Admissions Office warns, "nonresidents waste their time and money applying if their MCAT scores are below 30 and their GPA below 3.5." Talented out-of-state minority students may be given a little leeway, the Admissions Director tells us: "Minority students with slightly lower numbers who demonstrate exceptional leadership skills and exhibit strong extracurricular activities combined with either extensive medical-related or research experiences may be interviewed at the discretion of the Committee." Students who apply through EDP, much is open only to Alabama residents, should have a GPA of 3.4 or higher and an average MCAT score of at least 9, with no score lower than 9.

The Director of Admissions ranks quantitative values—MCAT scores, the science GPA, and the nonscience GPA, in that order—as the most important factors in admissions decisions. Decisions are also based in large part on the interview. The Admissions Committee assures prospective applicants that it strives to provide an "absolutely friendly atmosphere during interview days," adding, "We go all out of our way to meet personal needs and to have a relaxed environment." The interview day begins with a group meeting where the admissions director gives candidates information about the admissions process, curriculum, research activities, and the interview itself.

"Reasonable involvement in extracurricular activities and direct medical-related work experiences" are also considered important in the selection process. The committee "encourages all applicants to explore the medical field either by gainful employment or in a volunteer capacity." Special consideration may also be given to qualified students who are interested in practicing general medicine in underserved areas. Essays are not considered.

Special Programs for Members of Underrepresented Minorities: Students generally feel that minorities are treated fairly at U of A, but some resent the special programs the school provides. One such student (who said he falls into none of the categories he mentions) comments, "Minority students, females, and members of special interest groups are afforded better than equal treatment by faculty in the areas of admissions, scholarships, and special help programs by the school." These "special programs" include academic advising, review classes for the MCAT, a prematriculation summer session, and summer sessions for high school and college students. Despite students' intimations to the contrary, most of these programs do not restrict participation; the prematriculation summer session, for instance, is open to any student who is admitted to the school.

Transfer Policy: Alabama residents in good standing at other medical schools are eligible to apply for transfer into U of A.

eMail: GSHand@BMG.BHS.UAB.EDU

FINANCIAL AID

U of A ranks among the schools with the lowest tuition, but there are still a variety of loans and scholarship sources from which to solicit financial aid. The school awards some scholarships solely on the basis of merit.

ADMISSIONS FACTS

Demographics

% men	66
% women	34
% minorities	14

Deadline & Notification Dates

AMCAS	yes
Regular application	11/01
Regular notification	10/15-until filled
Early Decision application	8/01
	(EDP for AL residents only)
Early Decision notification	10/01

	In State	Out of State
Applied	525	1727
Interviewed	381	171
Matriculated	152	14

FIRST YEAR STATISTICS

Average GPA

Science	3.49	Nonscience	3.55

Average MCAT

Biology	9.7	Physical Science	9.4
Verbal	9.9	Essay	N/A

FINANCIAL FACTS

Tuition and Fees

In-state	$7,692	On-campus housing	N/A
Out-of-state	$18,362	Off-campus housing	$10,418

Financial Aid

% receiving some aid	67
Merit scholarships	yes
Average debt	$43,057

HITS AND MISSES

HITS	MISSES
Research effort	On-campus housing
Clinical facilities	Public transportation
Emphasis on ethics	Class size
Off-campus housing	Clinical exposure
	Campus safety
	Computer facilities

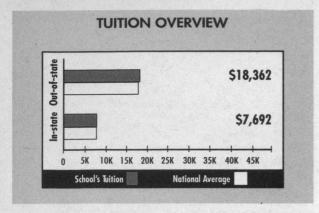

TUITION OVERVIEW

Out-of-state **$18,362**

In-state **$7,692**

0 5K 10K 15K 20K 25K 30K 35K 40K 45K

■ School's Tuition □ National Average

University of South Alabama College of Medicine

Office of Admissions, 2015 MSB, Mobile, AL 36688-0002
(205) 460-7176

OVERVIEW

The College of Medicine is part of the University of South Alabama in Mobile. As a state-supported school, USA's primary responsibility is to train clinicians to provide health care to Alabama residents, but the school also places considerable emphasis on research. Plus, with access to all the facilities of a very large undergraduate school, USA has other things to offer.

ACADEMICS

USA's curriculum and teaching methods are fairly traditional: the four years are split into two-year preclinical and clinical units and the majority of science classes are taught through lectures. During the first year, students spend most of their time learning the basic sciences, but they also take short courses in which they explore ethical and social aspects of medicine. Provision for patient contact is made from the first semester.

In the second year, students continue their study of the scientific basis of medicine, but the focus shifts from normal to abnormal functions. Courses in public health and behavioral sciences provide a psychosocial context. Throughout the year, students work with clinical problems and learn fundamental patient interaction skills in Introduction to Clinical Medicine (ICM). Juniors complete clerkships in the major disciplines and in Family Practice. Faculty-directed seminars and conferences highlight important issues. The fourth year is devoted primarily to electives.

Grading and Promotion Policy: For regular courses, A–F. For electives: Honors/Pass/Fail.

Additional Degree Programs: MD/Ph.D.

STUDENT LIFE

First- and second-year classes are held on the main campus of the University of South Alabama, so med students have access to the resources of a relatively large undergraduate school. The university offers a variety of housing options, including dorm rooms, apartments, and two- and three-bedroom houses.

ADMISSIONS

USA gives preference to residents of Alabama, but encourages nonresidents to apply. As the Admissions Committee gets AMCAS applications, it mails requests for supplementary information to all state residents and selected nonresidents. The most promising candidates are then invited to interview on campus.

The primary factors in the Admissions Committee's final decisions are the interview, the science and nonscience GPAs, MCAT scores (from the new test), letters of recommendation, and essays. Extracurricular activities and exposure to the medical field are also considered.

Special Programs for Members of Underrepresented Minorities: A minority affairs division coordinates the school's efforts to recruit underrepresented minority students. Among its offerings are summer sessions for college students, academic advising, tutoring, and counseling.

Transfer Policy: Applicants who are in good standing at their current med schools are considered for transfer into the second- and third-year classes.

ADMISSIONS FACTS

Demographics

% men	62
% women	38
% minorities	13

Deadline & Notification Dates

AMCAS	yes
Regular application	11/15
Regular notification	10/15-until filled
Early Decision application	8/01
	(EDP for AL residents only)
Early Decision notification	10/01

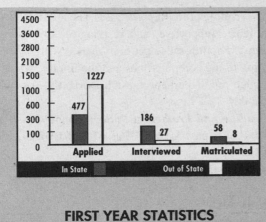

In State | Out of State

FIRST YEAR STATISTICS

Average GPA
Science   N/A   Nonscience   3.60

Average MCAT
Biology   9.28   Physical Science   9.08
Verbal   9.41   Essay   N/A

FINANCIAL FACTS

Tuition and Fees
In-state $6,375   On-campus housing   none
Out-of-state $12,183   Off-campus housing   N/A

Financial Aid
% receiving some aid   67
Merit scholarships   yes
Average debt   N/A

TUITION OVERVIEW

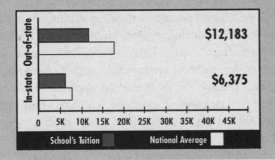

$12,183

$6,375

School's Tuition | National Average

University of Arizona College of Medicine

Admissions Office, Tucson, AZ 85724
(602) 626-6214

OVERVIEW

A friendly, noncompetitive atmosphere, a caring faculty, and a responsive administration are some of the features that make Arizona students among the happiest of the med students we surveyed. Other attractions are outstanding facilities and low tuition. The downside? If you're not from Arizona, Montana, Alaska, or Wyoming or you're not Native American, don't bother to apply.

ACADEMICS

During the first two years, students learn basic scientific principles, explore medical issues in behavioral and social contexts, and learn fundamental clinical skills. The last two years are devoted to required and elective clinical clerkships; students may also choose to do research or advanced study of the basic sciences.

Traditional lectures are the primary mode of instruction in basic science courses, but there is some time in each course devoted to alternative teaching methods. Students rate the quality of teaching as very good, but are even more impressed with the accessibility of the faculty outside of the classroom. Says one first-year student, "When they say 'come see me if you have a problem' they mean it."

Clinical exposure during the basic science years comes through Preparation for Clinical Medicine. In this course, students focus on clinical problem solving and learn patient evaluation skills. Although students like the degree to which scientific principles are correlated to the practice of medicine, they report that there is not much actual "hands-on experience" required in the first year. One student comments, "The clinical experience I've had has been through extracurricular activities.... Opportunities...are out there, you just have to make the effort to take advantage of them." Second-year exposure is more extensive; every student is required to complete a preceptorship in a physician's office in the last preclinical semester.

Students rate academic counseling and support services as very good, and feel that they have a voice in the way the school is run. Reports one, "The administration is available, supportive, and responsive...to students' concerns." Facilities also get high marks, with top honors going to the computer labs and the library, which is new, huge, and—perhaps most importantly—open 24 hours a day.

Grading and Promotion Policy: Honors/Pass/Fail. Students must pass USMLE Parts I and II in order to graduate.

Additional Degree Programs: MD/Ph.D.

STUDENT LIFE

Arizona's atmosphere is basically noncompetitive. Explains one second-year student, "I don't mean that students don't try to do their best, I mean they support each other." They also have lives outside the library; the University and the community offer a variety of social, educational, and recreational opportunities, and med students say their classmates are active participants. Although the University offers a variety of housing options, students rate the on-campus dorms and apartments as below par.

ADMISSIONS

Only Arizona residents, highly qualified residents of Alaska, Montana, and Wyoming (through WICHE), and Native Americans from states that border Arizona are eligible for admission. Others will not be considered and should not apply.

In making its decisions, the Admissions Committee considers the academic record, MCAT scores (from the new format test), essays, letters of recommendation, and the interview to be of primary importance. All Arizona residents receive the supplemental application and are invited to interview. Candidates will have four interviews, three with representatives of the medical school and one with a community physician.

Special Programs for Members of Underrepresented Minorities: Arizona has an active program for recruiting, admitting, educating, and graduating minority students. A prematriculation summer program is available.

Transfer Policy: Residents of Arizona who wish to transfer into the medical school will be considered. The Admissions Office can provide specific guidelines.

FINANCIAL AID

Arizona offers institutional, state, and federal loan and scholarship programs. Most financial aid is based on need, but some scholarships are awarded solely on merit. Determination of need is made after a student has been admitted.

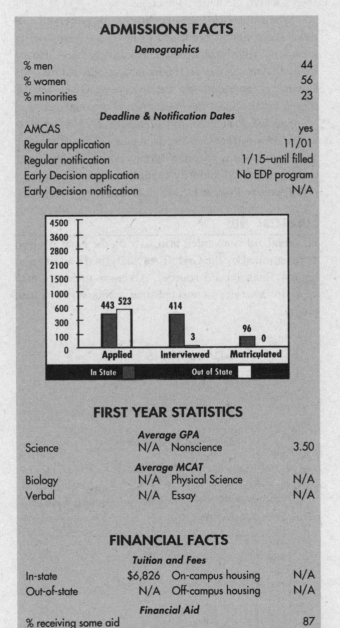

ADMISSIONS FACTS

Demographics

% men	44
% women	56
% minorities	23

Deadline & Notification Dates

AMCAS	yes
Regular application	11/01
Regular notification	1/15–until filled
Early Decision application	No EDP program
Early Decision notification	N/A

FIRST YEAR STATISTICS

Average GPA

Science	N/A	Nonscience	3.50

Average MCAT

Biology	N/A	Physical Science	N/A
Verbal	N/A	Essay	N/A

FINANCIAL FACTS

Tuition and Fees

In-state	$6,826	On-campus housing	N/A
Out-of-state	N/A	Off-campus housing	N/A

Financial Aid

% receiving some aid	87
Merit scholarships	no
Average debt	N/A

HITS AND MISSES

HITS	MISSES
Overall happiness	On-campus housing
Faculty accessibility	Lack of public transportation
Library	
Clinical facilities	
Noncompetitive, friendly classmates	
Extracurricular involvement	

TUITION OVERVIEW

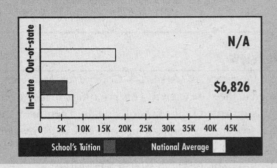

University of Arkansas for Medical Sciences College of Medicine

Office of Admissions
4301 West Markham Street, Little Rock, AR 72205
(501) 686-5354

OVERVIEW

The University of Arkansas College of Medicine is located in the state capital. This proximity to the government is reflected in the school's goals. Their main mission is to train physicians to provide care to the residents of Arkansas. Still, as evidenced by the school's MD/Ph.D. program, research is also a priority.

ACADEMICS

The curriculum at UAMS is fairly traditional. The first two years are primarily devoted to the basic sciences and the third and fourth years are spent in clerkships and electives. Patient contact begins during the first year, but it is extremely limited; the main focus is on departmental science courses. Clinical exposure intensifies during the second year as students investigate abnormal functions of the human body and learn physical examination and evaluation skills. Ethical and behavioral science issues in medicine are also investigated.

Most required clerkships are completed in the third year, but a primary care elective and a specialty rotation are mandatory in the fourth year. The balance of the fourth year is elective. Clinical teaching is done in the University Hospital and its affiliates, including six Area Health Education Centers around the state.

Grading and Promotion Policy: A–F for most courses; Pass/Fail for electives. Students must pass Part I of the USMLE.

Additional Degree Programs: MD/Ph.D.

STUDENT LIFE

The University of Arkansas reserves the right to require single students to live in on-campus residence halls. There are a number of housing options for both single and married students.

ADMISSIONS

Since no out-of-state applicants are accepted until all qualified Arkansas residents have been admitted, non-residents are discouraged from applying unless they have outstanding credentials. Those applying from out of state should have GPAs of 3.5 or higher and MCAT scores above the national average.

When the AMCAS application is received, all Arkansas residents are asked to interview with faculty members. Highly qualified nonresidents may also be invited. Among the selection factors the Admissions Committee considers are the interview, GPA, MCAT scores, letters of recommendation, and personal qualities.

Special Programs for Members of Underrepresented Minorities: UAMS participates in an affirmative action admissions program through which it encourages underrepresented minority candidates to apply.

Transfer Policy: UAMS does not accept transfers.

FINANCIAL AID

Financial aid is awarded primarily on the basis of need as determined by the GAPSFAS analysis. In addition to regular financial aid sources, Arkansas residents may apply for a service-connected state scholarship and loan program.

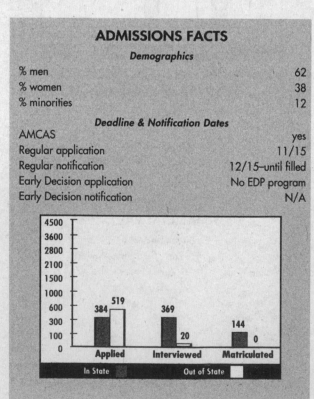

ADMISSIONS FACTS

Demographics

% men	62
% women	38
% minorities	12

Deadline & Notification Dates

AMCAS	yes
Regular application	11/15
Regular notification	12/15–until filled
Early Decision application	No EDP program
Early Decision notification	N/A

	Applied	Interviewed	Matriculated
In State	384	369	144
Out of State	519	20	0

FIRST YEAR STATISTICS

Average GPA
Science N/A Non-science 3.52 (93% above 3.0)

Average MCAT
Biology N/A Physical Science N/A
Verbal N/A Essay N/A

FINANCIAL FACTS

Tuition and Fees
In-state $7,729 On-campus housing N/A
Out-of-state $14,725 Off-campus housing N/A

Financial Aid
% receiving some aid 80
Merit scholarships N/A
Average debt N/A

TUITION OVERVIEW

Out-of-state $14,725
In-state $7,729

0 5K 10K 15K 20K 25K 30K 35K 40K 45K

School's Tuition National Average

University of California: Davis School of Medicine

Office of Admissions, Davis, CA 95616
(916) 752-2717

OVERVIEW

UC Davis explains its educational philosophy and goals in its admissions bulletin: "we are committed to instilling in our students the fundamental principles of medicine, along with a spirit of inquiry and a dedication to compassionate patient care." But how do these ideals hold up under the scrutiny of the students who attend this medium-sized California school? Very well indeed. The students we surveyed at UC Davis are among the happiest med students we talked to. An extremely diverse, laid-back student body, a faculty as interested in teaching as it is in research grants, and outstanding clinical training are the top reasons Davis students say they couldn't be happier with their choice of med school.

ACADEMICS

According to students, UC Davis's curriculum is "a balance between the academic and the clinical." Although the first two years are concerned primarily with developing in students the scientific knowledge and skills fundamental to the practice of medicine, courses emphasize the correlation between basic science principles and clinical practice. Courses are taught both departmentally and interdepartmentally, and, in the sophomore year, organization is largely systemic. A Physical Diagnosis practicum spans both preclinical years, and students are extremely satisfied with the opportunities this longitudinal course gives them to work with actual patients. "The high degree of early clinical exposure is a big plus," one second-year student tells us. But regular course requirements aren't the only vehicle by which students gain practical experience. A student explains, "One of the best things about the first two years at Davis is the opportunity to volunteer in one of the four clinics run by Davis students and faculty. It provides a chance to learn how to interview, examine, and present patients in a relaxed atmosphere. It also gives us a break from classwork and reminds us of why we're here."

In the third and fourth years, students complete clerkships in a variety of disciplines. While all of the rotations in the junior year are mandatory, there is a greater degree of flexibility in the senior year. All fourth-year students must take a two-week course which emphasizes physicians' social, ethical, and legal responsibilities. Clinical teaching takes place at the UC Davis Medical Center in Sacramento and in other affiliated facilities.

Students rate their instructors as outstanding, and laud members of the faculty and administration for their willingness to help students do their best. "The school provides excellent support, " says one student. "We have tutoring and many other services to help us in and out of class." Facilities, too, get high marks. Considering the general commendations students give to the school's clinical instruction, it is little surprise that they consider Davis's hospitals and other clinical teaching sites to be exceptional. Praise also extends to classrooms, labs, and computing facilities.

Grading and Promotion Policy: A–F. Students must take Parts I and II of the USMLE.

Additional Degree Programs: MD/Ph.D.

STUDENT LIFE

"Students are extremely diverse," reveals one second-year student. "Ages range from twenty-two to fifty. Some people are single, some are married, and some are parents. There is a mix of racial backgrounds and sexual orientations." Her classmates concur; their ratings of Davis place it among the most diverse schools in our survey. Luckily, the mix of people seems to work for Davis students. One third-year tells us, "The diversity makes for a richness of experience that's hard to find." Another adds, "There is a strong academic, personal, and social network here. There aren't many cutthroats." In fact, students rate competition among their classmates as low, saying that most people go out of their way to help those who are having trouble keeping up with their studies. This spirit of cooperation extends also to the community outside the med school. Students say that nearly everyone is involved in the volunteer clinics Davis sponsors.

Lest they give the impression that Davis is all work and altruism, students are quick to point out they know how to have fun and have plenty of opportunities to get away from their academic and professional pursuits. The University offers a number of on-campus diversions. Athletic facilities include a recreation center, swimming pools, an equestrian center, a bowling alley, and tennis, handball, racquetball, volleyball, and basketball courts. There is also a well-subscribed intramural program. Off-campus recreational activities abound, and the school rents a variety of sports equipment to students.

The University offers several different types of housing, some with mandatory meal plans, and maintains a list of off-campus rental units. Unlike students at most schools, those we surveyed at Davis were about equally satisfied with on- and off-campus offerings. They also report that public transportation is both accessible and safe.

ADMISSIONS

UC Davis shows preference to California residents, but non-residents may apply. The selection factors the Admissions Committee considers include the academic record, MCAT scores, letters of recommendation, exposure to the medical profession, extracurricular activities, community service, and motivation and suitability for the practice of medicine.

Current students add that the Admissions Committee seems to make a conscious effort to admit a diverse student body. "They want more than just numbers, research, and volunteer activities," reports one first-year who says that his experiences unrelated to academics and medicine tipped the balance when he applied to Davis. Others students stress that Davis gives non-traditional students a better chance for admission than do many other schools.

Special Programs for Members of Underrepresented Minorities: One Latina student tells us, "Davis is excellent in the recruitment and retention of students of color from disadvantaged backgrounds. There are many academic and psychological support systems." The Office of Minority Affairs coordinates these special services. Offerings include premedical development programs, a summer prematriculation session, review classes for Part I of the USMLE, academic advising, counseling, and tutoring. The extra effort has paid off; UC Davis is among the top med schools in minority admissions.

Transfer Policy: Transfer applicants in good standing at accredited U.S. or Canadian med schools will be considered on a space-available basis

FINANCIAL AID

Since UC Davis is a state school, there is no tuition for California residents. The majority of assistance is awarded on the basis of need, but there are some merit scholarships.

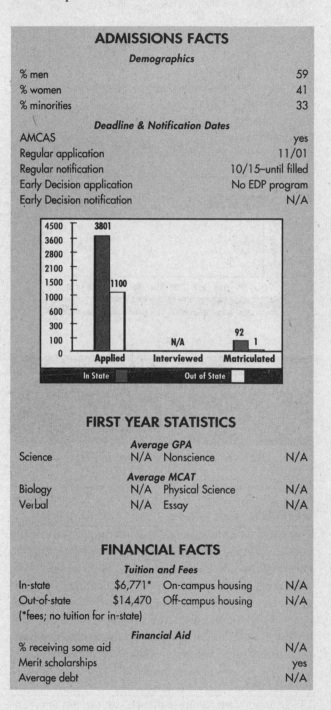

ADMISSIONS FACTS

Demographics

% men	59
% women	41
% minorities	33

Deadline & Notification Dates

AMCAS	yes
Regular application	11/01
Regular notification	10/15–until filled
Early Decision application	No EDP program
Early Decision notification	N/A

FIRST YEAR STATISTICS

Average GPA

Science	N/A	Nonscience	N/A

Average MCAT

Biology	N/A	Physical Science	N/A
Verbal	N/A	Essay	N/A

FINANCIAL FACTS

Tuition and Fees

In-state	$6,771*	On-campus housing	N/A
Out-of-state	$14,470	Off-campus housing	N/A
(*fees; no tuition for in-state)			

Financial Aid

% receiving some aid	N/A
Merit scholarships	yes
Average debt	N/A

HITS AND MISSES

HITS

Quality of teaching

Accessibility of faculty and administration
Academic support
Early clinical exposure
Diversity
Overall facilities
On- and off-campus housing
Public transportation

MISSES

There was no consensus among students about areas in which Davis needs to improve.

TUITION OVERVIEW

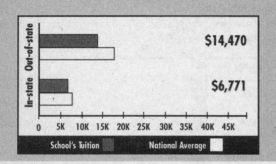

$14,470

$6,771

Out-of-state

In-state

0   5K 10K 15K 20K 25K 30K 35K 40K 45K

School's Tuition   National Average

University of California: Irvine College of Medicine

Admissions, 118 Med Surge I, Irvine, CA 92717
(714) 856-5388

OVERVIEW

The UC Irvine College of Medicine has grown rapidly both in size and reputation since its founding in 1968. Decidedly multicultural, its student body is one of the most diverse of any med school. According to the Admissions Office, only slightly more than a third of students are white. But no matter what your racial or ethnic background, if you're tempted by sun and an emphasis on primary care, this may be the place for you.

ACADEMICS

UC Irvine's curriculum is divided into traditional two-year basic science and clinical units. During the basic science years, a variety of teaching methods—including lectures, labs, interdisciplinary courses, problem-based learning, independent study, and computer-assisted learning—are employed.

Patient contact begins in the first year. During the second year, students learn physical diagnosis and participate in introductions to each of the third-year clinical clerkship areas. The third and fourth years are devoted to rotations and electives. A primary care rotation is required.

Grading and Promotion Policy: A–F.

Additional Degree Programs: MD/Ph.D.

STUDENT LIFE

Students at the med school have access to the facilities of the undergraduate campus. Living in southern California has its benefits, too. The terrific climate and the close proximity to the coast make UC Irvine an attractive spot for sun worshipers and water sports enthusiasts. On-campus housing is available for single and married students.

ADMISSIONS

Although it is UC Irvine's policy to accept only California residents, members of underrepresented minorities are encouraged to apply from out of state. According to the Admissions Office, primary selection factors are the interview, the science and nonscience GPAs, MCAT scores (from the new test), letters of recommendation, extracurricular activities, volunteer work, and exposure to the medical profession.

Special Programs for Members of Underrepresented Minorities: UC Irvine has an active recruitment program that is coordinated by its Minority Affairs division. Its offerings include a postbaccalaureate program for rejected applicants, community outreach programs, summer sessions for high school and college students, a prematriculation summer session, academic advising, tutoring, peer counseling, and review sessions for the USMLE Part I.

Transfer Policy: UC Irvine does not accept transfers.

FINANCIAL AID

There is no tuition for California residents, but there is financial aid available for students who need help in paying fees and expenses. Some merit scholarships are available.

ADMISSIONS FACTS

Demographics

% men	59
% women	41
% minorities	10

Deadline & Notification Dates

AMCAS	yes
Regular application	11/01
Regular notification	11/15-until filled
Early Decision application	No EDP
Early Decision notification	N/A

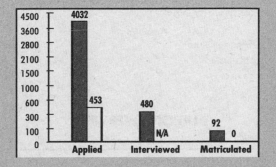

	Applied	Interviewed	Matriculated
	4032 / 453	480 / N/A	92 / 0

FIRST YEAR STATISTICS

Average GPA

Science	3.55	Nonscience	3.58

Average MCAT
Mean 10.20, no breakdown available

Biology	N/A	Physical Science	N/A
Verbal	N/A	Essay	N/A

FINANCIAL FACTS

Tuition and Fees

In-state	$7,259*	On-campus housing	N/A
Out-of-state	$14,958	Off-campus housing	N/A

(*fees; no tuition for in-state)

Financial Aid

% receiving some aid	87
Merit scholarships	yes
Average debt	N/A

TUITION OVERVIEW

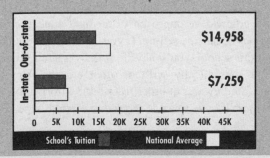

Out-of-state $14,958
In-state $7,259

School's Tuition � National Average ☐

University of California: Los Angeles, UCLA School of Medicine

Office of Admissions, Center for Health Sciences, Los Angeles, CA 90024
(310) 825-6081

OVERVIEW

UCLA is one of three California institutions often ranked among the top research-oriented med schools. But biomedical investigation isn't the school's only strength. Extensive early clinical exposure and fine teaching hospitals with a diverse patient base are other outstanding features.

ACADEMICS

UCLA's curriculum is divided into the usual preclinical and clinical units, but patient contact starts first year. In addition to traditional science courses, freshmen learn how to take patient histories and perform basic physical exams. A Preceptorship Program gives students the opportunity to practice these skills and to observe physicians at work. Even more clinical exposure can be gained in the spring quarter's Freshman Elective Program.

Second-year students continue their study of the scientific basis of medicine, but courses are structured around organ systems and taught by a multidisciplinary faculty. The clinical orientation of the first year intensifies in the sophomore curriculum and helps provide a transition to the third- and fourth-year clerkships. In addition to required rotations, junior and senior students may participate in a variety of electives.

Grading and Promotion Policy: A–F.

Additional Degree Programs: UCLA offers a Medical Scientist Training Program that leads to a combined MD/Ph.D.

STUDENT LIFE

The medical school is located on UCLA's main campus, so students have the amenities of a large university at their disposal. The urban location and the close proximity to the beach also provide numerous opportunities for social, recreational, and cultural activities. And, of course, the weather is wonderful.

The med school provides on-campus housing for both married and single students. Off-campus housing—though expensive—is plentiful.

ADMISSIONS

Preference is given to California residents, but highly qualified out-of-state students are encouraged to apply. The Admissions Committee considers the GPA, MCAT scores, letters of recommendation, and essays to be the most important factors in selecting candidates to invite to interview.

Special Programs for Members of Underrepresented Minorities: An admissions subcommittee coordinates UCLA's efforts to recruit underrepresented minority students and students from disadvantaged backgrounds. Among its offerings is a prematriculation summer session.

Transfer Policy: Applications for transfer into the third-year class are considered if the student is in good standing at an accredited U.S. med school.

FINANCIAL AID

Financial aid awards are primarily based on need, but academic merit is a consideration for some scholarships.

ADMISSIONS FACTS

Demographics

% men	57
% women	43
% minorities	28

Deadline & Notification Dates

AMCAS	yes
Regular application	11/01
Regular notification	1/15–until filled
Early Decision application	No EDP program
Early Decision notification	no EDP

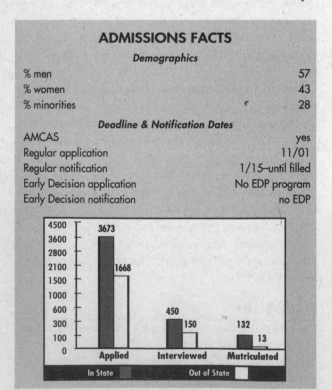

FIRST YEAR STATISTICS

Average GPA			
Science	3.57	Nonscience	3.64

Average MCAT			
Biology	N/A	Physical Science	N/A
Verbal	N/A	Essay	N/A

FINANCIAL FACTS

Tuition and Fees

In-state*	$7,144*	On-campus housing	N/A
Out-of-state	$14,843	Off-campus housing	N/A

(*fees; no tuition for in-state)

Financial Aid

% receiving some aid	N/A
Merit scholarships	yes
Average debt	N/A

TUITION OVERVIEW

$14,843

$7,144

0 5K 10K 15K 20K 25K 30K 35K 40K 45K

School's Tuition   National Average

University of California: San Diego School of Medicine

Admissions Office, 0621, 9500 Gilman Dr., La Jolla, CA 92093-0621
(619) 534-3880

OVERVIEW

Recognized as a top research-oriented school, UCSD offers a progressive approach to medical education in a gorgeous oceanside setting. If you want to find out more about this school, you'll have to fork over a few bucks to get its energetically written, often entertaining catalogue. But beware: in order to find the information you want, you'll have to wade through a myriad of personal essays, some of which are oh-so-California. A sample: "Out in the water, what seemed at first to be schools of seals turn humanoid as they lift onto day-glo surfboards and lean into five-foot curls. A hundred feet below me on the beach, nude joggers jog and naked frisbee-ers friz and volley-ballers volley *au naturel*." But don't get scared off. UCSD has a lot to offer.

ACADEMICS

The curriculum at UCSD is highly innovative. In all four years, students take courses from a required core and from a wide selection of electives. Instruction in the first two years emphasizes integration both within the basic sciences and between scientific principles and clinical applications. Courses are taught interdepartmentally, and much of the organization is based on organ systems. Preclinical students at UCSD don't spend all their time in lectures and labs; a significant amount of instruction is done in small groups, and there is ample time for electives.

Early clinical exposure comes through a five-quarter Introduction to Clinical Medicine (ICM) course. In ICM, first- and second-year students learn fundamental communication, examination, and diagnosis skills through lectures, demonstrations, group discussions, and hands-on experience with patients.

The third and fourth years make up the clinical portion of the curriculum. Required clerkships are spread out over the two years, and the balance of the time (which adds up to about one full year) is reserved for electives. All students must complete an independent study program in order to graduate.

Grading and Promotion Policy: Honors/Pass/Fail for requirements, Pass/Fail for electives. Students must pass Part I of the USMLE and take Part II in order to advance or graduate.

Additional Degree Programs: UCSD offers a funded Medical Scientist Training Program that leads to the MD/Ph.D. Other combined degree programs include MD/MA, MD/MPH, and a regular MD/Ph.D.

STUDENT LIFE

The med school is located on the university's campus in posh—and beautiful—La Jolla. The seaside site allows for water sports limited only by the imagination. Nearby San Diego was recently rated one of the most livable U.S. cities and offers plenty of cultural and recreational opportunities, including one of the world's most famous zoos. On-campus housing is available.

ADMISSIONS

UCSD gives preference to California residents and to applicants from western states without med schools (through the WICHE program). Highly qualified students from out of state are also invited to apply.

The Admissions Committee bases its evaluation of each candidate on a variety of factors: the academic record, with the GPA and the level and breadth of coursework taken into consideration; MCAT scores from the new format test; extracurricular and scholarly activities; letters of recommendation; and the interview.

Special Programs for Members of Underrepresented Minorities: A special Admissions Subcommittee evaluates and interviews underrepresented minority applicants and candidates from disadvantaged backgrounds. A prematriculation summer session is available.

Transfer Policy: UCSD does not accept transfers.

FINANCIAL AID

There is no tuition for Californians, and even nonresidents pay significantly less than they would at a private school. Most financial assistance is based on financial need. Regents scholarships are awarded on the basis of academic merit, but the amount of the scholarship depends on the recipient's financial status.

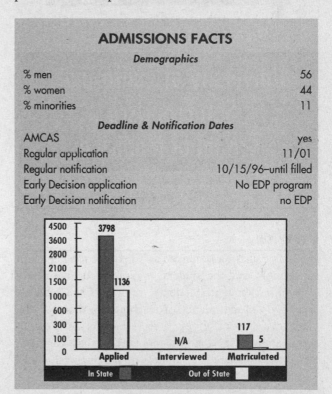

ADMISSIONS FACTS

Demographics

% men	56
% women	44
% minorities	11

Deadline & Notification Dates

AMCAS	yes
Regular application	11/01
Regular notification	10/15/96–until filled
Early Decision application	No EDP program
Early Decision notification	no EDP

In State / Out of State — Applied: 3798 / 1136; Interviewed: N/A; Matriculated: 117 / 5

FIRST YEAR STATISTICS

Average GPA

Science	N/A	Non-science	3.62

Average MCAT

Biology	N/A	Physical Science	N/A
Verbal	N/A	Essay	N/A

FINANCIAL FACTS

Tuition and Fees

In-state	$7,520*	On-campus housing	N/A
Out-of-state	$15,219	Off-campus housing	N/A

(*fees; no tuition for in-state)

Financial Aid

% receiving some aid	70
Merit scholarships	yes
Average debt	N/A

TUITION OVERVIEW

Out-of-state: $12,309

In-state: $4,610

0 5K 10K 15K 20K 25K 30K 35K 40K 45K

School's Tuition   National Average

University of California: San Francisco School of Medicine

Admissions, C-200, Box 0408, San Francisco, CA 94143
(415) 476-4044

OVERVIEW

UCSF is consistently ranked as one of the top ten medical schools, and the students we surveyed love nearly everything about it. Students' ratings of the school's diversity and the quality of teaching top those of any other school in our survey. In fact, students are so enthusiastic about UCSF that just about the harshest comment we got was, "There is absolutely *no* parking available! I wish someone had told me this earlier."

ACADEMICS

The first two years of the curriculum are devoted to the basic sciences. In this preclinical period, there is a large degree of integration between disciplines and attention to clinical correlations. Many courses are interdepartmental, and increasing emphasis is being put on small-group and problem-based learning. Clinical exposure begins first year, and students agree that they are pleased with the amount of early patient contact they have.

Students are nearly unanimous in giving the quality of teaching the highest rating possible, lauding also the accessibility of the faculty. Says one first-year student, "The faculty here at UCSF treats us extremely well. [They] know us by name and are extremely approachable."

"Progressive" and "receptive" are adjectives that come up over and over in students' comments about their teachers. Explains one second-year student, "If you want to come to a school that is excellent, but doesn't expect you to stop thinking about the world and medicine's relationship to it, this is the place. UCSF is an incredibly open atmosphere when it comes to acceptance of alternative ways to think about medicine."

Students give high marks to UCSF for the number of women and minority faculty members and the perspective this heterogeneity lends to teaching: "About fifty percent of lecturers and course directors are women; there are plenty of female researchers. We have more minority physicians in our faculty [than other schools], and there is sensitivity to cultural diversity and its relationship to the delivery of care."

Praise also extends to the academic counseling program. At UCSF, students choose advisors during the first year and those same faculty members serve as "advocates and mentors" for the entire four years. Reviews of facilities were more mixed, however, with commendations going to the outstanding clinical facilities and the "internationally known" library. Computer labs and classrooms didn't fare as well, with students rating them as only satisfactory.

Grading and Promotion Policy: First year, Pass/Fail. Afterwards, Honors/Pass/Fail. A passing grade on the USMLE Part I is required for promotion and graduation.

Additional Degree Programs: Among the combined degree programs UCSF offers are: The Medical Scientist Training Program (MD/Ph.D.), the MD with Thesis, MD/MS, MD/MA, MD/MPH, and the UC Berkeley-UC San Francisco Joint Medical Program (MS/MD).

STUDENT LIFE

The first thing most UCSF students mention when asked about their student body is that it's diverse: fifty-four percent of students are nonwhite, and twenty-two percent belong to traditionally underrepresented minorities. Another recurring theme, but one students don't agree on, is competition. Overall, students rate their classmates as moderately to very competitive, although some students disagree. Reports one, "Competition among students is minimal particularly since the first year is Pass/Fail. By the second year when Honors are introduced, positive interactions are already established." Another student was more cynical, suggesting that the unspoken rule is: "Be competitive, but don't look that way."

Outside of the classroom, students feel they have fairly active social lives and that students are very involved in UCSF's many clubs and activities. While they find the campus itself only moderately attractive, they are thrilled with San Francisco, its climate, and its public transit system. On-campus housing got the lowest rating of any item on the survey—students complain both about quality and availability—but students report plenty of off-campus housing exists within easy walking distance of the school.

ADMISSIONS

UCSF gives preference to residents of California, but up to 20 percent of students can come from out of state. Especially encouraged to apply as nonresidents are candidates with superior qualifications, members of underrepresented minorities, and students whose states participate in the Western Interstate Commission for Higher Education (WICHE). WICHE applicants are shown no preference in admission, but pay in-state fees.

UCSF is among the most selective medical schools in the country. Since the School of Medicine interviews only about 11 percent of its applicants and admits only about 3 percent of the total applicant pool, students are urged "to study carefully their own capacities and motivation; to consult with their counselors and with professionals in the field of their interest; and to compare thoroughly [UCSF's] entrance requirements with their records and courses." Successful applicants have strong academic backgrounds, experience in the medical field through volunteer, research, or work activities, and "superior personal qualities."

Special Programs for Members of Underrepresented Minorities: Committed to graduating physicians "who reflect the ethnic and cultural diversity of the communities they will serve and who are sensitive to the needs of a pluralistic society," UCSF is one of the most racially balanced schools in the country. Still, increased representation of minorities continues to be a top priority of the Admissions Office and Student Academic Services. Special programs available to minorities and students from disadvantaged backgrounds include tutoring and a comprehensive orientation program.

Transfer Policy: UCSF does not accept transfers.

eMail: JMCKINNE@MEDSCH.UCSF.EDU

FINANCIAL AID

California residents pay no tuition, and their yearly academic fees add up to under $4,000. Even out-of-state students get a huge break. Including fees, a year costs less than $12,000. Of course, students love how little they spend to go to one of the top-rated schools in the nation. Exclaims one, "[It's the] best bang for the buck! Harvard and Stanford can't be worth $20,000 a year more!" All financial aid is awarded on the basis of need as determined by the College Scholarship Service.

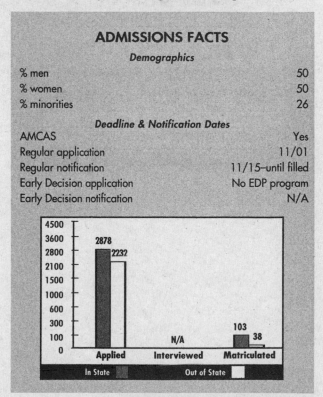

ADMISSIONS FACTS

Demographics

% men	50
% women	50
% minorities	26

Deadline & Notification Dates

AMCAS	Yes
Regular application	11/01
Regular notification	11/15–until filled
Early Decision application	No EDP program
Early Decision notification	N/A

FIRST YEAR STATISTICS

Average GPA

Overall	3.71	Science	3.72

Average MCAT

Biology	11	Physical Science	11
Verbal	11	Essay	N/A

FINANCIAL FACTS

Tuition and Fees

In-state	$6,621*	On-campus housing	N/A
Out-of-state	$14,320	Off-campus housing	N/A

(*fees; no tuition for in-state)

Financial Aid

% receiving some aid	N/A
Merit scholarships	yes
Average debt	N/A

HITS AND MISSES

HITS	MISSES
Diversity	On-campus housing
Quality of teaching	Competition can be intense
Accessibility of faculty	
San Francisco	
Research	
Library	

TUITION OVERVIEW

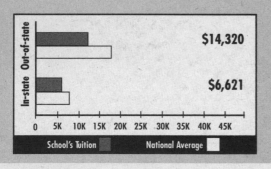

Out-of-state		$14,320
In-state		$6,621

0 5K 10K 15K 20K 25K 30K 35K 40K 45K

School's Tuition ▪   National Average ▫

Loma Linda University School of Medicine

Associate Dean for Admissions, Loma Linda, CA 92350
(800) 422-4558

OVERVIEW

The School of Medicine was founded in 1909 and is part of the Loma Linda University, an institution owned and operated by the Seventh-Day Adventist Church. According to LLU's literature, "The major objective of the School of Medicine is to prepare students who are well grounded in both the science and the art of medicine. It is the school's goal to prepare students with a solid foundation of medical knowledge, to assist them in the attainment of professional skills, and to motivate investigative curiosity and a desire to participate in the advancement of knowledge. It is the school's purpose that its graduates apply Christian principles in their service to mankind."

ACADEMICS

Although LLU's curriculum includes the courses found in most other U.S. medical schools, its religious affiliation adds another dimension. In addition to taking instruction in the basic sciences, freshmen and sophomores also participate in a Whole Person Formation continuum. The school's literature explains, "Courses and content are offered to emphasize Biblical, ethical, and relational aspects of the practice of medicine."

Aside from Whole Person Formation, first-year students take courses in the basic and behavioral sciences and begin to learn how to interact with patients. The year is divided into three quarters, with orientation to clinical medicine increasing in each segment. The first quarter is devoted to Gross Anatomy and Embryology; Histology; Biochemistry; and Human Behavior. Second-quarter students expand on their scientific knowledge through courses like Neuroscience and Molecular Biology & Genetics, but also begin to learn interviewing and fundamental diagnosis skills, a process that continues into the third quarter. In the final period, students begin to shift their basic science focus from the normal to the abnormal in preparation for the second year.

A course in pathology extends throughout the second year as students investigate the disease process; its effects on the body, mind, and spirit; and the ways in which a physician can intervene therapeutically. Introduction to Clinical Medicine begins in the third quarter and provides a transition to the third-year clerkships. Complementing basic and clinical science coursework is an investigation of psychosocial and preventative aspects of medicine.

The last two years are devoted to required and elective clinical experiences. In the junior year, students complete forty-eight weeks of rotations in obstetrics/gynecology, pediatrics, medicine, family medicine, surgery, radiology, and psychiatry. Didactic experiences highlight issues identified in clinical experiences. Although five months of the senior year are reserved for electives, students must complete clerkships in radiology, internal medicine, surgery, and neurology.

Grading and Promotion Policy: Pass/Fail. Students must pass Parts I and II of the USMLE.

Additional Degree Programs: MD/Ph.D.

ADMISSIONS

Loma Linda does not show preference to residents of California, but does give priority to members of the Seventh-Day Adventist Church. According to the school, however, "it is a firm policy of the Admissions Committee to admit each year a number of non-church-related applicants who have demonstrated a commitment to Christian principles and are best suited for meeting the educational goals of the school."

All candidates must submit both an AMCAS and a supplementary application. On the basis of this material, the Admissions Committee invites promising candidates for on-campus interviews. The committee's final selections are based on academic performance, MCAT scores, letters of recommendation, extracurricular activities, and the interview. Exposure to the medical field and volunteerism work in students' favor. According to school literature, "The Admissions Committee seeks individuals who have demonstrated a serious personal commitment to the practice of medicine and have altruistic goals and ideals."

Special Programs for Members of Underrepresented Minorities: Although the school subscribes to a nondiscrimination policy, it makes no mention of programs specifically geared to the recruitment or support of underrepresented minority students.

Transfer Policy: Students interested in transferring to LLU should contact the Admissions Office for more information about the current policy.

FINANCIAL AID

If you're interested in attending LLU and are short on funds, you can expect to graduate with a considerable amount of debt. Most federal and school funding is in the form of loans, and assistance from LLU is extremely limited. For the best chance of securing a favorable financial aid package, students should apply as early as possible.

ADMISSIONS FACTS

Demographics

% men	63
% women	37
% minorities	5

Deadline & Notification Dates

AMCAS	yes
Regular application	11/01
Regular notification	12/01–until filled
Early Decision application	8/01
Early Decision notification	10/01

FIRST YEAR STATISTICS

Average GPA

Science	N/A Non-science 3.57

Average MCAT

Biology	N/A	Physical Science	N/A
Verbal	N/A	Essay	N/A

FINANCIAL FACTS

Tuition and Fees

In-state	$21,770	On-campus housing	N/A
Out-of-state	$21,770	Off-campus housing	N/A

Financial Aid

% receiving some aid	N/A
Merit scholarships	N/A
Average debt	N/A

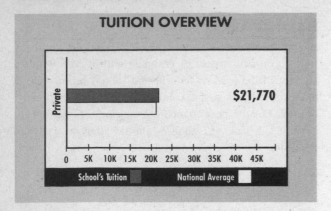

TUITION OVERVIEW

Private

$21,770

0   5K 10K 15K 20K 25K 30K 35K 40K 45K

School's Tuition ▨   National Average ☐

University of Southern California School of Medicine

Office of Admissions
1975 Zonal Avenue, Los Angeles, CA 90033
(213) 342-2552

OVERVIEW

The USC School of Medicine is part of the University's Health Science Campus, located in the heart of northeast Los Angeles. The med school's primary teaching facility is the Los Angeles County + USC Medical Center, a large hospital that provides a culturally and economically diverse patient base. School officials say that excellent teaching hospitals, nationally recognized research efforts, and "extremely dedicated teachers" are among the particular strengths of this popular California school.

ACADEMICS

USC has a modern curriculum that fosters integration among science disciplines, allows for early and extensive clinical exposure, and provides an active, student-oriented learning environment. There is also considerable emphasis on research. Although there is no research requirement in the formal coursework, students are encouraged to pursue investigative activities during elective and vacation time. Fellowships have been set aside to support these activities.

In the first two years, students study the sciences basic to medicine, but they also pay considerable attention to the clinical relevance of the principles they learn. Instruction in the fall semester of each year is arranged by discipline; in the spring, it is organized around organ systems. During basic science courses, clinical problems are used to illustrate key concepts. In addition, students have contact with patients and learn fundamental interaction skills in *Introduction to Clinical Medicine* (ICM). In ICM, small groups of students work with a faculty preceptor to develop and practice patient-interviewing, history-taking, physical examination, and evaluation skills.

The third and fourth years are actually a continuum during which students complete a series of required and elective experiences. Students have considerable freedom in designing of the program of the last two years. Although there are several mandatory clerkships, including those in the major disciplines, the order of these requirements and the selection of elective courses is up to the individual. Most rotations are done at the LA County + USC Medical Center, but a number of other affiliated hospitals act as secondary instruction sites. In addition to clinical experiences, a six-week *Basic and Clinical Science Review* is required of all juniors.

Grading and Promotion Policy: Unsatisfactory/Satisfactory/Near Honors/Honors

Additional Degree Programs: The med school offers a combined BS/MD in conjunction with the undergraduate division. An MD/Ph.D. is also available.

ADMISSIONS

USC shows no preference for residents of California. When the Admissions Office receives the AMCAS application, it asks each student to supply additional information. After evaluating the completed applications, members of the Committee invite the most promising candidates to LA for an interview. For the best chance of acceptance, students should apply as early as possible in the rolling admissions cycle.

According to admissions officials, the primary selection factors are the science GPA, MCAT scores, the interview, and the nonscience GPA. Letters of recommendation, extracurricular activities, exposure to the medical profession, essays, and volunteer activities are also considered important.

Special Programs for Members of Underrepresented Minorities: A minority affairs division coordinates USC's efforts to recruit and support underrepresented minority students. Among its special offerings are community outreach programs, academic advising, tutoring, and peer counseling. Qualified minority students also receive special consideration for admissions.

Transfer Policy: USC considers transfers who have completed the basic science curriculum at an accredited medical school, who have passed USMLE Part I, and who have a compelling reason for relocating to California.

FINANCIAL AID

Most financial assistance is awarded on the basis of documented need. University scholarship and loan programs augment standard federal sources.

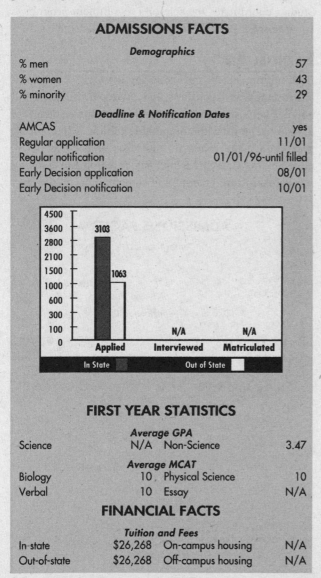

ADMISSIONS FACTS

Demographics

% men	57
% women	43
% minority	29

Deadline & Notification Dates

AMCAS	yes
Regular application	11/01
Regular notification	01/01/96-until filled
Early Decision application	08/01
Early Decision notification	10/01

FIRST YEAR STATISTICS

Average GPA

Science	N/A	Non-Science	3.47

Average MCAT

Biology	10	Physical Science	10
Verbal	10	Essay	N/A

FINANCIAL FACTS

Tuition and Fees

In-state	$26,268	On-campus housing	N/A
Out-of-state	$26,268	Off-campus housing	N/A

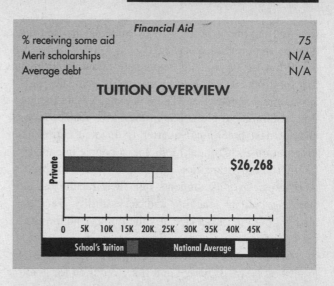

Financial Aid

% receiving some aid	75
Merit scholarships	N/A
Average debt	N/A

TUITION OVERVIEW

$26,268

Private

| 0 | 5K | 10K | 15K | 20K | 25K | 30K | 35K | 40K | 45K |

School's Tuition   National Average

Stanford University School of Medicine

Office of Admissions, 851 Welch Road, Room 154
Palo Alto, CA 94304 -1677
(415) 723-6861

OVERVIEW

If you're interested in research and aren't intimidated by an intense, competitive atmosphere, consider Stanford. At many institutions with comparable reputations, biomedical investigation is the purview of Ph.D. students and closeted faculty members most students never see. Not so at Stanford. Through a unique set of financial incentives, Stanford encourages all its students—regardless of whether their ultimate goal is academic medicine—to get involved in research.

ACADEMICS

Stanford loves research. Although the curriculum can be completed in four years, Stanford urges its students to take additional time for extra electives and/or research interests. Approximately 75 percent of students take at least five years. There are financial incentives for doing additional work: for any credits beyond the required thirteen quarters, students pay only 10 percent of the normal tuition. In addition, students who work as research assistants receive academic credit, tuition credit, stipends, or a combination of these benefits. Research assistantships can be undertaken at any point in the curriculum, but about 70 percent of students choose to do them in the preclinical years.

What many students appreciate about Stanford is that for all the research emphasis, it still provides excellent clinical preparation. There is considerable integration of clinical applications in the basic science years, and the last preclinical quarter is devoted entirely to Preparation for Clinical Medicine, a course intended to facilitate the transition to third- and fourth-year clerkships. Overall, students rate their faculty as outstanding both in teaching and accessibility. Facilities also get high marks, especially the library and the clinical facilities.

Grading and Promotion Policy: Pass/Fail. Passing grades on USMLE Parts I and II are required for graduation.

Additional Degree Programs: About twenty percent of students pursue combined degrees. Both MS/MD and MD/Ph.D. combined degrees are offered. A fully-funded Medical Scientist Training Program is available.

STUDENT LIFE

"The school is rather competitive," one first-year student reports. Her classmates agree. But despite the intensity of competition, students say they like their classmates and enjoy socializing with them. Beyond extracurricular activities sponsored by the medical school, students are welcome to participate in undergraduate organizations. Med students also have full use of the university's athletic facilities and are active in intramural sports. Nearby San Francisco offers a plethora of cultural and recreational opportunities. Both on- and off-campus housing opportunities are very good.

ADMISSIONS

Stanford is a private school and shows no preference for California residents. According to the admission bulletin, "Stanford...is interested in candidates who have a strong humanitarian commitment and who show evidence of originality, creativity, and a capacity for independent, critical thinking. Enthusiasm for the basic sciences and outstanding accomplishment in those areas are prerequisites for admission to the school, but the Committee on Admissions also looks for evidence of breadth of education and/or experience in the humanities and social sciences....The Committee values applications from those students who have tested their enthusiasm for working in the health-care environment,

both in the laboratory and in activities involving the care of others."

Stanford traditionally accepts less than two percent of applicants, making it one of the most selective schools in the country. On the basis of the AMCAS application, supplementary applications are sent to promising candidates, usually about half the total pool. About one-third of students who file supplemental applications are interviewed. Candidates have two one-hour interviews, one with a faculty member and one with a medical student.

Special Programs for Members of Underrepresented Minorities: Stanford recognizes that minorities are not only underrepresented in medicine, but more specifically, in medical education and research. Assistant deans in Student Affairs and the Office of Graduate Studies coordinates the school's recruitment programs.

Transfer Policy: Transfers are not accepted.

FINANCIAL AID

Both tuition and the cost of living are high at Stanford, but research assistantships and favorable financial aid policies help keep student indebtedness lower than it is at many schools with comparable tuition. Although all grants are made solely on the basis of need as determined by the GAPSFAS analysis, research and teaching assistantships are open to any student.

ADMISSIONS FACTS

Demographics

% men	58
% women	42
% minorities	14

Deadline & Notification Dates

AMCAS	yes
Regular application	11/01
Regular notification	10/15–until filled
Early Decision application	8/01
Early Decision notification	10/01

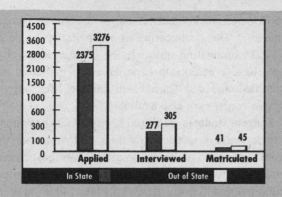

In State ▮ **Out of State** ☐

FIRST YEAR STATISTICS

Average GPA

Science	N/A	Non-science	3.6

Average MCAT

Biology	11	Physical Science	11
Verbal	10	Essay	N/A

FINANCIAL FACTS

Tuition and Fees

In-state	$23,731	On-campus housing	N/A
Out-of-state	$23,731	Off-campus housing	N/A

Financial Aid

% receiving some aid	80
Merit scholarships	none
Average debt	N/A

HITS AND MISSES

HITS	MISSES
Research opportunities	Academic advising
Location	Competition
Students have active social lives	
Clinical facilities	

TUITION OVERVIEW

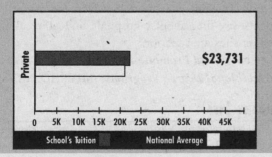

School's Tuition ▮ **National Average** ☐

University of Colorado School of Medicine

Medical School Admissions, 4200 East Ninth Avenue, Denver, CO 80262
(303) 270-4355

OVERVIEW

Attending med school in an area known for its gorgeous scenery and terrific year-round recreational activities might sound like paradise to the outdoor enthusiast. But, if you're not a state resident, don't get your heart set on Colorado just yet. Unless you have outstanding academic qualifications and a very healthy bank balance, this Denver school might not be an option. Only a handful of the spaces in each entering class are open to out-of-state students, and the non-resident tuition—over $40,000/year—makes Colorado the most expensive med school in the US.

ACADEMICS

Colorado's curriculum is divided into two-year preclinical and clinical units. Students spend the basic science period at the University of Colorado Health Sciences Center in Denver, a campus that the med school shares with the schools of dentistry, nursing, pharmacy, and the graduate school. Clinical teaching takes place at the University Hospital, the Colorado General Hospital, the VA Hospital, the Denver General Hospital and a number of other clinical facilities, including rural sites, throughout the state.

The curriculum is in the process of revision, but currently, the first two years focus primarily on the basic sciences. Freshmen begin their medical studies with Human Anatomy, Epidemiology & Biostatistics, and an investigation of Health Issues. Second- and third-quarter classes continue to center around the development of a scientific knowledge base, but an Introduction to Clinical Medicine (ICM) course begins in the second quarter. In the first-year segments of ICM, students learn interviewing and clinical problem-solving skills.

The second year combines of the basic and clinical sciences. There is more attention to the clinical relevance of scientific principles, and, as the year progresses, students have increased exposure to patients. In addition to the usual Pathology, Physiology, and Pharmacology courses, students study the non-bio-logical determinants and effects of disease in Human Behavior. The continuation of ICM teaches students physical examination skills. In the last quarter, sophomores have preclerkship experiences in pediatric and adult medicine and learn basic cardiac life support. Elective courses are also available.

Current students aren't too happy about the content of their basic science curriculum and welcome the school's efforts to revise the program. Foremost among their criticisms are what they perceive to be an "information overload" in the first two years and an inattention to the clinical relevance of the scientific principles they learn. Explains one first-year, "The focus of courses emphasizes tests too much. The emphasis should be taken off traditional tests and be put on clinical applications." Students do say, however, that this situation improves as they move into the end of the basic science curriculum and prepare for their clinical rotations.

In their third year, students begin their clerkships. Twelve weeks in Medicine and six weeks each in Obstetrics/Gynecology, Pediatrics, Psychiatry, Surgery and Surgery Subspecialties are required. Although twenty-eight weeks of the senior year are elective, all students must take a four-week Neurology clerkship and must spend six weeks either in Family Medicine or in Primary Care and Newborn Medicine.

Overall, teaching at Colorado gets high marks. "The faculty and deans are very supportive and are excited about teaching," says one first-year. Students also praise professors for their investigative efforts. Research strengths at Colorado, according to our respondents, are in the areas of neurobiology, immunology, pharmacology, and rural medicine.

Students are less enthusiastic about the school's facilities, most of which are rated as only satisfactory. There is a notable exception, however: the majority of students say the school's hospitals and other clinical teaching sites are superior.

Grading and Promotion Policy: Honors/Pass/Fail.
Additional Degree Programs: MD/PHD; MD/MS.

STUDENT LIFE

Overall, students are very happy at Colorado. Competition among classmates is moderate, and our respondents say that "students are extremely supportive of each other." Explains one first-year, "I've been pleasantly surprised by the attitudes of students. No one is ever too busy to stop and explain something you're having trouble with."

Although the students we surveyed say they don't lead stellar social lives, they do report a high degree of involvement in Colorado's plentiful school and extra-curricular activities. One second-year reports, "Our school has an outstanding variety of student government activities and excellent opportunities for student leadership."

Students also enjoy the recreational and cultural activities the med school's location in Denver affords; opportunities to engage in outdoor pursuits are especially plentiful. But not everyone is happy with the city. Paramount among their concerns is safety; students say crime is a problem, especially near the med school. Housing is also less than optimal. The med school offers no on-campus residences, and off-campus apartments can be expensive. Since all students commute, parking problems are inevitable; parking, students say, "is both expensive and scarce." Commuters do have other options, though. Those who choose to leave their cars at home find Denver's public transportation system to be relatively accessible and reasonably safe.

ADMISSIONS

First priority is given to Colorado residents, and more than eighty-five percent of students must come from instate. Among nonresidents, applicants from western states without med schools and candidates with exceptionally strong GPAs and MCAT scores are given primary consideration. Because the school admits students on a rolling basis, candidates are strongly encouraged to apply as early as possible. Students with strong credentials for whom Colorado is the first choice may apply through the Early Decision Program.

The primary selection factors include academic performance, MCAT scores, letters of recommendation, and the interview. On the basis of these factors, students who appear to "be the most highly-qualified in terms of intellectual achievement, character, motivation, maturity, and emotional stability" are offered places in the first-year class.

Special Programs for Members of Underrepresented Minorities: The University of Colorado encourages applications from underrepresented minority students. In addition to evaluating these students on the usual criteria, the Admissions Committee "carefully considers the student's social, economic and educational background."

Transfer Policy: Colorado considers transfers into the second and third year on a space-available basis. Students interested in applying for transfer should contact the school to discuss their eligibility.

FINANCIAL AID

Financial aid is awarded primarily on the basis of documented need. University loans and scholarships supplement federal and state aid programs. With nonresident tuition, fees, and expenses easily approaching or exceeding $50,000/year, out-of-state students should carefully plan their finances before matriculating.

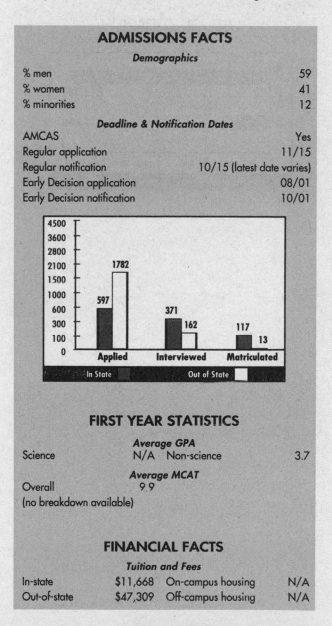

ADMISSIONS FACTS

Demographics

% men	59
% women	41
% minorities	12

Deadline & Notification Dates

AMCAS	Yes
Regular application	11/15
Regular notification	10/15 (latest date varies)
Early Decision application	08/01
Early Decision notification	10/01

In State / Out of State — Applied: 597 / 1782; Interviewed: 371 / 162; Matriculated: 117 / 13

FIRST YEAR STATISTICS

Average GPA

Science	N/A Non-science	3.7

Average MCAT

Overall (no breakdown available)	9.9

FINANCIAL FACTS

Tuition and Fees

In-state	$11,668	On-campus housing	N/A
Out-of-state	$47,309	Off-campus housing	N/A

Financial Aid

% receiving some aid .... N/A
Merit scholarships .... none
Average debt .... N/A

HITS AND MISSES

HITS	MISSES
Overall happiness	Early clinical exposure
Quality of teaching	Ethnic and cultural diversity
Teacher accessibility	No on-campus housing
Clinical facilities	Campus safety
Research efforts	
Plenty of campus activities	

TUITION OVERVIEW

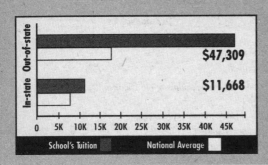

$47,309

$11,668

School's Tuition   National Average

University of Connecticut School of Medicine

Medical Student Affairs
263 Farmington Avenue, Room AG-062, Farmington, CT 06032
(203) 679-2152

OVERVIEW

Nearly all the U Conn students we surveyed say they're happy with their med school experience, though some fret about the conservatism of their classmates and the lack of diversity of the student body. The relatively noncompetitive atmosphere, an accessible administration and faculty, and extensive early clinical exposure are the things our respondents like most about their school.

ACADEMICS

Students are pleased with U Conn's "modern" curriculum. In the first two years, students study the usual basic sciences, but there is a mix of departmental and interdisciplinary courses, all taught by faculty teams. Throughout the two years, students investigate non-biological aspects of medicine through work in the behavioral and social sciences. In addition to lecture courses, students meet in small groups that use problem-based learning strategies. Clinical correlations are emphasized, especially in the second year.

Students are introduced to patients and "the health care team" though Introduction to Clinical Medicine (ICM), a course that starts first semester and continues throughout the preclinical years. In ICM, students learn history-taking, examination, and diagnosis skills. The freshmen and sophomores we surveyed are enthusiastic about their exposure to patients. Says one, "This school's greatest strength is its commitment to clinical medicine instruction during the first two years." Armed with the skills they developed as sophomores, juniors begin a series of clerkships and electives that stretch into the senior year.

U Conn's overall quality of teaching gets high marks, and students praise professors for creating "a cooperative, not competitive environment." Reports one sophomore, "The emphasis is on learning, not grades." Both the administration and the faculty also receive accolades for their approachability and receptiveness. Says one student, "We're not just numbers here. The

teachers and deans know our names and care about and respond to our concerns."

U Conn's humanistic bent extends beyond its treatment of students. To expose students to "diverse populations in the community setting and to broader health issues" and to encourage "a sense of professional responsibility to...low-income minority communities," U Conn requires all students to complete a community service requirement at some time during their four years of study.

Grading and Promotion Policy: Pass/Fail; Honors/Pass/Fail in third year only.

Additional Degree Programs: MD/PhD, MD/MPH.

STUDENT LIFE

"Supportive," "inquisitive," and "exciting to work with" are some of the terms U Conn students use to describe their classmates. But they add that they're not particularly diverse, and some say students tend to be "traditional and conservative." Involvement in community and school activities is moderate, but students say that is partially due to med school's relatively small selection of activities.

Most students are fairly pleased with the school's location in Farmington. Nearby Hartford, the state capital, offers many cultural and recreational attractions, and the mountains and the beach are both within easy driving distance. Off-campus housing opportunities are very good, but students warn that commuting without a car can be a hassle.

ADMISSIONS

U Conn shows preference to state residents, but a portion of each year's class can come from out of state. Nonresidents especially encouraged to apply are students with outstanding qualifications, members of underrepresented minorities, students with close ties to the state, and candidates who are interested in primary care.

The Admissions Committee is made up of faculty members, med students, and members of the medical community. Selection factors include the interview, science and nonscience GPAs, MCAT scores, difficulty of courses, breadth of academic experiences, extracurricular activities, and letters of recommendation.

Transfer Policy: Transfer applicants from U.S. med schools are considered for admission into the third-year class. Preference is given to Connecticut residents.

Special Programs for Members of Underrepresented Minorities: The Office of Minority Student Affairs coordinates U Conn's recruitment and support services for members of underrepresented minorities and for students with disadvantaged backgrounds. Among its offerings are summer programs for high school and college students, MCAT review, a prematriculation summer session, academic advising, tutoring, and peer counseling. Underrepresented minority applicants may also receive some special consideration for admission.

FINANCIAL AID

Financial aid awards are based primarily on need as determined by the GAPSFAS analysis. Long- and short-term loans and scholarships are the primary forms of assistance.

ADMISSIONS FACTS

Demographics

% men	51
% women	49
% minorities	14

Deadline & Notification Dates

AMCAS	yes
Regular application	12/15
Regular notification	10/15–until filled
Early Decision application	8/01
Early Decision notification	10/01

FIRST YEAR STATISTICS

Average GPA

Science	N/A	Nonscience	3.5

Average MCAT

Biology	9.5	Physical Science	9.8
Verbal	9.7	Essay	P

FINANCIAL FACTS

Tuition and Fees

In-state	$10,950	On-campus housing	None
Out-of-state	$20,525	Off-campus housing	N/A

Financial Aid

% receiving some aid	85
Merit scholarships	none
Average debt	$41,880

HITS AND MISSES

HITS	MISSES
Noncompetitive atmosphere	Diversity
Faculty accessibility	Few campus activities
Emphasis on ethics	Public transportation
Early clinical exposure	
Overall happiness	
Responsive administration	

TUITION OVERVIEW

Yale University School of Medicine

Office of Admissions, 367 Cedar Street, New Haven, CT 06510
(203) 785-2643

OVERVIEW

Since Yale is generally regarded as one of the top U.S. med schools, it's no surprise that the majority of the students we surveyed cite its reputation as the number one reason they applied. Though nearly all of our respondents intensely dislike New Haven, they love nearly everything else about Yale. Among its stand-out features, according to students, are its excellent faculty, cutting edge research, flexible curriculum, and its unique evaluation system. (There are no grades.)

ACADEMICS

According to the school bulletin, Yale's approach to medical education permits "the student to enjoy as large a degree of freedom in his or her preparation as is consistent with the fulfillment of requirements for the degree of Doctor of Medicine....Belief in the maturity and responsibility of the students is emphasized by creating a flexible program, through anonymous examinations, eliminating grades, and by encouraging independent study and research." The students we surveyed love Yale's system, but one warns, "The amazing amount of latitude gives you the opportunity and time to pursue personal interests, but requires more self-discipline than might be needed at other, more regimented schools."

The curriculum is divided into three phases, all of which provide the opportunity for students to explore individual interests. The initial phase occupies the first three semesters. During this time, students study the body's normal and abnormal structures and functions, investigate external determinants of health, and explore the history of medicine. To complement basic science coursework, three hours each week are set aside for clinical correlations. Students spend some of this time in lectures and the balance in small-group discussion sections which are conducted by a clinician in a hospital setting.

The fourth semester constitutes the second phase and is devoted primarily to Introduction to Clinical Medicine (ICM). ICM eases students into the clinical phase by teaching them how to take a medical history, perform a physical examination, conduct and interpret lab and other diagnostic tests, and make preliminary diagnoses.

The final phase consists of required and elective clerkships. In the last two years, students are assigned to rotations in the Yale–New Haven Hospital and the school's other clinical affiliates. In addition to clerkships in the major disciplines, students are required to complete a three-week stint in neuroscience and participate in a four-week ambulatory care experience. In addition to completing formal and elective coursework, all students must write a thesis in order to graduate.

As much as students like the way the curriculum is set up, they say they wouldn't be as happy if it weren't for the quality of the faculty. Teachers are rated as outstanding, in and out of the classroom. The learning environment, too, gets high marks, although many say they'd like to see improvements in computing facilities.

Outstanding clinical preparation is only part of the story; students are unanimous in giving Yale the highest possible rating for research. Some of this approbation can be explained by the degree to which students are encouraged to become involved in the school's investigative efforts, especially through the thesis requirement. Says one sophomore, "The thesis affords the opportunity to delve into an area in depth; to build a relationship with the faculty, principal investigator, and other students; and to publish independent research. The school provides funding for research, and there are numerous labs looking for med students to participate."

Grading and Promotion Policy: No grades are given. Students must pass Part I of the USMLE in order to be promoted to the third year and Part II in order to graduate.

Additional Degree Programs: Yale offers a National Institutes of Health-funded Medical Scientist Training Program that leads to a combined MD/Ph.D. Regular MD/Ph.D., MD/MPH, and MD/JD programs are also available.

STUDENT LIFE

One first-year student tells us, "I came to Yale because of the lack of grades. I expected there would be a lot of highly motivated, but not cutthroat students here; that's exactly what I found." His classmates agree. Based on their ratings, Yale places among the least competitive of the schools we surveyed, an atmosphere students attribute almost exclusively to the fact that they don't have to worry about their GPAs. The relaxed environment contributes to a general feeling of goodwill among classmates. Our respondents enjoy active social lives and report that they are very involved in school and community activities.

There's a lot to do at Yale, and students say they like to hang out at the "beautiful undergraduate campus." Educational, social, cultural, and recreational activities abound on the main campus, and many enjoy the full complement of athletic facilities, including weight rooms; exercise equipment; pools; rowing tanks; tennis, racquetball, and squash courts; saunas; steam rooms; and a golf course. Those who need a break from New Haven (and who wouldn't?), can travel to the University's 2,000-acre Recreation Center in East Lyme. The center features cabins, campsites, picnic groves, a dining hall, a lake, trout ponds, trap and skeet fields, and hiking trails.

Far and away the most common complaint about Yale is its location. "New Haven can be pretty depressing," says one student. According to his classmates, it can also be pretty scary. Only a handful of students say they feel safe on and around the med school campus. Although Yale offers some university housing, most of our respondents prefer off-campus offerings.

ADMISSIONS

No special consideration is given to residents of Connecticut. Since Yale does not participate in AMCAS, all students should obtain application materials directly from the school. When we asked the Director of Admissions what she would like to tell students about the admissions process, she responded:

"The Committee on Admissions in general seeks to admit students who best suit the philosophies and goals of the school....It also seeks to ensure an adequate representation of women and minority groups and a diversity of interests and backgrounds.... In considering applicants, the committee views the individual as a whole, taking into consideration each student's academic record, MCAT scores, premedical committee evaluations, letters of recommendation, outside accomplishments, and personal qualities."

"Interviews are arranged only by invitation of the admissions committee. A large number of applicants have attained a high level of academic achievement as indicated by grades and test scores. Activities and accomplishments are of considerable importance in distinguishing candidates as individuals and demonstrating the ability to make significant independent contributions."

Special Programs for Members of Underrepresented Minorities: The Office of Minority Affairs coordinates Yale's efforts to recruit and support members of underrepresented minorities. Among its offerings are community outreach programs, summer sessions for high school and college students, academic advising, peer counseling, and review sessions for Part I of the USMLE. Most of these programs are open to all students, regardless of ethnic background.

Transfer Policy: Because of its unusual curriculum, Yale does not accept transfers.

FINANCIAL AID

Financial aid is awarded solely on the basis of need as determined by the GAPSFAS analysis. Students who show need must take out a unit loan that consists of funding from a variety of loan sources. Yale will then award scholarships to students who still have unmet need.

ADMISSIONS FACTS

Demographics

% men	56
% women	44
% minorities	14

Deadline & Notification Dates

AMCAS	no
Regular application	10/15
Regular notification	3/15–until filled
Early Decision application	8/01
Early Decision notification	10/01

Bar chart:
- Applied: In State 137, Out of State 2558
- Interviewed: In State 37, Out of State 763
- Matriculated: In State 7, Out of State 93

In State / Out of State

FIRST YEAR STATISTICS

Average GPA

Science	N/A	Nonscience	N/A

Average MCAT

Biology	N/A	Physical Science	N/A
Verbal	N/A	Essay	N/A

FINANCIAL FACTS

Tuition and Fees

In-state	$22,175	On-campus housing	N/A
Out-of-state	$22,175	Off-campus housing	N/A

Financial Aid

% receiving some aid	N/A
Merit scholarships	none
Average debt	N/A

HITS AND MISSES

HITS	MISSES
Noncompetitive atmosphere	Computer labs
Quality of teaching	New Haven
Faculty accessibility	Safety
Facilities	Med school campus
Research efforts	On-campus housing
Overall happiness	Public transportation

TUITION OVERVIEW

Private: $22,175

School's Tuition / National Average

George Washington Univ. School of Medicine and Health Sciences

Office of Admissions, 2300 I Street NW, Washington, DC 20037
(202) 994-3506

OVERVIEW

GWU was recently ranked among the top comprehensive med schools. We asked students if it's living up to its reputation. This comment is representative of the response we got: "GWU has a lot to offer. Some of its best assets are a tremendous commitment to the student, emphasis on primary health care, and its location in the most politically active, informed city in the country." Add to this accessible professors and a noncompetitive student body, and you've got a place where you might want to spend a few years.

ACADEMICS

First-year instruction centers around normal human functions and several courses are taught interdepartmentally. The interdisciplinary approach continues into the second year as students focus on the effects of disease on the body. Patient contact begins during the first year and intensifies in the second-year Introduction to Clinical Medicine course, in which students learn historytaking, examination, and diagnostic skills. Overall, first- and second-year students are enthusiastic about the hands-on experience they get in the preclinical years.

The third year is devoted to extended clerkships in the major areas, with an additional required rotation in ambulatory primary care. Although required clerkships also make up about half of the fourth year, the balance of the time is free for electives, both on and off campus.

Students say the quality of teaching is very good, but even more praised is the faculty's attitude. "They don't want you to fail out or to be competitive with your classmates," reports one student. Professors' accessibility outside of class is rated as excellent.

Although students say the classrooms could be better, they are very satisfied with the rest of the school's facilities. GWU's location in the capital gives the added advantage of easy access to the resources of the National Library of Medicine and the National Institute of Health.

Grading and Promotion Policy: Honors/Pass/Conditional/Fail. A passing grade on Part I of the USMLE is required.

Additional Degree Programs: MD/Ph.D., MD/MPH.

STUDENT LIFE

Competition is moderate, and classmates are willing to help each other out. One indication of this cooperation is that 60 percent of the students we surveyed say they're in a study group—a much higher proportion than at most schools. There is also a student-run note service. Although students report less than stellar social lives, they like their classmates. "I picked GWU because I thought the students were happy and got along well together, and that is definitely true," says one fourth-year student.

The GWU campus isn't particularly popular, but Washington, D.C. is. Evidently, concerns about safety are outweighed by the city's considerable cultural and recreational opportunities. Off-campus living, though expensive, is made easier by the city's outstanding mass transit system.

ADMISSIONS

Special consideration is given to applicants from the D.C. area and to GWU undergraduates. In addition, GWU undergrads may apply to the med school through the early assurance program, in which academically talented students are granted admission after the sophomore year. Some students who apply through the regular admissions process may be admitted with the condition that they participate in a decelerated program for the basic science years.

The admissions office considers the following in making their admissions decisions: the interview; academic record, including GPA and level of coursework; MCAT scores; letters of recommendation; essays; extracurricular activities; research experience; and personal qualities. GWU offers regional as well as on-site interviews.

Special Programs for Members of Underrepresented Minorities: GWU encourages underrepresented minority students to apply. Special academic tutoring is available for students who are from educationally disadvantaged backgrounds.

Transfer Policy: GWU considers applications for transfer into the third year.

FINANCIAL AID

"Tuition stinks," says one otherwise happy fourth-year student. Indeed, it is expensive to attend GWU, but a large percentage of students receive some assistance through school-administered loan, grant, and scholarship programs.

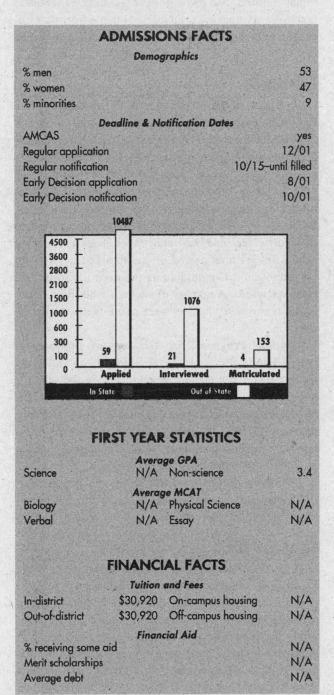

ADMISSIONS FACTS

Demographics

% men	53
% women	47
% minorities	9

Deadline & Notification Dates

AMCAS	yes
Regular application	12/01
Regular notification	10/15–until filled
Early Decision application	8/01
Early Decision notification	10/01

FIRST YEAR STATISTICS

Average GPA

Science	N/A	Non-science	3.4

Average MCAT

Biology	N/A	Physical Science	N/A
Verbal	N/A	Essay	N/A

FINANCIAL FACTS

Tuition and Fees

In-district	$30,920	On-campus housing	N/A
Out-of-district	$30,920	Off-campus housing	N/A

Financial Aid

% receiving some aid	N/A
Merit scholarships	N/A
Average debt	N/A

TUITION OVERVIEW

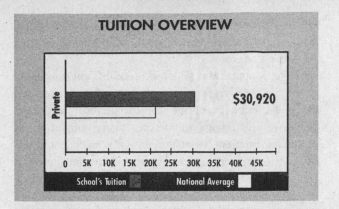

$30,920

School's Tuition   National Average

Georgetown University School of Medicine

Office of Admissions, 3900 Reservoir Road NW, Washington, DC 20007
(202) 687-1154

OVERVIEW

"A school's true value should be placed on how it prepares us...as physicians, something Georgetown has a fine track record of accomplishing," says one second-year student. While the vast majority of students we surveyed cite excellent clinical preparation as the school's major strength, students are also impressed with a curriculum that "emphasizes long-term learning rather than rote memorization" and a growing reputation in research. Add in the fact that it's in exciting Washington, D.C., and has a bunch of self-reported happy and noncompetitive students, and Georgetown is a tempting opportunity. If you can afford it.

ACADEMICS

Georgetown completed a revision of its curriculum in 1990. There is now more small-group, problem-based learning in the preclinical years, and segmented basic science lectures are giving way to interdepartmental courses that emphasize integration between the science and art of medicine. Students like the new curriculum and are especially enthusiastic about the amount of early hands-on experience they receive.

Patient interviews begin in the first month of school, and students are assigned ambulatory care preceptorships in both of the basic science years. Says one first-year student, "This [exposure to patients] has enabled me to keep my long-term vision of working with and helping people in mind while I tromp through the basic sciences."

The fundamental "doctoring skills" students learn in the first two years prepare them for the required and elective clerkships of the clinical period. Third- and fourth-year students laud the many opportunities and diverse patient base Georgetown's "excellent hospitals" afford and report feeling "confident about and well prepared" for their residencies. Several students complain, however, that too many of their classmates "are geared toward specialty fields." Reports one disgruntled student, "Family practice and primary care...are essentially scorned at Georgetown."

Although Georgetown has traditionally been acclaimed as "clinically oriented," students say emphasis on research is increasing. Reports one third-year student, "Our reputation for superior biomedical research is improving. We have...the chance to work with top-notch scientists on some of today's hottest research projects."

Quality of teaching throughout the four years is rated as superior and students report being impressed with the attention professors pay to moral and ethical issues in medicine. Both the faculty and the administration are perceived as "very caring" and "responsive to students' needs and suggestions."

Students agree that basic science classrooms, computer labs, and the library are very good, but say they'd like to have more space to study. Students can also take advantage of federal facilities; one fourth-year student points out that Washington is the home of the National Institute of Health and the National Library of Medicine.

Grading and Promotion Policy: Honors/High Pass/ Pass/Fail. For first- and second-year electives, Satisfactory/Unsatisfactory.

Additional Degree Programs: MD/Ph.D. An MD/ MBA is in the works. Georgetown also has an early assurance program for undergraduate students in their sophomore years.

STUDENT LIFE

"No one here is cutthroat," reports one second-year student. While this may be something of an overstatement, Georgetown students rate their classmates as surprisingly noncompetitive. Says one fourth-year student, "Students in each class are very willing to help each other learn." They also help each other play; students say that they and their classmates have very active social lives. In fact, no school topped Georgetown in this category.

Georgetown's location and a good public transportation system makes it easy to get out and about. By and large, students love Washington, D.C. and its educational, cultural, and recreational opportunities. There is no university housing available, but that's fine with students; off-campus housing, though expensive, is plentiful.

ADMISSIONS

Georgetown shows no preference for residents of any state. Competition is keen: the entering class of about 200 represents about 2.5 percent of the total applicant pool. All candidates who file an AMCAS application are mailed a supplemental application. The initial screening is based on information from both sources. Of particular interest to the Admissions Committee are grades, MCAT scores, letters of recommendation, essays, and extracurricular, and research experiences. Promising candidates are interviewed. If you're asked to talk with the Admissions Committee, be prepared for some personal questions. A number of students who interviewed at Georgetown report they were asked their opinion on abortion.

Special Programs for Members of Underrepresented Minorities: Students rate Georgetown extremely low on ethnic and racial diversity. Among the school's efforts to recruit qualified minority students is the Georgetown Experimental Medical Studies (GEMS) program. In this program, talented underrepresented minority students complete a postbaccalaureate year in preparation for medical school.

Transfer Policy: Transfers into the second- or third-year class are considered if space becomes available through attrition.

FINANCIAL AID

Although Georgetown's tuition has remained constant for the past six years, at $22,500 it's still very expensive. All financial assistance is awarded solely on the basis of need. In order to be eligible for school-administered funds and loan programs, students—even if married or otherwise independent—must supply parental information. A significant number of students have military scholarships. About 75 percent of students receive some form of assistance.

ADMISSIONS FACTS

Demographics

% men	67
% women	33
% minorities	10

Deadline & Notification Dates

AMCAS	yes
Regular application	11/01
Regular notification	10/15–until filled
Early Decision application	8/01
Early Decision notification	10/01

10873

4500		
3600		
2800		
2100		
1500		
1000		
600		
300		182
100	52	N/A	4
0		
	Applied	Interviewed	Matriculated

In State   Out of State

FIRST YEAR STATISTICS

Average GPA

Science	N/A	Non-science	3.51

Average MCAT

Biology	N/A	Physical Science	N/A
Verbal	N/A	Essay	N/A

FINANCIAL FACTS

Tuition and Fees

In-state	$22,500	On-campus housing	N/A
Out-of-state	$22,500	Off-campus housing	N/A

Financial Aid

% receiving some aid	N/A
Merit scholarships	yes
Average debt	N/A

HITS AND MISSES

HITS	MISSES
Clinical orientation	Not enough support for primary care
Quality of teaching	No on-campus housing
Approachable faculty and administration	Diversity
Students have active social lives	
Not a lot of "cutthroats"	
Washington, D.C. area	
Emphasis on ethics	

TUITION OVERVIEW

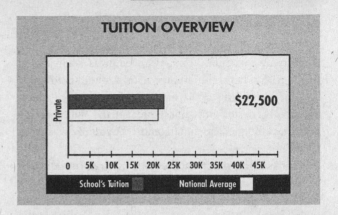

$22,500

School's Tuition   National Average

Howard University College of Medicine

Admissions Office, 520 W Street NW, Washington, DC 20059
(202) 806-6270

OVERVIEW

While Howard students complain about too much class time, an extremely heavy workload, and poorly maintained facilities, they say their classmates are terrific. "The best thing about Howard," says one second-year student, "is the people." But does a cooperative, friendly, predominantly African-American student body make up for all the things our respondents don't like about their school? For some, perhaps, but most students say they're only moderately satisfied with their Howard experience. In fact, for the category of students' overall happiness, this small D.C. school is at the bottom of those we surveyed.

ACADEMICS

Howard students spend most of their first two years studying the basic sciences. Although there are some interdisciplinary classes, most classes are taught departmentally, through large-group lectures. Students say they'd like more variety. Suggests one, "less time should be spent in lectures. That time could then be put into practical applications such as labs and seminars." Too little study time before exams and an "incomprehensible" written syllabus are also sources of frustration.

Complaints also extend to the instruction. Although students are satisfied with the overall quality of teaching and say that most faculty members are very accessible, they have problems with some of the basic science staff. Reports one student, "First-year lecturers seem out of touch with what's important for med students to know and their teaching skills are seriously lacking." Adds another, "The teachers don't present the material in a way that students can understand. They really waste our time!"

Early clinical exposure comes through Introduction to Patient Care, a three-part course that spans both preclinical years. This continuum is designed to give students a clinical context for their basic science studies and to prepare them for the third-year clerkships. Most students say the course falls short of its goals, however, particularly in the freshman year. One reports, "The clinical experience in the first year is little more than a tour of different areas of the hospital. We don't really *experience* anything." Overall, only about a third of the students we surveyed feel satisfied with the amount of exposure to patients in the preclinical years.

Although students are pleased with Howard's clinical facilities, the classrooms, labs, and—especially—the library receive very low marks. One student expresses a common gripe, "There are no adequate study facilities at this school, and this defeats the learning process."

Grading and Promotion Policy: Honors/Satisfactory/Unsatisfactory. Students must pass Parts I and II of the USMLE.

Additional Degree Programs: Howard's Early Entry Medical Education Program (EEMEP) allows talented college students to enter med school after their junior year. The med school also offers a combined BS/MD in conjunction with the undergraduate division. MS/MD and MD/Ph.D. programs are also available.

STUDENT LIFE

Students report that they like to get together outside of class, but say there is little time for socializing. Comments one, "I don't think many people are involved in school and community activities because we are in class almost eight hours a day." They also spend a lot of time preparing for class. Howard students, on average, spend more time studying than their counterparts at any other med school we surveyed. Although our respondents say the heavy workload makes for a fairly stressful atmo-

sphere, they report that classmates are supportive of each other. Evidence of this is the large number of students who say they participate in study groups, a much higher proportion that at most other schools we surveyed.

Howard's location in Washington, D.C. gets mixed reviews. While many students like the city and the cultural and recreational activities it offers, some say the school's neighborhood leaves much to be desired. "The area is very ugly, and there is a lot of crime," explains one sophomore. Security is a big concern; over three-fourths of the students we surveyed feel that the campus is unsafe. There is little on-campus housing, but students are pleased with off-campus offerings. Commuting without a car isn't a problem because the med school is accessible to the city's excellent public transportation system.

ADMISSIONS

Howard shows no preference in the admissions process to residents of D.C. or any state. All interested candidates are encouraged to apply, although candidates with GPAs under 3.0 will not be given primary consideration unless other credentials are outstanding.

The major factors in admissions decisions are the academic record, MCAT scores, letters of recommendation, and the motivation and suitability for studying and practicing medicine. Also considered is compatibility with the school's mission to provide care to the medically underserved.

Special Programs for Members of Underrepresented Minorities: Since the majority of students are African American, recruitment of members of underrepresented minorities is a priority of Howard's regular admissions program. Among special programs are a five-year medical track for students who experience academic difficulties and an Early Entry Medical Education program which allows talented students to enter med school after their junior undergraduate year.

Transfer Policy: Transfers into the third year are occasionally considered.

FINANCIAL AID

Most financial aid is awarded on the basis of need, though some merit scholarships are available.

ADMISSIONS FACTS

Demographics

% men	50
% women	50
% minorities	83

Deadline & Notification Dates

AMCAS	yes
Regular application	12/15
Regular notification	10/15-until filled
Early Decision application	No EDP program
Early Decision notification	N/A

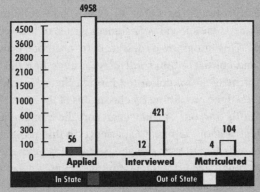

TUITION OVERVIEW

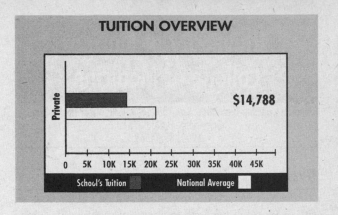

$14,788

School's Tuition   National Average

FIRST YEAR STATISTICS

Average GPA

Science	N/A	Nonscience	N/A

Average MCAT

Biology	N/A	Physical Science	N/A
Verbal	N/A	Essay	N/A

FINANCIAL FACTS

Tuition and Fees

In-district	$14,788	On-campus housing	N/A
Out-of-district	$14,788	Off-campus housing	N/A

Financial Aid

% receiving some aid	85
Merit scholarships	yes
Average debt	N/A

HITS AND MISSES

HITS	MISSES
Students support each other	Library
Faculty accessibility	Basic science facilities
Study groups	Early clinical exposure
Off-campus housing	Uneven quality of teaching
Public transportation	Campus area is unsafe

University of Florida College of Medicine

Medical Selection Committee, Box 100216, J. Hillis Miller Health Center, Gainesville, Florida 32610
(904) 392-4569

OVERVIEW

You can expect excellent clinical training at the University of Florida, thanks to its facilities and faculty, which are universally praised by students. Students at the University of Florida are a happy—if homogenous—group, and it's not simply due to the climes of their sunny state. The student body is enthusiastic about the school's emphasis on medical ethics and its strong research efforts. The campus is also very beautiful, but that beauty may be only skin deep; the campus gets low ratings for its safety. However, the quality of education makes UF very attractive. But be forewarned: fewer than 1 percent of students were accepted during the last admissions season.

ACADEMICS

Although the University of Florida's curriculum is split into traditional basic science and clinical units, the school tries to help students keep sight of the clinical relevance of basic science principles. To this end, UF says, "The basic science courses are taught in 'blocks' with a high level of integration of course materials and exams." The faculty also employs a combination of teaching strategies, ranging from traditional lectures to small group conferences, interdisciplinary courses, and computer-assisted learning. Students appreciate this variety. Says one, "[UF is] on the cutting edge when it comes to new and innovative teaching tools."

The quality of teaching at UF gets high praise, and students find the professors "extremely accessible" and caring. Comments one second-year, "There is a relaxed atmosphere when talking with faculty and deans." Students are also impressed by the emphasis faculty members place on ethics, giving UF one of the highest ratings in this category of any school we surveyed.

The school administration also earns high marks. Reports one student, "One of the nicest things about [UF] is that faculty/administration respond quickly to student recommendations about lectures, structure of courses, learning experience [and] teaching methods. Of the facilities, students reserve their highest praise for the clinical facilities; lowest marks go to the library.

Despite UF's efforts to provide early clinical exposure through preceptorships in rural clinics, students are only moderately satisfied with the amount of hands-on experience they have during the first year. Students who participate in the Program in Medical Science (PIMS) are notable exceptions. As an alternative to the regular curriculum, students can apply to PIMS, an option that allows students interested in practicing primary care to get early clinical exposure to family and community medicine. One second year student writes of the experience, "This program is designed to promote primary care and consists of 30 students/year attending the first year of medical school at the Florida State University. We joined the remaining 85 classmates at the University of Florida for our second year and the remainder of medical school. Clinical experience in this program is extensive and quite advantageous. My PIMS experience only strengthened my interest in medicine."

Grading and Promotion Policy: A through F. Parts I and II of the USMLE are required for graduation.

Additional Degree Programs: Students in good standing can elect to take the preclinical coursework over three years, either to pursue research or non-traditional coursework, or to make up for weaknesses in undergraduate preparation in the basic sciences. UF offers a seven-year Junior Honors Medical Program (BS/MD); applicants in their sophomore year at any school are considered. UF also offers an MD/Ph.D. program, which normally takes 7 years.

STUDENT LIFE

Students feel that their classmates are fairly competitive, but committed to helping each other out. Most report that they study hard, but say that all the work is worthwhile. One assures prospective students, "UF Medical school is very challenging and very rewarding. You make great friends and have time for a lot of fun. For anyone who is really interested in medicine, it is well worth it."

There is also a lot of enthusiasm for the number of clubs and activities there are on campus, and students rate their classmates as being involved to a significant degree in school and community activities. UF students agree that the campus is extremely attractive, but report that it's not particularly safe. Gainesville gets lukewarm reviews, but students greatly prefer off-campus living to university dorms. "On-campus housing," one student complained, "is horrifying."

ADMISSIONS

Students can apply to UF in one of three ways: through the regular admissions process, through the Junior Honors Medical Program (from sophomore year of undergraduate), or through the Program in Medical Sciences. Florida residents are given preference in admissions, but up to 5 percent of students can come from out of state. Especially encouraged to apply from out of state are students with outstanding academic qualifications, members of underrepresented minorities, or students with close ties to the state.

For regular admissions, science GPA, nonscience GPA, the interview, and MCAT scores were ranked as the most important factors in admissions. Letters of recommendation, volunteer activities, exposure to the medical profession, extracurricular activities, and essays are also considered. Adds the Admissions Office, "Many [successful applicants] have participated in significant research."

Transfer Policy: Transfers from an LCME accredited US or Canadian medical school are possible in some circumstances.

Special Programs for Members of Underrepresented Minorities: Students give UF extremely low marks for racial diversity, but the school is actively trying to improve its record. UF's efforts for recruiting and enrolling minority students include academic advising, tutoring, community outreach programs, a minority affairs division, peer counseling, and special consideration for admission. Other students are invited to participate in the appropriate programs.

eMail: Robert Watson@qm.server.ufl.edu

FINANCIAL AID

Although students like most everything else about UF, they are decidedly unhappy about financial aid. Says one, "Although not entirely the College of Medicine's fault, the financial aid services of the University of Florida are a complete disgrace. The budget that we, as professional students, are expected to live under is completely inadequate and borderline disgusting in its lack of recognition of basic needs of professional students aged 22-26." Another adds, "[There are] few scholarships."

ADMISSIONS FACTS

Demographics

% men	60
% women	40
% minorities	33

Deadline & Notification Dates

AMCAS	yes
Regular application	12/01
Regular notification	10/15-until filled
Early Decision application	N/A
Early Decision notification	N/A

Bar chart (In State / Out of State):
- Applied: 1225 / 967
- Interviewed: 290 / 16
- Matriculated: 81 / 4

FIRST YEAR STATISTICS

Average GPA

Science	3.55	Nonscience	3.66

Average MCAT

Biology	9.0	Physical Science	9.0
Verbal	9.0	Essay	P

FINANCIAL FACTS

Tuition and Fees

In-state	$8,172	On-campus housing	$7,923
Out-of-state	$21,172	Off-campus housing	$8,418

Financial Aid

% receiving some aid	72
Merit scholarships	yes
Average debt	$45,446

HITS AND MISSES

HITS	MISSES
Attractive campus	On-campus housing
Emphasis on research	Racial diversity
Ethics classes	Campus safety
Teaching	Public transportation
Clinical facilities	

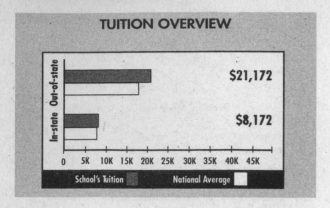

TUITION OVERVIEW

Out-of-state $21,172

In-state $8,172

0 5K 10K 15K 20K 25K 30K 35K 40K 45K

School's Tuition ▨ National Average ☐

University of Miami School of Medicine

Admissions, P.O. Box 016159, Miami, FL 33101
(305) 547-6791

OVERVIEW

If you are interested in a hot, sunny, clinically-oriented medical education, the University of Miami may be just the school. According to the students we surveyed, Miami's major strengths lie in its superior clinical training, excellent research efforts, and strong emphasis on medical ethics. What students most dislike is the area around the school's campus—only 30 percent of students feel that it's safe.

ACADEMICS

Although Miami divides its curriculum into the traditional two-year preclinical and clinical units, its program is progressive, especially in the basic sciences. During the first two years, only about half of students' time is spent in lectures; the remainder is devoted to labs and small group problem-based learning sessions. For better integration of the basic sciences, instruction is structured around organ systems, and some courses are interdisciplinary. In the third year, students complete required clinical rotations and four weeks of electives. The final year is entirely elective.

Students get their first exposure to patients in the first year. Patient contact intensifies in the second year when students learn the rudiments of physical diagnosis. Students rate the clinical exposure in all four years as outstanding. One student adds, however, "Clinical work

is definitely in a tertiary care setting. [There's] not much primary care exposure." Overall, clinical facilities are considered superior.

Reviews of the quality of teaching are more mixed, but the consensus is that the faculty does a good job, both in the classroom and in the lab. Students give high marks to Miami's research efforts. There is also praise for the "helpful and responsive" administration. Students are quite satisfied with lab, library, and computer facilities; classrooms could, however use some improvement.

Grading Policy: Years 1 and 2: A through F; Years 3 and 4: Honors/High Pass/Pass/Fail

Additional Degree Programs: Miami offers a six-year combined BS/MD. There is also an early assurance program for undergraduate sophomores. For students interested in research, an MD/Ph.D. program is available.

STUDENT LIFE

Ratings of the diversity of Miami's student body ranked the school near the top of all those we surveyed. Students say they like the multicultural atmosphere, and report that relations are good between their classmates. Competition is moderate.

By far students' biggest complaint is the lack of safety around the campus and in much of Miami. In fact, despite Miami's fabulous weather, students give the city tepid reviews. There is no on-campus housing. Although students say that off-campus housing is available and satisfactory, they warn that commuting without a car poses some problems and that public transportation is only moderately safe.

ADMISSIONS

Miami gives preference in admissions to Florida residents, so competition among out-of-state applicants is fierce. Over half of the 3,000 applicants for the 1993-94 school year were nonresidents; of those just 22 were accepted and eventually matriculated. Because the odds are so clearly against non-Floridians, the admissions office warns, "nonresidents are encouraged to apply only if they have a truly superior academic record and exceptional MCAT scores, or have other unique qualifications"

The interview, the science GPA, MCAT scores, and the non-science GPA are ranked by the admissions office as the most important selection factors. Also considered, in decreasing order of importance, are letters of recommendation, volunteer activities, extracurricular activities, exposure to the medical profession, and essays.

Miami is interested in maintaining its record for diversity among its student body and actively encourages women, candidates from socioeconomically disadvantaged backgrounds, and other non-traditional students to apply.

Transfer Policy: Transfers are accepted on a space-available basis. Transfers must be residents of Florida.

Special Programs for Members of Underrepresented Minorities: A Minority Affairs division coordinates programs for recruiting and graduating underrepresented minority students. Among its offerings are a prematriculation summer session, academic advising, tutoring, and peer counseling. According to the Admissions Office, only members of underrepresented minorities and students with disadvantaged backgrounds may participate in these programs.

FINANCIAL AID

Miami offers both scholarships and loans. Some scholarships are based on academic merit.

ADMISSIONS FACTS

Demographics

% men	58
% women	42
% minorities	9

Deadline & Notification Dates

AMCAS	yes
Regular application	12/15
Regular notification	10/15–until filled
Early Decision application	06/15-08/01
	(EDP for in-state applicants only)
Early Decision notification	10/01

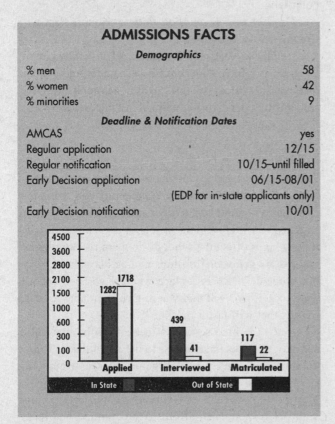

	In State	Out of State
Applied	1282	1718
Interviewed	439	41
Matriculated	117	22

FIRST YEAR STATISTICS

Average GPA

Science	3.51	Nonscience	3.56

Average MCAT

Biology	9.5	Physical Science	9.2
Verbal	9.5	Essay	P

FINANCIAL FACTS

Tuition and Fees

In-state	$22,050	On-campus housing	N/A
Out-of-state	$22,050	Off-campus housing	$14,000

Financial Aid

% receiving some aid	80
Merit scholarships	yes
Average debt	$68,000

HITS AND MISSES

HITS	MISSES
Diversity	Safety
Clinical facilities	No on-campus housing
Research	Public transportation
Emphasis on ethics	
Clinical exposure	

TUITION OVERVIEW

Private

$22,050

| 0 | 5K | 10K | 15K | 20K | 25K | 30K | 35K | 40K | 45K |

School's Tuition   National Average

University of South Florida College of Medicine

Medical School Admissions
12901 Bruce B. Downs Boulevard, Tampa, FL 33612-4799
(813) 974-2229

OVERVIEW

Located in Tampa, the University of South Florida College of Medicine (USF) is a big hit with students who go there. What's behind students' overwhelming vote of confidence for their school? Our respondents tell us that an excellent faculty, outstanding facilities, a vital research effort, a diverse and supportive student body, and a gorgeous location combine to make USF the med school of their dreams. But before you get ready to send in your application, be forewarned: if you're not a resident of Florida, your chances of being admitted are slim. Over ninety-nine percent of the student body comes from within the state.

ACADEMICS

USF has a fairly traditional curriculum, divided along the usual preclinical and clinical lines. First-year students focus most of their attention on the basic sciences, and are instructed in a variety of ways including lectures, labs, small-group conferences, and interdisciplinary instruction. In addition to completing science courses, first-year students investigate ethical and behavioral aspects of medicine. In the second semester, they begin to learn patient-interaction skills through a Physical Diagnosis course that extends into the second year.

Second-year students continue their investigation of scientific principles, but there is increased emphasis on clinical correlations, especially in pathology courses. The remainder of the Physical Diagnosis course and Introduction to Clinical Medicine further develop patient examination and evaluation skills and prepare students for the clinical phase of the curriculum. Third-year students complete five required clerkships in the major disciplines. There are eleven four-week rotations in the fourth year, nine of which are elective.

Students are enthusiastic about the quality of education at USF, praising both the content of their curriculum and the way material is presented. Nearly all of our respondents say they're satisfied with the amount of

clinical exposure they have in the basic science years and acknowledge that early contact with patients bolsters their confidence and skills for clinical rotations. Says one student, "As a fourth year, I've done externships at other facilities and have found my preparation to be superior for the clinical challenges I found there."

Praise extends also to USF's research efforts, which students feel is both comprehensive, which accessible to medical students. "There are numerous opportunities to get involved in research," says one student, "even in the preclinical years."

The encouragement from faculty to join USF's investigative efforts is typical of the way in which the staff interacts with students. Our respondents tell us that not only are professors competent teachers, they are also caring and involved advocates for their pupils. Reports one first-year, "I have the sense that students are valued, academically and personally."

USF's efforts to foster an environment conducive to preparing superior physicians include ensuring that facilities are first-rate. Although students applaud all components of USF's academic setting, they reserve their highest praise for clinical teaching sites and computer labs.

Grading and Promotion Policy: Honors/Pass with Commendation/Pass/Fail.

Additional Degree Programs: A University Honors Program is jointly sponsored by the undergraduate and medical school divisions of USF. Through the UHP, students may receive a combined baccalaureate/MD degree in either seven or eight years.

STUDENT LIFE

Those we surveyed say competition among members of USF's diverse student body is moderate and stress that classmates do their best to help each other out. A strong emphasis on involvement in school and community activities helps effect the school's cooperative atmosphere and fosters good relationships among classmates. Says one student, "USF is a place where I've been encouraged to get involved and where I've been able to make friends that will last a lifetime."

Since the med school is located on the main USF campus, students have access to the amenities of a large university as well as the organizations and activities sponsored by the med school. In addition, the school's location in Tampa, a city which is immensely popular with our respondents, affords many cultural and recreational opportunities.

Although off-campus housing is generally well-received, students admit that a high concentration of tourists and an inferior public transportation system make getting around town a somewhat frustrating and complicated endeavor.

ADMISSIONS

Over 99 percent of the students USF admits are Florida residents, so out-of-state students should not apply. After an initial evaluation of the AMCAS application, the Admissions Committee asks for supplementary information from highly-qualified candidates. The most promising applicants are then invited to interview. To insure the best chance for consideration, the Admissions Committee encourages candidates to apply as early as possible in the rolling admissions process.

The Director of Admissions ranks the science GPA, the non-science GPA, MCAT scores (from the new format test), and the interview as the primary selection factors. Also considered important are essays, letters of recommendation, exposure to the medical field, extracurricular activities, and volunteer work.

Special Programs for Members of Underrepresented Minorities: USF encourages qualified underrepresented minority students to apply. A Minority Affairs division coordinates the school's recruiting efforts and support services. Some special financial aid opportunities are available.

Transfer Policy: Applicants from LCME-accredited institutions are considered for transfer into the third year.

FINANCIAL AID

Financial aid is awarded solely on the basis of need. Limited loan and scholarship funds are available.

ADMISSIONS FACTS

Demographics

% men	62.5
% women	37.5
% minorities	31

Deadline & Notification Dates

AMCAS	yes
Regular application	12/01
Regular notification	10/15-until filled
Early Decision application	06/15-08/01
	(EDP for in-state applicants only)
Early Decision notification	10/01

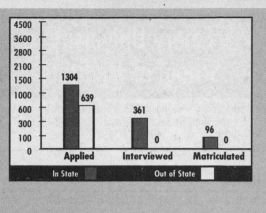

FIRST YEAR STATISTICS

Average GPA			
Science	3.7	Nonscience	3.5

Average MCAT			
Biology	9.8	Physical Science	9.6
Verbal	9.5	Essay	N/A

FINANCIAL FACTS

Tuition and Fees			
In-state	$8,245	On-campus housing	N/A
Out-of-state	$21,245	Off-campus housing	N/A

Financial Aid	
% receiving some aid	N/A
Merit scholarships	none
Average debt	$60,000

HITS AND MISSES

HITS	MISSES
Overall happiness	Public transportation
Quality of teaching	
Faculty accessiblity	
Research efforts	
Emphasis on ethics	
Overall facilities	
Diverse student body	
Plenty of campus activities	
Tampa	

TUITION OVERVIEW

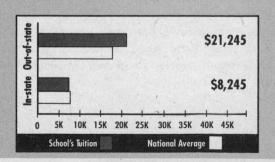

Emory University School of Medicine

Medical School Admissions, Room 303, Woodruff Health Sciences Center, Administration Building, Atlanta, GA 30322-4510
(404) 727-5660

OVERVIEW

According to the course bulletin, "The Emory University School of Medicine is committed to providing leadership in medicine and science through the development of recognized programs of excellence in medical education, biomedical research, and patient care." Emory is evidently not as dedicated to cooperating with people who want to find out more about their school, however. The Director of Admissions declined to participate in our survey and the Administration would not let us talk to current students. Here's what we do know.

ACADEMICS

Emory's curriculum is organized into the traditional two-year preclinical and clinical segments. In the first year, students focus primarily on the basic sciences. Some courses are taught interdepartmentally, and most include clinical correlation seminars. First-year students also explore preventative medicine and behavioral and social aspects of health care.

The basic science emphasis continues into the second year, but there is considerably more clinical orientation. In Clinical Methods, students learn fundamental clinical skills through lectures, discussion sections, videotapes, reading, and hands-on experiences with patients. During the second semester of this course, students begin the transition to the third-year clerkships through introductions to the major clinical disciplines. Required and elective rotations make up the majority of the third and fourth years; sixteen weeks of the senior year are free for electives.

Grading and Promotion Policy: A–F for most courses; Satisfactory/Unsatisfactory for electives. Students must take Parts I and II of the USMLE.

Additional Degree Programs: MD/Ph.D., MD/MPH.

STUDENT LIFE

Students have access to the organizations, events, and facilities of both the medical and the undergraduate schools. Sports and fitness enthusiasts may join intramural teams or may work out in the PE Center.

Emory students like Atlanta. Other area med students gave Atlanta high marks for its cultural and recreational opportunities. Emory offers a variety of university-owned housing, and there are plenty of off-campus apartments for rent.

ADMISSIONS

Emory shows preference to residents of Georgia, and gives some special consideration to residents of other southeastern states. About half the students come from out of state. Nonresidents should have a GPA of at least 3.3 to be considered competitive.

Among important selection factors are the GPA, the level and breadth of coursework, MCAT scores (from the new test), and the interview. Although all students are asked to submit a supplemental application—and, of course, the corresponding fee—only highly qualified candidates will be asked to interview. Among the students we surveyed at other schools were a number who interviewed at Emory; according to them, you should be prepared to tell what three people you would like to invite to a dinner party.

Special Programs for Members of Underrepresented Minorities: The Office of Minority Affairs coordinates the school's efforts to recruit, select, and retain underrepresented minority students. Special financial assistance is available for highly qualified minority students.

Transfer Policy: Transfer applicants from accredited U.S. schools will be considered on a space-available basis. Transfers are permitted only into the second and third years.

FINANCIAL AID

Since funds are limited, Emory encourages students who think they'll need assistance to submit all required documents as soon as possible after the interview. Most financial aid is awarded on the basis of documented need.

ADMISSIONS FACTS

Demographics

% men	59
% women	41
% minorities	10

Deadline & Notification Dates

AMCAS	yes
Regular application	10/15
Regular notification	10/15 to mid-March
Early Decision application	No EDP program
Early Decision notification	N/A

5806

Bar chart with values:
- Applied: In State 584, Out of State 5806
- Interviewed: In State 184, Out of State 597
- Matriculated: In State 60, Out of State 52

Legend: In State | Out of State

FIRST YEAR STATISTICS

Average GPA

Science	N/A	Non-science	3.62

Average MCAT

Biology	9.9	Physical Science	9.7
Verbal	9.9	Essay	N/A

FINANCIAL FACTS

Tuition and Fees

In-state	$20,200	On-campus housing	N/A
Out-of-state	$20,200	Off-campus housing	N/A

Financial Aid

% receiving some aid	71
Merit scholarships	yes
Average debt	N/A

TUITION OVERVIEW

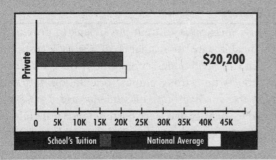

$20,200

School's Tuition | National Average

Medical College of Georgia School of Medicine

Office of Admissions, Augusta, GA 30912-4760
(706) 721-4792

OVERVIEW

One of the top comprehensive U.S. med schools, the Medical College of Georgia has recently revised its curriculum to include more interdepartmental courses and greater clinical correlation in the basic science years.

ACADEMICS

MCG's curriculum is divided into three phases. In the first phase, which lasts for the first year, students concentrate on the normal structure and function of the human body. Although there is considerable emphasis on the basic sciences, students also investigate the humanities and behavioral sciences. Clinical exposure begins in the second semester, when students work with patients to learn physical examination and evaluation skills. First-year students are also able to pursue their own interests through electives.

The focus on clinical medicine intensifies during the second year (Phase II). Courses include pathology, pharmacology, microbiology, community medicine, and Introduction to Clinical Medicine. During the final two years (Phase III), students complete required and elective clerkships. Most of the mandatory rotations are done in the third year, leaving about half of the fourth year free for electives.

Grading and Promotion Policy: A–F. Students must take Parts I and II of the USMLE.

Additional Degree Programs: MD/Ph.D.

STUDENT LIFE

The second largest city in Georgia, Augusta provides many cultural and recreational activities. It is perhaps most famous as the site for the annual Master's golf tournament, which you can think of as another, more subtle way to prepare for your impending doctor status. The school offers several different styles of reasonably priced on-campus housing.

ADMISSIONS

MCG gives preference to residents of Georgia, and only Georgians are permitted to apply through the Early Decision Program. A maximum of five percent of students can come from out of state. Primary considerations in the selection process are GPA, MCAT, letters of recommendation, the interview, and motivation and suitability for the practice of medicine.

Special Programs for Members of Underrepresented Minorities: The school strongly encourages members of underrepresented minorities to apply. A summer session for college students is among the special programs the school offers.

Transfer Policy: Transfers are considered on a space-available basis.

FINANCIAL AID

Although the majority of financial assistance is awarded on the basis of need, there are some merit scholarships available.

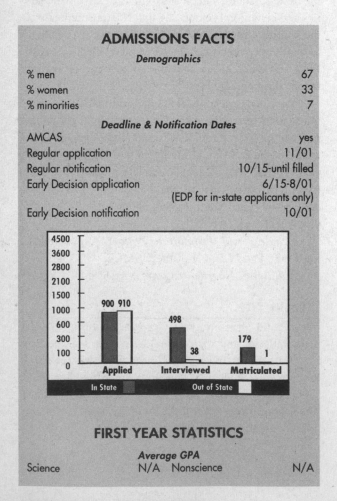

ADMISSIONS FACTS

Demographics

% men	67
% women	33
% minorities	7

Deadline & Notification Dates

AMCAS	yes
Regular application	11/01
Regular notification	10/15-until filled
Early Decision application	6/15-8/01
	(EDP for in-state applicants only)
Early Decision notification	10/01

First year statistics bar chart: Applied — In State 900, Out of State 910; Interviewed — In State 498, Out of State 38; Matriculated — In State 179, Out of State 1.

FIRST YEAR STATISTICS

Average GPA

Science	N/A	Nonscience	N/A

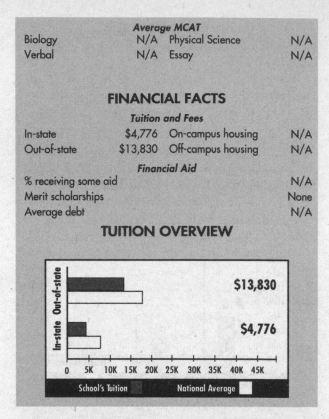

Average MCAT			
Biology	N/A	Physical Science	N/A
Verbal	N/A	Essay	N/A

FINANCIAL FACTS

Tuition and Fees

In-state	$4,776	On-campus housing	N/A
Out-of-state	$13,830	Off-campus housing	N/A

Financial Aid

% receiving some aid	N/A
Merit scholarships	None
Average debt	N/A

TUITION OVERVIEW

Tuition overview bar chart: Out-of-state $13,830; In-state $4,776. School's Tuition vs. National Average.

Mercer University School of Medicine

Office of Admissions, Macon, GA 31207
(912) 752-2542

OVERVIEW

Do you want to live in Georgia? Do you want to take care of Georgians? If so, this might be the school for you. A small class size, an entirely problem-based basic science curriculum, and a very specific mission are among Mercer's unusual features.

ACADEMICS

Mercer's mission is to train physicians to provide primary health care to residents of Georgia, especially those in rural and underserved areas. Mercer's curriculum reflects this strong clinical orientation. In the first two years, small groups of students use a case-study method to identify and learn basic science principles and to apply those principles to clinical problems. Clinical exposure begins in the first two years when students learn interviewing and examination skills through experiences with simulated patients.

The Community Office Practice Program (COPP) gives students the opportunity to practice their newly developed skills on real patients. Through preceptorships with community physicians, students experience the practice of primary care in rural settings, and explore issues such as preventative care. The third year and part of the fourth year are devoted to a mix of ambulatory and hospital-based clerkships. The remainder of the fourth year—about twenty weeks—is free for electives.

Grading and Promotion Policy: For the first and second years, Satisfactory/Unsatisfactory. For the clinical years, Honors/Satisfactory/Unsatisfactory. Passing grades on Parts I and II of the USMLE are required.

Additional Degree Programs: None.

STUDENT LIFE

Med students have access to all university events and facilities. In addition, Mercer has chapters of the major medical organizations. Although there is some university housing available, the school encourages students to explore Macon's off-campus housing options.

ADMISSIONS

Mercer gives preference in the admissions process to Georgia residents. As of this writing, out-of-state students have not been accepted. When the school receives the AMCAS application, all candidates who are state residents are asked to submit a supplementary application. Interviews are by invitation only.

Final selections are made on the basis of the interview, the information supplied on the applications, and the compatibility of the student's goals with the school's mission. The MCAT, in its new format, is required.

Special Programs for Members of Underrepresented Minorities: Mercer strongly encourages members of underrepresented minority groups to apply.

Transfer Policy: Applications for transfer into the third year will be considered if the candidate is a Georgia resident in good standing at an LCME-accredited med school.

FINANCIAL AID

Financial aid awards are primarily based on need as determined by the College Scholarship Service analysis. Merit is also a factor in some scholarships.

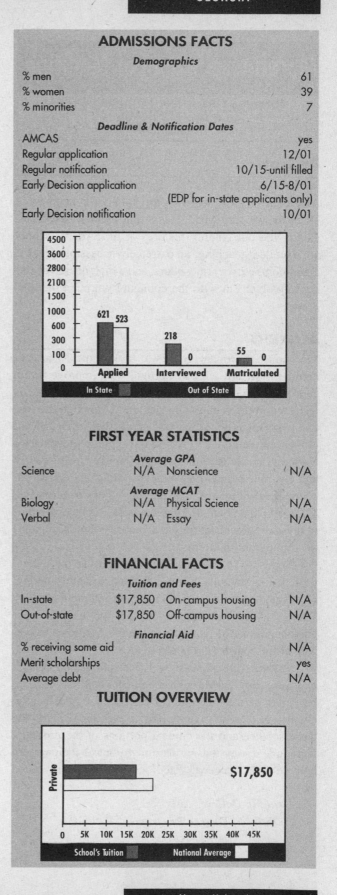

ADMISSIONS FACTS

Demographics

% men	61
% women	39
% minorities	7

Deadline & Notification Dates

AMCAS	yes
Regular application	12/01
Regular notification	10/15-until filled
Early Decision application	6/15-8/01
	(EDP for in-state applicants only)
Early Decision notification	10/01

Applied: In State 621, Out of State 523
Interviewed: In State 218, Out of State 0
Matriculated: In State 55, Out of State 0

In State / Out of State

FIRST YEAR STATISTICS

Average GPA

Science	N/A	Nonscience	N/A

Average MCAT

Biology	N/A	Physical Science	N/A
Verbal	N/A	Essay	N/A

FINANCIAL FACTS

Tuition and Fees

In-state	$17,850	On-campus housing	N/A
Out-of-state	$17,850	Off-campus housing	N/A

Financial Aid

% receiving some aid	N/A
Merit scholarships	yes
Average debt	N/A

TUITION OVERVIEW

Private: $17,850

School's Tuition / National Average

Morehouse School of Medicine

Admissions and Student Affairs, 720 Westview Drive SW,
Atlanta, GA 30310-1495
(404) 752-1657

OVERVIEW

Students at Morehouse, a predominately African-American medical school, were among the happiest of all those we surveyed. According to their responses, among the outstanding features of this Atlanta school are excellent teaching, an extremely accessible faculty, a non-competitive atmosphere, and a high degree of student involvement with the community around the med school.

ACADEMICS

Morehouse's primary goal is to train clinical and academic physicians who will provide and improve health care for the medically underserved, and this mission is reflected in the school's curriculum. Although the first two years focus on the basic sciences, there is significant clinical orientation. First-years explore preventative medicine in the Community and Family Health course and examine behavioral, socioeconomic and ethical aspects of medicine through Human Values in Medicine. They also spend an afternoon a week in preceptorships in diverse clinical settings and choose a family to monitor throughout the term.

Exposure to patients intensifies during the second year, when students learn and practice history-taking, physical diagnosis and other patient-interaction skills. These experiences prepare students for the third year clerkships, one of which is in Family Medicine. Over half of the fourth year is elective.

Students are pleased with the amount of clinical exposure they get through the curriculum, but feel the best part of their preclinical education is the faculty. Quality of teaching is reported as excellent in both the basic science and the clinical portions of the program, and students say that professors go out of their way to help students succeed. Facilities are consistently rated very good.

Grading Policy: A–F

Additional Degree Programs: MD/Ph.D.

STUDENT LIFE

Despite Morehouse's letter grading system, respondents indicate the atmosphere is more cooperative than competitive. Evidence of this is the large number of first- and second-year students who take part in study groups, something we didn't find at many other schools. Although students say the workload is heavy, they find enough free time to have active social lives and to get involved in community and school organizations.

Although there is no on-campus housing, students are very pleased with the accommodations Atlanta has to offer. Commuting without a car presents no major problems because the school is easily accessible by public transportation.

ADMISSIONS

Morehouse gives preference to Georgia and New Jersey residents, but up to 40 percent of students can be from out of state. Special consideration is given to members of underrepresented minorities. Since Morehouse has a rolling admissions policy, the Admissions Office advises that students who are seriously interested in the school apply as early as possible.

According to the Admissions Office, "Selection of students for admission is made by the committee on Admissions after consideration of many factors, none of which is assigned priority over the others. Selection factors include MCAT scores, the undergraduate academic record, the extent of academic improvement, balance and depth of the academic program, difficulty of courses taken, and other indications of maturation of learning ability. Additional factors considered by the committee include the nature of extracurricular activities, hobbies, the need to work, research projects and experiences, evidence of activities which indicate concurrence with the school's mission, and evidence of pursuing interests and talents in depth. Finally, the committee looks for evidence of those traits of personality and character essential to success in medicine: compassion, integrity, motivation, and perseverance."

Special Programs for Members of Underrepresented Minorities: Since Morehouse is a predominately black medical school, efforts to recruit, enroll, educate and graduate underrepresented minority students are a priority of the Student Affairs office. Recruitment vehicles and support services include community outreach programs, summer sessions for college students, a prematriculation summer program, academic advising, tutoring, peer counseling, and review sessions for the MCAT and Parts I and II of the USMLE. A decelerated program that gives students additional time to complete basic science requirements is also available for students who might benefit from a reduced workload.

Transfer Policy: Morehouse considers applicants for transfer into the second year on a space-available basis. Only students in good standing at U.S. medical schools will be considered.

FINANCIAL AID

Admission is need-blind. Although most of Morehouse's financial aid is awarded on the basis of academic need, the school offers some merit scholarships.

ADMISSIONS FACTS

Demographics

% men	42
% women	58
% minorities	100

Deadline & Notification Dates

AMCAS	yes
Regular application	12/01
Regular notification	1/15-until filled
Early Decision application	6/15-8/01
	(EDP for in-state applicants only)
Early Decision notification	10/01

	In State	Out of State
Applied	313	2486
Interviewed	117	86
Matriculated	22	14

FIRST YEAR STATISTICS

Average GPA

Science	3.11	Nonscience	3.32

Average MCAT

Biology	7	Physical Science	7
Verbal	7	Essay	N/A

FINANCIAL FACTS

Tuition and Fees

In-state	$16,811	On-campus housing	N/A
Out-of-state	$16,811	Off-campus housing	$15,344

Financial Aid

% receiving some aid	87
Merit scholarships	yes
Average debt	N/A

HITS AND MISSES

HITS	MISSES
Overall happiness	There was no consensus among our
Quality of teaching	respondents about areas that
Faculty accessibility	were less than satisfactory.
Extracurricular involvement	
Cooperative atmosphere	
Emphasis on academics	
Atlanta	

TUITION OVERVIEW

$16,811

School's Tuition   National Average

University of Hawaii: John A. Burns School of Medicine

Office of Admissions, 1960 East-West Road, Honolulu, HI 96822
(808) 956-5446

OVERVIEW

Wouldn't it be nice to combat stress by basking on Oahu's sandy beaches, scuba diving, surfing, or snorkeling? Before you get lost in a daydream about going to med school in the nation's most exotic state, consider this: Of the approximately 1,200 nonresidents who applied to the University of Hawaii School of Medicine in 1992, just three got in. Not very favorable odds. So, if you were thinking of applying from out of state but you don't have credentials that go beyond fantastic grades, you might want to set your sights elsewhere.

ACADEMICS

Hawaii's main mission is to provide and improve the health care of the state, and its approach to medical education reflects this goal. The medical school places a strong emphasis on primary care, with attention to multicultural issues. Students do portions of their clinical training in community health centers, and there are opportunities during vacation and elective periods to do preceptorships in rural areas of the Hawaiian and other Pacific islands.

Hawaii's curriculum is divided into two-year preclinical and clinical units, but it has many progressive features. Hawaii's recognition of the benefits of an active learning style have led the school to adopt a problem-based curriculum for the basic science years. The small size of each year's entering class—just over fifty students—keeps this approach manageable. In addition to studying the scientific principles that are the foundation for medicine, freshmen and sophomores investigate psychological and social aspects of medicine. The first two years also provide an introduction to clinical medicine; students learn the fundamentals of history-taking, patient examination, and physical diagnosis in preparation for the third-year clerkships.

Students spend their junior year in required clerkships in the major disciplines. Although requirements extend into the fourth year, seniors spend considerable time in electives that suit their individual interests. Clinical teaching is carried out in a variety of inpatient and outpatient settings. In addition to Leahi Hospital in Honolulu, the school is affiliated with ten community hospitals and three primary clinics spread throughout the islands.

Grading and Promotion Policy: Honors/Credit/No Credit. Students must pass Parts I and II of the USMLE.

Additional Degree Programs: MD/Ph.D.; MD/MS.

ADMISSIONS

Preference is given to Hawaiians and to residents of other Pacific islands. Since relatively few applicants who do not fit into one of these categories are accepted, nonresidents should carefully evaluate their chances of acceptance before taking the time to apply.

All candidates must apply through AMCAS. On the basis of the application, the Admissions Committee does a careful screening before inviting the most highly-qualified candidates to interview. Since a very small number of candidates are interviewed—about 10 percent of the total applicant pool—those who are asked to meet members of the committee stand a very good chance for admission.

Important selection factors include the academic record, MCAT scores, letters of recommendation, extracurricular activities, motivation for the study of medicine, and personal qualities. The school also considers the candidate's potential for contributing to provision of health care in the Pacific island region.

Special Programs for Members of Underrepresented Minorities: Hawaii has a diverse, multicultural faculty and student body. Through a special admissions program, it reserves eight spaces in each entering class for underrepresented minority and disadvantaged students.

Transfer Policy: Students who are interested in transferring should contact the Admissions Office for more information about the school's current policies.

FINANCIAL AID

Hawaii's in-state tuition is among the lowest of state-supported schools. Financial assistance is available in the form of grants, loans, and scholarships.

ADMISSIONS FACTS

Demographics

% men	57
% women	43
% minorities	2

Deadline & Notification Dates

AMCAS	yes
Regular application	12/01
Regular notification	10/15–until filled
Early Decision application	6/15-8/01
	(EDP for in-state applicants only)
Early Decision notification	10/01

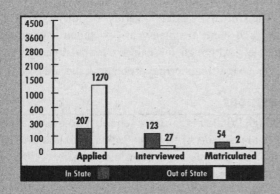

TUITION OVERVIEW

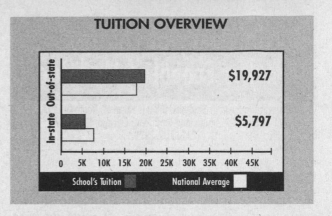

$19,927

$5,797

School's Tuition   National Average

FIRST YEAR STATISTICS

Average GPA

Science	N/A	Non-science	3.44

Average MCAT

Biology	9.6	Physical Science	9.3
Verbal	9.6	Essay	N/A

FINANCIAL FACTS

Tuition and Fees

In-state	$5,797	On-campus housing	N/A
Out-of-state	$19,927	Off-campus housing	N/A

Financial Aid

% receiving some aid	60
Merit scholarships	N/A
Average debt	N/A

University of Chicago: Pritzker School of Medicine

Office of the Dean of Students, Billings Hospital, Room G-115A, MC-1139, 5841 South Maryland Ave., Chicago, IL 60637
(312) 702-1939

OVERVIEW

If you're serious about research, make it your business to find out more about Pritzker. Consistently rated among the top 10 research-oriented schools, Pritzker is best known for producing academic physicians. A significant portion of each class is enrolled in combined MD/Ph.D. programs and about 90 percent of regular students engage in a laboratory or clinical project at some point during their four years. Pritzker's location on the campus of its well-respected parent school—the University of Chicago—offers other enticements for the student seeking intellectual challenges, and its location in a stable and diverse area of the midwest's largest city makes it a prime spot for social and cultural pursuits.

ACADEMICS

Pritzker has made recent innovations in its curriculum. More elective time has been incorporated into all four years, giving students the opportunity to better direct their education. Traditional first- and second-year basic science courses are complemented by exploration of ethical, behavioral science, and humanities aspects of medicine. Through the use of standardized patients and small group, problem-based learning, first-year students build a foundation in clinical skills.

Second-year courses continue to integrate scientific principles with clinical problems. A Physical Diagnosis course refines skills students learned in the first year and eases the transition into the third-year clerkships. Concurrently with the rotations in internal medicine, surgery, obstetrics/gynecology, psychiatry, pediatrics, and two electives, third-years meet in seminars and conferences to discuss the clinical relevance of the basic sciences. The fourth year is devoted to electives. During this time, students may complete additional clinical rotations, pursue research interests, or study at other medical centers.

Grading and Promotion Policy: Pass/Fail for the first two years, graded thereafter.

Additional Degree Programs: Pritzker offers a funded Medical Scientist Training Program that leads to a combined MD/Ph.D. MD/MBA, MD/JD, MD/MA and a regular MD/Ph.D. are also available.

STUDENT LIFE

Pritzker is located in Chicago's diverse Hyde Park neighborhood, about 12 miles south of the Chicago Loop. For extracurricular pursuits, students can take advantage of the University's organizations and facilities or partake of varied cultural, entertainment, and recreational opportunities available in the city.

The University offers a variety of housing arrangements, and there are plenty of off-campus apartments available. Although the campus has visible security, there is a significant crime problem in the area.

ADMISSIONS

Although Pritzker is a private school, it gives some preference to residents of Illinois. Still, approximately sixty percent of students come from out of state. Although any nonresident is welcome to apply, the Admissions Committee especially encourages women, members of underrepresented minorities, children of alumni, and students interested in pursuing academic and research careers to submit applications.

On the basis of their evaluation of both the AMCAS and supplemental applications, members of the Admissions Committee invite promising candidates to interview on campus. According to the Associate Dean of Students, this interview is the most important selection factor, with science and non-science GPAs, MCAT scores, and essays following close behind. Extracurricular activities, letters of recommendation, exposure to the medical profession, and volunteer activities are also reviewed. Of the overall goal of Pritzker's admissions process, the Associate Dean says, "Our ultimate aim is diversity among classmates who both learn from and teach each other."

Special Programs for Members of Underrepresented Minorities: Pritzker seeks to increase minority representation in its student body and gives some special consideration for admission to members of underrepresented minorities. Recruitment and support services include summer sessions for high school students, MCAT review classes, and academic tutoring.

Transfer Policy: Applications for transfer from students attending LCME-accredited schools are sometimes accepted if space is available and the candidate has a compelling need for the transfer.

FINANCIAL AID

Admission to Pritzker is need-blind. Scholarships and low-interest loans are awarded to all students who show need on the basis of the GAPSFAS analysis.

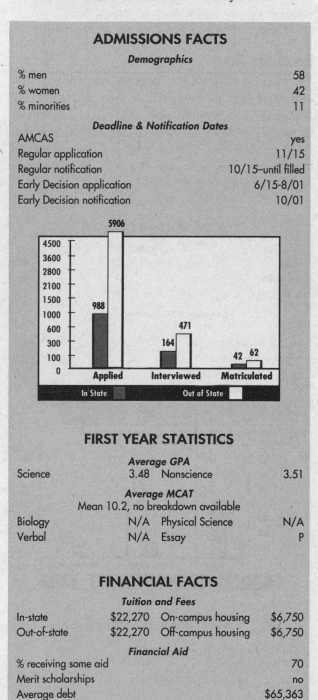

ADMISSIONS FACTS

Demographics

% men	58
% women	42
% minorities	11

Deadline & Notification Dates

AMCAS	yes
Regular application	11/15
Regular notification	10/15–until filled
Early Decision application	6/15-8/01
Early Decision notification	10/01

In State / Out of State bar chart:
- Applied: 988 (In State), 5906 (Out of State)
- Interviewed: 164 (In State), 471 (Out of State)
- Matriculated: 42 (In State), 62 (Out of State)

FIRST YEAR STATISTICS

Average GPA

Science	3.48	Nonscience	3.51

Average MCAT
Mean 10.2, no breakdown available

Biology	N/A	Physical Science	N/A
Verbal	N/A	Essay	P

FINANCIAL FACTS

Tuition and Fees

In-state	$22,270	On-campus housing	$6,750
Out-of-state	$22,270	Off-campus housing	$6,750

Financial Aid

% receiving some aid	70
Merit scholarships	no
Average debt	$65,363

TUITION OVERVIEW

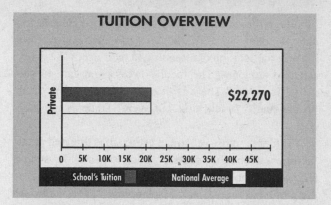

$22,270

School's Tuition | National Average

University of Health Sciences: Chicago Medical School

Office of Admissions, 3333 Green Bay Road, North Chicago, IL 60064
(708) 578-3206

OVERVIEW

Students say that growth at Chicago Medical School and its parent university is outpacing the school's ability to serve its students. Although students are generally satisfied with their experiences at CMS, complaints about packed lectures, cramped facilities, and an administration "that is slow to act" on the school's space problems are widespread.

ACADEMICS

CMS retains a relatively traditional curriculum that is divided into preclinical and clinical segments. Although the school has implemented some curricular revisions which foster more integration between the basic sciences and the clinical arts, scientific principles are still the main focus of the first two years. In some first-year courses, like Medical Ethics, discussion sections augment lectures, but students complain that because of the "expanded student population...small-group conferences are too large." Even so, students give the ethics course high marks.

In the second year, students continue to study the basic sciences and take Introduction to Clinical Medicine, a course designed to ease the transition into the required third-year clerkships. Despite this requirement, students are dissatisfied with the amount of clinical exposure they have during the first two years.

Regardless of the general feeling that there are "too many students" at CMS, students say the faculty is doing an excellent job of attending to their needs. Says one satisfied student, "The faculty takes great care in students' learning." There isn't quite as much enthusiasm for the quality of teaching, but overall students are satisfied.

Students' most vehement criticism is directed at the facilities, which they say are "much too small for such a large population." One student expresses frustration at the administration's lack of planning: "[The facilities] are way beyond capacity...yet the school has two buildings that are not being used. Why?"

Grading and Promotion Policy: A–F for required courses; Pass/Fail for electives. Passing grades on Parts I and II of the USMLE are required for graduation.

Additional Degree Programs: BS/MD (in conjunction with the Illinois Institute of Technology), MD/Ph.D., MS/MD.

STUDENT LIFE

CMS students spend more time studying than nearly all of their counterparts at the schools we surveyed. This heavy workload leaves little free time and students report that they very seldom socialize with classmates.

And beware: if you are looking for an inspiring urban experience, visit first. Despite its name, North Chicago is not a neighborhood in the Windy City. Rather, it is a somewhat depressed suburb considerably north of the city, and students intensely dislike it. There is no on-campus housing.

ADMISSIONS

CMS states no preference for residents of Illinois, and approximately eighty-one percent of students come from out of state. The Admissions Office reports that the average GPA of the most recent class was 3.2 and that the average MCAT score was between 8 and 9. To be considered competitive, students should be in the top third of their undergraduate class.

All applicants receive CMS's supplementary application. On the basis of both the AMCAS and the supplementary applications, promising candidates are invited to interview; these candidates usually represent ten to twelve percent of the total applicant pool. Students are interviewed by two or more members of the Admissions Committee. Final selections are made on the basis of factors that include academic achievement, MCAT scores, letters of recommendation, essays, activities, and personal qualities.

Special Programs for Members of Underrepresented Minorities: CMS says it is committed to increasing the numbers of underrepresented minorities in medicine and encourages all qualified applicants to apply. The school participates in community outreach programs in conjunction with other area schools.

Transfer Policy: CMS does not accept transfers.

FINANCIAL AID

By any standard, CMS is very expensive. The total cost of the first year, including tuition, fees, equipment, and living expenses, is estimated by the Financial Aid office to be over $38,000. Most financial assistance comes from outside programs, but there is some limited university funding. Approximately 75 percent of students receive some aid.

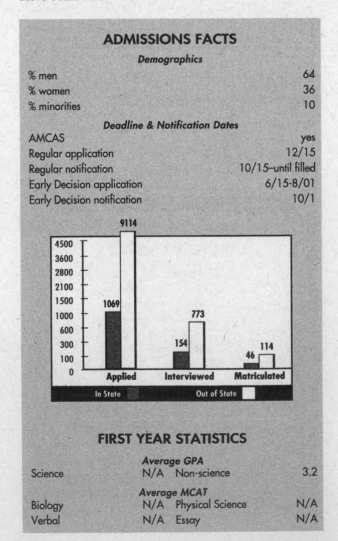

ADMISSIONS FACTS

Demographics

% men	64
% women	36
% minorities	10

Deadline & Notification Dates

AMCAS	yes
Regular application	12/15
Regular notification	10/15–until filled
Early Decision application	6/15-8/01
Early Decision notification	10/1

	Applied	Interviewed	Matriculated
In State	1069	154	46
Out of State	9114	773	114

FIRST YEAR STATISTICS

Average GPA		
Science	N/A	Non-science	3.2

Average MCAT		
Biology	N/A	Physical Science	N/A
Verbal	N/A	Essay	N/A

FINANCIAL FACTS

Tuition and Fees

In-state	$27,715	On-campus housing	N/A
Out-of-state	$27,715	Off-campus housing	N/A
(includes food and living expenses)			

Financial Aid

% receiving some aid	75
Merit scholarships	yes
Average debt	N/A

HITS AND MISSES

HITS	MISSES
Accessibility of faculty	Too many students
Emphasis on ethics	Overall facilities
Campus safety	Early clinical exposure
	Location

TUITION OVERVIEW

$27,715

School's Tuition / National Average

Private

0 5K 10K 15K 20K 25K 30K 35K 40K 45K

University of Illinois College of Medicine

Office of Medical College Admissions
Room 165 CME M/C 783, 808 S. Wood Street, Chicago, IL 60612
(312) 996-5635

OVERVIEW

With 300 first-year students and four separate campuses, the University of Illinois is the largest of the nation's medical schools. Each year's matriculants enter one of two different educational tracks: 175 students complete all four years of medical school at the Chicago campus, while the rest spend their first year in Champaign-Urbana. At the end of the freshman year, 25 of these students remain in Champaign-Urbana. Of the 100 remaining students, 50 go to the Rockford campus and 50 move on to Peoria. Assignments are made on the basis of students' preferences and space availability.

ACADEMICS

There are significant differences in the curricula at each of the campuses. Students in the Chicago program spend much of the first two years learning basic scientific principles underlying the functions of normal and abnormal organisms. Instructional methods include lectures, labs, clinical correlations conferences, and problem-based learning groups. An Introduction to Clinical Medicine course, which teaches problem-solving and patient interaction skills, provides a transition to the third-year clerkships. The senior year is devoted to a combination of requirements and electives.

The first year for students in the Champaign-Urbana track is arranged into eight month-long segments. In each of these segments, students investigate the basic sciences in the context of clinical problem themes. The most unusual aspect of this first-year program is a written curriculum that, according to the College of Medicine, "serves to set down in a comprehensive and systematic fashion those aspects of each subject that students are expected to study." The written curriculum is divided into learning units, each of which includes objectives, vocabulary, a list of learning resources, and a self-evaluation. Live instruction supplements the written learning units and takes the form of lectures, labs, and clinical correlation conferences.

Students who stay at Champaign-Urbana—usually those pursuing combined degree programs—finish their study of the basic sciences and learn fundamental clinical skills in the second year. The third and fourth years are devoted to required and elective clinical clerkships.

Students who are assigned to the Peoria campus spend their second year studying the basic sciences through instruction designed around organ systems. A clinical skills course covers fundamental patient examination and evaluation techniques. A special feature of the Peoria curriculum is the Monitor Program, in which each second-year student spends a day each week working with a practicing physician. The third and fourth years are devoted to required and elective clerkships.

The Rockford program is the most primary care-oriented of the four tracks. The second year focuses on the continued acquisition of scientific knowledge, but, more than the other three programs, provides significant hands-on patient contact. Beginning in the sophomore year and continuing throughout the remainder of med school, students spend two and one-half days a week experiencing the practice of primary care medicine in one of three Community Health Centers. In addition to this ambulatory care experience, students in the third and fourth years complete required and elective clinical clerkships.

Students in all four years are encouraged to pursue research activities in their free time and through electives. Independent study options are available at all but the Champaign-Urbana campus.

Grading and Promotion Policy: Passing grades in all clerkships and coursework are required for promotion. Students must also pass Parts I and II of the USMLE.

Additional Degree Programs: A variety of combined degree programs—including MD/Ph.D.—are offered at the Chicago and Champaign-Urbana campuses.

STUDENT LIFE

Although the Chicago and Champaign-Urbana campuses boast more campus organizations and recreational facilities, all locations offer extracurricular activities. University-owned residence halls and apartments are offered in Chicago and Champaign-Urbana, and plentiful off-campus housing is available at all sites.

ADMISSIONS

The College of Medicine gives preference to state residents, but up to 10 percent of students may come from out of state. All students must complete their baccalaureate degrees prior to matriculation.

Among the selection factors considered by the Admissions Committee are the GPA, MCAT scores, letters of recommendation, extracurricular activities, work experience, and personal qualities. An interview may be required.

Special Programs for Members of Underrepresented Minorities: The University of Illinois is among the top schools in minority admissions. The school is dedicated to continuing to recruit qualified members of underrepresented minorities and to providing counseling, academic advising, and other services to support enrolled students. A summer prematriculation session is offered to ease the transition to med school.

Transfer Policy: Transfers into the second and third years are considered on a space-available basis. Preference is given to residents of Illinois, and candidates must be in good standing at their current med school.

FINANCIAL AID

Most financial aid is awarded on the basis of financial need. Since grant money is limited, most assistance is in the form of long-term loans.

ADMISSIONS FACTS

Demographics

% men	37
% women	63
% minorities	24

Deadline & Notification Dates

AMCAS	yes
Regular application	12/01
Regular notification	10/15–until filled
Early Decision application	6/15-8/01
Early Decision notification	10/01

	Applied	Interviewed	Matriculated
In State	1969	86	267
Out of State	3721	30	33

FIRST YEAR STATISTICS

Average GPA

Science	N/A	Non-science	N/A

Average MCAT

Biology	N/A	Physical Science	N/A
Verbal	N/A	Essay	N/A

FINANCIAL FACTS

Tuition and Fees

In-state	$9,004	On-campus housing	N/A
Out-of-state	$24,250	Off-campus housing	N/A

Financial Aid

% receiving some aid	N/A
Merit scholarships	N/A
Average debt	N/A

TUITION OVERVIEW

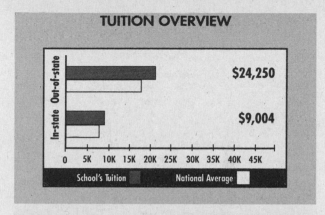

Out-of-state **$24,250**

In-state **$9,004**

| 0 | 5K | 10K | 15K | 20K | 25K | 30K | 35K | 40K | 45K |

School's Tuition ▮ National Average ▯

Loyola University Chicago: Stritch School of Medicine

Medical School Admissions
Room 1752, 2160 South First Avenue, Maywood, IL 60153
(708) 216-3229

OVERVIEW

Perhaps because of Loyola's Jesuit affiliation, the medical school places strong emphasis not only on producing skilled clinicians and academic physicians, but also on training medical humanists. According to the Admissions Office, "a spirit of volunteerism—giving back to the community and society" is one of the things that sets Loyola apart. The community interaction is not the only aspect that sounds tempting; think of the proximity to exciting Chicago.

ACADEMICS

Loyola's approach to medical education is fairly traditional. In the first two years, students spend the majority of their time acquiring a scientific knowledge base. Most courses are taught through lectures and augmented by small-group laboratory sessions. During the second of the four preclinical semesters, students begin to investigate patient care issues through an ethics class and training in emergency life support. The last basic science semester is intended to facilitate the transition to the clinical years. In this semester, students integrate scientific principles with clinical problems in a course organized around organ systems. A physical diagnosis course helps students develop fundamental patient examination and evaluation skills. Although hands-on experience is limited in the preclinical years, students are encouraged to practice their new skills through volunteer work in area clinics.

The last eight quarters are devoted to clinical clerkships and electives. Required rotations take up a little over half of the clinical period, with the remainder of the time free for students to pursue individual interests. Although training highly-skilled clinicians is part of Loyola's mission, the school is also dedicated to biomedical investigation. About half of Loyola students participate in a research project at some time during their four years, and there are several American Heart Association–funded fellowships for students who wish to spend a full year doing cardiovascular research.

Grading and Promotion Policy: Honors/High Pass/Pass/Fail. Students must take Parts I and II of the USMLE.

Additional Degree Programs: MD/Ph.D., MD/MS.

STUDENT LIFE

Community involvement is strongly encouraged at Loyola, and there are several student-initiated service projects in place. Ongoing programs include free health screening for disadvantaged populations and an AIDS education seminar students present in area schools.

For recreation, students can work out at the campus Fitness Center or participate in the many activities sponsored by the Medical Student Union. Those who need a break from the med school atmosphere can take advantage of the cultural and recreational opportunities of nearby Chicago. Although there are no university-owned residence halls or apartments, nearby off-campus housing is available and—by the standards of the Chicago area—reasonably inexpensive.

ADMISSIONS

Although Loyola is a private school, at least half of each class is reserved for residents of Illinois. Still, all qualified out-of-state students are encouraged to apply. After the AMCAS applications is received, students meeting the basic admissions requirements are asked to submit supplementary materials. Promising candidates are then invited to interview.

Final admissions decisions are based on the following factors: the academic record, particularly the GPA and the depth of coursework; MCAT scores from the new format test; the interview; letters of recommendation; essays; exposure to the medical profession; community and extracurricular activities; and work experience. For the best chance for acceptance, the

Admissions Committee recommends that students submit their applications as early in the rolling admissions cycle as possible.

Special Programs for Members of Underrepresented Minorities: Members of underrepresented minority groups are encouraged to apply.

Transfer Policy: Applications for transfer into the second- and third-year classes are considered. Candidates must be in good standing at accredited U.S. med schools.

FINANCIAL AID

Even though Loyola is a private school, Illinois residents get a significant break on tuition. For those who need help covering costs, the school provides assistance through a variety of loan, grant, and scholarship programs. The school's Financial Aid office provides excellent information on expense planning and aid programs. Special tuition scholarships are available to students from disadvantaged backgrounds.

ADMISSIONS FACTS

Demographics

% men	55
% women	45
% minorities	6

Deadline & Notification Dates

AMCAS	yes
Regular application	11/15
Regular notification	10/15–until filled
Early Decision application	6/15-8/01
Early Decision notification	10/01

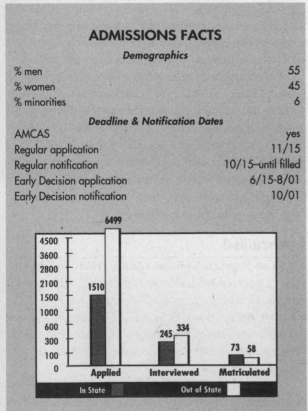

FIRST YEAR STATISTICS

	Average GPA		
Science	N/A	Non-science	3.47
	Average MCAT		
Biology	N/A	Physical Science	N/A
Verbal	N/A	Essay	N/A

FINANCIAL FACTS

Tuition and Fees

In-state	$24,392	On-campus housing	none
Out-of-state	$24,392	Off-campus housing	N/A

Financial Aid

% receiving some aid	90
Merit scholarships	yes
Average debt	N/A

TUITION OVERVIEW

$24,392

$24,392

School's Tuition   National Average

Northwestern University Medical School

Admissions Office, 303 East Chicago Avenue, Chicago, IL 60611
(312) 503-8206

OVERVIEW

Northwestern University Medical School (NUMS) is currently in the middle of a major curricular revision. Most of the changes will be in the basic sciences, and, according to the students we surveyed, things are going to get a whole lot better. The new curriculum is scheduled to be implemented in time for the entering class of 1997. Although the change in curriculum may cause some temporary growing pains at NUMS, students say that the quality of teaching and the school's ideal location on Lake Michigan should more than make up for this.

ACADEMICS

The new curriculum will continue to be divided into preclinical and clinical units, but it will feature a much greater degree of integration among basic science courses and will place considerably more emphasis on clinical correlations. The teaching methods, now almost exclusively lecture and lab, will be a combination of lectures and small group, problem-based learning formats. NUMS students who've been exposed to both methods are enthusiastic about the change. Says one, "In lectures, we get too much information too fast. They feed it to us and we spit it out. It's just regurgitation. The small group learning they've been experimenting with is a lot better....We learn to work as a team."

Early clinical exposure is also likely to increase. Currently, physical examinations and diagnoses are demonstrated in the basic science years, but for hands-on experience, students have to go beyond the required courses. Students are pleased with the clinically-oriented electives NUMS offers and the Patient Perspective program, where students monitor a patient through an entire hospital stay, is especially popular.

Students are also enthusiastic about the emphasis the faculty places on medical ethics. Students rate the overall quality of teaching as very good, but, because of the large class size, they don't always feel like they get individual attention. They are confident, however, that the new curriculum will allow them to have more personal interaction with the faculty.

Feedback on the facilities is generally positive, with one notable exception: students detest the medical library. One student reports, "It's small, it's cramped, and it's dangerous—part of it used to be a boiler room and there are pipes everywhere." Students solve the library problem by using Northwestern's Law Library, but this practice may come to an end. Complains one student, "The Law School is trying to kick us out." Welcome to the wonderful world of physician-attorney relations.

Grading and Promotion Policy: Pass/Fail. Students must take Part I of the USMLE.

Additional Degree Programs: Combined baccalaureate/MD, MD/Ph.D., MD/MPH, and MD/MM (Master of Management, in conjunction with the Kellogg School of Business).

STUDENT LIFE

Although there are plenty of heavy-duty studiers, overall, NUMS students spend less time preparing for class than any other students we surveyed. Students like the newly implemented Pass/Fail grading system. According to one student, "Getting rid of the Honors grade eliminated a lot of the cutthroat competition."

NUMS students have fairly active social lives, and they agree that they have a great city in which to play. "[The school] is in a great location right on the lake—the most beautiful part of Chicago." On-campus housing also receives enthusiastic reviews, but students warn that there is a significant difference in quality between the two residence halls. Students who choose to live off-campus generally have trouble finding affordable housing in the school's posh neighborhood, but an accessible—and relatively safe—public transportation system makes it easy to get around.

ADMISSIONS

Although it is a private med school, NUMS reserves 50 percent of each class for residents of Illinois. An additional third of each class is made up of students from the seven-year combined Baccalaureate/MD program the med school sponsors with the undergraduate school.

In evaluating applicants, NUMS looks at the interview, academic achievement, MCAT scores (from the new format), letters of recommendation, essays, extracurricular activities, and personal qualities.

Special Programs for Members of Underrepresented Minorities: NUMS encourages applications from members of underrepresented minorities.

Transfer Policy: NUMS considers transfers into its second and third year on a space-available basis.

FINANCIAL AID

All financial aid awards are made on the basis of need as determined by the GAPSFAS analysis. Approximately two thirds of students receive some form of assistance.

ADMISSIONS FACTS

Demographics

%men	51
%women	49
%minorities	4

Deadline & Notification Dates

AMCAS	yes
Regular application	11/15
Regular notification	10/15–until filled
Early Decision application	6/15-8/01
Early Decision notification	10/01

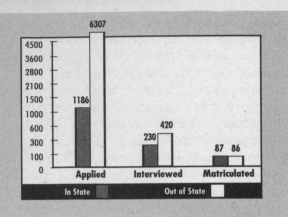

	6307
In State	Out of State

Applied: 1186 / 6307
Interviewed: 230 / 420
Matriculated: 87 / 86

FIRST YEAR STATISTICS

Average GPA
Science	N/A	Non-science	3.51

Average MCAT
Biology	N/A	Physical Science	N/A
Verbal	N/A	Essay	N/A

FINANCIAL FACTS

Tuition and Fees
In-state	$24,291	On-campus housing	N/A
Out-of-state (includes board)	$24,291	Off-campus housing	N/A

Financial Aid
% receiving some aid	60
Merit scholarships	no
Average debt	N/A

HITS AND MISSES

HITS	MISSES
New, improved curriculum	Library
Emphasis on ethics	Computer facilities too crowded
Chicago	
Public transportation	

TUITION OVERVIEW

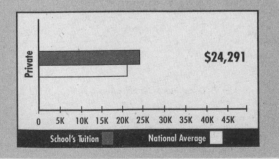

$24,291

School's Tuition	National Average

Rush Medical College of Rush University

Office of Admissions, 524 Academic Facility,
600 South Paulina Street, Chicago, IL 60612
(312) 942-6913

OVERVIEW

Even though state residents have a decided advantage in this private school's admissions process, non-residents—who each year compete for a small percentage of spots in the freshman class—make up about three quarters of the applicant pool. What makes Rush such a popular choice among med school applicants? According to current students, Rush's extremely supportive faculty, its cohesive student body, its large complex of urban, suburban, and rural hospitals, and its location in vibrant Chicago make it "an excellent place to go to med school."

ACADEMICS

Although all Rush students cover the same basic material in the preclinical first two years, between 15 and 20 percent of each year's entering class participates in the Alternative Curriculum—a small group, problem-based learning track. In the traditional curriculum, freshmen investigate normal human structure, function, and behavior in courses arranged by scientific discipline. The second year builds on this knowledge as students explore the disease process and its effects on the individual and society. Patient interaction begins when students learn the fundamentals of interviewing, history-taking, and examination.

The Alternative Curriculum offers a more integrated approach. Material is organized into multidisciplinary units, and case studies that correlate basic, clinical, and behavioral sciences are the primary mode of instruction. Although students meet in small groups with faculty facilitators to identify and discuss learning issues, much of their time is spend in independent or collaborative study. Written "learning guidebooks," which highlight key basic science concepts, list reference citations, and include learning exercises, provide a framework for each unit. Although there are no formally-scheduled lectures, individuals or groups of students may meet with faculty members to discuss aspects of cases or cover material in more depth. Labs are also available for Alternative Curriculum students' use.

At the end of the preclinical years, students from the traditional and alternative curricula reunite for clinical clerkships. Over the final two years, students are required to complete rotations in family practice, medicine, neurology, pediatrics, psychiatry, obstetrics/gynecology, and surgery and must do a sub-internship in family practice, pediatrics, or medicine. A minimum of twenty weeks of electives are also required in the clinical period.

Although students in both learning tracks report being very satisfied with the amount of clinical exposure they get in the first two years, participants in the Alternative Curriculum are slightly more enthusiastic about the extent of clinical correlation than their peers in the traditional program. There is no significant difference in their attitudes towards professors, however. All of the Rush students we surveyed say instructors do an outstanding job of conveying material. Perhaps more importantly, say our respondents, professors are extraordinarily supportive of students and give them every opportunity to succeed in their studies—even when that means that instructors must spend considerable time outside of class to help those who are struggling with material.

The learning environment, too, is given outstanding reviews. Although students have few complaints about any of Rush's facilities, they are especially enthusiastic about the school's clinical teaching sites. The large variety of hospital and ambulatory settings expose students to a culturally and socioeconomically diverse patient base and give them experience with a wide array of health problems and issues.

Grading and Promotion Policy: Honors/Pass/Fail. Students must take Parts I and II of the USMLE.

Additional Degree Programs: MD/Ph.D.

STUDENT LIFE

Rush students are among the happiest we surveyed. Although much of our respondents' enthusiasm about their school can be credited to the academic environment, quality of life issues also play a role. Students enjoy the noncompetitive atmosphere at Rush and say relations among classmates are excellent. Involvement in school and community activities is high, and students say they have a wide variety of extracurricular pursuits from which to choose. The school's location in Chicago

is also a big plus; our respondents were nearly unanimous in giving the Windy City and its enormous array of accessible cultural, social, educational, and recreational activities the highest possible ratings.

Students are also pleased with the on- and off-campus housing options available to them. For those who choose to make independent living arrangements, the city's excellent public transportation system makes commuting a breeze. Using mass transit is not without drawbacks, however; safety is a big concern for nearly all of our respondents.

ADMISSIONS

Although it is a private med school, Rush shows a strong preference for candidates from Illinois. In the 1992–93 school year, fewer than one percent of out-of-state applicants were accepted and eventually matriculated. Presently, only about 15 percent of spaces in the entering class are available to out-of-state students, but, according to the school's literature, more places will soon be reserved for nonresidents.

Only candidates who are thought to be exceptionally well-qualified—usually between 12 and 15 percent of the total pool—are invited to interview. During the interview day, students meet with two faculty members and take a student-conducted tour of the school's facilities. Although there is currently no provision for regional interviews, those candidates who are invited to come to campus but who live a great distance from Chicago are given first priority for vacation-time interviews.

Among the final considerations in admissions decisions are the academic record, MCAT scores, the interview, maturity, integrity, motivation, extracurricular activities, and the suitability for the practice of medicine. Factors that influence the Admissions Committee's evaluation of the scholastic record include the difficulty of the undergraduate institution, the level and breadth of coursework, and the ways in which the individual's cultural, social, or economic background may have influenced his or her academic achievement.

Special Programs for Members of Underrepresented Minorities: According to school literature, "Rush Medical College seeks to attract candidates who can help make the student body more representative of our national population and more realistically informed about social problems affecting the delivery of health care in this country." To encourage young minority and economically disadvantaged students to develop their interests in medicine, Rush participates in the Chicago Area Health Careers Opportunity Program.

Transfer Policy: Students interested in transferring to Rush should contact the Admissions Office to discuss their individual circumstances.

FINANCIAL AID

Financial aid is awarded primarily on the basis of need as determined by the College Scholarship Service analysis. Loans are the most common form of assistance, and students with documented need must borrow a set amount (a unit loan) before becoming eligible for scholarships and grants. Residents of Illinois who are interested in practicing primary care specialties in underserved areas of the state may want to investigate the Illinois Department of Health's Medical Student Scholarship program. Through this program, students receive full tuition and a monthly stipend in exchange for postresidency service in a designated area experiencing a physician shortage.

ADMISSIONS FACTS

Demographics

% men	48
% women	52
% minorities	9

Deadline & Notification Dates

AMCAS	yes
Regular application	11/15
Regular notification	10/15–until filled
Early Decision application	6/15-8/01
Early Decision notification	10/01

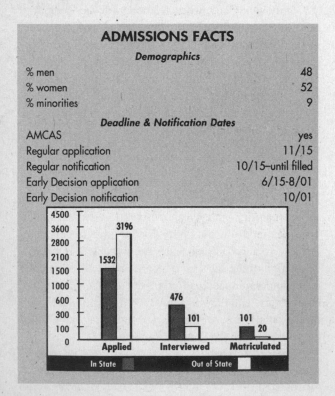

FIRST YEAR STATISTICS

Average GPA

Science	N/A	Non-science	N/A

Average MCAT

Biology	N/A	Physical Science	N/A
Verbal	N/A		
		Essay	
			N/A

FINANCIAL FACTS

Tuition and Fees

In-state	$23,436	On-campus housing	N/A
Out-of-state	$23,436	Off-campus housing	N/A

Financial Aid

% receiving some aid	80
Merit scholarships	N/A
Average debt	N/A

HITS AND MISSES

HITS	MISSES
Overall happiness	Campus safety
Quality of Teaching	Safety of public transportation
Teacher accessibility	
Involved, committed student body	
Noncompetitive atmosphere	
Plenty of school-sponsored activities	
Empsis on ethics	
Chicago	
Housing options	
Accessible public transportation	

TUITION OVERVIEW

$23,436

School's Tuition   National Average

Southern Illinois University School of Medicine

Student Affairs, P.O. Box 19230, Springfield, IL 62794-9230
(217) 782-2860

OVERVIEW

Although SIU is committed to training physicians as scientists, producing superior clinicians is its main goal. Students appreciate this objective. Reports one, "I chose this school because of the emphasis placed on making good, caring, and compassionate doctors." Advises another, "Anyone who is from Illinois and is looking for a medical school which emphasizes clinical skills as well as academic skills should apply to SIU."

ACADEMICS

Students at SIU spend their first year in Carbondale and the remainder of their training in Springfield. To foster more continuity and assimilation in the basic sciences, the curriculum is organized around organ systems, and early clinical training is required. Problem-based learning is incorporated into the regular curriculum; in addition, a separate Problem-based Learning Curriculum (PBLC) is available to eighteen students a year.

In this program, students use case studies to learn and apply basic science principles. Says one student of the PBLC experience, "We are placed in groups [consisting of] six students and one tutor. All of our learning is self-directed. There are no scheduled lectures or required reading. I really enjoy this type of learning because it is very clinically oriented. We have required clinical experiences and our learning is set up around a case which we follow and derive learning issues from." In addition to studying the basic sciences, first- and second-year students in both curricular tracks investigate psychosocial aspects of medicine and participate in required clinical experiences. SIU students are extremely happy with the amount of early clinical exposure they receive.

Students rate faculty accessibility as outstanding and are very satisfied with the quality of teaching. Clinical facilities are also rated as excellent. Students are not as pleased with the basic science facilities, however, rating classrooms, labs, and the library as only satisfac-

tory. They reserve their harshest criticism for the computer facilities.

Grading and Promotion Policy: Honors/Pass/Fail. A passing grade on Part I of the USMLE is required for graduation.

Additional Degree Programs: MD/JD.

STUDENT LIFE

Students say their classmates aren't overly competitive. As one student says, "The environment here at SIU School of Medicine is very relaxing. The Pass/Fail system makes life much less stressful and everyone is not out to outdo each other." SIU students like each other, and they make time to socialize. Reports one, "All of our classmates get along amazingly well." But another feels that there is too much partying: "My classmates are brilliant, but on the whole are very immature and seem to treat their first year of medical school as if it's an extended undergraduate period."

ADMISSIONS

Illinois residents are given preference, but up to ten percent of each year's class can be from out of state. Out-of-state applicants should have outstanding academic qualifications, be members of an underrepresented minority, have close ties to the state, or be interested in primary care. All out-of-state students must apply early decision or through the combined MD/JD program.

The interview, the science GPA, MCAT scores (from the new format test), and letters of recommendation are the most important factors in admissions decisions. Also considered are the nonscience GPA, extracurricular activities, volunteer activities, exposure to the medical profession, and essays. Students are sent a supplemental application if their GPA is at least 3.0 on a 4.0 scale and their MCAT scores in the verbal and biological sciences are at least in the 60th percentile. Candidates who look promising on the basis of the supplemental application are given two interviews, one with an Admissions or Student Affairs staff member and another with a faculty member. The Admissions Committee includes faculty and students from both campuses.

Special Programs for Members of Underrepresented Minorities: SIU offers MEDPREP, a nondegree undergraduate or postbaccalaureate program designed to assist minority, disadvantaged, or postbaccalaureate students in developing the knowledge and qualities they need to be successful in medical school. Academic advising, MCAT review, and assistance in applying to medical school are some features of the MEDPREP program. Participation in MEDPREP does not guarantee admittance to the medical school. SIU also offers a prematriculation program for accepted students. Some members of the majority seem to resent what they see as special opportunities. Complains one such student, "Minority students aren't given equal treatment. They are given much better treatment."

Transfer Policy: Transfers are considered in "hardship cases requiring a move to Springfield, Illinois." Transfer applicants must be in good academic standing at a U.S. LCME-approved medical school.

FINANCIAL AID

Students are impressed that SIU provides quality education while containing costs. One points out, "Money is an important issue. [SIU] is one of the most affordable medical schools in Illinois." This affordability extends only to residents of Illinois, however; nonresidents pay three times the in-state tuition rate. Approximately 85 percent of students receive some sort of financial aid. Besides the usual variety of federal loans, SIU offers Watson Family Assistant Loans, Emergency Loans, and Illinois Health Improvement Association Loans.

FIRST YEAR STATISTICS

Average GPA			
Science	N/A	Non-science	N/A
Average MCAT			
Biology	N/A	Physical Science	N/A
Verbal	N/A	Essay	N/A

FINANCIAL FACTS

Tuition and Fees

In-state	$11,240*	On-campus housing	N/A
Out-of-state	$31,310	Off-campus housing	N/A
*(includes fees)			

Financial Aid

% receiving some aid	88
Merit scholarships	no
Average debt	$44,498

HITS AND MISSES

HITS	MISSES
Faculty accessibility	Computer facilities
Clinical facilities	Research emphasis
Early clinical exposure	Campus activities
Attractive campus	

TUITION OVERVIEW

$31,310

$11,240

School's Tuition   National Average

ADMISSIONS FACTS

Demographics

% men	55
% women	45
% minorities	11

Deadline & Notification Dates

AMCAS	yes
Regular application	11/15
Regular notification	10/15-until filled
Early Decision application	6/15-8/01
Early Decision notification	10/01

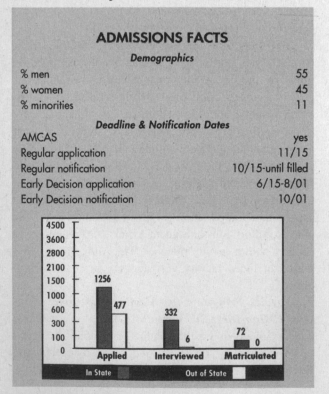

Indiana University School of Medicine

Medical School Admissions Office, Fester Hall 213, 1120 South Drive,
Indianapolis, IN 46202-5113
(317) 274-3772

OVERVIEW

Like its midwestern rival, the University of Illinois, Indiana's med school has an unusual setup. Students spend their first two, basic science years at one of nine campuses located in various regions of the state. After the preclinical period, most students transfer to the main campus in Indianapolis. Of the other locations, only Bloomington—home of Indiana U's main undergraduate division—has a four-year curriculum. Most Bloomington students are in a combined-degree Medical Science Program. Matriculants are assigned to campuses on the basis of student preferences and the availability of space.

ACADEMICS

Although Indiana has a relatively traditional curriculum, it has several progressive features. The preclinical program is pretty much the same at all locations, but because some campuses are on a semester schedule and others are on a quarter system, the timing varies somewhat. Basic science lectures are complemented by interdisciplinary seminars and small group discussions. Clinical correlation conferences help students understand the relevance of scientific principles, and a first-year behavioral science course highlights out psychological and social issues in medicine.

Although there is not a lot of patient contact in the first year, students can take electives to receive hands-on experience. There is considerably more clinical orientation in the second year. Students learn history-taking and physical diagnosis skills in Introduction to Medicine, a course that eases the transition into the third-year clerkships. Juniors complete rotations in the major disciplines and in family medicine. Additional clerkships and a research segment are required in the senior year, with the remainder of the time free for electives.

Grading and Promotion Policy: High Honors/Honors/Pass/Fail. Students must pass Parts I and II of the USMLE.

Additional Degree Programs: MS/MD, MD/Ph.D.

STUDENT LIFE

The main medical center is in Indianapolis, but there are preclinical students at each of the other Statewide Medical Education System locations. The other campuses are Indiana University, Purdue, Notre Dame, Ball State, Indiana State, Gary's Northwest Center for Medical Education, University of Evansville, and the Fort Wayne Center for Medical Education. At all locations, med students have access to the resources of the parent universities. Student organizations and the availability of housing vary from one campus to the next.

ADMISSIONS

Indiana gives preference to state residents, but well-qualified candidates from out of state are encouraged to apply. Applicants who pass an initial review will be asked to submit supplementary materials. Any Indiana resident with a GPA of at least 3.0 is eligible for an interview.

The Admissions Committee makes its final selections on the basis of the interview, GPA, MCAT scores, letters of recommendation, character, and personal qualities.

Special Programs for Members of Underrepresented Minorities: Indiana encourages members of underrepresented minorities to apply.

Transfer Policy: Indiana considers applications for transfer into the second or third year from Indiana residents who are in good standing at U.S. or foreign med schools. Nonresident applications are accepted only from students at U.S. med schools.

FINANCIAL AID

Most financial aid is awarded on the basis of need as determined by the CSS analysis, and there are some merit scholarships available.

ADMISSIONS FACTS

Demographics

% men	62
% women	38
% minorities	6

Deadline & Notification Dates

AMCAS	yes
Regular application	12/15
Regular notification	10/15–until filled
Early Decision application	6/15-8/01
Early Decision notification	10/01

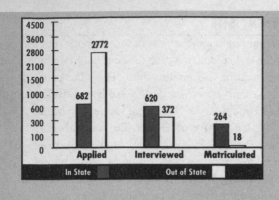

FIRST YEAR STATISTICS

Average GPA

Science	N/A	Non-science	3.61

Average MCAT

Biology	9.4	Physical Science	9.4
Verbal	9.4	Essay	N/A

FINANCIAL FACTS

Tuition and Fees

In-state	$9,161	On-campus housing	N/A
Out-of-state	$20,728	Off-campus housing	N/A

Financial Aid

% receiving some aid	N/A
Merit scholarships	yes
Average debt	N/A

TUITION OVERVIEW

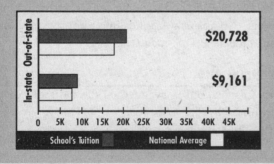

University of Iowa College of Medicine

Coordinator of Admissions, 108 CMAB, Iowa City, IA 52242
(319) 335-8052

OVERVIEW

Since it is the only med school in the state, one of the University of Iowa College of Medicine's major goals is to train clinicians to provide health care to Iowans. But this is only part of the school's mission. Iowa is is also highly committed to research; in addition to its efforts in the basic and clinical sciences, the school has a Center for Health Science Research that investigates the organization, delivery, efficacy, and financing of health care services.

ACADEMICS

One of the most unusual features of the academic experience at Iowa is the first-semester Human Dimensions in Medicine (HDM) course. In HDM, freshmen are assigned to an eight-member group that meets to share ideas and discuss issues related to med school and the health care delivery system. More importantly, perhaps, this group promotes teamwork and acts as a support network for its members as they progress through their education.

The first year and a half at Iowa is devoted to the basic sciences. In some courses, especially those in the second and third semesters, students use a small group case study method to identify and learn scientific principles. Third-semester students also investigate social, economic, and ethical aspects of medicine.

The fourth-semester Introduction to Clinical Medicine course (ICM) provides a transition into the clinical clerkships. In ICM, students learn interviewing and examinations skills through work with mannequins, simulated patients, and real patients. In addition, they participate in a preceptorship at the university hospitals. Lectures that introduce the clinical specialties they will encounter in the third year are also part of the curriculum.

In the third year, students complete required clerkships in a variety of disciplines. While most rotations are done in the university hospitals, students can take some in affiliated sites, including ambulatory care centers. The family practice clerkship must be done in a private physician's office. Nearly all of the fourth year is elective.

Grading and Promotion Policy: For the first three years, Honors/Pass/Fail. For the fourth year, Pass/Fail.

Additional Degree Programs: Iowa offers a funded Medical Scientist Training Program that leads to a combined MD/Ph.D. Regular MD/Ph.D. and MD/MS programs are also offered.

STUDENT LIFE

The University of Iowa is an integral part of Iowa City, and the town has a distinct college flavor. Med students participate in their own organizations and join in the activities of the large university community. Athletically-minded students can work out in the campus fitness center, or if they'd rather stay on the sidelines, they can help raucous Hawkeye fans cheer on their Big Ten teams.

Although on-campus housing is available, most students live off campus. City and campus bus services help students without cars get around.

ADMISSIONS

Preference is given to Iowa residents, but nonresidents with outstanding qualifications are encouraged to apply. Students who the Admissions Office believe to be highly qualified will be asked for supplemental information. For the best chance of admission, candidates should apply as early as possible in the admissions cycle.

Since applicants are generally not interviewed, the primary selection factors are the GPA, MCAT scores, and letters of recommendation. Although students with GPAs over 2.5 will be considered, almost 90 percent of successful applicants had GPAs of 3.2 or above.

Special Programs for Members of Underrepresented Minorities: Iowa's Educational Opportunity Program (EOP) provides financial and academic assistance to members of underrepresented minorities and students from disadvantaged backgrounds.

Transfer Policy: Iowa considers applicants for transfer.

FINANCIAL AID

Most financial aid is awarded on the basis of need as determined by the ACT analysis. Long-term loans are the primary source of assistance.

ADMISSIONS FACTS

Demographics

% men	64
% women	34
% minorities	9

Deadline & Notification Dates

AMCAS	yes
Regular application	11/15
Regular notification	10/15–8/15
Early Decision application	6/15-8/01
Early Decision notification	10/01

Bar chart:

	In State	Out of State
Applied	358	2942
Interviewed	N/A	N/A
Matriculated	149	26

FIRST YEAR STATISTICS

Average GPA

Science	3.6	Non-science	3.6

Average MCAT
Mean 9-10 on each subject test

Biology	N/A	Physical Science	N/A
Verbal	N/A	Essay	N/A

FINANCIAL FACTS

Tuition and Fees

In-state	$8,487	On-campus housing	N/A
Out-of-state	$21,387	Off-campus housing	N/A

Financial Aid

% receiving some aid	N/A
Merit scholarships	N/A
Average debt	N/A

TUITION OVERVIEW

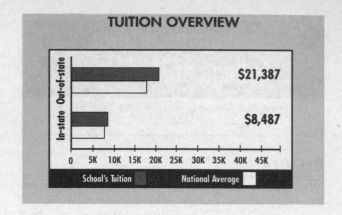

Out-of-state $21,387

In-state $8,487

■ School's Tuition   □ National Average

University of Kansas School of Medicine

Associate Dean for Admissions,
3901 Rainbow Blvd., Kansas City, KS 66160-7301
(913) 588-5245

OVERVIEW

Recognized as one of the top comprehensive U.S. med schools, the University of Kansas School of Medicine is dedicated to providing and improving health care for residents of the state. Because of the school's mission—and because of the funding it receives from Kansas taxpayers—which state you call home may have a lot to do with your chances of being admitted. In the 1992–93 school year, over half of in-state applicants were accepted, while only about 2 percent of nonresidents got in.

ACADEMICS

The structure of Kansas's curriculum is fairly classical, but the school has modified it to help students better integrate the basic, clinical, and behavioral sciences. While the first two years remain primarily devoted to the acquisition of the scientific knowledge base necessary for the study and practice of medicine, students also investigate psychosocial issues and develop fundamental patient interaction skills. Like their counterparts at most other U.S. med schools, Kansas students spend their freshman year studying normal human structures and functions and their second year investigating the disease process. Clinical exposure begins during the first semester and intensifies throughout the basic science years. The sophomore year's Introduction to Clinical Medicine provides a transition to the clinical clerkship phase.

Before the end of their sophomore year, students work with their advisors to plan their third- and fourth-year schedule of core requirements and electives. During the clinical period, all students must complete clerkships in medicine, surgery, pediatrics, obstetrics/gynecology, psychiatry, family medicine, and geriatrics. They must also work for one month with a practicing community physician, a requirement that is normally fulfilled in a small town setting. Although most students do the majority of their clinical work at the Medical Center in Kansas City, about one-fourth of students move to the med school's campus in Wichita to complete their rotations.

Grading and Promotion Policy: Superior/High Satisfactory/Satisfactory/Low Satisfactory/Unsatisfactory. Students must pass Parts I and II of the USMLE.

Additional Degree Programs: MD/Ph.D.

ADMISSIONS

Although Kansas accepts only a small percentage of out-of-state candidates, the Admissions Committee encourages highly qualified nonresidents to apply. According to the Associate Dean for Admissions, those accepted from out of state for the 1992–93 school year had outstanding academic credentials, including an average GPA of 3.67 and average MCAT scores of 10.25.

In making its final selections, the Admissions Committee considers a variety of academic and nonacademic factors. Among the criteria on which each student is evaluated are GPA, MCAT scores (from the new test), letters of recommendation, the interview, "the applicant's motivation, capability, preparation, and suitability for a career in medicine," extracurricular and civic activities, and accomplishments.

Special Programs for Members of Underrepresented Minorities: Kansas encourages members of underrepresented minorities to apply and offers several scholarships for qualified minority students.

Transfer Policy: Applications for transfer into the third year are considered on a space-available basis.

FINANCIAL AID

Financial aid is awarded primarily on the basis of documented need and consists of a variety of loan, scholarship, and grant programs. Kansas residents interested in primary care specialties may want to look into the Kansas Medical Student Loan Program. In this program, students receive full tuition and a monthly stipend in exchange for postresidency practice in a medically underserved area of the state.

ADMISSIONS FACTS

Demographics

% men	59
% women	41
% minorities	10

Deadline & Notification Dates

AMCAS	yes
Regular application	11/01
Regular notification	2/01–until filled
Early Decision application	6/15-8/01
Early Decision notification	10/01

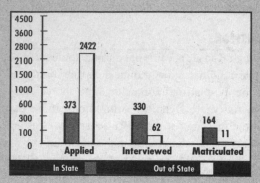

FIRST YEAR STATISTICS

Average GPA

Science	N/A	Non-science	3.5

Average MCAT
Mean subject scores at least at 60th percentile

Biology	N/A	Physical Science	N/A
Verbal	N/A	Essay	N/A

FINANCIAL FACTS

Tuition and Fees

In-state	$8,460	On-campus housing	N/A
Out-of-state	$19,618	Off-campus housing	N/A

Financial Aid

% receiving some aid	75
Merit scholarships	yes
Average debt	N/A

TUITION OVERVIEW

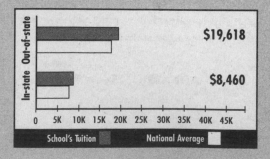

University of Kentucky College of Medicine

Admissions Office, Room MN104, Office of Education, 800 Rose Street, Lexington, KY 40536-0084
(606) 233-6161

OVERVIEW

The University of Kentucky was recently rated among the country's top ten comprehensive schools. But the College of Medicine isn't resting on its laurels; exciting changes are going on.

ACADEMICS

"In 1992 the Robert Wood Johnson Foundation awarded the College of Medicine a $2.5 million grant to institute sweeping changes in the way the institution educates physicians." Students have mixed feelings about the curricular changes, but most are satisfied with their Kentucky experiences.

Kentucky's new curriculum, which is intended to allow more clinical exposure during the first two years of medical school, went into effect with the class entering the fall of 1993. Reviews are mixed. One respondent remarks: "The [Robert Wood Johnson] curriculum is helpful in fostering our decision-making skills, but its implementation (at least here) has been sketchy and problematic; i.e. very confusing objectives and scheduling."

Whatever their feelings about the new curriculum, most UK students think their professors are doing a good job. Some complain, however, that a lot of the reading in the basic science years is unnecessary. Comments one second-year student, "There is no need to do the assigned reading. Studying lecture notes and the handouts given for each class is sufficient to obtain a full grasp of the material."

Feedback on the school's facilities is largely positive, but complaints about the "lack of adequate study space for individuals and groups" are widespread. Explains one student, "The majority of medical students that I know cannot study effectively in a small study carrel in the library, and it is next to impossible to find a room to study in on a regular basis." Computer and clinical facilities receive consistently high ratings.

Grading and Promotion policy: A–F. Passing grades on USMLE Parts I and II are required.

Additional Degree Programs: MD/Ph.D. (7 years), MD/MA (5 years), MD/MPH (5 years).

STUDENT LIFE

Students agree that, overall, they are pretty happy at UK, but some women express concern about what they perceive to be a lack of support for female students. Complains one, "The problem is that the 'Old Boy's Network' still runs the school. To illustrate this is the fact that there is only one female departmental chairperson." These students do add, though, that the school is working to improve conditions.

UK's atmosphere is competitive. First- and second-year students report they spend a lot of time hitting the books, leaving them little freedom or inclination to get involved in school and community activities. Spectator sports are a release for some. According to one third-year student, "A wonderful feature about the school is that we get tickets for UK basketball. Not great seats, but they are obtained for us. I don't have to wait in line."

Students like Lexington and agree that the campus is both attractive and safe. They are dissatisfied with the dorms, however, and vastly prefer off-campus housing opportunities. A downside to commuting to school? "Parking here," one student says, "sucks."

ADMISSIONS

UK gives preference to in-state applicants, but up to 10 percent of its students can be nonresidents. Students with outstanding academic qualifications, members of underrepresented minorities, students with close ties to the state, and alumni children are especially encouraged to apply from out of state.

The Admissions Office ranks the science GPA, MCAT scores (from the new format test), the interview, and letters of recommendation as the most important selection factors. Also considered, in descending order of importance, are exposure to the medical profession, nonscience GPA, extracurricular activities, and volunteer activities. Essays are considered only for out-of-state applicants.

Special Programs for Members of Underrepresented Minorities: Kentucky students give the school extremely low ratings on diversity, a situation the admissions office is hoping to change through special programs. Among its offerings are special consideration for admissions, a prematriculation summer session for accepted students, academic advising, tutoring, peer counseling, and review sessions for Parts I and II of the

USMLE. With the exception of special consideration for admission (which applies also to rural students), programs are open to any enrolled students.

Transfer Policy: UK accepts transfers when space is available.

FINANCIAL AID

UK uses the College Scholarship Service to evaluate need for grant and loan funds. There are some merit scholarships. About 74 percent of students obtain Stafford Loans.

ADMISSIONS FACTS

Demographics

% men	69
% women	31
% minorities	9

Deadline & Notification Dates

AMCAS	yes
Regular application	11/01
Regular notification	After interview -until filled
Early Decision application	6/15-8/01
Early Decision notification	10/01

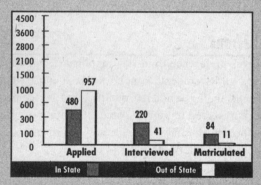

In State	Out of State

FIRST YEAR STATISTICS

Average GPA

Science	N/A	Nonscience	3.44

Average MCAT

Biology	N/A	Physical Science	N/A
Verbal	N/A	Essay	N/A

FINANCIAL FACTS

Tuition and Fees

In-state	$7,420*	On-campus housing	N/A
Out-of-state	$17,050	Off-campus housing	N/A
*(includes fees)			

Financial Aid

% receiving some aid	85
Merit scholarships	yes
Average debt	$35,360

HITS AND MISSES

HITS	MISSES
Clinical facilities	Diversity
Faculty accessibility	Competitive atmosphere
Computer labs	Extracurricular involvement
Lexington	Study space

TUITION OVERVIEW

Out-of-state $17,050

In-state $7,420

School's Tuition	National Average

University of Louisville School of Medicine

Admissions, Health Sciences Center, Louisville, KY 40292
(502) 588-5193

OVERVIEW

Do you want to practice primary care in Kentucky? That is what University of Louisville School of Medicine wants to train its students to do. Located in Kentucky's largest city, the University of Louisville School of Medicine strives to meet the needs of the surrounding metropolitan area and the state. The school's mission is threefold, encompassing direct health care services, education, and research. The school assumes a major responsibility for educating the commonwealth's physicians—42 percent of Kentucky's physicians are Louisville graduates.

ACADEMICS

Louisville's curriculum is divided along the usual preclinical and clinical lines. The primary focus of the first two years is on the basic sciences, but students also investigate topics in humanities, behavioral sciences, and medical computing. The Clinical Diagnosis course in the second year shifts the emphasis toward clinical medicine as students learn examination and evaluation skills. In both of the preclinical years, students take electives which they may use to explore the basic sciences in greater depth or to gain early clinical experience.

The third year consists of required clerkships in the major disciplines and in ophthalmology, neurology, and family practice. Although most of the fourth year is devoted to clinical electives, students must complete rotations in advanced medicine and surgery and take a course in advanced cardiac life support.

Grading and Promotion Policy: A–F

Additional Degree Programs: BS/MD; MD/Ph.D.

STUDENT LIFE

Ranked as one of the nation's most livable cities, Louisville offers plenty of urban amenities. For the culturally minded, there is an orchestra, theaters, and ballet and opera companies. Sports fans can cheer for the university teams, take in a minor league baseball game, or bet on the races at nearby Churchill Downs, home of the Kentucky Derby.

The University offers several different styles of on-campus housing, and there are plenty of reasonably priced off-campus rental units available.

ADMISSIONS

Louisville gives preference to Kentucky residents, but up to six percent of students can come from out of state. Nonresidents especially encouraged to apply are students with outstanding qualifications, women, members of underrepresented minorities, candidates with close ties to the state, and children of alumni. Out-of-state applicants are urged to apply Early Decision.

The Director of Admissions ranks as the primary selection factors the science and nonscience GPAs, MCAT scores (from the new test), and the interview. Also considered important are extracurricular activities, essays, exposure to the medical field, and volunteer activities. Special consideration is given to students who are interested in primary care and/or in practicing in ru-

ral communities.

Special Programs for Members of Underrepresented Minorities: The Office of Health Careers Programs coordinates recruiting efforts and support services for members of underrepresented minorities. Among its offerings are community outreach programs, summer sessions for college students, a prematriculation summer session, academic advising, tutoring, peer counseling, and review classes for Parts I and II of the USMLE.

Transfer Policy: Louisville considers transfers in exceptional circumstances.

eMail: @ULKYUM.Louisville.edu

FINANCIAL AID

Most awards are made on the basis of documented need, but the school offers some merit scholarships.

ADMISSIONS FACTS

Demographics

% men	54
% women	46
% minorities	10

Deadline & Notification Dates

AMCAS	yes
Regular application	11/01
Regular notification	10/15–until filled
Early Decision application	6/15-8/01
Early Decision notification	10/01

FIRST YEAR STATISTICS

	Average GPA		
Science	N/A	Non-science	3.5
	Average MCAT		
Biology	N/A	Physical Science	N/A
Verbal	N/A	Essay	N/A

FINANCIAL FACTS

Tuition and Fees

In-state	$7,300	On-campus housing	N/A
Out-of-state	$16,930	Off-campus housing	N/A

Financial Aid

% receiving some aid	90
Merit scholarships	yes
Average debt	$32,614

TUITION OVERVIEW

Out-of-state $16,930

In-state $7,300

0   5K   10K   15K   20K   25K   30K   35K   40K   45K

School's Tuition   National Average

Louisiana State University: School of Medicine in New Orleans

Office of Admissions, 1901 Perdido St.,
New Orleans, LA 70112-1393
(504) 568-6262

OVERVIEW

According to students who go there, LSU School of Medicine in New Orleans (LSUNO) has a lot to recommend it to prospective applicants. A strong clinical emphasis, a focus on primary care, solid teaching, and excellent facilities are among the things our respondents like best about their school. But unless you have money to burn—as over 400 applicants in a recent admissions season apparently did—don't bother applying to LSUNO if you're not a resident of Louisiana. Out-of-state candidates are not considered for admission to this primary care-oriented state school, and the policy is unlikely to change.

ACADEMICS

Like most other U.S. med schools, LSUNO divides its curriculum into two-year preclinical and clinical units. The first two years are devoted primarily to the basic sciences, but there is significant attention to the clinical correlations of scientific principles. There is also considerable time for electives in the freshman year, and many students choose to get a head start on developing their clinical skills. For those who do not choose electives that include hands-on experiences, exposure to patients comes in the second year through the Introduction to Clinical Medicine course (ICM). In ICM, students use case studies and real experiences with patients to apply their basic science knowledge to clinical problems. They also learn fundamental interviewing, history-taking, physical examination, and diagnosis skills.

Our respondents praise the school's emphasis on early, meaningful contact with patients, saying that these experiences have a profound impact on their success in their clerkships and in their eventual practices. Furthermore, the school's affiliation with the state-supported Charity Hospital gives students a diverse patient base on which to practice their burgeoning skills. Explains one second-year, "Charity is in need of as many helping hands as possible, which affords even inexperienced medical students the chance for a lot of hands-on experience with patient care, tests, and procedures."

Armed with the skills they learned in the basic science years, students enter the clinical phase. The third and fourth years are divided into blocks during which students take a variety of required and elective clerkships. In addition to completing rotations in the major disciplines, students spend time in more specialized areas like geriatrics, substance abuse, and ophthalmology. All juniors must also complete a four-week family medicine clerkship in a community physician's office. An acting internship and discussions of practice-related issues round out the core requirements. Twenty-four weeks of the senior year are reserved for free electives.

Students praise their faculty, giving teachers high marks for their ability to convey difficult material and for their willingness to help students outside the classroom. Facilities, too, are well-received, with top honors going to LSUNO's hospitals and science labs.

Grading and Promotion Policy: Honors/High Pass/Pass/Fail.

Additional Degree Programs: LSUNO offers combined BS/MD and MD/Ph.D. programs.

STUDENT LIFE

Although students say the atmosphere at LSUNO is pretty intense, competition is reserved for the classroom, making relations among classmates friendly and casual. A plethora of on-campus activities gives students the opportunity to pursue their professional, cultural, and recreational interests, and the school's location in New Orleans affords students a robust and varied social life. But living and working in a city known for its party atmosphere has its drawbacks.

Although most students enjoy the school's setting, many express concerns about crime and admit frustration with the throngs of tourists who descend upon the city, particular during Mardi Gras. Public transportation is also a concern; mass transit gets poor marks both for accessibility and safety.

ADMISSIONS

Although nonresidents are not admitted, the acceptance rate for state residents is fairly high. In the most recent admissions season, about one-half of the in-state candidates were interviewed; of those, over half were accepted and eventually matriculated.

According to the Associate Dean for Admissions, the Committee evaluates each applicant on the basis of a variety of factors. Among the most important of these are the science GPA, MCAT scores, the interview, letters of recommendation, and the non-science GPA. Extra curricular activities, exposure to the medical profession, volunteer activities, and essays are also considered important.

Special Programs for Members of Underrepresented Minorities: A Minority Affairs division coordinates LSUNO's efforts to recruit, enroll, retain, and graduate members of underrepresented minorities. Among its offerings are community outreach programs, summer sessions for high school students, a prematriculation summer session for enrolled students, academic advising, and peer counseling. Minority students are also given some special consideration in the admissions process.

Transfer Policy: Transfer applicants are considered on a space-available basis.

FINANCIAL AID:

Although most assistance is awarded on the basis of documented need, LSUNO also offers some merit scholarships. Scholarship, loan, grant, and work-study programs are available to students who require aid.

FIRST YEAR STATISTICS

Average GPA			
Science	3.4	Nonscience	N/A

Average MCAT			
Biology	N/A	Physical Science	N/A
Verbal	N/A	Essay	N/A

FINANCIAL FACTS

Tuition and Fees			
In-state	$6,924	On-campus housing	N/A
Out-of-state	$6,924	Off-campus housing	N/A

Financial Aid	
% receiving some aid	N/A
Merit scholarships	yes
Average debt	N/A

HITS AND MISSES

HITS	MISSES
Overall happiness	Competitive atmosphere
Quality of teaching	Campus safety
Faculty accessibility	Public transportation
Research efforts	
Emphasis on ethics	
Early clinical exposure	
Overall facilities	
Plenty of campus activities	

TUITION OVERVIEW

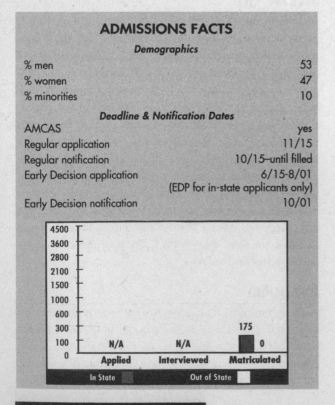

ADMISSIONS FACTS

Demographics	
% men	53
% women	47
% minorities	10

Deadline & Notification Dates	
AMCAS	yes
Regular application	11/15
Regular notification	10/15–until filled
Early Decision application	6/15-8/01
	(EDP for in-state applicants only)
Early Decision notification	10/01

Louisiana State University: School of Medicine in Shreveport

Admissions Office, 1501 Kings Highway, P.O. Box 33932,
Shreveport, LA 71130-3932
(318) 674-5190

OVERVIEW

Like the other Louisiana state med school, LSU in Shreveport gets numerous applications each year from out-of-state candidates—even though it is emphatic in its warning that it does not and cannot accept non-residents. So, if you're not a state resident, learn from your predecessors and don't waste your time and money applying to this small but growing school. For those who are bona fide state residents, however, read on. If you're the type that enjoys shaping your own education and are interested in lots of hands-on contact with patients, you might want to take a closer look.

ACADEMICS

Although LSU in Shreveport's curriculum retains a classical structure, it has many progressive features. Among the most attractive is its flexibility, even in the preclinical years. During the first and second years, students have a total of thirty-six weeks of electives in which to pursue their own interests, providing them with a much greater degree of freedom than their counterparts at most other med schools enjoy.

Aside from elective time, students spend much of their first two years studying the basic sciences and the clinical applications of scientific principles. Traditional lectures, labs, small group discussions, interdisciplinary courses, independent study, and computer-assisted learning are among the teaching formats students and teachers use to cover basic, clinical, and behavioral science material. There is extensive patient contact in the preclinical years, much of it coming through the school's comprehensive care clinic. Sophomore year training in physical diagnosis eases the transition into the clinical period.

The third and fourth years consist of a series of required and elective clerkships. During those years, students have twenty weeks free for electives, some of which may be taken outside of the medical school. Most clinical teaching takes place in the LSU Hospital, the Shreveport Veterans' Administration Hospital, and the Comprehensive Care Clinic.

Although the school has a strong clinical bent, there are plenty of opportunities to pursue research interests, and many students use some of their elective time for scientific investigation. For those who want in-depth involvement in a research area, but don't want to commit to the full MD/Ph.D. program, the school offers an Honors Research program through which participants earn a special designation on their diploma.

Grading and Promotion Policy: A–F
Additional Degree Programs: BS/MD; MD/Ph.D.

ADMISSIONS

Only Louisiana residents are considered for admission. Upon receipt of a candidate's AMCAS application, the Admissions Committee—made up of basic and clinical science faculty members and local physicians—requests supplemental information. On the basis of the completed application, the committee invites the most promising candidates to interview. The Assistant Dean for Admissions describes the interview process: "There is an hour orientation at each interview group, consisting of a discussion with clinical and basic science faculty, the financial aid director, and medical students. These are followed by two closed-book interviews (in which the interviewer does not have the student's application file in front of her during the meeting) and one open-book interview."

After the interview, the committee makes a final determination on each candidate. Among the primary selection factors in this decision are the science GPA, MCAT scores (from the new test), the interview, and the nonscience GPA. Other important criteria include essays, letters of recommendation, and extracurricular activities.

Special Programs for Members of Underrepresented Minorities: LSU in Shreveport encourages members of underrepresented minorities to apply and gives these students some special consideration in the admissions process. A minority affairs division coordinates recruitment and support services that include community outreach programs, academic advising, tutoring, and peer counseling.

Transfer Policy: Applications for transfer are considered on a space-available basis.

eMail: biofsk@mail-sh.lsumc.edu

FINANCIAL AID

Although most financial aid is awarded on the basis of documented need, the school offers some merit scholarships.

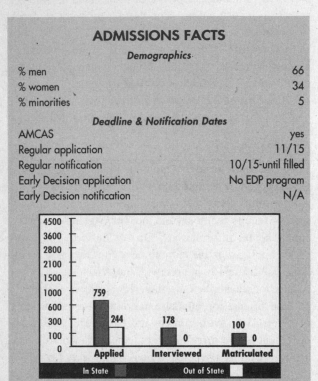

ADMISSIONS FACTS

Demographics

% men	66
% women	34
% minorities	5

Deadline & Notification Dates

AMCAS	yes
Regular application	11/15
Regular notification	10/15-until filled
Early Decision application	No EDP program
Early Decision notification	N/A

In State / Out of State

- Applied: 759 / 244
- Interviewed: 178 / 0
- Matriculated: 100 / 0

FIRST YEAR STATISTICS

Average GPA

Science	3.4	Nonscience	3.4

Average MCAT

Biology	N/A	Physical Science	N/A
Verbal	N/A	Essay	N/A

FINANCIAL FACTS

Tuition and Fees

In-state	$6,927	On-campus housing	N/A
Out-of-state	$14,827	Off-campus housing	N/A

Financial Aid

% receiving some aid	81
Merit scholarships	yes
Average debt	$34,980

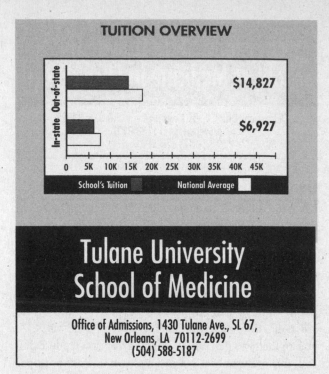

TUITION OVERVIEW

- Out-of-state: $14,827
- In-state: $6,927

School's Tuition / National Average

Tulane University School of Medicine

Office of Admissions, 1430 Tulane Ave., SL 67,
New Orleans, LA 70112-2699
(504) 588-5187

OVERVIEW

Tulane has recently adopted a medium-range strategic plan that will have far-reaching effects on the Medical Center's educational, research, and patient care programs. Included in this plan are major revisions in the med school curriculum, especially in the preclinical years. According to the Tulane students we surveyed, many of these changes have already been implemented, resulting in a more integrated, clinically relevant, and student-friendly approach to the basic sciences.

ACADEMICS

Although the basic sciences are the main focus of Tulane's preclinical curriculum, teaching centers not only on the acquisition of a knowledge base, but also on the clinical relevance of scientific principles. In the recent revisions, the structure and methods of instruction were revamped. Interdisciplinary courses, problem-based learning, computer-assisted teaching, and a new Introduction to Clinical Medicine course (ICM) now augment—and in some cases replace—traditional departmental science lectures. Classroom hours have been cut, leaving freshmen and sophomores with more free time for study and electives.

The two-year ICM course allows students to explore sociological, behavioral, and ethical aspects of medicine and fosters the early development of clinical skills. Through practice with standardized and real patients, students learn history-taking, examination, and physical diagnosis skills. Students at Tulane are pleased with the way ICM helps them correlate the basic and clinical sciences, and appreciate the opportunities they have for early hands-on contact with patients. Says one representative student, "Taking care of patients during the first and second year has made studying the textbooks more understandable, more realistic, and more interesting." The location of these early clinical experiences is also an asset. According to one student, "Charity, the public hospital adjacent to the school, is an excellent place for students to see an enormous and diverse patient population."

Armed with the skills they developed in their sophomore years, third-year students complete a series of required clerkships. These rotations extend into the senior year, but the now-experienced fourth-years are given greater responsibility in patient care. A four-week community medicine clerkship is mandatory; seniors may choose to complete this requirement in locations as mundane as rural Oklahoma or as exotic as Belize. The remaining twenty weeks are reserved for electives.

Teaching is a strength at Tulane, according to students, and professors are "eager to help outside the classroom." Our respondents also admire their instructors' research activities, and tell us that students have the chance to begin their own research projects as early as the first year.

Tulane's facilities don't fare quite as well as its teachers. Although clinical sites and computer labs are acknowledged as outstanding, classrooms, science labs, and the library receive only lukewarm praise.

Grading and Promotion Policy: Honors/High Pass/Pass/Conditional/Fail.

Additional Degree Programs: BS/MD; MD/MS; MD/Ph.D.

STUDENT LIFE

Perhaps the greatest test of motivation and self-discipline for Tulane students is in resisting the temptations of delightful, decadent New Orleans. Known for world-famous bars, the Jazz and Heritage Festival, and—of course—Mardi Gras, "the Big Easy" offers plenty of opportunities to party, and Tulane students say they make time to play. Those we surveyed report that they have relatively active social lives, and that they enjoy spending time with their classmates. Relationships among members of the student body, even among members of different classes, are friendly, according to our respondents. "Everyone truly seems to care about each other. Even the upperclassmen do a lot to make us feel at home," one first-year told us. A cooperative rather than competitive academic environment contributes to students' overall feeling of well-being.

Many of the students we surveyed were thrilled to live and learn in the Crescent City. Still, New Orleans isn't for everyone. A steady stream of tourists who come to the city to "let it all hang out" (sometimes literally) can make the atmosphere resemble that of a port of call for sailors who've spent many lonely months at sea. Concerns about safety—on campus and around town—are abundant. Public transportation is neither very accessible nor very safe, a problem made more significant to students because of a severe parking shortage on campus.

ADMISSIONS

According to the Admissions Office, Tulane shows no preference to residents of Louisiana or other southern states. As the Admissions Committee receives AMCAS applications, it automatically sends out supplementary materials to all applicants. Once all application materials are on file, the Committee decides whether or not to invite the candidate for an interview. Although Tulane will make arrangements for regional interviews, students should make every effort to travel to the campus.

The Admissions Office bases its final decisions on a variety of factors. An evaluation is made of each applicant's scholastic achievement and promise; information pertinent to this assessment includes overall and science GPAs, the level and breadth of coursework, the rigors of the undergraduate school, trends in grades, MCAT scores, and letters of recommendation. Students are also rated on their character and achievements, judged in part by the interview, extracurricular activities, and life experiences.

Special Programs for Members of Underrepresented Minorities: Tulane offers a Medical Education Reinforcement and Enrichment Program (MedREP) to help increase opportunities for members of minority groups traditionally underrepresented in medicine. Among MedREP's offerings are summer programs for college students, a prematriculation summer session, tutoring, workshops, counseling, and review classes for USMLE Parts I and II.

Transfer Policy: Tulane considers applications for transfers into the second and third years.

FINANCIAL AID

Most financial aid is awarded on the basis of need as determined by GAPSFAS, but Tulane offers some merit scholarships.

ADMISSIONS FACTS

Demographics

% men	60
% women	40
% minorities	8

Deadline & Notification Dates

AMCAS	yes
Regular application	12/15
Regular notification	10/15–until filled
Early Decision application	No EDP program
Early Decision notification	N/A

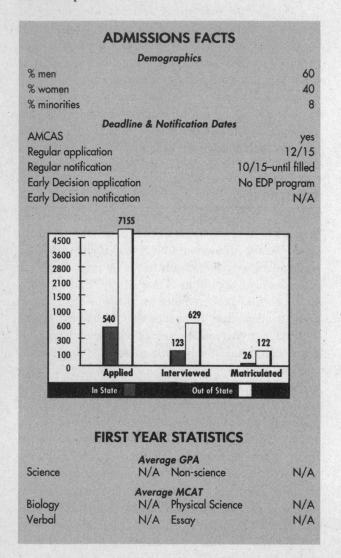

FIRST YEAR STATISTICS

Average GPA

Science	N/A	Non-science	N/A

Average MCAT

Biology	N/A	Physical Science	N/A
Verbal	N/A	Essay	N/A

FINANCIAL FACTS

Tuition and Fees

In-state	$26,080	On-campus housing	N/A
Out-of-state	$26,080	Off-campus housing	N/A

Financial Aid

% receiving some aid	80
Merit scholarships	yes
Average debt	N/A

HITS AND MISSES

HITS	MISSES
Overall hapiness	Campus safety
Cooperative atmosphere	Public transportation
Quality of teaching	Library
Teacher accessibility	
Early clinical exposure	
Plenty of activities	

TUITION OVERVIEW

$26,080

School's Tuition   National Average

Johns Hopkins University School of Medicine

Committee on Admission, 720 Rutland Avenue,
Baltimore, MD 21205-2196
(410) 955-3182

OVERVIEW

In almost any rating of U.S. med schools, Johns Hopkins is near the top, and the students we surveyed say the school deserves its fabulous reputation. Comments one enthusiastic second-year student, "Hopkins has an incredible...history of excellence in medicine which makes studying here awesome." In fact, most of our respondents claim that this venerable Baltimore institution is the best med school in the country, regardless of what the students of a certain Boston school might say to the contrary. Competition with Harvard—the school with which Hopkins most often jockeys for top position—is a big issue among those we surveyed. Actually, competition in general is a hot topic, and one of the major sources of students' complaints. Still, most say excellent teaching, cutting-edge research, and a new, more student-centered curriculum make the intense atmosphere worthwhile.

ACADEMICS

Hopkins's revised curriculum emphasizes integration between the basic and clinical sciences and places a large degree of responsibility for learning on the student. One sophomore describes some of the features of the new approach: "[It] provides more and sooner clinical exposure, less class time, and more individual creativity only one period no classes."

In the first two years, students develop the scientific knowledge base necessary for the study of medicine, explore nonscience aspects of health care, and begin to learn clinical skills. The basic sciences are presented in an integrated format, and there is strong emphasis on clinical correlations. Complementing instruction in the sciences is the beginning of a four-year Physician and Society continuum. In this course, students investigate ethical, social, humanities, and economic aspects of medical practice. Traditional lectures occupy only a small portion of the preclinical phase; much of the first two years is spent in labs, seminars, discussion sections, and clinical groups, all of which are made up of teams of between five and twenty students.

Freshmen and sophomores are very happy with the amount exposure to clinical medicine they get. To give their basic science studies a practical perspective, students work with community physicians. Through this experience (which begins in the first semester) and through instruction in the fundamental clinical skills of history-taking, physical examination, and preliminary diagnosis, students have hands-on contact with patients and begin to make the transition to the clerkship phase. The third and fourth years consist of a combination of required and elective experiences.

Overall, students say that the quality of education at Hopkins is "superior." Much of the credit for this rating goes to the faculty. Reports one sophomore, "The clinicians and researchers actually enjoy teaching, and are readily accessible." Another adds, "They are not only interested in developing an MD, but developing a physician, a complete person. In order to do this, they help students in any way possible to help nip problems—both academic and personal—in the bud." But not everyone is in complete agreement; a few students say that Hopkins's emphasis on top-notch biomedical investigation exacts a price in the classroom. Complains one student, "The faculty's first commitment is to their research, not teaching. Students do well as a consequence of their own motivation."

Hopkins's administration and support services are generally applauded. Says one appreciative freshman, "The school is good about making the hassles of medical school, such as financial aid and registrar services, as easy as possible. They are also good at providing amenities such as tutoring when needed." Facilities, too, are rated as excellent. Students praise classrooms, labs, and the library, and are nearly unanimous in giving clinical training sites the highest rating possible. Computer labs, however, are not as popular.

Grading and Promotion Policy: Hopkins uses a letter grading system for required courses and clerkships and Honors/Pass/Fail for electives.

Additional Degree Programs: MD/Ph.D. Students may also arrange individual courses of study with the undergraduate and other graduate divisions.

STUDENT LIFE

Overall, our respondents report that they're happy at Hopkins, but most say student life could be better. Almost 50 percent of those we surveyed feel their classmates are extremely competitive, and most say they study very hard. Says one sophomore, "The coursework is not for the fainthearted. There is a lot of work required of everyone—even to just pass." The competition, heavy workload, and the letter-grading system for required courses lead some to say that the school is "very stressful," and many say they don't have much time for a social life.

Hanging out with classmates is further complicated by "the commuter nature of the school." Because Hopkins is in an "unsafe, unattractive part of town," much of the med school community lives a distance from the campus. Although some students say you "need a car if you want to be at Hopkins," others say the university's shuttle system takes the hassle out of getting around, especially between the med school and undergrad campuses. Recreational facilities on the main campus, especially the gym, track, and pool, are popular places to blow off steam.

Although students appreciate Baltimore's relatively low cost of living, they aren't too pleased with the city. One student reports, "The campus and the town are very unsafe. Very visible security is in place, but it has no effect on crime." His classmates agree; all of the students we surveyed say that the crime problem is a big drawback of the school. Still, one student says it could be worse (and takes a potshot at two other top-ten schools, Yale and Penn): "East Baltimore isn't the safest place in the world, but it's a hell of a lot better than New Haven or West Philadelphia."

ADMISSIONS

Since Hopkins is a private school, it does not give special consideration to state residents. It is also something of a maverick in med school admissions: it does not participate in AMCAS, nor does it require the MCAT. To meet the standardized test requirement, students may choose to submit either SAT, ACT, GRE, or MCAT scores.

Students may apply to Hopkins in one of four ways: the regular admissions process; the Flex Med Senior Program, which allows accepted students to defer admission for up to three years; the Flex Med Junior Program, which provides undergraduates in their junior years with advanced assurance of admission; or the MD/Ph.D. program. In all programs, admission is extremely competitive.

Because of Hopkins's reputation, its applicant pool is self-selective. In other words, most students who have less-than-stellar qualifications don't bother to apply. Still, almost 3,500 people submitted applications in 1992; of those, fewer than 20 percent were interviewed and between three and four percent were accepted and eventually matriculated.

Important selection factors include the academic record, scholastic and personal achievements, letters of recommendation, extracurricular activities, motivation and suitability for the study of medicine, and the interview. Although Hopkins will make arrangements for regional interviews, we've found that it is generally in your best interest to make the effort to travel to the campuses of the schools to which you are invited to interview.

Special Programs for Members of Underrepresented Minorities: As part of its continuing effort to recruit members of underrepresented minorities, Hopkins offers summer programs for college students and a prematriculation session for accepted students.

Transfer Policy: Hopkins considers transfers into the second or third year on a space-available basis.

eMail: http://infonet.welch.jhu.edu/

FINANCIAL AID

Financial aid is awarded solely on the basis of need. Individual awards are made in the form of loans, scholarships, and grants and are usually sufficient to cover 100 percent of a student's documented need.

ADMISSIONS FACTS

Demographics

% men	59
% women	41
% minorities	13

Deadline & Notification Dates

AMCAS	yes
Regular application	11/01
Regular notification	11/01–3/31
Early Decision application	6/15-8/01
Early Decision notification	10/01

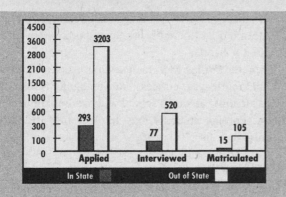

	In State	Out of State
Applied	293	3203
Interviewed	77	520
Matriculated	15	105

FIRST YEAR STATISTICS

Average GPA

Science	N/A	Nonscience	N/A

Average MCAT

Biology	N/A	Physical Science	N/A
Verbal	N/A	Essay	N/A

FINANCIAL FACTS

Tuition and Fees

In-state	$22,564	On-campus housing	N/A
Out-of-state	$22,564	Off-campus housing	N/A

Financial Aid

% receiving some aid	80
Merit scholarships	N/A
Average debt	N/A

HITS AND MISSES

HITS	MISSES
Quality of teaching	Very competitive atmosphere
Faculty accessibility	Campus safety
Basic science facilities	Computer facilities
Clinical facilities	Baltimore
Library	
Research efforts	
Prestigious faculty actually teach	

TUITION OVERVIEW

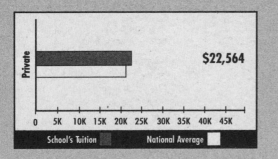

$22,564

University of Maryland School of Medicine

Committee on Admissions, Room 14-015
655 West Baltimore Street, Baltimore, MD 21201
(410) 706-7478

OVERVIEW

Maybe there's not as much patient contact as some people would like. And many of the students we surveyed complain of a very competitive atmosphere, a killer workload, and "atrocious" crime problems in Baltimore. But the bottom line is they are happy at Maryland. Good teaching, excellent research efforts, a diverse student body, and outstanding clinical facilities help make it all worthwhile.

ACADEMICS

The four years at Maryland are divided into the traditional two-year basic science and clinical units, but the school has made an effort to update its curriculum, especially in the preclinical years. Among the innovations are an interdisciplinary approach to some of the basic sciences, required behavioral and social science courses, and an emphasis on clinical correlations. These changes have met with mixed reviews: comments range from "fantastic" to "a real disappointment." Regardless of its shortcomings, however, the new curriculum stresses independent learning and leaves students with more free time than they had under the old curriculum. Maryland has also augmented its clinical clerkships with a required rotation in ambulatory care.

Students are introduced to interviewing techniques, diagnosis, and medical ethics though the Introduction to Clinical Practice course they take in both basic science years. While students like the experience, freshmen especially would like more patient contact. Clinical facilities, however, are beyond reproach; students rate them as superior.

Students are also enthusiastic about the school's research efforts. Maryland encourages students to participate in biomedical investigation through its Short Term Research Training Program (STRTP). Student fellowships, which are jointly funded by the school and the National Institute of Health, enable students—usually in the summer after freshman year—to see first-hand how laboratory research connects with clinical applications.

The quality of teaching is very good, according to students, and most professors are helpful and supportive. A few respondents single out the administration as unresponsive to students' concerns. Many of those we surveyed complain that too much time is spent in class, and reading assignments are often excessive. The new curriculum may lessen these burdens, though. Overall, our respondents stress that Maryland is a great deal for the money, especially for in-state students. Facilities are generally rated as very good, but students say that the library could use major improvement.

Grading and Promotion Policy: A–F. Students must pass USMLE Part I.

Additional Degree Programs: MD/Ph.D.

STUDENT LIFE

Students rate UMSM as very diverse and say that, though the atmosphere is intense, students generally treat their classmates well. They do not socialize very often, however; first- and second-year students complain that their full academic schedules and "endless" workload leave them little free time.

While they generally like Baltimore, students have serious concerns about its safety. Says one freshman, "I think everyone I know has been affected [by crime] in one way or another. The school is working to improve this situation; a new shuttle service has been implemented." Although Maryland makes dorms and apartments available, most students prefer to live off-campus.

ADMISSIONS

Residents of Maryland are given preference in admissions, but out-of-state applicants are encouraged to apply. According to the admissions bulletin, "Academic achievement, extracurricular activities, personal characteristics, recommendations...scores on the MCAT and personal interviews all are considered in the committee's evaluation of an applicant....Of significant concern to the committee...are the applicant's character, personality, and potential to perform as a medical student and as a future physician."

Special Programs for Members of Underrepresented Minorities: Maryland is among the top schools in minority admissions, and it is dedicated to continuing to increase representation. Recruitment and enrichment programs are conducted at the high school, undergraduate and med school level and are coordinated by the Office of Minority Affairs. Outreach programs, such as paid summer research programs available to undergraduate minority students, are an important aspect of the school's efforts.

Transfer Policy: Maryland accepts transfers into its third- and fourth-year classes. Transfer students must be in good standing at a med school with a compatible curriculum. Foreign students may transfer into the third year only.

FINANCIAL AID

Financial aid is based solely on documented need. University grants are made only to residents, but Dean's Scholarships are awarded primarily to nonresidents. Minority students from Maryland are eligible for Desegregation Grants.

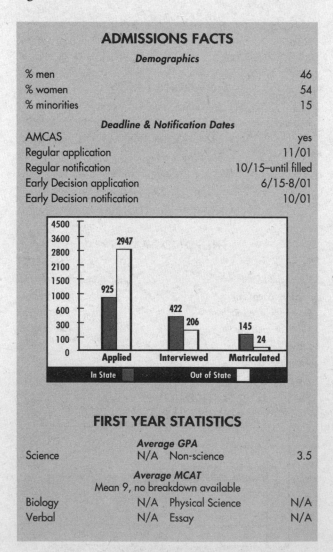

ADMISSIONS FACTS

Demographics

% men	46
% women	54
% minorities	15

Deadline & Notification Dates

AMCAS	yes
Regular application	11/01
Regular notification	10/15–until filled
Early Decision application	6/15-8/01
Early Decision notification	10/01

In State / Out of State bar chart:

	Applied	Interviewed	Matriculated
In State	925	422	145
Out of State	2947	206	24

FIRST YEAR STATISTICS

Average GPA

Science	N/A	Non-science	3.5

Average MCAT
Mean 9, no breakdown available

Biology	N/A	Physical Science	N/A
Verbal	N/A	Essay	N/A

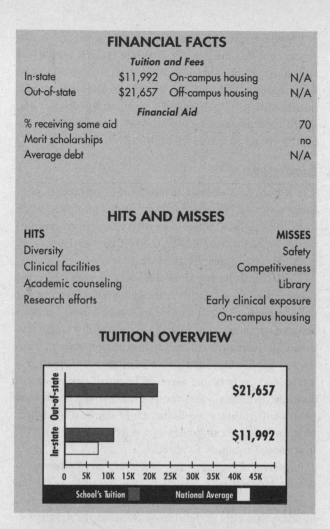

FINANCIAL FACTS

Tuition and Fees

In-state	$11,992	On-campus housing	N/A
Out-of-state	$21,657	Off-campus housing	N/A

Financial Aid

% receiving some aid	70
Merit scholarships	no
Average debt	N/A

HITS AND MISSES

HITS	MISSES
Diversity	Safety
Clinical facilities	Competitiveness
Academic counseling	Library
Research efforts	Early clinical exposure
	On-campus housing

TUITION OVERVIEW

$21,657

$11,992

0 5K 10K 15K 20K 25K 30K 35K 40K 45K

School's Tuition   National Average

Uniformed Services University of the Health Sciences F. Edward Hébert School of Medicine

Admissions Office, 4301 Jones Bridge Road, Bethesda, MD 20814-4799
(800) 772-1743

OVERVIEW

"USUHS is one of the best-kept secrets in medical education," say students. "It's the only school in the country where students are paid to attend medical school. Not only are the benefits great, the quality of the education is unbeatable!" USUHS students aren't just enthusiastic about their school, they're downright fired-up. Their fervent praise put the school at the top of those we surveyed in an unparalleled twelve categories, including overall happiness, accessibility of professors, and emphasis on medical ethics. The school was in the top five in ten other areas.

USUHS was created in 1972 to prepare young men and women for careers as health care professionals in the Army, Navy, Air Force, and the Public Health Service. Because the school is government funded, there are no tuition fees and even equipment and books are provided free of charge. In addition, students receive a salary and other perks while they're in school. Considering the expense of other med schools, it's quite a deal. So, what's the catch?

In return for the cost of their education, students agree to serve in the military for seven years after graduation; time spent in residency and other post-graduate education doesn't count. This obligation is a major deterrent for many prospective applicants, but students say it shouldn't be. Advises one student, "Look at this school and don't be intimidated by the armed forces." USUHS students argue that the emphasis on military medicine and the service requirement are not so much obligations as opportunities. Asks one student, "How many civilian physicians get to study [things like] dive medicine and aerospace medicine, and still fulfill a fellowship in cardiology without mounting a huge debt? How many civilian physicians can just pick up their practice and move to Germany, Australia, Hawaii, Alaska, etc.?" Despite the attractions, one student warns that USUHS is not for everyone: "Do not come here if you don't want to serve your nation and be a military officer as well as a physician. There are privileges and responsibilities with both titles."

ACADEMICS

The structure of the curriculum at USUHS is fairly traditional, but because of the school's unique mission—to train primary care, military physicians—unique aspects of military medicine are also emphasized. According to one student, there are other aspects of the curriculum that set USUHS apart: "There is a strong commitment to public health, preventative medicine, and tropical medicine." The curriculum is sufficiently well rounded, however, that students can pursue their individual interests and qualify for any residency.

Contact with patients begins in the first semester of the first year and intensifies over the four years.

Students rate the amount of clinical training as outstanding. Says one, "I believe that USUHS is strongest in the clinical experience—very hands on." Another adds, "With Bethesda Naval Hospital, Walter Reed Army Medical Center, and Malcolm Grow Hospital all in the local area, the clinical opportunities and diversity are outstanding."

Not only do students like what they learn, they like how they're being taught; professors receive outstanding ratings for quality of teaching and accessibility. Just as the military affiliation draws classmates together, so, too, does it connect students with faculty. Explains one, "Both faculty and students here are committed to being physicians and serving their country. It creates a camaraderie and teamwork that I don't think many schools have." There is also considerable praise for the care professors take to make sure that students are really learning and to the commitment teachers make to helping students succeed. One second-year student comments, "Our classes are taught by the experts, and they are dedicated to teaching us well. Professors are here to make us be the best doctors we can be; they are not here to weed us out." Academic support services also receive accolades.

Grading and Promotion policy: A–F and Pass/Fail. Students must pass USMLE Parts I and II.

Additional Degree Programs: none.

STUDENT LIFE

Of the schools we surveyed, USUHS was the leader in overall student happiness. Contributing to this is a lack of cutthroat competition and an emphasis on teamwork. "The best part of this school is the spirit of cooperation. There is little direct competition," reports one second-year student.

This feeling of collegiality extends beyond the classroom. Students report that they enjoy hanging out with their classmates, and that there are plenty of activities to get involved in. While students say USUHS is not particularly diverse, one reports, "The school is outstanding in its treatment of minorities, and for the most part students are sensitive to issues of a cultural nature. The isolated incidents of perceived insensitivity have much more to do with ignorance than with intent." There are also not many women at the school, but according to the mostly male respondents, students of both sexes are treated equally by faculty and classmates.

Students give high marks to the campus and its location near Washington, D.C. While there is no university housing, students are pleased with what they can find nearby. Although an excellent and safe public transportation system makes commuting around the metro area pleasant, some students complain that the cost of living is relatively high.

ADMISSIONS

The School of Medicine is a federal government-sponsored program. Therefore, there are no quotas by state of residence. In addition to regular admissions requirements, students must also be U.S. citizens and meet age, physical, and security standards.

The admissions office declined to rank selection factors, saying instead, "Although grades are not the only criterion used in making decisions, college achievements are scrutinized very carefully since academic performance reflects achievement potential, interests, motivation, and self-discipline. All applicants are judged on personal merit in terms of demonstrated aptitude, potential, and motivation for the study and practice of military medicine. Only the best qualified, most promising candidates are selected." The MCAT, in its new format, is required.

Special Programs for Members of Underrepresented Minorities: USUHS is striving to increase the number of women and traditionally underrepresented minority students at the school. A Minority Affairs Division coordinates this effort. Among special programs are a prematriculation summer session, academic advising, and review classes for the USMLE Parts I and II. These programs are also available to other students.

Transfer Policy: Transfers are not accepted.

FINANCIAL AID

Since there is no tuition or educational fees, students at USUHS have no need for financial aid. In fact, the financial picture is quite favorable. Upon matriculating, students become active reserve officers in one of the service branches and have the benefits of that rank. These include full salary, free health coverage for the student and his or her family, a housing allowance, commissary privileges, and thirty days' paid leave.

ADMISSIONS FACTS

Demographics

% men	73
% women	27
% minorities	7

Deadline & Notification Dates

AMCAS	yes
Regular application	11/01
Regular notification	11/01–until filled
Early Decision application	No EDP program
Early Decision notification	N/A

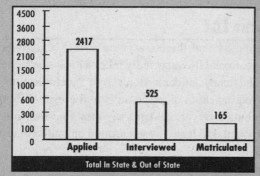

Total In State & Out of State

FIRST YEAR STATISTICS

Average GPA

Science	N/A	Nonscience	3.4

Average MCAT
(mean MCAT of 9.6 no breakdown available)

FINANCIAL FACTS

Tuition and Fees

In-state	0	On-campus housing	N/A
Out-of-state	0	Off-campus housing	N/A

Financial Aid

% receiving some aid	N/A
Merit scholarships	N/A
Average debt	N/A

HITS AND MISSES

HITS	MISSES
Faculty accessibility	Minimal emphasis on research
Academic counseling	Diversity
Emphasis on ethics	Homosexuals not admitted
Overall facilities	No on-campus housing
Quality of life	
Fellow students	

Boston University School of Medicine

Admissions Office, Building L, Room 124, 80 East Concord Street,
Boston, MA 02118
(617) 638-4630

OVERVIEW

The BU admissions bulletin says, "Prospective candidates are attracted by the dual advantages of comparatively small classes that afford opportunity for considerable personal contact with members of the faculty, and the benefits of study in a great medical center where there are unlimited possibilities for clinical instruction." They're right. The students we surveyed give BU high marks for teaching excellence and an "awesome" clinical program. And the school's location in Boston only contributes to the medical school experience.

ACADEMICS

BU's curriculum is divided into the usual two-year preclinical and clinical segments. In the basic science years, BU augments traditional lectures and labs with interdepartmental courses. Students also investigate the behavioral and sociological aspects of medicine. In the second semester of the sophomore year, all students take The Biology of Disease. This interdisciplinary course focuses on the functions of abnormal organ systems and integrates scientific principles with clinical problem-solving. Third-year students are required to complete rotations in the major clinical disciplines. During the fourth year, students complete requirements and choose from a variety of electives.

Clinical exposure begins in the first year and intensifies during the second. As sophomores, students learn medical interviewing and physical diagnosis skills in a variety of settings, including hospitals, outpatient clinics, and physicians' offices. An unusual feature of BU's clinical program is the required clerkship in Home Medical Service. In this clerkship, students are responsible for primary care of geriatric patients. BU's students applaud these experiences and the school's diverse teaching sites rating both exposure and facilities as outstanding.

Students are equally enthusiastic about the quality of teaching. "Professors," says one second-year student, "are not only excellent teachers, they are also physicians who are genuinely motivated by a desire to alleviate suffering." The faculty also gets high marks for accessibility.

Unfortunately, this praise does not extend to BU's basic science, library, and computer facilities. All are given low ratings, with the harshest criticism reserved for the classrooms.

Grading and Promotion Policy: Honors/Pass/Fail

Additional Degree Programs: BU has a number of different combined BA/MD programs. Ph.D./MD and MD/MPH programs are also available.

STUDENT LIFE

Students say that the atmosphere at BU is fairly competitive. Social life reportedly takes a back seat to studying, and many students don't find much time to get involved in school or community activities. When they do go out, however, students say they find lots to do in the city and find it easy to get around on public transportation.

Students are almost unanimous in giving Boston the highest possible rating. BU's campus, on the other hand, does not fare as well. Students find it unattractive and relatively unsafe. There is no on-campus housing.

ADMISSIONS

BU states no preference for the residents of Massachusetts. Since approximately one-third of every class is reserved for students who are enrolled in one of the combined BA/MD programs BU sponsors, competition for the remaining spots is keen. For the best chance for consideration, candidates are encouraged to apply as early in the admissions cycle as possible.

In making its final selections, the Admissions Committee considers the interview, the academic record, MCAT scores, letters of recommendation, activities, and personal qualities.

Special Programs for Members of Underrepresented Minorities: The Office of Minority Affairs coordinates efforts to recruit underrepresented minority students. One of its offerings is the Early Medical School Selection Program. In this program, minority students secure early acceptance to the medical school and spend their senior year in a transitional program at BU.

Transfer Policy: Transfers into the second or third year are considered. Students must be in good standing at an accredited medical school.

FINANCIAL AID

BU is an expensive school, and the cost of living is high in Boston. The financial aid office coordinates a variety of aid sources to help students secure financing. Although grants are available, about 90 percent of need is met through loans. Most financial assistance is based on need as determined by the College Scholarship Service analysis.

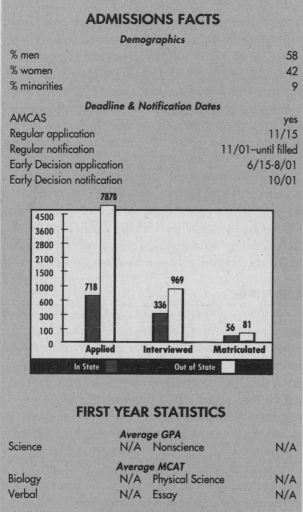

ADMISSIONS FACTS

Demographics

% men	58
% women	42
% minorities	9

Deadline & Notification Dates

AMCAS	yes
Regular application	11/15
Regular notification	11/01–until filled
Early Decision application	6/15-8/01
Early Decision notification	10/01

	Applied	Interviewed	Matriculated
In State	718	336	56
Out of State	7878	969	81

FIRST YEAR STATISTICS

Average GPA

Science	N/A	Nonscience	N/A

Average MCAT

Biology	N/A	Physical Science	N/A
Verbal	N/A	Essay	N/A

FINANCIAL FACTS

Tuition and Fees

In-state	$29,275	On-campus housing	none
Out-of-state	$29,275	Off-campus housing	N/A

Financial Aid

% receiving some aid	90
Merit scholarships	N/A
Average debt	N/A

HITS AND MISSES

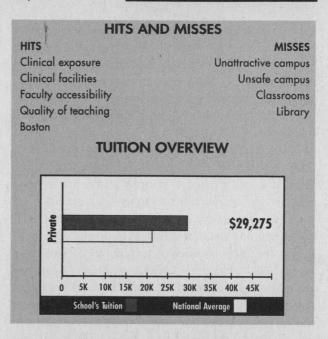

HITS	MISSES
Clinical exposure	Unattractive campus
Clinical facilities	Unsafe campus
Faculty accessibility	Classrooms
Quality of teaching	Library
Boston	

TUITION OVERVIEW

$29,275

School's Tuition National Average

Harvard Medical School

Office of Admissions, 25 Shattuck Street, Building A-210,
Boston, MA 02115-6092
(617) 432-1550

OVERVIEW

Harvard is consistently rated as one of the best med schools in the country, and the students we surveyed say it's an exciting place to be. Innovative curricula, cutting-edge research, excellent teaching, and some of the nation's best hospitals top their list of the school's best features.

ACADEMICS

Harvard revamped its approach to medical education in 1987 and now offers two distinct curricula leading to the MD. One is the New Pathway program, which, according to the students we surveyed, "is very clinically oriented and meshes the basic, clinical, and social sciences very well." The other is the Health Sciences and Technology track Harvard offers in conjunction with the Massachusetts Institute of Technology. The HST program is designed for "students with a strong interest in the science of medicine and research-oriented medical careers"; about 20 percent of students choose this option.

The New Pathway and HST programs are different only in the first two years. Participants in HST focus on the scientific and quantitative underpinnings of clinical and lab problems. The program is organized in a semester format and students are encouraged to conduct research in addition to completing their required coursework.

New Pathway students use a problem-based, case-study approach to investigate the basic and clinical sciences that are the foundation for medicine. Small-group tutorials and self-directed learning are augmented by lectures, labs, and conferences. Through this combination of learning styles, students take the primary responsibility for their education. According to Harvard, they are expected to learn to "analyze problems, locate relevant material in library and computer-based resources, and develop habits of lifelong learning and independent study." Longitudinal courses that emphasize the acquisition of clinical skills and cover behavioral, social, and ethical perspectives run throughout the first two years.

Students love the "active learning style" of the New Pathway curriculum. Says one freshman, "It's a great way to learn medicine." The main advantage of the case-study approach over traditional departmental formats is that it helps students "learn and retain the materials better" and assigns clinical relevance to scientific principles. Those we surveyed are also extremely enthusiastic about their degree of involvement with patients in the first two years.

HST and New Pathway students join up for the last two years. All juniors and seniors are required to take 52 weeks of core clerkships, spend eight weeks in an advanced science or independent study project, and participate in a longitudinal course that explores physicians' roles and responsibilities. In addition to fulfilling these requirements, upperclassmen choose from a wide variety of electives to design a program that reflects their own interests and goals.

Despite Harvard's emphasis on self-motivated learning, the success of its curricula ultimately depends on the faculty. Students give their professors extremely high marks, both for quality of teaching and for their willingness to help students outside the classroom. One of the reasons relationships with the faculty are so good is Harvard's unusual organizational system. Members of each entering class are assigned to one of five Academic Societies. These groups bring together faculty members and students from all four years and, through academic and social activities, foster a collegial atmosphere.

Grading and Promotion Policy: Honors/Pass/Fail.

Additional Degree Programs: MD/Ph.D., MD/MPH.

STUDENT LIFE

Harvard students are among the happiest we surveyed, not just because they attend one of the most prestigious med schools in the world (though they are quick to point that out), but because of the people they have found there. "My classmates are down-to-earth, fun-to-be-with people who each bring something unique and wonderful...to the school," says one pleased-as-punch freshman. The school and the Academic Societies bring students together through a wide variety of organizations and events. Because they "don't have to be in class all day long," respondents say they have fairly active social lives.

Boston is also a veritable playground for students looking for a break from academia, and most of those we surveyed say they are thrilled with the city. On-campus housing doesn't quite measure up; students prefer off-campus living and say getting around is easy. Boston's mass transit system gets an enthusiastic "thumbs-up."

ADMISSIONS

Harvard does not show preference for the residents of any state, nor does it participate in AMCAS. All applicants are expected to have scholastic records that indicate "academic excellence." Although Harvard publishes minimum course requirements, it is also expected that students pursue in-depth study in some area—whether in scientific or other disciplines—through advanced level courses and, if possible, through independent work.

Among important considerations in the admissions decisions are the academic record, the essay, MCAT scores, extracurricular activities, exposure to the medical profession, work and research experience, letters of recommendation, and personal qualities. Performance during the interview is also a decisive factor.

Special Programs for Members of Underrepresented Minorities: Harvard encourages applications from qualified minority members.

Transfer Policy: Transfers into the third year are considered on a space-available basis.

FINANCIAL AID

Admissions decisions are made without regard to financial status. All aid is awarded based on need as determined by the GAPSFAS analysis.

ADMISSIONS FACTS

Demographics

% men	60
% women	40
% minorities	19

Deadline & Notification Dates

AMCAS	yes
Regular application	10/15
Regular notification	Latest date: last day of February
Early Decision application	No EDP available
Early Decision notification	N/A

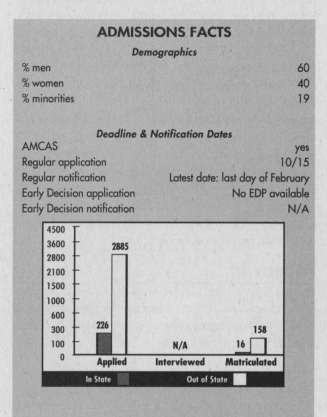

In State ▮   Out of State ▯

Applied: In State 226, Out of State 2885
Interviewed: N/A
Matriculated: In State 16, Out of State 158

FIRST YEAR STATISTICS

Average GPA

Science	N/A	Non-science	3.7

Average MCAT

Biology	11.3	Physical Science	11,3
Verbal	10.5	Essay	N/A

FINANCIAL FACTS

Tuition and Fees

In-state	$23,883	On-campus housing	none
Out-of-state	$23,833	Off-campus housing	N/A

Financial Aid

% receiving some aid	N/A
Merit scholarships	N/A
Average debt	N/A

HITS AND MISSES

HITS	MISSES
Overall happiness	Campus safety
New Pathway curriculum	No on-campus housing
Quality of teaching	
Faculty accessibility	
Student relations	
Early clinical exposure	
Research emphasis	
Clinical facilities	
Boston	

TUITION OVERVIEW

$23,883

School's Tuition ▮   National Average ▯

University of Massachusetts Medical School

Associate Dean for Admissions, 55 Lake Avenue North, Worcester, MA 01655
(508) 856-2323

OVERVIEW

One of the most attractive aspects of U Mass is its low cost; the students we surveyed prefaced almost every comment with "U Mass is one of the least expensive med schools in the country." The financial picture is made even better by Massachusetts' "Learning Contract" program through which students may defer up to two-thirds of their tuition until after they complete residency training. At that time, they can either choose to repay the deferred amount through a loan repayment schedule, or have it forgiven in exchange for a two-year service obligation to the state. But a bargain is no bargain if the product isn't good. Students say that's not a problem at U Mass.

ACADEMICS

Although the curriculum at U Mass is divided into the usual two-year preclinical and clinical units, it has many progressive features, particularly in the basic science years. Freshmen concentrate most of their efforts on acquiring an understanding of the normal function of cells and organisms, but there is considerable clinical correlation. Clinical exposure also begins first year through coursework in emergency medicine, medical interviewing, and physical diagnosis. For hands-on experience, all students are required to take a three-week family and community medicine clerkship.

While the focus on the basic sciences continues in the sophomore year, the curriculum also emphasizes behavioral, social, and ethical issues. During this year, students refine and augment their clinical skills through examination, evaluation, and diagnosis exercises with standardized patients. During the third and fourth years, students complete a core of required clerkships. In addition to the mandatory rotations, seniors take twenty-four weeks of electives. Overall, students are pleased with the amount of clinical exposure they get at U Mass, and upperclassmen say the fundamental skills they learned in the basic science years helped prepare them for the more intense patient contact of the clinical years.

The faculty, too, gets high marks. Students say the overall quality of teaching is very good, and most have found professors "flexible and supportive" outside of the classroom. The library and hospitals are particular standouts among facilities.

Grading and Promotion Policy: Honors/Near Honors/Satisfactory/Marginal/Unsatisfactory. Students are required to take Parts I and II of the USMLE.

Additional Degree Programs: MD/Ph.D.

STUDENT LIFE

Students say they're extremely happy at U Mass. There is minimal competition among classmates, and student relations are reportedly quite good. Most respondents say they are relatively involved in extracurricular activities, although the school doesn't offer a large selection.

What students like least about U Mass is its location. "A very blue collar and industrial town," Worcester offers few cultural and entertainment opportunities. There is also no university housing, and students say that commuting without a car can be complicated.

Though a city bus line serves the medical center, it is not easily accessible in all parts of town.

ADMISSIONS

Admission to U Mass is restricted to state residents. Selection factors include academic performance, MCAT scores, the interview, and letters of recommendation. The Admissions Committee is made up of faculty members and medical students.

Special Programs for Members of Underrepresented Minorities: Students give U Mass extremely low marks for diversity, but the school says it is committed to increasing minority representation through an active recruiting program. State residents who are members of underrepresented minorities are strongly encouraged to apply.

Transfer Policy: Applications for transfer are accepted only from residents of Massachusetts and are considered only if space is available.

FINANCIAL AID

Though students are pleased with the financial benefits of the Learning Contract, they complain that additional financial aid opportunities are scarce. Awards are made primarily in the form of loans.

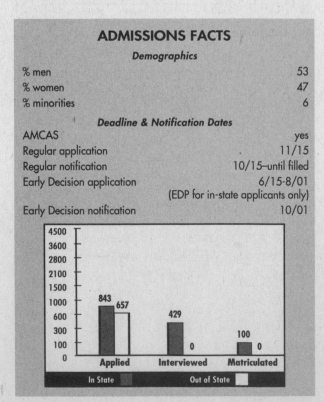

ADMISSIONS FACTS

Demographics

% men	53
% women	47
% minorities	6

Deadline & Notification Dates

AMCAS	yes
Regular application	11/15
Regular notification	10/15–until filled
Early Decision application	6/15-8/01
	(EDP for in-state applicants only)
Early Decision notification	10/01

	Applied	Interviewed	Matriculated
In State	843	429	100
Out of State	657	0	0

FIRST YEAR STATISTICS

Average GPA

Science	3.5	Non-science	N/A

Average MCAT

Biology	N/A	Physical Science	N/A
Verbal	N/A	Essay	N/A

FINANCIAL FACTS

Tuition and Fees

In-state	$10,222	On-campus housing	none
Out-of-state	N/A	Off-campus housing	N/A

Financial Aid

% receiving some aid	75
Merit scholarships	N/A
Average debt	N/A

HITS AND MISSES

HITS	MISSES
Learning Contract program	Diversity
Faculty accessibility	Academic advising
Noncompetitive atmosphere	Worcester
Library	Unnecessary reading assignments
Clinical facilities	
Research emphasis	
Overall happiness	

TUITION OVERVIEW

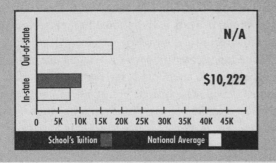

N/A

$10,222

| 0 | 5K | 10K | 15K | 20K | 25K | 30K | 35K | 40K | 45K |

School's Tuition ▪ National Average ▫

Tufts University School of Medicine

Office of Admissions, 136 Harrison Avenue, Stearns 1, Boston, MA 02111
(617) 956-6571

OVERVIEW

In its promotional material, Tufts says, "The goal is to give our medical students a total educational experience which is enjoyable, of the highest quality, and helps individual students to achieve their full potential as healers, researchers, teachers, and public citizens." Most of the students we surveyed report that Tufts is doing a good job of achieving this aim. Students applaud the quality of teaching and give high marks to faculty and administration for responding to students' needs—in and out of the classroom. Comments one, "Tufts is dedicated to ensuring a well-rounded development of doctor and person. They are very concerned about students being happy with life and not overwhelmed with the tasks ahead."

ACADEMICS

Tufts calls its curriculum "dynamic," and students agree that the school works hard to be flexible in how and what it teaches. Tufts updates the traditional, divided preclinical curriculum by using a systems approach to the basic sciences and augmenting lectures and labs with integrative small group, problem-based learning experiences. Again, students are enthusiastic: "Problem-based learning case studies are great. We have a lot of small group conferences—not lecture all day like some schools." Reports another, "There is good integration of information between courses, the course directors are very open to student critiques, and the faculty are very responsive to students' criticism and requests."

One of the most striking elements in Tufts' curriculum is its Preclinical Elective Program. Through this program, all first- and second-year students select some of their own preclinical experiences. Over 100 different electives are offered. Students give the program and the faculty preceptors who serve as mentors and advisors rave reviews. Says one first-year student, "The preclinical electives here at Tufts are awesome! It's nice to work in a hospital, doctor's office, or lab from the first semester." Whether it's because of the wealth of opportunities afforded by the elective program, or Tufts's emphasis on "more than just the physical treatment of patients," students are among the happiest of any we surveyed with the amount of early clinical exposure they receive.

Students aren't quite as spirited in their praise of the school's facilities. While they are well satisfied with classrooms, labs, and especially hospitals, they give low marks to the library. Computer facilities also received lukewarm reviews, but one student says that, "with the addition of new Mac labs," things are getting better.

Grading and Promotion Policy: Honors/High Pass/ Pass/Low Pass/Fail. Parts I and II of the USMLE are required.

Additional Degree Programs: Tufts offers the VAMC-Tufts Hospital Based Practicum, which provides in-depth exposure to tertiary care medicine. This program allows students, through summer and school-year work-study, to get hands-on clinical experience while earning tuition credits. Students apply to the practicum after acceptance into the medical school. Tufts also offers a combined MD/Ph.D. and a four-year MD/MPH program.

STUDENT LIFE

Women are well represented at Tufts and students generally believe that females are treated equitably by faculty and classmates. Students rate their classmates as fairly competitive. Not everyone agrees with this assessment, however. Explains one, "The students here are extremely intelligent and friendly, and while they are very competitive with themselves (want to do as well as they can), there is no evidence here of cutthroat competition."

Even though one student reports that there is "time to play hard," Tufts students are only moderately active socially compared to those at the other schools we surveyed. They are satisfied by the number of school activities available and commend the involvement of the administration and faculty: "The Tufts administration fully supports students in all extracurricular endeavors, both academic and pleasure-related. We have an excellent faculty that motivates students to do research and form clubs, such as journal clubs, family medicine groups, etc." Still, many go off campus for most of their extracurricular pursuits.

One of the points on which most students agree is that they like going to med school in Boston, which is

not surprising since a large number of Tufts students attended a Boston-area school as undergrads. One comments, "There are plenty of opportunities for fun as well as learning in Boston, with easy access to all." This "easy access" is afforded by an excellent—and relatively safe—public transportation system. Despite the general accolades for Boston, however, many students are unimpressed with Tufts's campus—"just a collection of buildings"—and the "not very safe" area around the campus. Students gave on-campus housing lousy reviews, perhaps because of safety issues; they much prefer off-campus offerings.

ADMISSIONS

Tufts states no preference for residents of Massachusetts. According to the admissions bulletin, "The selection of candidates for admission is based not only on performance in premedical courses, but also on the applicant's entire academic record and extracurricular experiences. Letters of recommendation and additional information...are reviewed for indications of promise and fitness for a medical career." Tufts also strongly recommends "real-life experience in the health care field." The MCAT is required and should be taken in the spring of the year of application. Candidates are encouraged to apply as early as possible.

Special Programs for Members of Underrepresented Minorities: Students rated Tufts low on diversity, a situation Tufts is addressing through special programs for recruiting, enrolling, retaining, and graduating underrepresented minorities. Among the offerings are scholarships, attention in the regular curriculum to diseases that disproportionately affect minorities, and outreach programs to expose minority high school students to medical careers. There is also a prematriculation summer program that introduces students to first-semester courses and teaches study, testing, and time-management skills.

Transfer Policy: Tufts considers transfers into the second or third year if space is available.

FINANCIAL AID

By any standard, it's costly to attend Tufts. The tuition is only part of the story. Including tuition, housing, and expenses, the financial aid office estimates the total bill for the first year at close to $34,000. Making the financial picture even more grim is the fact that only about one-third of students receive Tufts-administered funds.

(It is interesting to note that, in the admissions bulletin, the "sample" financial aid award for a student who shows a need of almost $30,000 is entirely made up of loans.) Remember, too, that Boston's high cost of living is usually rated second only to New York's.

HITS AND MISSES

HITS	MISSES
Supportive administration	Diversity
Caring faculty	Library
Boston	Attractiveness of campus
Public transportation	

TUITION OVERVIEW

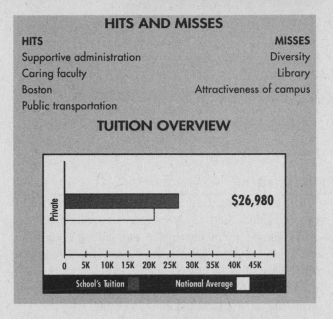

ADMISSIONS FACTS

Demographics

% men	55
% women	45
% minorities	13

Deadline & Notification Dates

AMCAS	yes
Regular application	11/01
Regular notification	10/15–until filled
Early Decision application	6/15-8/01
Early Decision notification	10/01

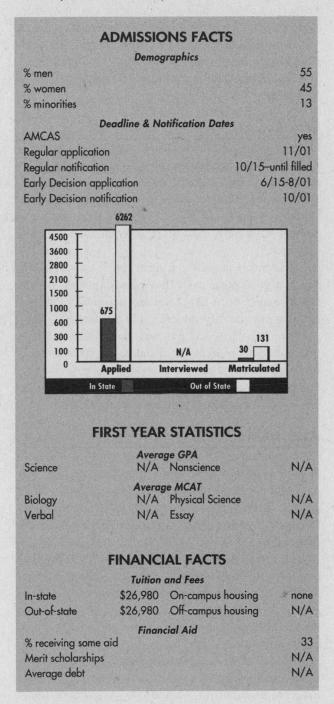

FIRST YEAR STATISTICS

Average GPA

Science	N/A	Nonscience	N/A

Average MCAT

Biology	N/A	Physical Science	N/A
Verbal	N/A	Essay	N/A

FINANCIAL FACTS

Tuition and Fees

In-state	$26,980	On-campus housing	none
Out-of-state	$26,980	Off-campus housing	N/A

Financial Aid

% receiving some aid	33
Merit scholarships	N/A
Average debt	N/A

University of Michigan Medical School

Admissions Office
M4130 Medical Science Building , Ann Arbor, MI 48109-0611
(313) 764-6317

OVERVIEW

Michigan is recognized as a top research-oriented med school, and students say it deserves its great reputation. Although their rankings place the school among the most "cutthroat" of those in our survey, respondents say that its excellent faculty, ample opportunities to participate in research, and involved, diverse student body make the intense atmosphere worthwhile.

ACADEMICS

Michigan revamped its curriculum in 1992. The program is now divided into four distinct phases, one for each year of study. In Component I, students learn basic science fundamentals in preparation for the more integrated approach of Component II. In the second phase, students continue their basic science study, but in a clinical context. Courses are structured around organ systems, and the instruction is interdisciplinary. As students learn about pathology, they discuss clinical approaches to patients with diseases. Also required in both preclinical years is Introduction to the Patient. In this course, students observe physicians and work with standardized and actual patients to gain an understanding of the health care environment and to develop fundamental clinical skills. Most Michigan students say they are satisfied with the amount of clinical exposure they get in the basic science years.

The skills students develop in the second year help them make the transition to the clerkship experiences of Component III. In addition to completing required rotations and electives, students attend conferences that emphasize the clinical application of scientific principles. The fourth year is largely elective, though a basic science experience is mandatory.

Students are extremely pleased with Michigan's new curriculum and are confident that, "when all the bugs are worked out," it will be even better. The quality of teaching also gets excellent reviews, and students are impressed with the number of "prominent faculty mem-

bers" who actually teach. Most respondents say that professors are accessible outside of class.

Praise extends to the school's facilities. Science labs, the library, and clinical teaching sites are rated as outstanding, and students say that the Learning Resource Center, which provides a variety of instructional media, including computer software, is top-notch.

Grading and Promotion Policy: In the first year, Pass/Fail. In other years: Honors/High Pass/Pass/Fail.

Additional Degree Programs: BS/MD, MD/Ph.D., MD/MPH.

STUDENT LIFE

Despite the intense atmosphere, respondents say they find time to get involved in the school's many extracurricular activities. Student relations are also very good, and most of those we surveyed like their classmates. Comments one sophomore, "Although there are a fair number of gunners, most people are extremely cool and laid-back."

Students "outside the mainstream" also say Michigan is a good place to be. Says a gay freshman, "The faculty and students have been very accepting...Ann Arbor also provides a good gay social atmosphere."

The university campus and Ann Arbor get high marks, and accessible school and public transportation make it easy to get around. Although students say both on-campus and off-campus housing is very good, some complain that in-town apartments are expensive.

ADMISSIONS

Michigan shows preference to state residents, but up to 30 percent of each class can come from out of state. Any interested nonresident is encouraged to apply. Up to 20 percent of each class may be admitted through Early Decision. Students applying through EDP should have outstanding GPAs and MCAT scores.

In making its decisions, the Admissions Committee considers the GPA, MCAT scores, the personal statement, letters of recommendation, and the interview to be of primary importance. Also considered are exposure to the medical profession, extracurricular activities, and volunteer work.

Special Programs for Members of Underrepresented Minorities: A minority affairs division coordinates recruiting efforts. Among the programs it offers are special consideration for admissions, a prematriculation summer session, and tutoring services.

Transfer Policy: Michigan does not accept transfers.

FINANCIAL AID

Financial aid is awarded primarily on the basis of need, but the school offers some merit scholarships.

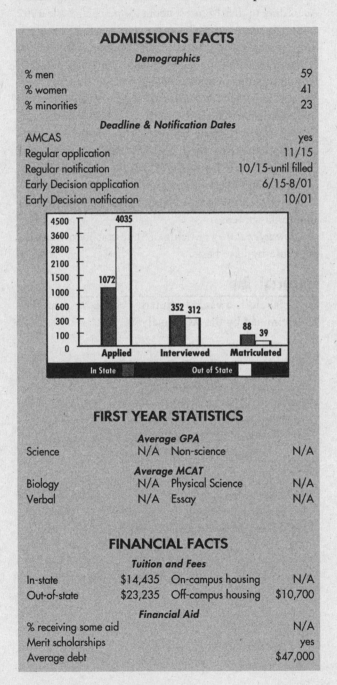

ADMISSIONS FACTS

Demographics

% men	59
% women	41
% minorities	23

Deadline & Notification Dates

AMCAS	yes
Regular application	11/15
Regular notification	10/15-until filled
Early Decision application	6/15-8/01
Early Decision notification	10/01

FIRST YEAR STATISTICS

Average GPA

Science	N/A	Non-science	N/A

Average MCAT

Biology	N/A	Physical Science	N/A
Verbal	N/A	Essay	N/A

FINANCIAL FACTS

Tuition and Fees

In-state	$14,435	On-campus housing	N/A
Out-of-state	$23,235	Off-campus housing	$10,700

Financial Aid

% receiving some aid	N/A
Merit scholarships	yes
Average debt	$47,000

HITS AND MISSES

HITS	MISSES
Quality of teaching	Competitive atmosphere
Extracurricular involvement	
Overall facilities	
Emphasis on research	
Ann Arbor	
Public transportation	

TUITION OVERVIEW

Out-of-state: $23,235
In-state: $14,435

School's Tuition   National Average

Michigan State University College of Human Medicine

Admissions Office, A-239 Life Sciences, East Lansing, MI 48824-1317
(517) 353-9620

OVERVIEW

The mission of the Michigan State med school is to educate compassionate, humane physicians, and the focus is on primary care. The College of Medicine endeavors to make quality health care a reality for everyone in the state, including rural and inner-city populations. To achieve the mission, students do their clinical work in one of six Michigan communities.

ACADEMICS

Michigan State's curriculum is divided into three "blocks." Blocks I and II, which encompass the first two academic years, are taught on the Michigan State University, East Lansing campus. Block I features basic science and psychosocial courses and an integrative clinical course that applies the basic sciences to patient cases. Students get early exposure to patients through a clinical skills course and a unique mentor program. In the mentor program, small groups of students work with a preceptor to explore patient care and the complex roles of the physician.

Block II covers advanced basic science concepts. Courses are taught in a small group, problem-based format and science instruction is presented within the social context of a clinical decisions course. The clinical skills experience and the mentor program continue throughout the second year.

Block III, which is taken during the third and fourth years, is taught in one of six Michigan communities. The community-based clinical experience features a series of required and elective clerkships that are completed in both hospital and ambulatory settings.

Michigan State uses a variety of traditional and non-traditional teaching styles, including lectures, labs, problem-based learning, interdisciplinary courses, independent study, and computer-assisted learning. Throughout the curriculum, small classes facilitate a collegial relationship between students and their professors. The mentor program and the clinical skills continuum link students with clinical faculty preceptors and give students extensive, hands-on experiences with patients.

Grading and Promotion Policy: Pass/Fail.

Additional Degree Programs: BS/MD; MD/Ph.D.; MD/MA.

STUDENT LIFE

Students in their preclinical years can take advantage of the considerable resources of a Big Ten university. Within the medical school, there are numerous opportunities to get involved. Michigan State provides ample opportunities for students to participate in the administrative decision-making process and sponsors chapters of the major national medical associations.

Students have a good deal of choice in their living arrangements. The university offers on-campus residence halls and apartments, and off-campus accommodations in Lansing and East Lansing are plentiful.

ADMISSIONS

Michigan State gives preference to state residents, but up to 20 percent can be from out of state. Because the school has a rolling admissions policy, candidates are encouraged to apply as early as possible.

In making final admissions decisions, the admissions office ranks as the primary selection factors the interview, the science GPA, MCAT scores (from the new test), letters of recommendation, essays, exposure to the medical field, volunteer activities, and the stu-

dents' compatibility with the mission of the school. Also considered important are the nonscience GPA and extracurricular activities.

Special Programs for Members of Underrepresented Minorities: The Admissions Office says it "values diversity in the composition of the entering class." According to their figures, about 20 percent of the 1992 entering class are members of underrepresented minorities. Among the recruitment and support services the school offers minority students are community outreach programs, summer programs for college students, special consideration for admission, a prematriculation session, academic advising, tutoring, and review sessions for Parts I and II of the USMLE. The school also offers a postbaccalaureate program, Advanced Baccalaureate Learning Experience (ABLE). Black, Mexican-American, Mainland Puerto Rican, and Native American students are selected for this program through the regular admissions process.

Transfer Policy: Michigan State considers transfers on a case-by-case basis.

FINANCIAL AID

Financial aid is awarded primarily on the basis of need as determined by the ACT analysis.

ADMISSIONS FACTS

Demographics

% men	52
% women	48
% minorities	20

Deadline & Notification Dates

AMCAS	yes
Regular application	11/15
Regular notification	10/15–until filled
Early Decision application	6/15-8/01
Early Decision notification	10/01

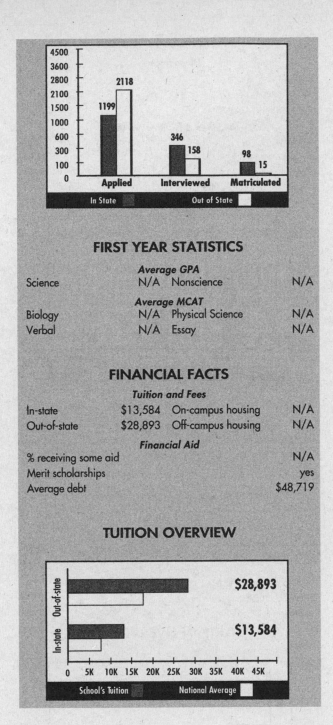

FIRST YEAR STATISTICS

Average GPA
Science	N/A	Nonscience	N/A

Average MCAT
Biology	N/A	Physical Science	N/A
Verbal	N/A	Essay	N/A

FINANCIAL FACTS

Tuition and Fees
In-state	$13,584	On-campus housing	N/A
Out-of-state	$28,893	Off-campus housing	N/A

Financial Aid
% receiving some aid	N/A
Merit scholarships	yes
Average debt	$48,719

TUITION OVERVIEW

Wayne State University School of Medicine

Admissions, 540 East Canfield, Detroit, MI 48201
(313) 577-1466

OVERVIEW

Wayne State is dedicated to improving the health of the residents of Detroit and its surrounding communities through education, research, and service programs. Most students share this goal; the majority stay in Michigan at least through residency, and about 50 percent enter primary care.

ACADEMICS

Wayne State's curriculum is divided into the usual two-year preclinical and clinical units. During the first year, students study the basic sciences to gain an understanding of the normal structures and functions of the human body. In addition to departmental science courses, students investigate social and behavioral issues in medicine.

During the second year, the focus shifts to the effects of disease on the organism. The first portion of this year is devoted to traditional science courses and is followed by an interdisciplinary study of the organ systems in which instructors stress both integration between the sciences and the clinical relevance of scientific principles. Sophomores also explore psychological and ethical aspects of medical care and learn fundamental history-taking, examination, and evaluation skills.

Third-year students complete clerkships in both ambulatory and hospital settings. In addition to those in the major disciplines, rotations in ophthalmology, otolaryngology, and family medicine are required. The senior year is wholly elective.

Grading and Promotion Policy: Honors/Pass/Fail. Students must take Parts I and II of the USMLE.

Additional Degree Programs: MS/MD, MD/Ph.D.

STUDENT LIFE

Wayne State is located in Detroit's cultural center, within walking distance of a variety of city attractions, including the Institute of the Arts, the Historical Museum, the Science Center, and the Children's Museum.

Students can also take advantage of the resources of the university; the med school is connected to the main university campus by a city bus service.

Although Detroit has notorious crime problems, Wayne State boasts that, thanks to the combined efforts of the University Department of Public Safety and the Detroit Police Department, the area around the school is among the safest in the city.

ADMISSIONS

Wayne State gives preference to Michigan residents, but considers exceptionally well-qualified out-of-state applicants. Both nonresidents and residents may apply through the Early Decision Program, but candidates should have GPAs of 3.4 or above and average MCAT scores of 8.5 or better to be considered competitive. Students who apply through the regular admissions process should apply as early as possible.

Students who are asked to interview have passed through two initial screenings, one before and one after submitting a supplementary application. Wayne State makes final admissions decisions primarily on the basis of GPA, MCAT scores, the interview, extracurricular activities, and work experience.

Special Programs for Members of Underrepresented Minorities: Wayne State is among the leaders in minority enrollment. The Recruitment Office coordinates efforts to increase representation of minority groups. Among its offerings are a postbaccalaureate program for students who have been denied admission and a summer prematriculation session for accepted students.

Transfer Policy: Wayne State considers applications for transfer into the second and third years from students who are in good standing at U.S. med schools. Exceptional candidates from foreign med schools are also sometimes considered.

FINANCIAL AID

The school offers assistance through loans, scholarships, grants, and work-study. Financial aid is awarded primarily on the basis of documented need.

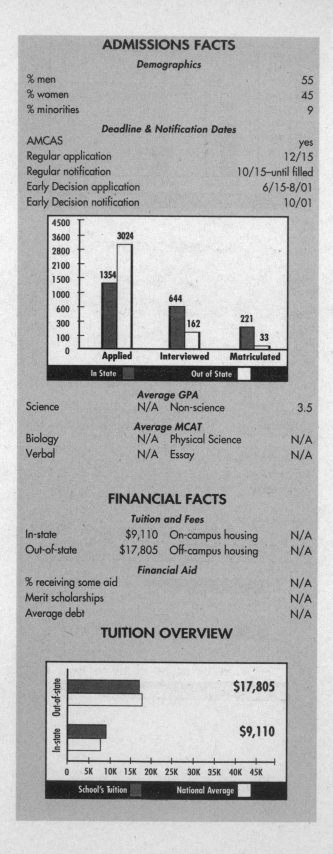

ADMISSIONS FACTS

Demographics

% men	55
% women	45
% minorities	9

Deadline & Notification Dates

AMCAS	yes
Regular application	12/15
Regular notification	10/15–until filled
Early Decision application	6/15-8/01
Early Decision notification	10/01

Average GPA

Science	N/A	Non-science	3.5

Average MCAT

Biology	N/A	Physical Science	N/A
Verbal	N/A	Essay	N/A

FINANCIAL FACTS

Tuition and Fees

In-state	$9,110	On-campus housing	N/A
Out-of-state	$17,805	Off-campus housing	N/A

Financial Aid

% receiving some aid	N/A
Merit scholarships	N/A
Average debt	N/A

TUITION OVERVIEW

Out-of-state $17,805
In-state $9,110

School's Tuition   National Average

Mayo Medical School

Admissions Committee, 200 First Street SW, Rochester, NM 55905
(507) 284-3671

OVERVIEW

If you are looking for a progressive medical education, Mayo's approach fits into a long-standing spirit of innovation: Dr. William Mayo and his two sons were pioneers in the concept of group medical practice, and the world-renowned clinic they founded has been a leader in patient care for decades. An extremely small class size, a collegial relationship between students and the faculty, and attention to the founders' dual objectives of healing the sick and advancing medical science are hallmarks of the Mayo experience.

ACADEMICS

Mayo's curriculum emphasizes both basic and clinical sciences in all four years. In the first semester of their freshman year, students learn the basic sciences through concentrated, departmental courses. During the second semester, they take interdisciplinary courses that emphasize clinical correlations and integration between the sciences. Patient contact begins the first year and intensifies during a spring course in which students learn fundamental history-taking and examination skills.

In the sophomore year, students continue their basic science study and have extensive hands-on patient contact. Both didactic experiences and introductions to major clinical disciplines are incorporated into the second year. Lecture courses, seminars, preceptorships, and introductory rotations are among the methods of instruction.

The third year is divided into two segments: clerkships and the research semester. In the clerkship portion, students expand on their second-year experiences through more intense rotations in internal medicine, obstetrics and gynecology, surgery, neurology, and pediatrics. During the research semester, students investigate topics of particular interest, write formal research papers, and present their findings.

Fourth-year students complete clerkship requirements in medicine, primary care, and surgery. The rest of the year is free for electives offered at Mayo's campuses in Rochester, Jacksonville, and Scottsdale. Seniors may also elect to spend a portion of their time in off-campus experiences.

Grading and Promotion Policy: Honors/Pass/Marginal Pass/Fail. Students must take Parts I and II of the USMLE.

Additional Degree Programs: MD/Ph.D.

STUDENT LIFE

The Mayo Medical Center's Activity Program sponsors social, recreational, and cultural events for med students and their significant others. There's something for just about everyone. Performers can participate in musical groups or show their stuff in the annual talent show; athletes can join intramural teams and compete in school-sponsored tournaments; and altruists can get involved in a variety of community service projects. Rochester offers fewer outlets for socializing than many students would like, but does provide extracurricular opportunities for the sports-minded.

Although respondents rate their colleagues as somewhat competitive, they note that the school's small size fosters cooperation.

Mayo does not offer any on-campus housing, but off-campus housing is both available and affordable.

ADMISSIONS

Although Mayo offers in-state tuition rates to residents of Minnesota, Florida, and Arizona, the admissions office says it doesn't show preference to applicants from those states. In each entering class, the majority of spaces are reserved for MD students, but several places are reserved for those pursuing combined degrees.

Among the primary factors the Admissions Committee relies on in making its final decisions are the academic record, MCAT scores, letters of evaluation, and the interview. Also considered are extracurricular activities, exposure to the health care field, and motivation and suitability for the practice of medicine.

Special Programs for Members of Underrepresented Minorities: The Admissions Committee strongly encourages underrepresented minority students to apply. Full tuition grants are available for qualified students.

Transfer Policy: Mayo does not accept transfers.

FINANCIAL AID

Mayo's goal is to provide full tuition support to all of its students by the year 2005. Currently, Mayo provides grants to supplement extramural loan and grant programs.

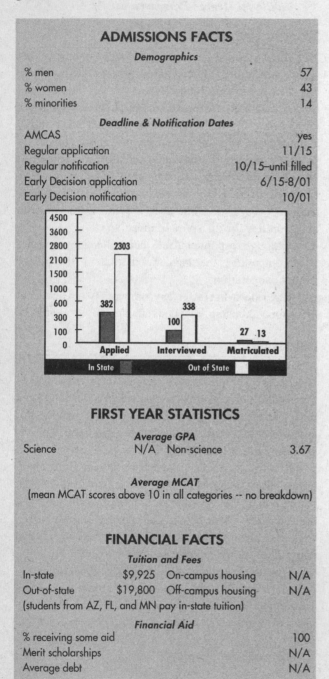

ADMISSIONS FACTS

Demographics

% men	57
% women	43
% minorities	14

Deadline & Notification Dates

AMCAS	yes
Regular application	11/15
Regular notification	10/15–until filled
Early Decision application	6/15-8/01
Early Decision notification	10/01

Applied: In State 382, Out of State 2303
Interviewed: In State 100, Out of State 338
Matriculated: In State 27, Out of State 13

FIRST YEAR STATISTICS

Average GPA

Science	N/A	Non-science	3.67

Average MCAT
(mean MCAT scores above 10 in all categories -- no breakdown)

FINANCIAL FACTS

Tuition and Fees

In-state	$9,925	On-campus housing	N/A
Out-of-state	$19,800	Off-campus housing	N/A

(students from AZ, FL, and MN pay in-state tuition)

Financial Aid

% receiving some aid	100
Merit scholarships	N/A
Average debt	N/A

TUITION OVERVIEW

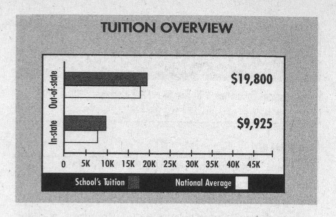

Out-of-state $19,800
In-state $9,925

School's Tuition — National Average

University of Minnesota–Duluth School of Medicine

Admissions Room 107, 10 University Drive, Duluth, MN 55812
(218) 726-8511

OVERVIEW

UMD School of Medicine is the nation's only remaining two-year medical school. After completing the two basic science years in Duluth, students transfer to the University of Minnesota-Twin Cities campus in Minneapolis for an additional two years of clinical medical education. Most students at UMD are interested in primary care, and warn that if you're not you're unlikely to be happy there: "The school does an excellent job of achieving its mission—preparing people for rural primary care. Prospective students should strongly consider this when applying. If someone is not interested in rural primary care, they may not want to apply."

ACADEMICS

UMD employs a variety of teaching formats, including traditional lectures, labs, small group learning, interdisciplinary courses, and computer-assisted learning. They also have recently introduced some problem-based learning in the first-year curriculum. Although UMD has only about 45 full-time faculty members, over 250 area physicians teach part time or participate in preceptorships, helping to augment basic science preparation with practical clinical knowledge. By and large, students are extremely pleased with the quality of teaching and the accessibility of the faculty. Says one, "Duluth is a great place to go to medical school if you want a supportive, noncompetitive environment with easy access to faculty."

UMD students get early clinical exposure through the Family Practice Preceptorship. Both first- and second-year students rate this experience, and the rest of their clinical training, as outstanding; only one school got higher marks in this category.

The UMD Admissions Office boasts, "UMD is of comparatively small size, but has the resources of one of the nation's largest universities at its disposal." Overall, students rate the school's facilities as excellent. Students give glowing reviews to the classroom, lab, computer, and clinical facilities, but complain that the library leaves a lot to be desired.

Grading and Promotion Policy: Honors/Pass/Fail. A passing grade on Part I of the is required for promotion to the third year at the UM-Minneapolis.

Additional Degree Programs: Because it is a two-year school, UMD has no combined degree programs.

STUDENT LIFE

UMD students are much more socially active than their counterparts at most other schools. Explains one, "Students here have a life. The attitude seems to be that med school is important, but not necessarily the center of your life." Although students feel that UMD offers plenty of school clubs, much of the extracurricular activity is centered around recreational opportunities afforded by the school's location.

Students sound like the Chamber of Commerce when they describe the area around their campus: "Duluth provides a lot of opportunities for the student who enjoys outdoor recreational activities—cycling, running, skiing, hiking, camping, canoeing, etc. And all are easily accessible within or around the city." Another student adds, "Outdoor enthusiasts love [UMD's] very close proximity to the Boundary Waters, many state parks, and the Superior National Forest." Overall, students say, "Quality of life is excellent in Duluth."

ADMISSIONS

Residents of Minnesota, North Dakota, South Dakota, Iowa, Wisconsin, and the Upper Peninsula of Michigan are considered for admission. UMD also invites underrepresented minority students who are interested in practicing family medicine in rural communities to apply. Students who do not fall into one of these categories will not be considered, and should not apply.

Science GPA, MCAT scores (from the new format test), letters of recommendation, and the interview are ranked as the most important selection factors. Also considered in decreasing order of importance are exposure to the medical profession, volunteer activities, nonscience GPA, and extracurricular activities. Compatibility with the school's mission is also considered: "In reviewing applicants to the school, the Committee on Admissions selects those individuals whose career objectives clearly indicate the greater probability to a) become family practice physicians and b) practice in rural or small town areas of this state or similar regions experiencing a physician shortage."

Special Programs for Members of Underrepresented Minorities: Since UMD is a state school, the racial mix is influenced by the demographics of Minnesota. It is, therefore, not surprising that "the racial mix is European origin and American Indians." UMD is committed to providing minority group members with the opportunity to study medicine and devotes much of its efforts to recruiting American Indian students. Among special programs the school offers minority students are academic advising, tutoring, community outreach programs, a decelerated basic science program, and summer sessions for high school and college students. UMD has also established the Center for American Indian and Minority Health. Special programs are not open to other students, and some majority students find this disturbing. Says one, "Native American students receive unequal treatment at UMD in that they receive extra special treatment above and beyond that of other students."

Transfer Policy: No transfer students are accepted.

FINANCIAL AID

Ninety percent of UMD students receive some financial assistance. The admissions office encourages those who will need financial aid to apply for it immediately upon acceptance.

ADMISSIONS FACTS

Demographics

% men	47
% women	53
% minorities	10

Deadline & Notification Dates

AMCAS	yes
Regular application	11/15
Regular notification	10/15-until filled
Early Decision application	6/15-8/01
Early Decision notification	10/01

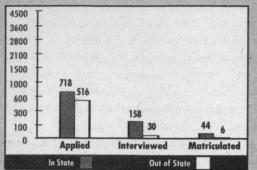

In State / Out of State

718 516 / 158 30 / 44 6

Applied / Interviewed / Matriculated

FIRST YEAR STATISTICS

Average GPA

Science	N/A	Non-science	3.45

Average MCAT

Biology	8.9	Physical Science	8.3
Verbal	9.0	Essay	N/A

FINANCIAL FACTS

Tuition and Fees

In-state	$14,212	On-campus housing	N/A
Out-of-state	$27,892	Off-campus housing	8,900

(resident tuition is granted to high-priority minority nonresidents)

Financial Aid

% receiving some aid	93
Merit scholarships	yes
Average debt	$55,000

(includes 3rd and 4th year at UM-MN)

HITS AND MISSES

HITS	MISSES
Noncompetitive atmosphere	Library
Women treated equitably	Racial diversity
Quality of teaching	Emphasis on research
Accessibility of faculty	Academic advising
Clinical facilities	On-campus housing
Early clinical exposure	
Overall happiness	
Duluth	

TUITION OVERVIEW

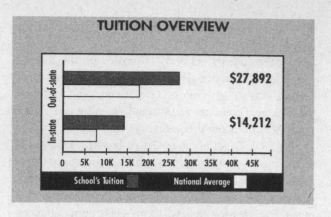

Out-of-state $27,892
In-state $14,212

School's Tuition | National Average

University of Minnesota Medical School—Minneapolis

Office of Admissions, Box 293-UMHC
420 Delaware Street SE, Minneapolis, MN 55455-0310
(612) 624-1122

OVERVIEW

School officials say, "The Medical School at Minnesota has a rich tradition of research and clinical achievements.... The pursuit of research in all departments has infused the whole school with a spirit of scientific inquiry." The students who responded to our survey agree; their highest ratings go to the school's investigative efforts. One sophomore summarizes, "Extraordinary opportunities are readily available." Minnesota's research efforts don't come at the expense of clinical training, however. Students are pleased with the effort the school makes to produce caring, skilled physicians.

ACADEMICS

Minnesota's curriculum is progressive. The first year consists of four quarters, the first three of which are primarily devoted to developing knowledge of the basic sciences. Normal structure and biochemical processes are the subjects of instruction in the fall, and as the year progresses, the focus shifts to organ systems and the effects of disease. Clinical correlations, aspects of the behavioral sciences, and topics in preventative medicine are also covered. In the summer quarter, students learn history-taking and physical diagnosis skills in the first part of a Clinical Medicine course.

Although Minnesota students continue their basic science studies throughout the second year, they have considerably more clinical exposure than their counterparts at most other schools. Concurrently with science courses, sophomores take a series of clinical tutorials. The first of these is a continuation of the general introduction begun the previous summer. This segment is followed by four six-week tutorials in internal medicine, family practice, pediatrics, and neurology. In these sessions, students spend two half-days a week meeting with tutors to evaluate and discuss assigned patients. Not surprisingly, students give early clinical exposure high marks, and third-year students say these experiences help ease the transition to clerkships.

The third and fourth years are comprised of required clerkships and electives, but students have considerable freedom in planning the sequence of programs. Comments one student, "There's a lot of free time for research, self-directed learning, work, or whatever." As an alternative to the regular clinical curriculum, juniors may choose to enter the Rural Physician Associate Program (RPAP). In RPAP, students work closely with physician preceptors to provide primary care to residents of nonurban communities around the state.

Overall, students are pleased with their educational experience and give the faculty high marks both for the quality of instruction and for accessibility outside the classroom. Basic science and clinical teaching facilities, too, are rated as outstanding, but students say the mediocre library and computer labs make studying more difficult than it should be.

Grading and Promotion Policy: Outstanding/Excellent/Satisfactory/No Credit. Students must pass Parts I and II of the USMLE.

Additional Degree Programs: Minnesota has a funded Medical Scientist Training Program that leads to a combined MD/Ph.D.

STUDENT LIFE

Students' general enthusiasm about Minnesota extends to their feelings about their classmates. Says one freshman, "There is an excellent sense of community.... This contributes greatly to the students' desires to help others." Although most students say they're too busy to have great social lives, student organizations and medical fraternities provide extracurricular activities.

University housing is reportedly adequate, but most of our respondents say they prefer to make their own living arrangements off-campus. The school's location is extremely popular; students say the Twin Cities' varied cultural, recreational, and entertainment offerings more than make up for the long, cold winters.

ADMISSIONS

Preference is given to residents of Minnesota, but students with outstanding qualifications are encouraged to apply from out of state. Students who want to apply through the Early Decision Program should have a GPA of 3.5 or better and score an average of 10 or above on the MCAT.

In addition to grades and MCAT scores, the Admissions Committee considers the interview, letters of recommendation, extracurricular activities, the breadth of coursework, and personal qualities.

Special Programs for Members of Underrepresented Minorities: Although students gave Minnesota low marks for diversity, the school says it is committed to increasing represented minority groups and has an active recruitment program.

Transfer Policy: Minnesota accepts all students transferring from the two-year program in Duluth. Other transfers from LCME accredited U.S. or Canadian med schools will be considered on a space-available basis.

FINANCIAL AID

Minnesota offers financial assistance through school and government programs. Additional loans and scholarships are provided by the Minnesota Medical Foundation. All forms of assistance are coordinated by the med school Financial Aid office. Although most aid is awarded on the basis of demonstrated need, there are some merit scholarships.

ADMISSIONS FACTS

Demographics

% men	53
% women	47
% minorities	6

Deadline & Notification Dates

AMCAS	yes
Regular application	11/15
Regular notification	11/15–5/15
Early Decision application	6/15-8/01
Early Decision notification	10/01

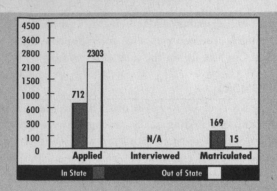

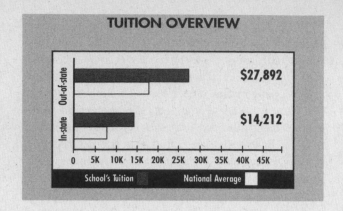

TUITION OVERVIEW

$27,892

$14,212

FIRST YEAR STATISTICS

Average GPA

Science	N/A	Non-science	3.53

Average MCAT

Biology	N/A	Physical Science	N/A
Verbal	N/A	Essay	N/A

FINANCIAL FACTS

Tuition and Fees

In-state	$14,212	On-campus housing	N/A
Out-of-state	$27,892	Off-campus housing	N/A

(resident tuition is granted to high-priority minority nonresidents)

Financial Aid

% receiving some aid	N/A
Merit scholarships	N/A
Average debt	N/A

HITS AND MISSES

HITS	MISSES
Basic science facilities	Diversity
Clinical facilities	Library
Research efforts	Computer facilities
Activities	Excessive reading assignments
Minneapolis-St. Paul	
Lots of nontraditional students	

University of Mississippi School of Medicine

Chairman, Admissions Committee
2500 North State Street, Jackson, Mississippi 39216-4505
(601) 984-5010

OVERVIEW

The School of Medicine is part of the University of Mississippi Medical Center in Jackson, the state capital. In addition to the med school, the schools of Nursing, Health Related Professions, and Dentistry and the graduate programs in medical sciences make up the medical center community. Since the med school is state funded, a large part of its mission is to provide and improve health care for state residents. Its admissions policies reflect these goals, putting nonresidents at a decided disadvantage in the application process.

ACADEMICS

Mississippi divides its curriculum along traditional lines but makes an effort to integrate the basic and clinical sciences from the first year. Freshmen focus most of their efforts on studying anatomy, physiology, and biochemistry to gain an understanding of the normal structures and functions of the human body. To supplement these courses, students are presented with clinical correlations that help them to understand the application of scientific principles to patient problems. Emphasis on thought and behavioral processes is covered in psychiatry and behavioral science segments.

In the second year, students continue to study the scientific basis of medicine but focus on the disease process and therapeutic intervention strategies. A psychiatry course emphasizes the effects of disease on the behavior of the patient and his or her environment. Clinical correlations continue, working up to the final segment of the sophomore year, a six-week Introduction to Clinical Medicine (ICM) course. In ICM, students learn history-taking, examination, and diagnosis skills through classroom presentations and small group sessions.

The ICM experience helps prepare students for the clinical phase of the curriculum. In the third year, students complete clerkships in obstetrics/gynecology, pediatrics, medicine, psychiatry, surgery, and family medicine. Requirements continue into the fourth year, and include rotations in the neurosciences, internal medicine, and a surgery subspecialty. Advanced work is also required in two of three major fields: obstetrics/gynecology, surgery, or pediatrics. Teaching sites include the University Hospital, the VA Hospital, and the Mississippi State Hospital.

Grading and Promotion Policy: Numerical. Students must take Parts I and II of the USMLE.

Additional Degree Programs: MD/Ph.D.

ADMISSIONS

Mississippi shows a strong preference for state residents: in the 1992–93 admission season, no out-of-state candidates were even interviewed. Further, no nonresidents may apply though the Early Decision Program.

Aside from state residence, the Admissions Committee considers candidates' academic record, MCAT scores, interviews, letters of recommendation, maturity, integrity, stability, and personal achievements to be important.

Special Programs for Members of Underrepresented Minorities: Mississippi's Office of Minority Student Affairs coordinates recruitment and support programs aimed at increasing the number of underrepresented minority physicians. A summer prematriculation program is available to students to ease the transition to medical school.

Transfer Policy: Transfers are considered on a space-available basis. Applicants must be in good standing at their current med school.

FINANCIAL AID

Most financial aid is based on need, but Mississippi offers a few merit scholarships. For students who are interested in practicing in underserved areas of Mississippi, the state offers a Medical Education Scholarship Loan Program.

ADMISSIONS FACTS	
Demographics	
% men	78
% women	22
% minorities	11

Deadline & Notification Dates

AMCAS	yes
Regular application	11/01
Regular notification	10/15-until filled
Early Decision application	6/15-8/01
	(EDP for in-state residents only)
Early Decision notification	10/01

	Applied	Interviewed	Matriculated
In State	346	260	100
Out of State	367	0	0

In State / Out of State

FIRST YEAR STATISTICS

Average GPA

Science	N/A	Non-science	3.6

Average MCAT

Biology	N/A	Physical Science	N/A
Verbal	N/A	Essay	N/A

FINANCIAL FACTS

Tuition and Fees

In-state	$6,715	On-campus housing	N/A
Out-of-state	$12,715	Off-campus housing	N/A

Financial Aid

% receiving some aid	N/A
Merit scholarships	yes
Average debt	$24,000

TUITION OVERVIEW

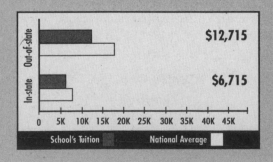

Out-of-state $12,715
In-state $6,715

0 5K 10K 15K 20K 25K 30K 35K 40K 45K

School's Tuition / National Average

University of Missouri, Columbia: School of Medicine

Admissions Office, MA202 Medical Sciences Building,
One Hospital Drive, Columbia, MO 65212
(314) 882-2933

OVERVIEW

Recognized as one of the leading comprehensive med schools, University of Missouri, Columbia (Mizzou) "is committed to developing physicians who will meet Missourians' health care needs." Although the school emphasizes primary care, it also prepares students for specialized training and academic medicine.

ACADEMICS

Mizzou's curriculum is divided into the usual two-year preclinical and clinical units. The first two years focus on the basic sciences, but there is considerable attention to the behavioral, social, and ethical aspects of medicine. Although there are some traditional lectures, small-group instruction and interdisciplinary courses are emphasized.

Students get their first exposure to patient care through the Introduction to Clinical Medicine course (ICM) that begins in the second semester. Through lectures, labs, and small-group clinical experiences, students learn fundamental problem-solving, examination, and evaluation techniques. Armed with these skills, students embark on the third- and fourth-year clinical experiences.

During the third year, students rotate through the major disciplines and complete a four-week Community Health Preceptorship in a private physician's office. About half of the senior year is devoted to required clerkships; the remainder of the time is reserved for electives. During this and other free periods, students are encouraged to participate in research projects. Some funding is available for students who wish to do long-term research.

Grading and Promotion Policy: A–F

Additional Degree Programs: BS/MD, MA/MD, MD/Ph.D.

STUDENT LIFE

Students can get involved in a variety of school organizations, including branches of the major national medical student associations. One of the more popular offerings, the Mizzou chapter of the American Medical Student Association (AMSA), coordinates academic, social, and cultural events. It also sponsors a number of community service projects, including Students Teaching AIDS to Students (STATS). Through STATS, AMSA members travel to local schools and community youth groups to present educational seminars about the disease. In addition to medically-related activities, students can take advantage of the considerable resources of the undergraduate campus. Columbia, a quintessential college town, is located within a few hours of both Kansas City and St. Louis.

ADMISSIONS

Preference is given to residents of Missouri, but some positions are available for nonresidents. On the basis of the AMCAS application and supplemental letters of recommendation, the Admissions Committee invites promising candidates—usually about 40 percent of the total applicant pool—to interview on campus.

In making its final decisions, the Admissions Committee considers the interview, the GPA, MCAT scores, letters of recommendation, extracurricular and work activities, and personal qualities.

Special Programs for Members of Underrepresented Minorities: Mizzou is committed to recruiting and educating underrepresented minority students. All interested candidates are encouraged to apply.

Transfer Policy: Applications from Missouri residents who wish to transfer into the second and third years are considered on a space-available basis.

FINANCIAL AID

Most financial aid is awarded on the basis of documented need.

ADMISSIONS FACTS

Demographics

% men	56
% women	44
% minorities	12

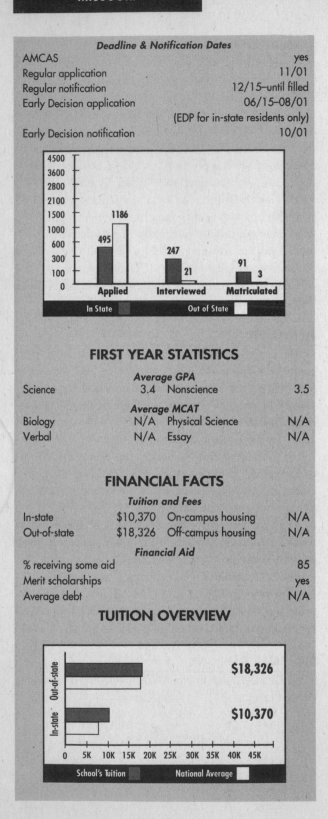

Deadline & Notification Dates

AMCAS	yes
Regular application	11/01
Regular notification	12/15–until filled
Early Decision application	06/15–08/01
	(EDP for in-state residents only)
Early Decision notification	10/01

In State / Out of State bar chart:

	Applied	Interviewed	Matriculated
In State	495	247	91
Out of State	1186	21	3

FIRST YEAR STATISTICS

Average GPA
Science	3.4	Nonscience	3.5

Average MCAT
Biology	N/A	Physical Science	N/A
Verbal	N/A	Essay	N/A

FINANCIAL FACTS

Tuition and Fees
In-state	$10,370	On-campus housing	N/A
Out-of-state	$18,326	Off-campus housing	N/A

Financial Aid
% receiving some aid	85
Merit scholarships	yes
Average debt	N/A

TUITION OVERVIEW

Out-of-state: $18,326
In-state: $10,370

School's Tuition / National Average

University of Missouri: Kansas City School of Medicine

Council on Selection, 2411 Holmes, Kansas City, MO 64108
(816) 235-1870

OVERVIEW

The School of Medicine and the College of Arts and Sciences at UMKC offer a unique, intense, six-year combined BA/MD program. UMKC does not offer a traditional four-year program, so if you're a junior in college, you can turn the page. On the other hand, if you are currently in high school, are completely committed to becoming a physician, and can handle year-round education, the students we surveyed say you should definitely look into UMKC.

ACADEMICS

There are a number of things to recommend the UMKC approach to medical education. Of course, students save time and money by compressing the usual eight years of college and med school into just six years. But there are other, more qualitative benefits. From the onset of the program, students experience the medical profession first-hand. They do this with the help of a clinical-scholar, called a Docent. In the beginning of the first year, small groups of students are assigned to a Docent who will act as their mentor, guide, and preceptor throughout the entire six years.

During the first two years, students focus most of their efforts on working toward their baccalaureate degree through Arts and Science coursework. Around a quarter of the time is spent in a longitudinal Introduction to Medicine course that is conducted by the Docent in community hospitals. During the first-year clinical experiences, students learn medical vocabulary; observe the effects of disease on patients; become acclimated to the hospital setting; investigate social, behavioral, and economic aspects of medicine; and begin to develop clinical problem-solving skills. In addition to covering undergraduate coursework, the second year provides training in Physical Diagnosis, introductions to clinical specialties, and the first courses in biochemistry and physiology.

During the last four years, the focus shifts to medical training. Although students continue undergraduate coursework throughout this time, the main emphasis is on instruction in the basic and clinical sciences. Two months of each year are spent with the Docent and a small number of other students working with a selected group of patients. The remainder of the time is spent in required and elective coursework. There is a considerable amount of flexibility in the sequence of the program. At the end of the second year, students meet with their Docents to plan the best sequence of courses and clerkships.

The best part of the UMKC program, according to the students we surveyed, is the extensive early exposure to patients; in fact, students were nearly unanimous in giving their clinical experiences the highest possible rating. Says one student. "We see patients in our own outpatient clinic starting the first year. I have met many students [from other schools] and discussed their experiences. I am confident that UMKC is unparalleled in its clinical preparation."

The school's emphasis on the ethical practice of medicine also gets high marks. What doesn't fare as well with UMKC students is the school's record for biomedical investigation. In contrast to their enthusiastic approbation of the school's emphasis on clinical practice, students rate UMKC's research efforts as mediocre. Classroom, laboratory, and computing facilities, too, receive only lukewarm praise.

Grading and Promotion Policy: Pass/Fail. Students must pass Parts I and II of the USMLE.

Additional Degree Programs: Exceptionally qualified students may participate in a combined BA/MD/Ph.D. program.

Student Life

Before you decide to apply to UMKC, warns one student, "Make sure you have enough desire and commitment" to attend classes nearly year-round for all six years. Those we surveyed describe the atmosphere as "intense," and report that competition can be significant. Still, students enjoy fairly active social lives and say that they like to spend time with their classmates. Although there is not too much time for extracurricular pursuits, students have the resources of both the undergraduate campus and Kansas City at their disposal.

Students are expected to live on campus for the first two years, a requirement that is none too popular with students. Off-campus housing is much more well-received, though students say it's wise to live within walking distance if you don't have a car because public transportation is poor.

Admissions

Since students enter the UMKC program directly from high school, the admissions process is different from that at other medical schools. Preference is given to residents of Missouri, but up to 15 percent of the class can come from out of state. Nonresidents with exceptional qualifications are invited to apply. Most applicants have strong science and math backgrounds and rank near the top of their classes.

According to the Admissions Coordinator, students are judged on essays, letters of recommendation, extracurricular activities, interviews, ACT or SAT scores, and High School class rank. Since the curriculum is intense, students should show high levels of maturity and motivation, possess strong study skills, and have a genuine commitment to medicine.

Special Programs for Members of Underrepresented Minorities: UMKC encourages applications from members of underrepresented minorities and seeks to identify minority and disadvantaged high school students who are interested in medicine through community outreach programs and special summer sessions.

Transfer Policy: Transfers are seldom accepted, but, if space becomes available, Missouri residents who have completed their baccalaureate degrees will be considered for placement into the third year.

Financial Aid

Although the savings of students taking six years instead of the usual eight to finish both the undergraduate and medical degrees are still considerable, the cost of attending UMKC has increased considerably in the past year. There is some help for students who have trouble making ends meet, however. Most financial aid is awarded on the basis of need, but the school offers some merit scholarships for Missouri residents.

ADMISSIONS FACTS	
Demographics	
% men	45
% women	55
% minorities	10

Deadline & Notification Dates

AMCAS	yes
Regular application	12/01
Regular notification	03/15–until filled
Early Decision application	N/A
Early Decision notification	N/A

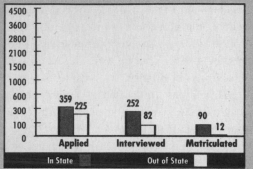

FIRST YEAR STATISTICS

Average GPA: 93% average high school class rank

Science	N/A	Nonscience	N/A

Average MCAT: 90% average ACT score

Biology	N/A	Physical Science	N/A
Verbal	N/A	Essay	N/A

FINANCIAL FACTS

Tuition and Fees

In-state	$13,756 (1st yr)	On-campus housing	$4,000
Out-of-state	$27,292 (1st yr)	Off-campus housing	N/A

Financial Aid

% receiving some aid	N/A
Merit scholarships	for MO residents only
Average debt	N/A

HITS AND MISSES

HITS	MISSES
Early clinical exposure	Research emphasis
Clinical facilities	Science facilities
Emphasis on ethics	Library
Diversity	Public transportation

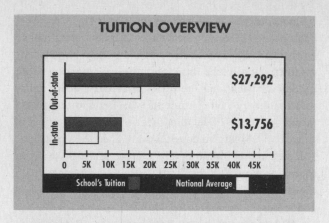

Saint Louis University School of Medicine

Nancy Peters, Admissions Committee, 1402 S. Grand Boulevard, St. Louis, MO 63104
(314) 577-8205

OVERVIEW

SLU School of Medicine is recognized as a leading comprehensive med school. Supported, in part, by the Jesuit order, "The School of Medicine strives to graduate physicians who manifest in their personal and professional lives a special appreciation for what may be called humanistic medicine." The pursuit of this ideal can be seen in SLU's emphasis on nonbiological aspects of medicine and in the programs offered by the Center for Health Care Ethics.

ACADEMICS

Although SLU's curriculum is divided along the classical preclinical and clinical lines, it has some modern features. In the first two years, students study the basic sciences and investigate social and behavioral issues relevant to health. Some courses are taught by a multidisciplinary faculty and demonstrations, labs, discussion groups, and preceptorships augment traditional lectures.

Training in the "art" of medicine begins in the first semester with the Medical Communication Skills course that runs throughout the basic science years. Other clinically oriented courses focus on ethics, decision-making, and basic patient interaction skills. Students have the opportunity to practice their clinical techniques in a controlled environment: the school's Clinical Simulation

Complex recreates health care settings and activities. In the third year, SLU students complete clerkships in the major disciplines. Seniors divide their time between required clerkships and electives.

SLU encourages students to participate in the faculty's research efforts. Elective periods in the first and second years may be used for this purpose, and there are fellowships available for summer work. In addition to regular research fellowships, the school offers summer research preceptorships in gerontology and geriatrics.

Grading and Promotion Policy: Honors/Pass/Fail. Students must pass Parts I and II of the USMLE.

Additional Degree Programs: MD/MA; MD/Ph.D.

STUDENT LIFE

SLU students can pursue their health-related interests by taking part in research forums or by participating in the school's many organizations. Those who need a break from academic and career pursuits can take advantage of the resources of the main campus, including the award-winning Simon Recreation Center or the well-subscribed intramural program.

St. Louis also offers a wide variety of extracurricular pursuits. Tower Grove Park and the Missouri Botanical Gardens are just a few blocks away from the medical school. Nearby Forest Park, one of the nation's largest metropolitan parks, is the home of the St. Louis Zoo, the Art Museum, and the Science Center. Admission to these attractions is free—an added benefit for starving med students. For the more well-heeled student, St. Louis offers opera, theater, ballet, and—for less highbrow tastes—professional baseball and hockey teams.

The cost of living in St. Louis is extremely reasonable for a city of its size. Although the school offers some university housing, students can save money by making their own living arrangements off-campus. Commuting without a car can be inconvenient, though.

ADMISSIONS

SLU shows no preference for Missouri residents. Upon receipt of the AMCAS application, SLU requests supplemental information from all candidates. Promising applicants are then invited for an on-campus interview. These candidates will be informed of the Admissions Committee's decision one week after the interview.

According to the Dean of Admissions, the primary selection factors are the science and nonscience GPAs, MCAT scores (from the new test), the interview, and letters of recommendation. Also considered important are volunteer activities, exposure to the medical profession, extracurricular activities, and essays.

Special Programs for Members of Underrepresented Minorities: A Minority Affairs division coordinates recruiting and support services for underrepresented minority students. Among special offerings are community outreach programs, summer sessions for high school students, special consideration for admissions, academic advising, tutoring, and peer counseling.

Transfer Policy: Transfer applicants are considered on a space-available basis. Special consideration is given to students with compelling reasons for wanting to attend school in St. Louis.

FINANCIAL AID

All financial aid is awarded on the basis of documented need.

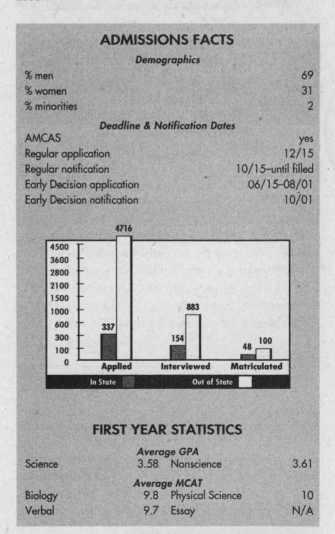

ADMISSIONS FACTS

Demographics

% men	69
% women	31
% minorities	2

Deadline & Notification Dates

AMCAS	yes
Regular application	12/15
Regular notification	10/15–until filled
Early Decision application	06/15–08/01
Early Decision notification	10/01

	Applied	Interviewed	Matriculated
In State	337	154	48
Out of State	4716	883	100

FIRST YEAR STATISTICS

Average GPA

Science	3.58	Nonscience	3.61

Average MCAT

Biology	9.8	Physical Science	10
Verbal	9.7	Essay	N/A

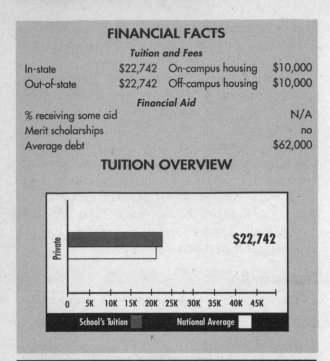

FINANCIAL FACTS

Tuition and Fees

In-state	$22,742	On-campus housing	$10,000
Out-of-state	$22,742	Off-campus housing	$10,000

Financial Aid

% receiving some aid	N/A
Merit scholarships	no
Average debt	$62,000

TUITION OVERVIEW

$22,742

Private

| 0 | 5K | 10K | 15K | 20K | 25K | 30K | 35K | 40K | 45K |

School's Tuition   National Average

Washington University School of Medicine

Office of Admissions, Campus Box 8107,
660 South Euclid Avenue #8107, St. Louis, MO 63110
(314) 362-6857

OVERVIEW

Wash U is consistently rated among the top research-oriented med schools. An outstanding complex of affiliated hospitals, an internationally-renowned faculty, and state-of-the art research facilities are some of the med school's most attractive features. An added benefit to students wrestling with the high cost of medical school is the school's location in affordable St. Louis.

ACADEMICS

Wash U's curriculum is divided along the usual preclinical and clinical lines, but there is an emphasis on integration of the basic and clinical sciences throughout the four years. During the first year, students focus on the basic sciences, medical humanities, and psychosocial aspects of medicine. Instruction in the freshman and sophomore years is a mix of the traditional and the progressive; teaching methods include lectures, small lab groups, seminars, and problem-based learning.

Computer imaging and other technological applications are used extensively. Throughout the basic science years, clinical correlations are stressed through the use of case studies.

After the first year, the focus shifts to clinical medicine. Although students continue their study of the basic sciences in the second year, they also acquire and practice clinical skills, facilitating the transition into the third-year clerkships. Juniors complete a core of clerkships in the traditional disciplines with required rotations in neurology, neurosurgery, ophthalmology, and otolaryngology. Fourth-year students, with the help of faculty advisors, structure their own courses of study through electives.

Students are also encouraged to participate in basic science and clinical research, and the school offers a lot of opportunities to do so. Wash U ranks among the top med schools in National Institute of Health funding. Additional funding comes from a variety of sources.

Grading and Promotion Policy: For the first semester, P/F. For all other semesters, Honors/High Pass/Pass/Fail.

Additional Degree Programs: Wash U has a funded Medical Scientist Training Program, which leads to a combined MD/Ph.D. An MA/MD degree is also offered.

STUDENT LIFE

Wash U offers a variety of clubs and activities, including chapters of the major national medical organizations. Med students can also take advantage of events and facilities on the University's main campus, a short distance from the Medical Center. Especially popular is the intramural sports program, which is housed in the school's new athletic field house. A free shuttle service connects the two campuses.

St. Louis has a lot of attractive features, not the least of which is a low cost of living. The Medical Center is located near the Central West End neighborhood, an area of beautiful homes, gaslit streets, shops, and restaurants. Forest Park, one of the nation's largest metropolitan parks, borders the med school campus and offers numerous cultural and recreational opportunities, including the city zoo, the Art Museum, and a public golf course. Downtown is just a few miles away. Despite St. Louis' large-city amenities, the city is not for everyone. Easterners, especially, complain about the extreme weather conditions, the slow "Southern" pace, and the distance from other metropolitan areas.

Wash U offers residence halls for single students. Since rent is low in St. Louis, though, students generally find they can save money by making their own living arrangements off campus.

ADMISSIONS

Wash U shows no preference for residents of Missouri and seeks a diverse student population. The school is among the most selective in the country. Since it has a rolling admissions policy, students should apply as early as possible.

Final selection factors include the interview; the level and breadth of coursework, GPA, MCAT scores, letters of recommendation, extracurricular activities, exposure to the medical field, and motivation and suitability for the practice of medicine.

Special Programs for Members of Underrepresented Minorities: The school's Dean of Minority Affairs coordinates efforts to recruit members of underrepresented minorities. Summer sessions for high school and college students, a prematriculation summer session for accepted students, academic advising, tutoring, peer counseling, and review courses for Parts I and II of the USMLE are among the special programs Wash U offers.

Transfer Policy: Highly-qualified applicants in good standing at U.S. med schools are considered for transfer into the third year, but transfers are normally granted only to those students with a compelling need to attend Wash U.

FINANCIAL AID

Although most financial aid is awarded solely on the basis of documented need, Wash U awards several full-tuition merit scholarships. Five Distinguished Student Scholarships, four Distinguished Alumni Scholarships, and two Distinguished African-American Scholarships are awarded to members of the first-year class on the basis of academic and personal achievement.

ADMISSIONS FACTS

Demographics

% men	54
% women	46
% minorities	7

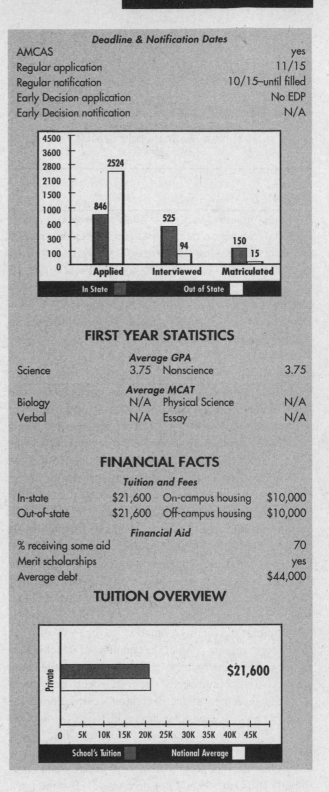

Deadline & Notification Dates

AMCAS	yes
Regular application	11/15
Regular notification	10/15–until filled
Early Decision application	No EDP
Early Decision notification	N/A

Applied: In State 846, Out of State 2524
Interviewed: In State 525, Out of State 94
Matriculated: In State 150, Out of State 15

FIRST YEAR STATISTICS

Average GPA

Science	3.75	Nonscience	3.75

Average MCAT

Biology	N/A	Physical Science	N/A
Verbal	N/A	Essay	N/A

FINANCIAL FACTS

Tuition and Fees

In-state	$21,600	On-campus housing	$10,000
Out-of-state	$21,600	Off-campus housing	$10,000

Financial Aid

% receiving some aid	70
Merit scholarships	yes
Average debt	$44,000

TUITION OVERVIEW

Private: $21,600

School's Tuition | National Average

Creighton University School of Medicine

Medical School Admissions Office
California at 24th Street, Omaha, NE 68178
(800) 325-4405

OVERVIEW

A commitment to quality teaching, a caring and accessible staff, and a strong emphasis on the ethical practice of medicine are a few of the reasons Creighton students say you should take a serious look at their school. But if you're looking for a diverse, multicultural student body and are itching to work with patients from the first days of med school, Creighton students suggest you explore other options.

ACADEMICS

Creighton divides its curriculum into three phases: the basic science core, an introduction to clinical medicine, and the clinical clerkships. During the one-and-a-half year basic science period, students learn scientific principles and investigate social, behavioral, and ethical aspects of medicine. During the second semester of the sophomore year, students learn fundamental patient interviewing and diagnostic skills.

In the third year, students complete fifty weeks of rotating clerkships at the medical center's hospitals. Electives, which may be taken in the basic or the clinical sciences, comprise the entire fourth year; research projects and extramural assignments are also encouraged during this period.

Students give high marks to the faculty at Creighton, reporting that the quality of teaching is strong and that instructors are extremely accessible outside of class. A number of our respondents have some problems with the way the Creighton's curriculum is set up, however. "Some of the classes just aren't structured well," reports one second-year. Another adds, "I feel the traditional approach Creighton uses is not the most effective. The learning process is physically and emotionally difficult. That's not necessary." But the most common complaint by far is what students judge as a lack of early clinical exposure. Students would like to see more clinical correlations in the first segment of the curriculum and, especially, to have more opportunities for hands-on contact with patients. Although exposure to actual patients does increase in the second phase, some students feel that such experiences are "too little, too late." Many first and second years would also like to have more research involvement in the early stages of med school. By contrast, those we surveyed are extremely enthusiastic about the emphasis Creighton puts on ethics, reporting that Creighton does a good job of stressing the humanitarian aspect of medicine.

Students are generally satisfied with Creighton's facilities, with top honors going to the school's library and clinical facilities. Most clinical teaching is done at Saint Joseph Medical Center, located on the University campus. Additional clinical facilities include the Saint Joseph Center for Mental Health, Childrens Hospital, Omaha Veterans Medical Center, and Bergan Mercy Medical Center. New ambulatory clinics are in the works.

Grading and Promotion Policy: A–F for required courses, Pass/Fail for electives. Students take both Parts I and II of the USMLE.

Additional Degree Programs: MD/Ph.D.

STUDENT LIFE

Students report that they are happy at Creighton, but a number of our first- and second-year respondents say they're pretty stressed out. "Outside people don't understand what we go through in med school. We give up our lives to go into medicine, at least in the first two years," says one particularly overwhelmed second-year. Despite comments like these, however, students say they have relatively active social lives and are involved in extracurricular pursuits. Since the medical school is part of Creighton University, med students have access to all of the school's facilities and special events. There are also a number of organizations and activities sponsored by the med school itself—many of which have a strong humanitarian bent.

Omaha is not simply the home of the famed sponsors of television's Wild Kingdom; it also has big-city amenities and a relatively low cost of living (which, according to the Admission Office's bulletin, is about 12 percent under the national average). Most students are satisfied with the school's location, although there are a handful of staunch supporters of the town, and a few harsh critics. There is more consensus about housing options, however; students say both school-sponsored and off-campus offerings are good. On-campus housing is available only for single students, but there are plenty of off-campus apartments within walking distance. For students who choose to live farther away, public transportation is an accessible and safe option.

ADMISSIONS

Preference in admissions is given to residents of the Midwest and to applicants whose states do not have medical schools, but all qualified students are encouraged to apply. Successful candidates from recent years have had average GPAs of 3.5 or above. Selection standards are high; students with GPAs lower than 3.2 or whose MCAT scores are below the 50th percentile are discouraged by the Admissions Office from applying.

In making its selections, the Admissions Committee considers the interview, academic record, MCAT scores, letters of recommendation, and personal qualities.

Special Programs for Members of Underrepresented Minorities: Creighton's student body is not currently very diverse, a condition that both the administration and the students would like to see improve. A few programs exist to increase minority representation. The Admissions Office gives special consideration to applications from qualified underrepresented minority students, and a summer prematriculation program is available for students with educationally disadvantaged backgrounds.

Transfer Policy: Transfers into the second and third years will be considered on a space-available basis.

FINANCIAL AID

Most financial aid assistance is awarded on the basis of need. In addition to federally-funded loan programs, a limited number of scholarships are available.

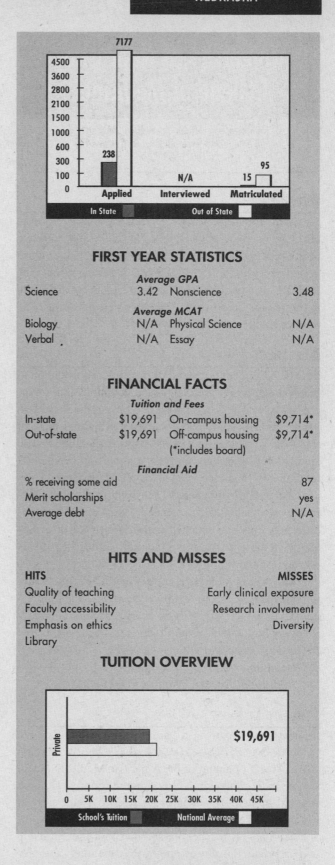

FIRST YEAR STATISTICS

	Average GPA		
Science	3.42	Nonscience	3.48
	Average MCAT		
Biology	N/A	Physical Science	N/A
Verbal	N/A	Essay	N/A

FINANCIAL FACTS

	Tuition and Fees		
In-state	$19,691	On-campus housing	$9,714*
Out-of-state	$19,691	Off-campus housing	$9,714*
		(*includes board)	

Financial Aid	
% receiving some aid	87
Merit scholarships	yes
Average debt	N/A

HITS AND MISSES

HITS	MISSES
Quality of teaching	Early clinical exposure
Faculty accessibility	Research involvement
Emphasis on ethics	Diversity
Library	

TUITION OVERVIEW

$19,691

ADMISSIONS FACTS

Demographics	
% men	60
% women	40
% minorities	8

Deadline & Notification Dates	
AMCAS	yes
Regular application	12/01
Regular notification	10/15–until filled
Early Decision application	06/15–08/01
Early Decision notification	10/01

University of Nebraska College of Medicine

Office of Academic Affairs, Room 4004 Conkling Hall,
600 South 42nd Street, Omaha, NE 69198-4430
(402) 559-4205

OVERVIEW

As a state-supported school, UNMC's primary responsibility is to train physicians to provide and improve health care for the residents of the state, including those in underserved areas. Still, UNMC is serious about biomedical investigation and strongly encourages students to participate in research projects sometime during their four years.

ACADEMICS

UNMC has recently revised its preclinical curriculum to incorporate more problem-based learning and to increase early clinical exposure. During the first two years, students study basic scientific principles through traditional lectures and in the context of clinical case studies. Also presented in both years is an Introduction to Clinical Medicine course. In ICM, students learn physical examination and diagnosis skills through experiences with simulated patients. For real clinical experience, students are matched with a physician preceptor and have the opportunity to monitor a group of patients throughout the four years.

Third-year students complete clerkships in the major disciplines. In the senior year, all students are required to do an eight-week preceptorship in Family Practice. Beyond this requirement, the fourth year is free for basic science and clinical electives.

Grading and Promotion Policy: A–F
Additional Degree Programs: MD/Ph.D.

STUDENT LIFE

Students participate in a variety of local and national medical organizations. Despite the school's medium size, UNMC's chapter of the American Medical Student Association is the eighth largest in the country. Through AMSA, students in their basic science years can get early clinical exposure by making arrangements to volunteer in an ER or spend a summer in a preceptorship with a practicing physician. AMSA members are also involved in diverse community service projects and organize educational and social activities.

ADMISSIONS

UNMC gives preference to residents of Nebraska, but nonresidents are invited to apply. Special consideration is also given to students interested in practicing in underserved areas of the state. After the AMCAS application is received, all state residents and selected out-of-state applicants are asked to complete a supplementary application.

Among the selection factors the Admissions Committee considers in making its final decisions are the GPA, the level and breadth of coursework, MCAT scores, the interview, letters of recommendation, and motivation and suitability for the practice of medicine.

Special Programs for Members of Underrepresented Minorities: The Office of Minority Student Affairs coordinates recruiting efforts and support services for members of underrepresented minorities. Among the Office's offerings are community outreach programs, summer sessions for college students, and counseling services.

Transfer Policy: Applications for transfer from students in good standing at LCME-accredited schools are considered.

FINANCIAL AID

Most financial aid is awarded on the basis of documented need. Assistance is in the form of scholarships, loans, and part-time employment.

ADMISSIONS FACTS

Demographics

% men	53
% women	47
% minorities	5

Deadline & Notification Dates

AMCAS	yes
Regular application	11/15
Regular notification	01/04/95–until filled
Early Decision application	No EDP
Early Decision notification	N/A

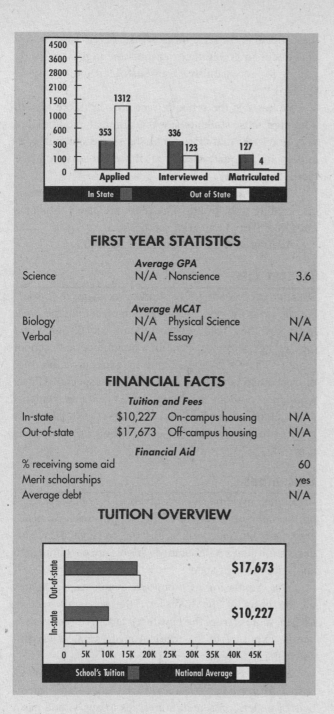

FIRST YEAR STATISTICS

Average GPA

Science	N/A	Nonscience	3.6

Average MCAT

Biology	N/A	Physical Science	N/A
Verbal	N/A	Essay	N/A

FINANCIAL FACTS

Tuition and Fees

In-state	$10,227	On-campus housing	N/A
Out-of-state	$17,673	Off-campus housing	N/A

Financial Aid

% receiving some aid	60
Merit scholarships	yes
Average debt	N/A

TUITION OVERVIEW

University of Nevada School of Medicine

Office of Admissions, Reno, NV 89557-0046
(702) 784-6063

OVERVIEW

One sophomore student summarizes our general findings about this Western school: "University of Nevada is the place to be if you desire one-on-one attention, direct access to the faculty, early access to patients, an administration who listens and cares, and high ethical...standards." Still, there is a lot about Nevada that students don't like; a competitive atmosphere, a relatively stagnant social scene, and sub-par computing and library facilities are the major sources of complaint.

ACADEMICS

The first two years at Nevada focus on the basic sciences, but give considerable attention to psychological and social issues. There is also a high degree of clinical correlation. Students use case studies to identify clinical applications of scientific principles and to develop the problem-solving skills necessary to the practice of medicine. Concurrent with basic and behavioral science coursework, students learn fundamental patient interaction, examination, and evaluation skills.

Nevada students are enthusiastic about the preclinical curriculum. Comments one sophomore, "In comparison to other medical students, we have more clinical exposure, earlier. This lets us integrate our basic sciences with clinical sciences more smoothly." For those who want still more patient contact, there are ample opportunities to work with area physicians or volunteer at the university hospitals.

These early patient-care experiences ease the transition into third- and fourth-year clerkships and electives. In addition to rotations in the major clinical disciplines, there is a strong emphasis on primary care. Clinical teaching is done in Reno, Las Vegas, and rural communities around the state.

The small student body— just over fifty students per class—is one of the things our respondents like best about Nevada. Says one, "You don't feel like a number here." Another adds, "You get specialized attention from the professors." Most of their classmates share these feelings; in fact, those we surveyed were nearly unanimous in giving their teachers the highest possible ratings for accessibility. They also laud the quality of teaching.

Reviews of the school's facilities are more mixed. Although most students say that clinical facilities are very good and that classrooms, labs, and computer facilities are adequate, nearly all those we surveyed rate the library as poor.

Grading and Promotion Policy: Letter and numerical grading and Honors/Pass/Fail are used. Students must take Parts I and II of the USMLE.

Additional Degree Programs: MD/Ph.D.

STUDENT LIFE

Students say Nevada's size allows classmates to "bond," but they rate the atmosphere as somewhat competitive. Most say they lead relatively dull social lives, and they're not very involved in community and school groups. There's a bright spot in extracurricular life, though. Reno is popular with students, especially those who enjoy outdoor activities. And, of course, students who can afford the financial risk can always take their chances in the casinos. Off-campus housing is rated as superior.

ADMISSIONS

Preference in admissions is given to Nevada residents, but a small number of out-of-state applicants are considered. Only students with strong ties to Nevada and students from states without med schools are encouraged to apply from out of state.

The Admissions Committee evaluates candidates on the basis of the interview, the academic record, MCAT scores (from the new test), letters of recommendation, exposure to the medical profession, and extracurricular activities.

Special Programs for Members of Underrepresented Minorities: Nevada strongly encourages members of underrepresented minorities to apply, and has a minority student affairs division to coordinate recruiting and support programs.

Transfer Policy: Transfers into the second and third years are accepted on a space available basis. Only students in good standing at U.S. or Canadian med schools are considered.

FINANCIAL AID

More than 50 percent of students receive some form of assistance. In addition to loans and scholarships awarded on the basis of need, there are some merit scholarships available.

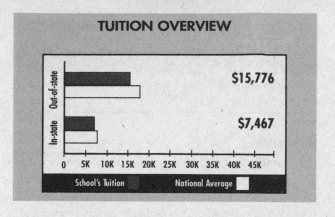

TUITION OVERVIEW

$15,776

$7,467

School's Tuition   National Average

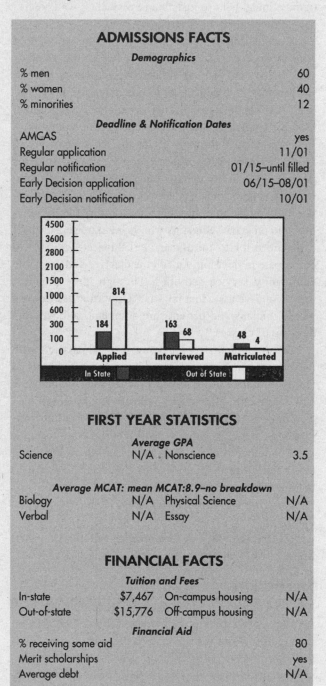

ADMISSIONS FACTS

Demographics

% men	60
% women	40
% minorities	12

Deadline & Notification Dates

AMCAS	yes
Regular application	11/01
Regular notification	01/15–until filled
Early Decision application	06/15–08/01
Early Decision notification	10/01

In State   Out of State

FIRST YEAR STATISTICS

Average GPA

Science	N/A	Nonscience	3.5

Average MCAT: mean MCAT:8.9–no breakdown

Biology	N/A	Physical Science	N/A
Verbal	N/A	Essay	N/A

FINANCIAL FACTS

Tuition and Fees

In-state	$7,467	On-campus housing	N/A
Out-of-state	$15,776	Off-campus housing	N/A

Financial Aid

% receiving some aid	80
Merit scholarships	yes
Average debt	N/A

Dartmouth Medical School

Admissions Office, 7020 Remsen, Room 306, Hanover, NH 03755-3833
(603) 650-1505

OVERVIEW

Dartmouth's first year begins with a series of workshops designed to orient students to the med school experience and foster positive, cooperative relationships among the student body. Whether it is because of this type of program, the small class size, the isolated location of the school, or a unique combination of complementary personalities, the atmosphere is decidedly noncompetitive. This comment is indicative of many we heard: "Medical school is grueling enough, so it's so refreshing to learn in such a nurturing, supportive, and noncompetitive environment. We are here as colleagues and friends—to learn from and to help each other." Of the schools we surveyed, Dartmouth is the least cutthroat.

ACADEMICS

Since 1985, Dartmouth has been revising its curriculum to provide more small-group, problem-based learning in the basic sciences. Currently, over half of the courses are taught in seminar format. There is also an effort to increase integration of the preclinical and clinical years. For some students, this is welcome news. Comments one second-year student, "I have some complaints about the conservative curriculum, but many changes are going on and will improve the school dramatically within a few years."

In the new curriculum, first-year students investigate the basic sciences and psychosocial issues in medicine. A Clinical Exposure course introduces the doctor-patient relationship. The main course of the second year is Scientific Basis of Medicine, an interdisciplinary course that focuses on and correlates aspects of the basic sciences, disease, and clinical medicine. A psychiatry curriculum that explores scientific aspects of behavior is integrated with the Preparation for Clinical Medicine course. In addition to traditional clerkships, third- and fourth-year students are required to do a seven-week rotation in primary care. A large percentage of clerkships are done in an ambulatory setting. Over the two years, twelve to sixteen weeks are available for electives.

Overall, students are impressed by how much the faculty and administration "really care" and give them outstanding ratings for accessibility. Praise for the quality of teaching is not quite so emphatic, although the consensus is that it is generally good. Students are pleased with the emphasis professors put on the doctor-patient relationship, however. One reports, "The extreme clinical bent to just about every class we take has been a most pleasant surprise."

Considering the positive tone of comments about clinical experiences, the relatively low rating students gave the amount of early clinical exposure is surprising. Two factors may contribute to this disparity. First, students can choose a "Family Medicine Longitudinal Elective" which allows them to spend time with a physician preceptor throughout the basic science years. Since this experience is not required, not all students take the opportunity to have extensive "hands-on" experience. Second, some students object, "There is a strong family practice bent, but there are too few family practitioners on staff." Students who want extensive clinical exposure prior to third-year clerkships are advised to participate in the family medicine elective and available community service activities. Through these pursuits, one second-year student reports, "Opportunities to work with clinicians and patients are abundant, almost from day one of classes."

While students report being merely satisfied with the classroom, library, lab, and computer facilities at Dartmouth, they positively gush when they evaluate the new Dartmouth-Hitchcock Medical Center. Raves one, "Dartmouth-Hitchcock Medical Center is absolutely incredible—huge, brand-new, with cutting edge technology." Another goes on, "It's fantastic—there's nothing else even close to it anywhere. You have to see it to believe it."

Grading and Promotion Policy: Honors/High Pass/ Pass/Fail.

Additional Degree Programs: MD/Ph.D., MD/ MBA (5 or 6 years).

STUDENT LIFE

The noncompetitive atmosphere at Dartmouth, students say, makes it a great place to go to school. Cooperation among the classes is fostered by a "Big Sibs" peer counseling program in which second-year students help first-year students learn the ropes. Says one first-year student, "Big sibs are indispensable resources and friends." This interaction leads to generally excellent student relations, but there is some criticism of the lack of diversity in the student body.

Students agree that Dartmouth isn't exactly racially or ethnically diverse, but some go further in their criticism of Dartmouth's uniformity. Says one second-year student, "New Hampshire is one of the most homogeneous states in the country. Dartmouth very much reflects the community in which it's located. For white males, that may be considered a great thing. For the rest of us, it's not." Agrees another, "This place is steeped in East Coast conservatism. It is full of [instances of] the 'old boy network.'"

Students give their classmates high marks for being committed to and involved in community service and school activities. "The typical [Dartmouth student]," says one first-year student, "is the well-rounded individual." To blow off steam, they take advantage of the recreational opportunities afforded by the school's location. Reports one student, "We are very much engaged in outdoor activities. Skiing, ice skating, swimming, and rollerblading are common pastimes."

Dartmouth's geographic location and its small-town setting are two of the main reasons a lot of students say they applied. Despite its lack of some urban amenities, they give Hanover high marks: "Northern New England is absolutely beautiful year-round. The atmosphere is extremely relaxed both in the med school and in the community. It's highly conducive to studying, since there aren't many outside stresses." But students warn applicants to keep the rural setting in mind when considering Dartmouth. "Hanover is in the boonies; you shouldn't come here if you want to be in a big city."

ADMISSIONS

Although Dartmouth is a private school and there are, therefore, no residency requirements, the school is committed to "providing opportunities for residents of [New Hampshire] to study medicine." In addition to the four-year curriculum at Dartmouth, Dartmouth offers a joint program with Brown in which students spend the basic science years at Dartmouth and the clinical years at Brown. Of the entering class of eighty-four, twenty are admitted through the Brown-Dartmouth program.

In selecting students, Dartmouth "looks for individuals who will do well academically, enjoy the commitment to lifelong learning, communicate well with patients and colleagues, respect and uphold the role of the physician, and handle well the problem-solving and decision-making role of the physician, often in time-constrained and stressful environments." Dartmouth is one of the few schools that does not *require* the MCAT;

however, the test is waived only in unusual circumstances. Students applying to the Brown-Dartmouth program must take the MCAT. If the test is taken, it must be in the new format.

Special Programs for Members of Underrepresented minorities: Despite Dartmouth's claim that nine percent of its students are members of minorities, Dartmouth students gave the school poor marks for diversity. Minority applicants are encouraged to "identify themselves to the Admissions Office so that additional information can be forwarded." Among special programs Dartmouth offers to minority students are a pre-matriculation summer session and special consideration for admissions.

Transfer Policy: Transfers are accepted occasionally on a space-available basis and when there is a compelling reason for transfer.

FINANCIAL AID

Many students complain about the expense of attending Dartmouth. Including tuition, fees, and living expenses, the student budget tops $34,000. Although about 75 percent of students receive financial assistance, the average debt of a Dartmouth student is around $70,000.

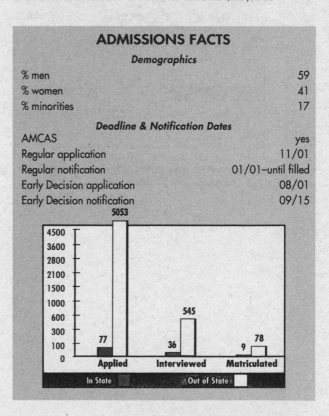

ADMISSIONS FACTS

Demographics

% men	59
% women	41
% minorities	17

Deadline & Notification Dates

AMCAS	yes
Regular application	11/01
Regular notification	01/01–until filled
Early Decision application	08/01
Early Decision notification	09/15

FIRST YEAR STATISTICS

Average GPA

Science	N/A	Nonscience	N/A

Average MCAT

Biology	N/A	Physical Science	N/A
Verbal	N/A	Essay	N/A

FINANCIAL FACTS

Tuition and Fees

In-state	$23,380	On-campus housing	N/A
Out-of-state	$23,380	Off-campus housing	N/A

Financial Aid

% receiving some aid	70
Merit scholarships	no
Average debt	$70,000

HITS AND MISSES

HITS	MISSES
Noncompetitive atmosphere	Diversity
Extracurricular involvement	Research
Safe campus	Classrooms
Beautiful location	On-campus housing
Faculty accessibility	

TUITION OVERVIEW

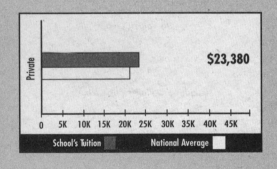

$23,380

0   5K   10K   15K   20K   25K   30K   35K   40K   45K

School's Tuition   National Average

UMDNJ:
New Jersey Medical School

185 South Orange Avenue, Newark, NJ 07103-4631
(201) 982-4631

OVERVIEW

In 1991, UMDNJ-NJMS introduced a revised curriculum. Features of the new program include greater clinical correlation in the basic science years, increased emphasis on behavioral, social, and environmental aspects of medicine, and earlier exposure to patient care.

ACADEMICS

Basic science instruction is arranged from cell to organism. In the first year, the focus is on the normal structure and functions of the human body, while the second year centers on the abnormal. Problem-based learning is employed in the first two years, helping students see the clinical relevance of scientific principles. Through a clinical skills program, freshmen and sophomores learn examination and evaluation skills. Students also get hands-on experience with patients through required office-based preceptorships. Beyond the mandatory courses, students have time for electives in the preclinical years, and many students use this opportunity to volunteer at the school's Student Family Health Care Clinic, which provides comprehensive care to medically underserved residents of Newark.

The clinical portion of the curriculum lasts the final two years, during which time students spend sixty-four of the eight-four total weeks in required clerkships. The remaining weeks are free for electives in which students may complete additional clerkships and preceptorships or pursue research in the basic or clinical sciences.

Grading and Promotion Policy: Honors/High Pass/ Pass/Fail. Students must take Parts I and II of the USMLE.

Additional Degree Programs: BS/MD (in conjunction with several undergraduate schools); MD/Ph.D.

STUDENT LIFE

NJMS has chapters of the major state and national medical associations. Although the offices of these and other organizations are located in the student lounge area of the Medical Science Building, students complain that there isn't much to do on campus. Things may be changing, though. The school is still working on developing campus recreational facilities. Currently, students who want to keep fit may use the gym at the Community Mental Health Center or can pay to use the athletic facilities at the nearby New Jersey Institute of Technology. For athletes looking for a real workout (or, perhaps, spectators looking for first-hand exposure to orthopedics and head trauma) the school offers a well-established rugby club that competes with teams from local colleges, rugby clubs, and other med schools.

There is no on-campus housing, but the Office of Student Affairs maintains a listing of rental units available off campus.

ADMISSIONS

NJMS gives preference to New Jersey residents, but between five and 10 percent of students can come from out of state. Nonresidents especially encouraged to apply are those with outstanding academic qualifications, women, and members of underrepresented minorities.

According to the Admissions Office, primary selection factors include science and nonscience GPA, MCAT scores, letters of recommendation, and the interview. Also considered important are extracurricular activities, exposure to the medical profession, and volunteer activities. Essays are not considered.

Special Programs for Members of Underrepresented Minorities: NJMS encourages members of underrepresented minorities to apply and has a minority affairs division to coordinate recruiting efforts and support services. Among its offerings are community outreach programs, summer sessions for high school and college students, a prematriculation summer session, academic advising, and peer counseling. These programs are also open to educationally and economically disadvantaged students.

Transfer Policy: Transfer applicants are considered when space is available.

FINANCIAL AID

Financial aid is awarded on the basis of need as determined by the GAPSFAS analysis. The primary source of assistance is long-term loans.

ADMISSIONS FACTS

Demographics

% men	62
% women	38
% minorities	20

Deadline & Notification Dates

AMCAS	yes
Regular application	12/15
Regular notification	10/15–until filled
Early Decision application	06/15–08/01
	(EDP for in-state residents only)
Early Decision notification	10/01

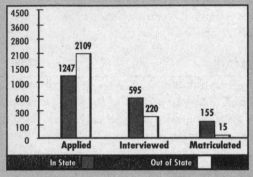

	Applied	Interviewed	Matriculated
In State	1247	595	155
Out of State	2109	220	15

In State   Out of State

FIRST YEAR STATISTICS

Average GPA

Science	N/A	Nonscience	3.35

Average MCAT

Biology	N/A	Physical Science	N/A
Verbal	N/A	Essay	N/A

FINANCIAL FACTS

Tuition and Fees

In-state	$13,033	On-campus housing	N/A
Out-of-state	$16,821	Off-campus housing	N/A

Financial Aid

% receiving some aid	70
Merit scholarships	no
Average debt	N/A

TUITION OVERVIEW

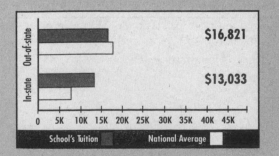

Out-of-state	$16,821
In-state	$13,033

0 5K 10K 15K 20K 25K 30K 35K 40K 45K

School's Tuition   National Average

UMDNJ:
Robert Wood Johnson
Medical School

Office of Admissions, 675 Hoes Lane, Piscataway, NJ 08854-5635
(908) 235-4576

OVERVIEW

Until it was renamed in 1986, UMDNJ-RWJ was called the UMDNJ-Rutgers Medical School, and basic science instruction is still carried out on the Rutgers University campus. After the preclinical years, students move to one of two clinical campuses located in New Brunswick or Camden. In accordance with the school's increasing emphasis on primary and ambulatory care, a combination of university hospitals, major clinical affiliates, and community-based facilities is used at both locations.

ACADEMICS

UMDNJ-RWJ's curriculum combines elements of the classical approach to medical education with a more modern, interdisciplinary style. Departmental and integrated basic science courses occupy much of the first two years, but students also study nonbiological aspects of health through behavioral science and environmental medicine courses. To show the clinical relevance of scientific material, the school incorporates a Clinical Correlations course into the first year; in this segment, students use case studies to identify and explore patient problems that relate to the concepts they learn in other coursework. There is, however, no direct patient contact in the first year.

Armed with their newly acquired knowledge of the body's normal structures and functions, sophomores shift their focus to the disease process and begin to make the transition from the basic to the clinical sciences. Although second-year students take other courses, the majority of their time is spent in an interdisciplinary pathology course and in Introduction to Clinical Medicine (ICM).

In ICM, students learn to obtain a medical history, perform a physical examination, and conduct and interpret lab tests. Teaching is done both in labs and at the bedside, and, by the end of the course, students are expected to be able to make fundamental diagnoses. The students we surveyed are pleased with the experiences they get through ICM, but say UMDNJ-RWJ takes too long to get them involved with patients. Complains one student, "RWJ needs to start clinical education in the first year!"

Although most students complete their clinical years at the Piscataway/New Brunswick RWJ University Hospital and its affiliates, about one-third of the junior class moves to Camden for training at the Cooper Hospital and other South Jersey clinical teaching sites. Requirements are essentially the same at both locations: students complete clerkships in the major disciplines, family medicine, neurology, and ambulatory medicine. About half of the fourth year is free for electives.

Overall, the students we surveyed say the quality of their educational experience is very good. They applaud the faculty for their teaching, research, and accessibility outside of the classroom. Enthusiasm extends to the school's computing facilities, which students rate as outstanding. The Kessler Teaching Laboratories, located in the Medical Science Complex at Piscataway, house new equipment for word processing, computer-assisted learning, and self-testing.

Grading and Promotion Policy: Honors/High Pass/Pass/Low Pass/Fail.

Additional Degree Programs: UMDNJ-RWJ offers a combined BS/MD in conjunction with Rutgers University. MD/Ph.D. and MD/MPH programs are also available.

Student Life

Although students say UMDNJ-RWJ's atmosphere is fairly competitive, they are positive about their relationships with their peers. Those we surveyed say they like to hang out with their classmates and—despite a heavy workload—find time for socializing. Several complained, however, that the school's lack of on-campus housing makes it a little difficult to get together with friends.

Medical clubs and organizations give students the opportunity to discuss professional issues, explore career options, and hang out with their classmates. Those who want to try out their newly acquired knowledge and skills can take part in the Bernard Kessler Student Volunteer Program. Through some of the community-service projects sponsored by this program, students can organize area blood drives, teach health-education seminars to children and teenagers, follow a woman through the various stages of her pregnancy, or help hearing-impaired patients secure medical care. For a break from academic and professional pursuits, students can take advantage of the social, cultural, and recreational offerings of Rutgers University.

Admissions

New Jersey residents are given preference in admissions, but between ten and fifteen percent of students can come from out of state. Although any interested candidate is invited to apply, most nonresidents who are accepted have exceptional qualifications. Since UMDNJ-RWJ has a rolling admissions policy, all candidates are encouraged to apply as early as possible.

According to admissions officials, "UMDNJ-Robert Wood Johnson seeks to admit a diverse class of students who have demonstrated excellence in their previous endeavors and who are committed to providing excellent health care and advancing scientific knowledge. We value a broad undergraduate education and we actively seek those who have demonstrated leadership qualities." Among other factors the Admissions Committee considers in making its selections are science and nonscience GPA, MCAT score, the interview, letters of recommendation, and essays.

Special Programs for Members of Underrepresented Minorities: The school's efforts to recruit and support traditionally underrepresented students are coordinated by a minority affairs division. Among its offerings are community outreach programs, summer sessions for college students, special consideration for admission, a prematriculation summer session, tutoring, and peer counseling.

Transfer Policy: Transfers into the second and third years are considered if a space becomes available through attrition.

Financial Aid

Most financial aid is awarded on the basis of documented need. Since there is a limited amount of grant money available, most awards consist of a combination of long-term loans. A few merit scholarships are available.

ADMISSIONS FACTS

Demographics

% men	63
% women	37
% minorities	24

Deadline & Notification Dates

AMCAS	yes
Regular application	12/15
Regular notification	10/15–until filled
Early Decision application	06/15–08/01
Early Decision notification	10/01

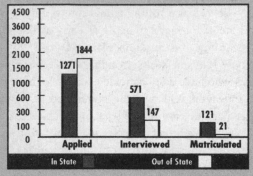

FIRST YEAR STATISTICS

Average GPA

Science	N/A	Nonscience	3.37

Average MCAT

Biology	N/A	Physical Science	N/A
Verbal	N/A	Essay	N/A

FINANCIAL FACTS

Tuition and Fees

In-state	$13,033	On-campus housing	none
Out-of-state	$16,821	Off-campus housing	N/A

Financial Aid

% receiving some aid	75
Merit scholarships	yes
Average debt	$50,300

HITS AND MISSES

HITS	MISSES
Diversity	Early clinical exposure
Student relations	Lack of on-campus housing
Computer labs	Public transportation
Research efforts	
Overall happiness	

TUITION OVERVIEW

$16,821

$13,033

School's Tuition   National Average

University of New Mexico School of Medicine

Office of Admissions, Basic Medical Sciences Building, Room 107,
Albuquerque, NM 87131-5166
(505) 277-4766

OVERVIEW

Much of University of New Mexico's reputation as a leader among comprehensive med schools stems from its innovative approach to medical education. Over the past several years, New Mexico has gradually revised its curriculum to emphasize problem-based instruction in the basic science years and to incorporate more ambulatory and community-based experiences in the clinical phase. Although students from all over the country are eager to take advantage of New Mexico's exciting curriculum and extremely low tuition, most nonresidents have little chance of getting in. So, unless you're from New Mexico, be ready to apply Early Decision and make sure you have a back-up choice.

ACADEMICS

New Mexico's progressive new curriculum, introduced in the fall of 1993 and scheduled to be fully implemented by 1997, reflects the national trend toward an active learning process. Innovations include a high degree of integration of the basic and clinical sciences, intensive early exposure to patients, extensive community-based learning experiences, peer teaching, and computer-assisted instruction. The school has also taken steps to ensure that students feel they are a part of the med school community. "Learning Families" that consist of small groups of students from each year, house officers, faculty, community physicians, and other health professions meet biweekly to provide support, discuss medical issues, and plan social functions.

New Mexico's curriculum is divided into three phases. Phase I comprises the first eighteen months of med school. During this time, instruction is structured around organ systems and incorporates biological, behavioral, and social perspectives. In addition to attending traditional lectures, students learn through laboratory exercises, seminars, and problem-based tutorials.

Exposure to clinical medicine in Phase I comes through skills workshops and a weekly continuity clinic.

At the end of the first year, students are required to spend one to three months in a clinical Practical Immersion Experience (PIE) either in a rural or urban community. About half of students' time in Phase I is reserved for electives.

Phase II begins in February of the second year and extends to December of the third year. In this period, students spend approximately twenty weeks working in an ambulatory setting and twenty weeks rotating through the major disciplines at inpatient facilities. Phase II students continue to meet in small-group tutorial sessions that integrate the basic and clinical sciences. Problems presented by patients seen during rotations serve as a learning base.

Phase III comprises the last fifteen months of medical school. During this time, students choose from clinical selectives in which they have substantial responsibility for patient care. A month-long community-based preceptorship is also required, in which students work alongside a primary care physician who serves as a mentor.

In addition to fulfilling basic science and clinical requirements, all students must present a scholarly or creative work prior to graduation.

Grading and Promotion Policy: Outstanding/Good/Satisfactory/Marginal/Unsatisfactory. Students must take Parts I and II of the USMLE.

Additional Degree Programs: MD/Ph.D.

STUDENT LIFE

Since the medical school is located on the north campus of the University of New Mexico, students can take advantage of the considerable resources of the University. The city also provides an outlet for students who need a break from studying. The greater Albuquerque metropolitan area is home to nearly a third of the state's population and offers numerous cultural and recreational opportunities. Housing is available in neighborhoods near the med school.

ADMISSIONS

First priority is given to New Mexico residents, but the school also participates in the Western Interstate Commission for Higher Education (WICHE). Through WICHE, residents of Alaska, Montana, and Wyoming are given special consideration. All nonresidents, including WICHE candidates, must apply through the Early Decision Program. Traditionally, only a small number of out-of-state applicants are accepted.

Although all state residents receive supplementary applications, only those nonresidents who are under serious consideration for admission will be asked for supplemental materials. According to the Admissions Office, the primary selection factors are the science and nonscience GPA, MCAT scores, the interview, and letters of recommendation. Exposure to the medical field, extracurricular activities, and volunteer work are also considered.

Special Programs for Members of Underrepresented Minorities: New Mexico encourages applications from members of underrepresented minorities and offers programs to recruit and support such students. Special offerings include community outreach programs, summer sessions for high school and college students, special consideration for admissions, a prematriculation summer session for accepted students, academic advising, and review classes for Part I of the USMLE.

Transfer Policy: Transfer students are accepted in cases in which there is a compelling need for students to attend med school in New Mexico.

FINANCIAL AID

New Mexico is among the least expensive U.S. med schools, but financial aid is available to those who show documented need. Most assistance is in the form of long-term loans, but after a student has borrowed a set amount—called a unit loan—he or she is eligible for scholarship funds.

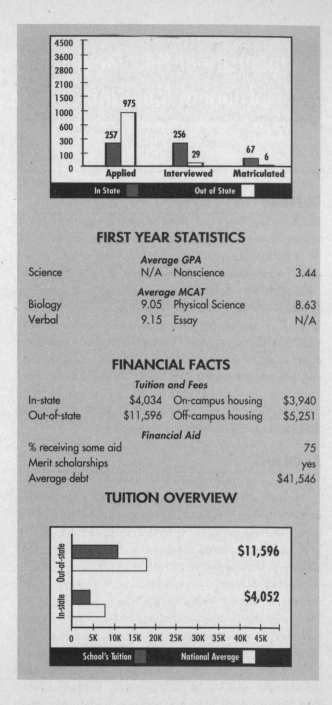

FIRST YEAR STATISTICS

	Average GPA		
Science	N/A	Nonscience	3.44
	Average MCAT		
Biology	9.05	Physical Science	8.63
Verbal	9.15	Essay	N/A

FINANCIAL FACTS

	Tuition and Fees		
In-state	$4,034	On-campus housing	$3,940
Out-of-state	$11,596	Off-campus housing	$5,251
	Financial Aid		
% receiving some aid			75
Merit scholarships			yes
Average debt			$41,546

TUITION OVERVIEW

ADMISSIONS FACTS

Demographics	
% men	31.5
% women	68.5
% minorities	29
Deadline & Notification Dates	
AMCAS	yes
Regular application	11/15
Regular notification	12/15–until filled
Early Decision application	06/15–08/01
(Nonresidents must apply through EDP)	
Early Decision notification	10/01

Albany Medical College

Office of Admissions, 47 New Scotland Avenue, Albany, NY 12208
(518) 445-5521

OVERVIEW

Founded in 1839, Albany Medical College is one of the oldest med schools in the U.S. The College and its main teaching hospital are combined into one complex, the Albany Medical Center. Major construction at the center has just been completed. New additions include a seven-story patient tower, an ambulatory care facility, an updated emergency department, and several surgery suites, including some designed specifically for open-heart surgery.

ACADEMICS

You should know ahead of time that Albany's curriculum is fairly traditional. In the first two years, students study the basic sciences that are the foundation for medical practice. Lectures, conferences, and lab sessions are the major modes of instruction, but patient presentations that highlight clinical correlations are also incorporated. In the freshman-year Focal Problems course, students investigate issues central to patient care. A sophomore Behavioral Science segment lends social and psychological perspectives. This means there's not a lot of interaction with patients early on, something many see as a drawback.

In the sophomore-year Introduction to Medicine and Physical Diagnosis courses, students learn fundamental communication, examination, and evaluation skills, and explore other aspects of clinical medicine. These courses also help ease the transition into the third- and fourth-year clerkships.

In their junior year, students complete required rotations at the Albany Medical Center Hospital and other affiliated clinical settings. Mandatory clerkships continue in the final year, but much of seniors' time is free for electives. With the help of an advisor, students may choose from a full range of offerings, including community preceptorships and research work.

For those of you interested in issues beyond the clinical, Albany encourages its students to get involved in research not only in their final year, but throughout med school. The summer between the freshman and sophomore year is a popular time to take part in on-going projects, and some stipends are available for such activities. Depending on their level of commitment to scientific investigation, Albany students may also pursue a combined MD/Ph.D. or work toward an MD with Distinction in Research.

Grading and Promotion Policy: Albany uses a modified Pass/Fail grading system. Students must take Parts I and II of the USMLE.

Additional Degree Programs: The med school offers a combined BS/MD program in conjunction with Rensselaer Polytechnic Institute and Union College. An MD/Ph.D. program is also available.

STUDENT LIFE

Students who need a break from their studies can find a lot to do on and around the campus. The med school sponsors an active student government, a student newspaper, and numerous academic, social, and cultural organizations. Athletes can practice their squash and tennis skills on the school's courts or join the rugby and crew teams.

Albany also offers plenty of diversions. New York's capital is a midsize town with many big-city amenities, including a ballet company, a symphony, and a minor league baseball team. Skiers and hikers find the location among the Berkshire, Catskill, and Adirondack mountains especially attractive. For those looking for a more cosmopolitan environment, Boston and New York are just a few hours away.

The Medical College provides suite-style housing for single students. Married students or others who prefer to make their own living arrangements can find plenty of rental units in the city.

ADMISSIONS

Although most students are residents of New York, Albany is a private school and welcomes applications from all interested candidates. Since the school has a rolling admissions policy, all students should apply as early as possible.

Final selections are made on the basis of qualitative and quantitative factors. Important selection factors include the interview, GPA, MCAT scores, letters of recommendation, extracurricular activities, work experience, exposure to the health care field, and motivation and suitability for the practice of medicine.

Special Programs for Members of Underrepresented Minorities: A minority affairs division coordinates efforts to recruit and support qualified minority students. A summer prematriculation session is available for admitted students.

Transfer Policy: Applications for transfer into the second or third year are evaluated on a case-by-case basis.

FINANCIAL AID

New York students get a slight break on tuition, but it is still relatively expensive to attend Albany. In addition to financial assistance based on demonstrated need, the college offers partial- and full-tuition merit scholarships.

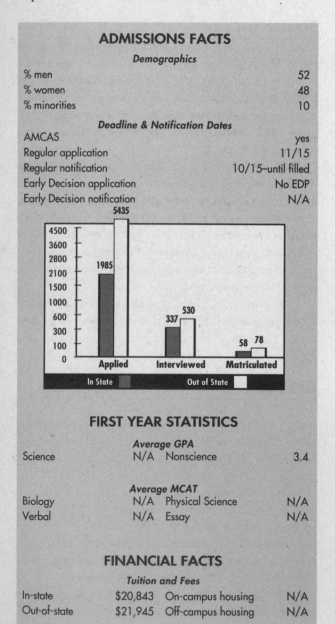

ADMISSIONS FACTS

Demographics

% men	52
% women	48
% minorities	10

Deadline & Notification Dates

AMCAS	yes
Regular application	11/15
Regular notification	10/15–until filled
Early Decision application	No EDP
Early Decision notification	N/A

FIRST YEAR STATISTICS

Average GPA

Science	N/A	Nonscience	3.4

Average MCAT

Biology	N/A	Physical Science	N/A
Verbal	N/A	Essay	N/A

FINANCIAL FACTS

Tuition and Fees

In-state	$20,843	On-campus housing	N/A
Out-of-state	$21,945	Off-campus housing	N/A

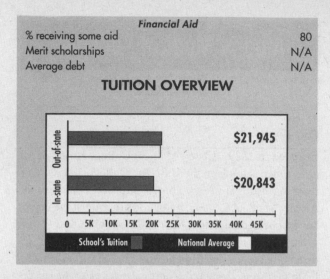

Financial Aid

% receiving some aid	80
Merit scholarships	N/A
Average debt	N/A

TUITION OVERVIEW

Out-of-state: $21,945
In-state: $20,843

School's Tuition · National Average

Albert Einstein College of Medicine of Yeshiva University

Office of Admissions, Jack and Pearl Resnick Campus,
1300 Morris Park Avenue, Bronx, NY 10461
(718) 430-2106

OVERVIEW

Albert Einstein College of Medicine is widely regarded as one of the nation's best medical schools. School officials describe the College as "a community in which students, faculty, and administrators share...the challenges of learning, teaching, providing clinical care to a diverse urban population, managing health care delivery systems, and exploring the newest vistas of biomedical research." By and large, students at Einstein agree with this description; teaching and research efforts get high marks, and the clinical facilities are rated as outstanding. If your academic credentials are strong enough for you to be competitive in a very selective admissions process, and you don't mind the intensity of living and working in the nation's largest city, you may want to look into what Einstein has to offer.

ACADEMICS

Einstein's curriculum is marked by organizational and instructional innovations. During the preclinical phase, which encompasses most of the first two years, students study the basic sciences mainly through traditional lectures, labs, and conferences. Since Einstein considers a multidisciplinary faculty important to students' understanding of the integrity of the biomedical foundations of medicine, much of the teaching is interdepartmental.

Freshmen investigate normal biological structures and functions in a series of science courses. Concurrently, they take Introduction to Clinical Medicine (ICM). ICM is not so much one course as a combination of modules which builds a foundation of skills and attitudes necessary in a competent, compassionate physician. Much of the instruction is carried out through seminars, small-group conferences, and experiences in clinical settings. A selective portion allows students to pursue their own interests and to have more hands-on contact with patients.

In the second year, students continue their study of the basic sciences, but shift their focus from the normal to the abnormal. The major science course in the sophomore year is an interdisciplinary, organ system-based study of Pathology and Physiology. The study of disease is integrated with clinical applications through the second segment of ICM. In the main component of the sophomore ICM, students expand on the history-taking and interviewing skills they developed in the first year and learn the fundamentals of physical examinations and diagnosis.

Prepared by their preclinical experiences, students enter the third-year clerkships. Juniors rotate though a variety of disciplines in both ambulatory and inpatient settings. Periodically, students meet in Human Values Groups in which they discuss and clarify their responses to their experiences with patients. Although there are a few requirements in the fourth year, seniors have six months of elective time. In this period, they may choose to complete advanced clerkships or participate in research projects.

Overall, students are pleased with the quality of teaching and say that professors are more than willing to help those who are having trouble keeping up in class. There is less enthusiasm for the methods of communicating material, however. "The speed of education and the expected rate of absorption of new information is too high," says one student. Another adds, "More problem-based learning would be better in the basic sciences. I hate the lecture, memorization, exam format." Although students may have some reservations about Einstein's choice of instructional methods in some classes, they have nothing but good things to say about Einstein's research efforts.

Einstein strongly encourages independent learning and a spirit of inquiry. For this reason, the school requires all students to pursue an in-depth study in some area of interest. This project can be based on a literature review, a clinical problem, or labwork.

Grading and Promotion Policy: In the basic science years, Honors/Pass/Fail; in the clinical years, Honors/High Pass/Pass/Low Pass/Fail.

Additional Degree Programs: MD/Ph.D.

STUDENT LIFE

In addition to the myriad opportunities afforded by Einstein's location in New York City, the school offers a variety of extracurricular activities. Among the College's unusual offerings is the Albert Einstein Symphony Orchestra, a performance group composed of students, house staff, and faculty. The Student Activities Committee sponsors a variety of academic, recreational, and cultural organizations and outings. Some activities are easy on the budget: sports fans can take advantage of complimentary tickets to Yankee and Mets games, while culture vultures may prefer discount tickets for theatrical and musical events. The college also recently opened an athletic center with a full range of facilities and services, including a swimming pool, squash courts, weight rooms, an indoor jogging track, and steam rooms.

In a city known for its extremely high cost of living, the College offers reasonably-priced housing. Most students live either in the on-campus Eastchester Road Residence or in the nearby Rhinelander Residence. Our respondents are satisfied with the studio, one-bedroom, and two-bedroom apartments that are available through the school; in fact, Einstein was one of the few schools we surveyed at which students prefer on-campus to off-campus housing. They are not enthusiastic about the area around the school, however. One student sums up the general opinion of his classmates: "Help me, I'm trapped! I hate the Bronx!"

ADMISSIONS

Einstein shows no preference for New York residents and welcomes applications from all interested candidates. Upon receipt of the AMCAS application, Einstein requests that each candidate submit supplemental information. On the basis of the completed application, the Admissions Committee invites promising candidates to interview.

GPAs, MCAT scores (from the new test), the interview, and letters of recommendation are weighed heavily in the selection process, but there are other important factors, as well. The Associate Dean for Admissions told us, " We also give great weight to students' non-academic activities.... This includes a broad array of scholarly projects, including research, and helping-caring activities for the community or individuals-in-need. We probably give greater weight to students with non-traditional backgrounds, i.e. students who are somewhat older, have been doing interesting things since graduating college and have had unusual life experiences that should make them better prepared for the study and practice of medicine."

Special Programs for Members of Underrepresented Minorities: Einstein strongly encourages members of underrepresented minorities to apply, and a minority affairs division coordinates recruitment and support programs. Among special offerings are community outreach programs, summer sessions for high school and college students, a prematriculation summer session for accepted students, academic advising, tutoring, and peer counseling.

Transfer Policy: Einstein does not accept transfers.
eMail: admissions@aecom.yu.edu

FINANCIAL AID:

Although most financial assistance is based on documented need, Einstein offers some merit scholarships.

ADMISSIONS FACTS

Demographics

% men	53
% women	47
% minorities	8

Deadline & Notification Dates

AMCAS	yes
Regular application	11/15
Regular notification	01/15–until filled
Early Decision application	06/15–08/01
Early Decision notification	10/01

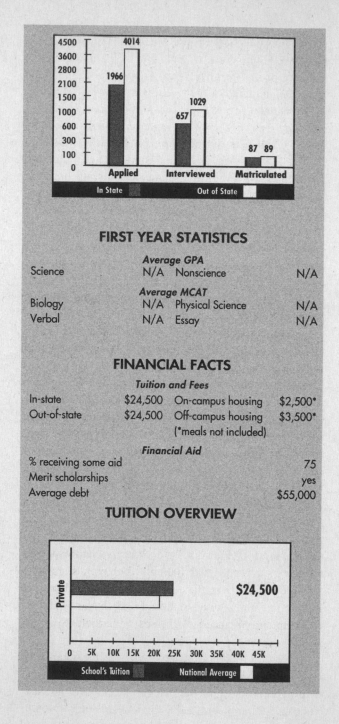

FIRST YEAR STATISTICS

	Average GPA		
Science	N/A	Nonscience	N/A

	Average MCAT		
Biology	N/A	Physical Science	N/A
Verbal	N/A	Essay	N/A

FINANCIAL FACTS

Tuition and Fees

In-state	$24,500	On-campus housing	$2,500*
Out-of-state	$24,500	Off-campus housing	$3,500*
		(*meals not included)	

Financial Aid

% receiving some aid	75
Merit scholarships	yes
Average debt	$55,000

TUITION OVERVIEW

Columbia University College of Physicians and Surgeons

Admissions Office, Room 1-416,
630 West 168th Street, New York, NY 10032
(212) 305-3595

OVERVIEW

The Columbia College of Physicians and Surgeons (P&S) is one of the oldest and most highly regarded U.S. med schools. Of the philosophy behind its approach to medical education, the school says, "The acquisition of knowledge and skills is important...but far more vital is a profound understanding of the science, the art, and the ethic within which both knowledge and skill are applied." Pretty high-minded stuff, but they actually back it all up with a diverse and thorough preparation in all aspects of the medical education. And all of this in that mecca of culture, New York City!

ACADEMICS

Freshmen and sophomores begin their medical education with a study of the basic sciences. There is considerable variety in the instructional methods of the preclinical years; lectures, labs, small group conferences, demonstrations and seminars are all widely used. In addition to basic science coursework, first-year students attend correlation clinics and explore economic, social, behavioral, and ethical issues in health care and health care delivery.

During the second year, there is an increased emphasis on the clinical relevance of basic scientific principles, and students begin to develop fundamental patient care skills. Physical examination and evaluation techniques are taught in a four-week clerkship at the end of the second year. This experience serves also as an introduction to the hospital setting and eases the transition into the third and fourth years. Throughout the preclinical phase, students may take electives to explore their particular interests.

The third year is composed of required clinical clerkships. In rotations through the various disciplines, juniors refine their history-taking, examination, and diagnostic skills and learn to work as part of the health care team.

Students continue their clinical experience in the final year. Although seniors must complete a one-month experience in ambulatory care, the majority of their time is reserved for electives. Up to three months may be spent at another med school and through the School of Public Health, students may arrange to study overseas.

Grading and Promotion Policy: Honors/Pass/Fail.

Additional Degree Programs: MD/Ph.D.; MD/MPH.

STUDENT LIFE

Extracurricular programs and events are coordinated by the P&S club, the school's main student organization. There's something for everyone, including academic and service projects, cultural outings, athletic events, and parties. The club also sponsors musical and other performance groups.

Outside the med school, students are faced with an almost overwhelming array of diversions. Whether you prefer museums, theater, sporting events, shopping, nightlife, or people watching, there's always something to do in "the city that never sleeps." Of course, living in New York isn't for everyone. For many, the drawbacks—most notably, congestion, crime, the extremely high cost of living and, of course, New Yorkers—outweigh the benefits.

Because affordable apartments are hard to find in the city, all single students who want to live on campus are guaranteed a room in Bard Hall, a high-rise dormitory-style residence. Inside the building is the Bard Athletic Club, a recently renovated facility that houses a pool, squash courts, exercise equipment, and saunas. One-, two-, and three-bedroom apartments are available in the other residence facility, the Bard Haven Towers, but most of these units are reserved for married students and upperclassmen.

ADMISSIONS

P&S shows no preference for residents of New York. Since the school does not participate in AMCAS, interested candidates can obtain applications directly from the school. A little less than half of the applicant pool was interviewed for admission to the 1992 entering class. Of these, about 13 percent were ultimately accepted and matriculated.

The interview, MCAT scores, the academic record, letters of recommendation, and extracurricular activities are among the most important selection factors. Personal qualities, including the evidence of a commitment to self-education, maturity, leadership, and motivation to study and practice medicine, are also considered.

Special Programs for Members of Underrepresented Minorities: P&S encourages qualified members of underrepresented minorities to apply.

Transfer Policy: Applications for transfer into the second or third years are considered on a space-available basis.

FINANCIAL AID

All financial aid is awarded on the basis of need. Students with need must borrow a standard sum (called a unit loan) before becoming eligible for scholarship funds. There are, however, some full-tuition scholarships for students who show a combination of need and extraordinary academic promise.

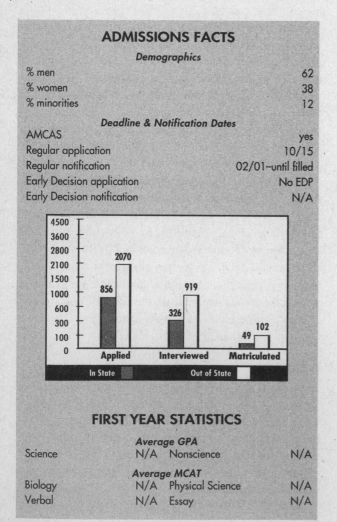

ADMISSIONS FACTS

Demographics

% men	62
% women	38
% minorities	12

Deadline & Notification Dates

AMCAS	yes
Regular application	10/15
Regular notification	02/01–until filled
Early Decision application	No EDP
Early Decision notification	N/A

	Applied	Interviewed	Matriculated
In State	856	326	49
Out of State	2070	919	102

FIRST YEAR STATISTICS

Average GPA

Science	N/A	Nonscience	N/A

Average MCAT

Biology	N/A	Physical Science	N/A
Verbal	N/A	Essay	N/A

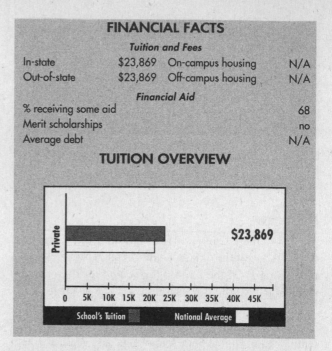

FINANCIAL FACTS

Tuition and Fees

In-state	$23,869	On-campus housing	N/A
Out-of-state	$23,869	Off-campus housing	N/A

Financial Aid

% receiving some aid	68
Merit scholarships	no
Average debt	N/A

TUITION OVERVIEW

$23,869

School's Tuition   National Average

Cornell University Medical College

Office of Admissions, 445 East 69th Street, New York, NY 10021
(212) 746-1067

OVERVIEW

Although its undergraduate division is located in Ithaca, Cornell's med school is located in the heart of New York City, a site which is extremely popular with the Cornell students we surveyed. Among other attractive features of this top-ranked school are an outstanding research effort, a prestigious faculty, terrific facilities, and a large array of extracurricular activities. The downside? The majority of our respondents say they are less than completely satisfied with the amount of clinical exposure they get in their first year.

ACADEMICS

Cornell boasts a recently revamped curriculum that includes more problem-based learning, less memorization, a greater emphasis on self-education, and fewer class hours. One of the most obvious results of Cornell's recent curricular revision is the large amount of free time in the basic science years. During unscheduled time, students can pursue independent study and augment formal coursework with electives.

The study of the basic sciences is the central focus of the preclinical years, but Cornell is placing increased emphasis on the clinical relevance of the scientific foundations. Small-group conference sessions serve to highlight clinical applications, and paper patients give students the opportunity to develop problem-solving and critical thinking skills. A parallel Clinical Curriculum lends behavioral, social, economic, and ethical perspectives.

In the sophomore year, a Physical Diagnosis segment teaches students patient-interaction skills such as history-taking, physical examination, and physical diagnosis. Instruction in this course is accomplished through lectures, demonstrations, and small-group clinical experiences. Basic science correlations are stressed throughout. Although students are generally pleased with the curriculum in the first two years, nearly all of our respondents say that they would like to have more opportunities to practice their developing skills on real patients.

After completing the first two years, students move on to the clinical phase of the curriculum. The junior year begins with an Introduction to the Clinical Years. In this course, students use case studies to develop their diagnostic skills and become acclimated to hospital procedures and settings. After this orientation, juniors complete fourty-eight weeks of clerkships in the major disciplines and in public health. These rotations are intended to give students a grounding in patient care and to provide exposure to the medical specialties.

At the end of the junior year, students plan their programs for the senior year. Although there are some requirements—including a one-month teaching or research assignment—seniors have considerable time for electives.

The quality of teaching is solid at Cornell, and students say professors do more than just bombard them with facts. "Instructors emphasize detail, but they really make you learn how to think critically. That's probably why they turn out such good doctors," says one student. In addition to the accolades they get for their teaching skill, members of the faculty also earn high marks for their accessibility outside of the classroom and their research activities.

Research is perceived as a major strength at Cornell, both by the medical community at large and the students who attend the school. Top-notch facilities help support investigative efforts; hospitals, labs, computing facilities, and the library are all rated as outstanding.

Grading and Promotion Policy: Honors/Pass/Fail

Additional Degree Programs: An MD/Ph.D. program is offered in conjunction with Rockefeller University and the Memorial Sloan-Kettering Cancer Center.

STUDENT LIFE

A substantial portion of Cornell students come from Ivy League schools, and some say this contributes to a moderately high level of competition among classmates. "Still," says one first year, "Students here aren't 'rocket science' types with no social skills. People get along well with one another." Although our respondents report that a heavy workload keeps them from being social butterflies, they report a very high degree of involvement in extracurricular and community activities. Perhaps that's because there's plenty to do at Cornell, both on and off campus. To foster professional development, the school sponsors chapters of the major national med student organizations. These groups and other special-interest clubs promote social, cultural, and recreational activities that are open to all students. A special Cultural Committee helps students secure discounted tickets to a variety of cultural events throughout the city. For those with less highbrow tastes, Cornell fields a rugby team that competes with clubs from other med schools.

But school activities are only a small part of the story. Cornell's location on the Upper East side of Manhattan provides more numerous and varied diversions than any med student could hope to sample in four years. According to our respondents, the school's site was a major factor in most students' decisions to apply and contributes greatly to the satisfaction they find in their med school experience. Of course, living in New York has its price.

Cornell addresses one of the city's major drawbacks–Manhattan's high cost of living. On-campus housing is guaranteed; while it may not be luxurious, it is inexpensive and, students say, more than adequate for their needs. Dormitory-style rooms go for about $265/ month, and the monthly rent per student of shared apartments is a little over $325. One of the residence buildings, Olin Hall, houses a gym, a student lounge, and a library. Accessible public transportation makes it easy to get around the city; most Cornell students consider New York's mass transit system to be nearly as safe as it is convenient.

ADMISSIONS

Since it is a private school, Cornell does not show preference to New York residents. All candidates are asked to submit supplementary materials after their AMCAS applications have been received. On the basis of the completed application, the Admissions Committee invites the most highly-qualified applicants to interview—usually about 25 percent of the total pool.

Since there is space in the first-year class for only about two percent of applicants, the selection process is extremely competitive. The Committee considers a host of factors in making its decisions. Of them, the interview, academic achievement, MCAT scores, letters of recommendation, and personal qualities are the most important. Only exceptionally-qualified candidates are encouraged to apply through the Early Decision Program.

Special Programs for Members of Underrepresented Minorities: Cornell subscribes to an equal opportunity philosophy and takes disadvantaged educational backgrounds into consideration in its admissions decisions. A Summer Fellowship Program for underrepresented minority students gives undergraduates the opportunity to explore their medical interests through coursework and research projects.

Transfer Policy: Applicants who wish to transfer into the second or third year will be considered if they are in good standing at accredited med schools and if there is space available.

FINANCIAL AID

Since Cornell offers no merit scholarships, all financial aid is awarded on the basis of documented need. Students are expected to meet most of their educational costs through loans. After they have borrowed a set amount (called a unit loan), Cornell will grant funds to cover unmet need.

ADMISSIONS FACTS

Demographics

% men	54
% women	46
% minorities	13

Deadline & Notification Dates

AMCAS	yes
Regular application	10/15
Regular notification	10/15–until filled
Early Decision application	06/15–08/01
Early Decision notification	10/01

Bar chart — In State / Out of State:
- Applied: 1319 (In State), 3983 (Out of State)
- Interviewed: 360 (In State), 846 (Out of State)
- Matriculated: 36 (In State), 65 (Out of State)

FIRST YEAR STATISTICS

Average GPA

Science	3.53	Nonscience	N/A

Average MCAT

Biology	10.5	Physical Science	10.5
Verbal	10.5	Essay	N/A

FINANCIAL FACTS

Tuition and Fees

In-state	$22,050	On-campus housing	N/A
Out-of-state	$22,500	Off-campus housing	N/A

Financial Aid

% receiving some aid	65
Merit scholarships	no
Average debt	N/A

HITS AND MISSES

HITS	MISSES
Research efforts	Early clinical exposure
Clinical facilities	Off-campus housing
Science labs	
Library	
Computer Labs	
Plenty of activities	
Extracurricular involvement	
New York	

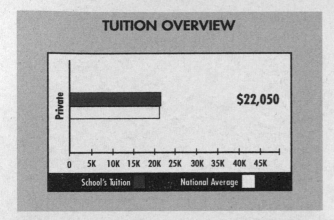

TUITION OVERVIEW

Private

$22,050

0 5K 10K 15K 20K 25K 30K 35K 40K 45K

School's Tuition   National Average

Mount Sinai School of Medicine of the CUNY

Director of Admissions, Annenberg Bldg. Room 5-04,
One Gustave L. Levy Place, Box 1002, New York, NY 10029-6574
(212) 241-6696

OVERVIEW

Yet another school in the middle of exciting New York City. So what makes this one stand out? Asked what he'd like to tell students about Mount Sinai, an Admissions official quoted the med school dean: "We are committed to providing...education that equips students not only with knowledge, but with the skills, values, and attitudes you will need throughout your professional careers. Our programs are based on the concept that the retention of facts is only one step in the learning process which emphasizes using those facts to solve the diverse problems encountered in a career in medicine. As a consequence, a very special type of teaching is a major priority at Mount Sinai. We increasingly emphasize small group seminars that stimulate creative thinking and encourage students to explore complex links between apparently dissimilar events." Recent curricular revisions fit into a long-standing spirit of innovation at Mt. Sinai.

ACADEMICS

Although Mt. Sinai's curriculum is divided along the usual preclinical and clinical lines, the school has made some recent improvements. Says the assistant dean for student affairs, "The educational process includes programs offered at few other schools, such as multi-disciplinary laboratories, interactive computer-assisted learning, and a standardized patient program." There is also a strong emphasis on the integration of the basic and clinical sciences.

During the first two years, students spend much of their time in departmental and multidisciplinary science courses. Interdisciplinary courses are structured around organ systems and include significant clinical correlations. In addition, freshmen and sophomores investigate social and ethical issues in medicine and begin to acquire fundamental clinical skills. An innovative method of instructing students in clinical care gives students the chance to practice their "bedside manner" in the school's new Morchand Center for Clinical Competence. At the center, students take histories from and examine surrogate patients who, in turn, evaluate students' efforts and offer advice.

The curriculum in the first two years has been revised to include significant time for electives. Students may take electives at the medical school or at the undergraduate and graduate divisions of the branches of the City University of New York system.

In the third and fourth years, students complete clinical clerkships in both inpatient and ambulatory settings. Among other requirements is a rotation in Geriatric Medicine. Some of the junior year and most of the senior year are reserved for electives. During this time, students are free to pursue advanced clinical experiences or complete research in the basic or clinical sciences.

Grading and Promotion Policy: In the basic sciences, Mt. Sinai uses an anonymous Pass/Fail grading system. In the Clinical years, Honors/Pass/Fail is used. Students must pass Parts I and II of the USMLE.

Additional Degree Programs: Mt. Sinai offers a combined BS/MD in conjunction with the City Colleges of New York. An MD/Ph.D. program is also available.

STUDENT LIFE

The Recreation Office and the Student Relations Committee coordinate Mt. Sinai's many activities. While there are numerous campus organizations and events, much of students' extracurricular life is centered around the wide array of cultural, recreation, and social offerings of the nation's largest city.

In recognition of students' tight budgets, the Recreation Office provides free or low-priced tickets to a range of events, including theater, operas, concerts, and movies. Students concerned about their physical, as well as their intellectual, development during med school can take advantage of free memberships at the local YMHA or YWHA.

Mt. Sinai also makes an effort to ease the financial strain of living in Manhattan. The school offers dorm-style rooms and standard apartments for single and married students at costs significantly lower than the New York standard.

ADMISSIONS

Mt. Sinai shows no preference for residents of New York and welcomes applications from any interested student. Since the school has a rolling admission policy, candidates should submit their applications as early as possible. When the Admissions Committee receives the AMCAS application, it asks the student to submit supplementary materials. Promising candidates are then invited to campus for a pair of personal interviews.

According to the assistant dean of admissions, the primary selection factors are the interview, the science and nonscience GPA, MCAT scores, letters of recommendation, and essays. Extracurricular activities, volunteer work, and exposure to the medical field are also considered.

Special Programs for Members of Underrepresented Minorities: Mt. Sinai encourages members of underrepresented minorities to apply and offers a number of special programs to recruit and support students. Among these offerings are community outreach programs, summer sessions for high school and college students, a prematriculation summer session, academic advising, tutoring, peer counseling, and review classes for Parts I and II of the USMLE.

Transfer Policy: Applications for transfer into the third-year class are considered on a space-available basis.

FINANCIAL AID

Financial aid is awarded on the basis of need. The school offers assistance in the form of loans, scholarships, grants, and work-study.

ADMISSIONS FACTS

Demographics

% men	47
% women	43
% minorities	11

Deadline & Notification Dates

AMCAS	yes
Regular application	11/01
Regular notification	11/15–until filled
Early Decision application	06/15–08/01
Early Decision notification	10/01

	Applied	Interviewed	Matriculated
In State	1500	430	74
Out of State	2229	375	41

FIRST YEAR STATISTICS

Average GPA

Science	N/A	Nonscience	3.5

Average MCAT

Biology	N/A	Physical Science	N/A
Verbal	N/A	Essay	N/A

FINANCIAL FACTS

Tuition and Fees

In-state	$21,825	On-campus housing	N/A
Out-of-state	$21,825	Off-campus housing	N/A

Financial Aid

% receiving some aid	75
Merit scholarships	no
Average debt	$69,000

TUITION OVERVIEW

$21,825

| School's Tuition | National Average |

New York Medical College

Office of Admissions, Room 127, Sunshine Cottage, Valhalla, NY 10595
(914) 993-4507

OVERVIEW

Students at New York Medical College (NYMC) spend their first two, basic science years at the school's campus in Westchester county. Clinical teaching is done in the school's numerous affiliated hospitals, including major Catholic Church-sponsored facilities in New York City. The wide range of clinical settings expose NYMC students to a culturally and economically diverse patient base.

ACADEMICS

Students spend their first two years investigating the sciences basic to medicine. Many courses are interdisciplinary, and instructors place considerable emphasis on the clinical relevance of scientific material. Although lectures are used extensively, other more engrossing and interactive teaching methods—such as labs, small-group tutorials, seminars, and demonstrations—are also employed. Five weeks at the end of the first year are devoted to a Behavioral Science course. During the mornings in this period, freshmen attend lectures that highlight psychiatric and sociological issues. In the afternoons, students have their first extensive patient contact; in small groups, students learn fundamental communication and interaction skills by interviewing patients and their families. Relevant social and emotional practice-related issues, such as death and dying and medical ethics, are explored through panel discussions. The first-year curriculum also allows time for electives.

The main course in the second year is an interdisciplinary study of pathology and physiology. Through lectures, demonstrations, tutorials, externships, and self-directed learning, students investigate abnormal structures and functions. Pharmacology, Microbiology, and a year-long Clinical Skills course are also required. In Clinical Skills, students expand on their first-year experiences in history-taking and interviewing and learn to conduct a thorough physical examination, to make fundamental diagnoses, and to communicate their findings.

NYMC uses a lottery system to assign third-year students to clerkships at one of its affiliated hospitals. During rotations in the major disciplines, juniors are expected to refine their clinical skills and to function as part of the health care team. In addition to learning at the bedside during "rounds," students integrate the basic and clinical sciences through lectures, tutorials, seminars, and conferences. The fourth year consists of three months of required clinical experiences and five months of electives.

Grading and Promotion Policy: Honors/Pass/Fail. Students must pass Part I of the USMLE.

Additional Degree Programs: MD/Ph.D.

STUDENT LIFE

In addition to medically-oriented organizations and activities, NYMC sponsors on-campus events for its students, including parties, dances, picnics, and happy hours. The campus and surrounding area provide plenty of opportunities for the active set: golf, tennis, skating, horseback riding, skiing, and hiking are all readily accessible. Although students can find things to do in the suburban Westchester area, those looking for a wide range of cultural events and an active nightlife can make the trip into New York City.

NYMC offers a residence hall that features dorm-style rooms and on-site recreational facilities. Also available are a small number of one- and two-bedroom apartments. Both complexes are located within walking distance of the campus.

ADMISSIONS

NYMC is a private institution and shows no preference for New York residents. All students who apply through AMCAS are asked to submit additional information, but only highly qualified candidates—usually a little under forty percent of the total applicant pool—are invited to interview. According to the students we surveyed at other schools, some NYMC interviewers asked a lot of personal questions, especially about relationships with significant others. Be prepared, especially if you're a woman.

Selection factors include GPAs, MCAT scores, the interview, letters of recommendation, intellectual curiosity, maturity, integrity, and the motivation to practice medicine. Exceptionally qualified students for whom NYMC is the first choice are encouraged to apply through the Early Decision Program. And if you're not accepted through EDP, you can be reconsidered in the regular admissions process.

Special Programs for Members of Underrepresented Minorities: An Office of Minority Affairs coordinates NYMC's efforts to recruit and support underrepresented minority students. Among recruitment offerings is a summer training program for undergraduates. The school also offers a combination scholarship/loan program for minority students who demonstrate both academic promise and financial need.

Transfer Policy: Transfers are considered on a case-by-case basis.

FINANCIAL AID

Most financial aid is awarded on the basis of documented need. In addition to regular loan and scholarship programs, NYMC coordinates a number of service-obligated loans and scholarships. The school's brochure provides an excellent description of available assistance.

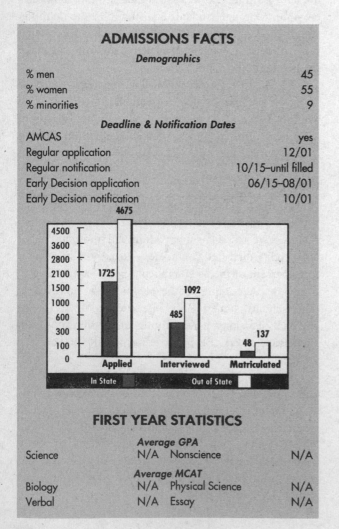

ADMISSIONS FACTS

Demographics

% men	45
% women	55
% minorities	9

Deadline & Notification Dates

AMCAS	yes
Regular application	12/01
Regular notification	10/15–until filled
Early Decision application	06/15–08/01
Early Decision notification	10/01

FIRST YEAR STATISTICS

Average GPA

Science	N/A	Nonscience	N/A

Average MCAT

Biology	N/A	Physical Science	N/A
Verbal	N/A	Essay	N/A

FINANCIAL FACTS

Tuition and Fees

In-state	$24,565	On-campus housing	N/A
Out-of-state	$24,565	Off-campus housing	N/A

Financial Aid

% receiving some aid	85
Merit scholarships	N/A
Average debt	N/A

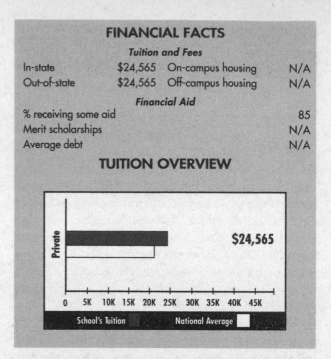

New York University School of Medicine

Office of Admissions, P.O. Box 1924, New York, NY 10016
(212) 263-5290

OVERVIEW

Although NYU hesitates to label its approach to medical education—fussily complaining that such categorizations are often nothing more than "esoteric pedagogical shop talk," its course bulletin describes its curriculum as "correlative." NYU explains, "the basic structure of the classical system is followed but, when possible, relationships among the disciplines are reviewed, stressed, and restressed." Translation: basic science material is still conveyed, in part, through lectures and labs, but NYU seeks integration among the sciences and between biological principles and clinical practice.

ACADEMICS

Though you may see some integration, for the most part the curriculum remains rigidly traditional. First-year students study normal structures and functions, investigate the clinical relevance of molecular and cellular biology, and explore psychological, sociological, and ethical aspects of medicine. Courses are interdisciplinary, and a variety of teaching methods, including self-directed learning, are employed.

Sophomores turn their attention to the abnormal human structures and functions; the major course in the second year is Pathology. Students spend some of their time in lectures, but small group conferences, problem-based learning, lab work, and clinical correlations are also emphasized. Coordinated with Pathology and other science courses are "Medical Seminars" that serve as introductions to the practice of medicine. In these seminars, students apply their knowledge of physiology and pathology to clinical case studies. Sophomores also learn the fundamentals of history-taking, physical examination, and diagnosis.

After the two-year preclinical period, students begin a series of Core Clerkships and Clinical Electives. Juniors and seniors complete rotations in the traditional disciplines, but ambulatory care experiences in each area are also required. While most of the instruction is "bedside," NYU continues to emphasize the connection between the basic and clinical sciences though seminars, conferences, demonstrations, lectures, and correlation discussions.

Students who want more in-depth work in the sciences may choose to participate in the Honors Program. Under this option, students spend about 10 percent of their four years in laboratory work, with most research completed in the summer between freshman and sophomore year. In addition to opportunities to work in the labs, Honors students can attend enrichment lectures that cover important aspects of the basic, clinical, and behavioral sciences.

Grading and Promotion Policy: Pass/Fail, letter, and numerical grading systems are used.

Additional Degree Programs: MD/Ph.D.

STUDENT LIFE

Studying is only part of med school. NYU students have a multitude of on-and off-campus extracurricular opportunities. The med school has its own recreational facilities, including basketball and paddleball courts. For those looking for a wider range of fitness services and activities, the Washington Square campus's Sports Center is just a short distance away. If athletics aren't your style, you can take in a free movie at the med school's weekly film festival. Or, of course, you can venture off campus.

NYU's location offers outstanding cultural and entertainment opportunities. The well-established Student Activities Program, which provides complementary and discounted tickets for the opera, theater, ballet and other attractions, makes taking advantage of many of these diversions easy on a med student's usually-strained finances.

The school also tries to mitigate living costs by providing affordable on-campus housing. Several styles of apartments are available, but new students are encouraged to look for a place as early as possible after acceptance.

ADMISSIONS

NYU does not state a preference for in-state students, nor does it participate in AMCAS. To apply to NYU, write or call the admissions office to request materials. In addition to the completed application, candidates are asked to submit transcripts from all undergrad and graduate schools they attended and to secure recommendations from their premedical committees or faculty members. Promising candidates—traditionally between one-fourth and one-third of the entire applicant pool—are invited to interview.

The Admissions Committee makes its final decisions on the basis of qualitative and quantitative factors. Important considerations include the interview, GPA, MCAT scores, letters of recommendation, and personal qualities.

Special Programs for Members of Underrepresented Minorities: NYU encourages members of underrepresented minorities to apply.

Transfer Policy: Applications for transfer into the third year are considered on a space-available basis. Applicants must be in good standing at accredited U.S. med schools.

FINANCIAL AID

Financial aid is awarded on the basis of demonstrated need. Although most of the assistance is in the form of loans, students with exceptional need are eligible to apply for scholarships.

ADMISSIONS FACTS

Demographics

% men	60
% women	40
% minorities	5

Deadline & Notification Dates

AMCAS	no
Regular application	12/01
Regular notification	12/20–08/30
Early Decision application	No EDP
Early Decision notification	N/A

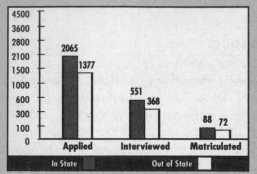

Applied: In State 2065, Out of State 1377
Interviewed: In State 551, Out of State 368
Matriculated: In State 88, Out of State 72

FIRST YEAR STATISTICS

Average GPA

Science	N/A	Nonscience	N/A

Average MCAT

Biology	N/A	Physical Science	N/A
Verbal	N/A	Essay	N/A

FINANCIAL FACTS

Tuition and Fees

In-state	$23,160	On-campus housing	N/A
Out-of-state	$23,160	Off-campus housing	N/A

Financial Aid

% receiving some aid	N/A
Merit scholarships	N/A
Average debt	N/A

TUITION OVERVIEW

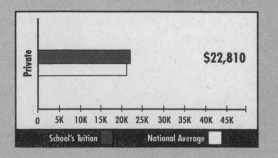

Private: $22,810

School's Tuition / National Average

University of Rochester School of Medicine and Dentistry

Office of Admissions, Medical Center Box 601
Rochester, NY 14642-8601
(716) 275-4539

OVERVIEW

Do you fear the MCAT? (Who doesn't?) Well, here's an alternative. One of the very few schools that doesn't require the MCAT, Rochester may be a good option for an applicant with a solid GPA but a fear of standardized tests. But even if you have top scores, Rochester has much to offer: it recently adopted a progressive curriculum that stresses integrated, multidisciplinary teaching and early clinical exposure.

ACADEMICS

Rochester's curriculum was revised in 1985 and is under continuous evaluation. Although the first two years are primarily geared to the acquisition of scientific knowledge, Rochester updates traditional preclinical education with alternative teaching methods, clinical correlations, and emphasis on ethical and psychosocial issues. Much of the instruction comes through interdisciplinary courses and case studies. During the second year, students focus on the mechanisms of disease and their effects on patients. In Introduction to Physical Diagnosis, students develop interaction, examination, and evaluation skills and work with a variety of patients. Both first- and second-year students have the opportunity to take electives.

The third year begins with a general clerkship, followed by required rotations in the major disciplines. Fourth-year students finish their mandatory clerkships and spend half a day per week in an ambulatory-care preceptorship. A significant portion of the senior year is elective. All students must complete an independent study project to graduate.

Grading and Promotion Policy: Rochester uses three grading systems: Satisfactory/Fail; Honors/Satisfactory/Fail; and Honors/Good/Satisfactory/Poor/Fail.

Additional Degree Programs: MD/MS, MD/Ph.D.

STUDENT LIFE

Med students have access to the resources of the undergraduate division of the university and participate in its educational, cultural, and recreation programs. Although it's not on the main campus, the medical school is just a short walk away.

Rochester is a good place for those who like the outdoors. Lake Ontario and the Finger Lakes provide opportunities for fishing, boating, and other water sports. Of the town itself, the school's bulletin says, "With a flavor and appeal all its own, it has been rated among the East's most livable cities: small and clean enough to be comfortable, but large and cosmopolitan enough to afford a variety of diversions, whether tastes run to symphony orchestras and jazz concerts, planetariums and museums, or sports."

ADMISSIONS

No preference is given to residents of New York; instead, the school seeks to admit a geographically diverse student body. Applications from nontraditional students are welcome.

Since Rochester doesn't participate in AMCAS, interested students should get application materials directly from the school. Although the MCAT is not required, candidates who have taken the test for other schools are asked to submit their scores. Among the selection factors the Admissions Committee considers are academic achievement, including the level and breadth of coursework; exposure to the medical field; extracurricular activities; and personal qualities.

Special Programs for Members of Underrepresented Minorities: The Office of Minority Affairs coordinates the school's efforts to recruit, admit, and educate underrepresented minority students. Among its offerings are several summer research programs for college students, a prematriculation summer session, and an Academic Careers Development Program.

Transfer Policy: Transfers are not normally accepted, but exceptions may be made in unusual cases.

FINANCIAL AID

Financial aid is awarded on the basis of need as determined by the GAPSFAS analysis. Students must meet a portion of that need through a unit loan, after which Rochester will supply scholarship assistance to make up the balance.

ADMISSIONS FACTS

Demographics

% men	52
% women	48
% minorities	14

Deadline & Notification Dates

AMCAS	yes
Regular application	10/15
Regular notification	01/15–until filled
Early Decision application	No EDP
Early Decision notification	N/A

Bar chart. In State / Out of State

- Applied: 900 / 1731
- Interviewed: 259 / 407
- Matriculated: 39 / 59

FIRST YEAR STATISTICS

Average GPA

Science	N/A	Nonscience	N/A

Average MCAT

Biology	N/A	Physical Science	N/A
Verbal	N/A	Essay	N/A

FINANCIAL FACTS

Tuition and Fees

In-state	$22,810	On-campus housing	N/A
Out-of-state	$22,810	Off-campus housing	N/A

Financial Aid

% receiving some aid	80
Merit scholarships	N/A
Average debt	N/A

TUITION OVERVIEW

Private: $22,810

School's Tuition / National Average

SUNY Health Science Center at Brooklyn: College of Medicine

Office of Admissions, 450 Clarkson Avenue-Box 60M,
Brooklyn, NY 11203-2098
(718) 270-2446

OVERVIEW

The largest of the State University of New York medical schools, SUNY Brooklyn admits approximately 230 students each year. Students spend their preclinical years taking classes at the Basic Sciences Building in Brooklyn and spend their clinical period doing rotations at the university hospital, the Kings County Hospital, and several other patient-care settings.

ACADEMICS

SUNY Brooklyn's fairly traditional curriculum has been updated by the incorporation of elective time into three of the four years. In the preclinical phase, students spend most of their time studying the basic sciences. Each week in this period, students have one afternoon free to pursue experiences that relate to their own interests.

During the second year, students begin to make the transition to clinical medicine. The relevance of the basic sciences to patient problems is highlighted in clinical correlation sessions. Sophomores also begin to learn to take thorough medical histories, perform physical examinations, conduct and interpret lab tests, and make fundamental physical diagnoses.

The second-year preclinical experiences help students prepare for the third-year clerkships. Juniors complete rotations in six major disciplines. Although requirements continue into the fourth year, twenty weeks are reserved for electives. During this time, students may participate in experiences in the basic, behavioral, and clinical sciences and may engage in research activities.

Grading and Promotion Policy: Honors/Pass/Fail.

Additional Degree Programs: SUNY Brooklyn offers an eight-year BS/MD program in conjunction with the Sophie Davis School of the City College of New York. A combined MD/Ph.D. is also available, and the school is in the process of developing an MD/MPH program.

ADMISSIONS

Even though SUNY Brooklyn is state-supported and therefore shows a preference for New York residents, out-of-state students make up a portion of each year's entering class. Although any interested out-of-staters may submit an application, the Admissions Office especially encourages students with outstanding qualifications, women, children of alumni, and members of underrepresented minorities to apply.

There are several ways to apply to the med school. High school students may apply through the eight-year BS/MD program; sophomores attending the Sophie Davis School of the City College of New York may seek early assurance of admission to the med school; and other applicants may apply though the regular or Early Decision programs. Highly-qualified candidates are invited to interview at the College of Medicine.

Among the selection factors the Admissions Committee considers most important are GPA, MCAT scores (from the new format test), the interview, letters of recommendation, essays, character, and motivation.

Special Programs for Members of Underrepresented Minorities: SUNY Brooklyn's Minority Affairs division coordinates recruitment and support programs for members of underrepresented minorities. Among its offerings are community outreach programs, a summer prematriculation program, academic advising, tutoring, peer counseling, and review sessions for Part I of the USMLE. In addition, first-year minority students are paired with a faculty member who serves as a mentor throughout their medical education.

Transfer Policy: Applications for transfer from students in good standing at U.S. or foreign medical schools are considered on a case-by-case basis.

FINANCIAL AID

Most financial aid is awarded on the basis of need as determined by the College Scholarship Service analysis and is primarily in the form of long-term student loans. New York residents may be able to augment federal assistance with funding from the state's Tuition Assistance Program.

ADMISSIONS FACTS

Demographics

% men	65
% women	35
% minorities	13

Deadline & Notification Dates

AMCAS	yes
Regular application	12/15
Regular notification	10/15–until filled
Early Decision application	06/15–8/01
Early Decision notification	10/01

Bar chart — Applied, Interviewed, Matriculated (In State / Out of State):
- Applied: 2343 (In State), 2213 (Out of State)
- Interviewed: 821 (In State), 225 (Out of State)
- Matriculated: 178 (In State), 22 (Out of State)

FIRST YEAR STATISTICS

Average GPA

Science	N/A	Overall	N/A

Average MCAT

Biology	N/A	Physical Science	N/A
Verbal	N/A	Essay	N/A

FINANCIAL FACTS

Tuition and Fees

In-state	$8,670	On-campus housing	N/A
Out-of-state	$17,320	Off-campus housing	N/A

Financial Aid

% receiving some aid	N/A
Merit scholarships	N/A
Average debt	N/A

TUITION OVERVIEW

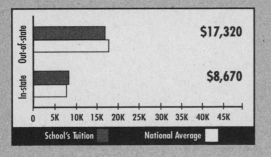

Out-of-state: $17,320
In-state: $8,670

(School's Tuition / National Average)

SUNY Buffalo School of Medicine and Biomedical Sciences

Office of Medical Admissions
CFS Building, Rm. 35, Buffalo, NY 14214-3013
(716) 829-3465

OVERVIEW

Recognized as one of the leading comprehensive U.S. med schools, SUNY Buffalo has a strong commitment to "combining the elements of scientific preparation with an appreciation for the patient as a human being." Early clinical exposure, an emphasis on family medicine, and a diversified patient base are notable features of the school. But research is also gaining prominence. The construction of a modern research building is evidence of the SUNY Buffalo's pledge to "provide an academic environment capable of preparing students...as biomedical scientists and teachers." While snow and boredom are big parts of life in Buffalo, the challenge of the studies and the high caliber of the students with whom you will associate can provide a powerful lure.

ACADEMICS

In the first two years, students study the basic sciences and build clinical foundations for the practice of medicine. They study not only science but also the psychological, social, and economic determinants and effects of disease. Although lectures remain a major method of instruction, laboratory exercises and small-group conferences lend variety. Some required and elective courses are taught by a multidisciplinary faculty.

One of the strengths of SUNY Buffalo's curriculum is that it provides early and extensive clinical exposure. Beginning in the first year, students have biweekly sessions with physician preceptors. These on-going experiences give students hands-on contact with patients and allow them to investigate and discuss the practical applications of their scientific training. During the first two years, students also learn the rudiments of history-taking, physical examinations, and physical diagnosis. Elective opportunities allow freshmen and sophomores to augment their formal coursework with in-depth study in the basic, clinical, computer, and behavioral sciences.

After a summer break (during which some students choose to do research), the clinical clerkships begin. Among the junior year requirements are eleven weeks of Internal Medicine; seven weeks each of surgery, obstetrics/gynecology, and psychiatry; four weeks of a surgery specialty or family medicine; and a one-week selective in basic science–clinical science correlations. Lectures, demonstrations, group conferences, and ward rounds complement bedside teaching. With the help of faculty advisors, students plan their fourth year course of study.

Grading and Promotion Policy: Honors/High Satisfactory/Satisfactory/Unsatisfactory. Students must pass Part I of the USMLE.

Additional Degree Programs: SUNY Buffalo offers a combined BS/MD program to which students from any undergraduate school may apply during their sophomore year. The med school also offers a combined MD/Ph.D.

STUDENT LIFE

The first year begins with an orientation week. During this "get-acquainted period," students from all four years take part in a variety of activities, including a school-wide picnic and athletic competition. Don't worry if you're not an athlete; the whole point is for students to work together. Cooperation among the classes is further fostered by an advising/support network in which two members from each class are teamed with at least two faculty members.

To break the monotony of their studies, SUNY Buffalo students pursue numerous extracurricular activities. Polity, the med school's student government, coordinates social, political, and academic events. Performers may be interested in participating in the annual talent show, Medical School Follies, or the school's *a cappella* singing group. Community service projects, sponsored by med student associations, give students an opportunity to put their developing medical skills to use. Those who seek recreational opportunities won't be disappointed, either; a ski club, intramural sports teams, and fitness facilities give athletes the chance to play as hard as they work.

ADMISSIONS

SUNY Buffalo shows a strong preference for New York residents, but up to four percent of students can come from out of state. In order to be competitive, nonresidents should have GPAs of 3.5 or above and a composite MCAT of 30 or better. The Admissions Office especially encourages nonresident members of underrepresented minorities and children of alumni to apply.

Although the Admissions Committee uses no stringent cutoffs in their decisions, GPAs and MCAT scores (from the new test) are important selection factors. Other considerations are the interview, letters of recommendation, essays, exposure to the medical field, extracurricular activities, and volunteer work. Like most other schools, SUNY Buffalo encourages undergraduates to pursue a well-rounded liberal arts education while satisfying the basic premedical science requirements.

Special Programs for Members of Underrepresented Minorities: SUNY Buffalo strongly encourages members of underrepresented minorities to apply and provides a number of support services to enrolled students. Among the school's special offerings are a summer prematriculation program, academic counseling, enrichment sessions after the first year, and review classes for Parts I and II of the USMLE.

Transfer Policy: Applications for transfer from students in good standing at foreign and U.S. medical schools are considered. A compelling reason for the transfer must exist.

FINANCIAL AID

Financial aid is awarded on the basis of need as determined by the College Scholarship Service analysis. In addition to the standard federal loans and scholarships, SUNY Buffalo coordinates institutional and state funding. Special opportunities for New York residents include the Regents Physician Loan Forgiveness Program, the Tuition Assistance Program, and the Regents Health Care Opportunity Scholarships. There are specific criteria for the Regents programs, including a promise to serve in areas currently experiencing a physician shortage.

ADMISSIONS FACTS

Demographics

% men	59
% women	41
% minorities	12

Deadline & Notification Dates

AMCAS	yes
Regular application	12/01
Regular notification	10/15–until filled
Early Decision application	06/15–08/01
Early Decision notification	10/01

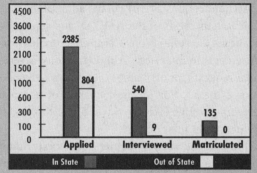

FIRST YEAR STATISTICS

Average GPA

Science	N/A	Nonscience	N/A

Average MCAT

Biology	N/A	Physical Science	N/A
Verbal	N/A	Essay	N/A

FINANCIAL FACTS

Tuition and Fees

In-state	$8,809	On-campus housing	N/A
Out-of-state	$17,459	Off-campus housing	N/A

Financial Aid

% receiving some aid	N/A
Merit scholarships	yes
Average debt	$60,000

TUITION OVERVIEW

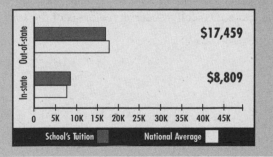

SUNY Stony Brook Health Sciences Center School of Medicine

Committee on Admissions, Level 4, Room L47
Health Sciences Center, Stony Brook, NY 11794-8434
(516) 444-2113

OVERVIEW

The School of Medicine is part of SUNY Stony Brook's Health Sciences Center. Other divisions are Allied Health Professions, Dental Medicine, Nursing, and Social Welfare. Med school officials say the HSC environment is cooperative: "Whenever possible, faculties in other schools of the HSC...participate in instructional experiences, as will students from the other health disciplines." Over 150 hospitals, clinics, and social and political agencies provide education and training for the student body.

ACADEMICS

In response to changing priorities in medical education, SUNY Stony Brook has just implemented a new curriculum that "stress[es] the interweaving of basic and clinical sciences." Stony Brook officials describe some of the revisions: "The integration of individual courses into multidisciplinary blocks makes the organization of the material and learning more efficient. Greater emphasis is placed on small group instruction and self-instruction."

During the first two years, students study the sciences in departmental and interdisciplinary courses and are introduced to patient care. Freshman-year science courses concentrate on the normal structures and functions of the body, but students also begin to investigate the disease process. Nontechnical courses include Preventative Medicine, Basic Life Support, the first half of Introduction to Clinical Medicine (ICM), and the first segment of the four-year Medicine in Contemporary Society continuum. In Medicine in Contemporary Society, students explore social, ethical, legal, and economic aspects of health care.

In the sophomore year, students focus on pathophysiology in Systems Approach to Medicine. While the main goal of this block is to foster students' understanding of the scientific underpinnings of medicine, there is a strong emphasis on the integration of the basic and clinical sciences. In the second half of ICM, sophomores learn how to take a patient history, to conduct a physical examination, and to use their knowledge of pathology and physiology to solve clinical problems.

The clinical experiences of the second year provide a transition to the third-year clerkships. At the university hospital and the school's affiliates, juniors rotate through the major disciplines. About half of the fourth year is devoted to clinical electives; the remainder is free for electives.

Stony Brook students who are interested in biomedical investigation are encouraged to work on research projects during the summer after their freshman year and in elective periods. An MD with Distinction in Research is offered for those who want in-depth involvement in research, but who don't want to pursue a combined MD/Ph.D.

Grading and Promotion Policy: Honors/Pass/Fail. Students must take Parts I and II of the USMLE.

Additional Degree Programs: The med school offers an eight-year combined BS/MD to which Stony Brook students in their sophomore undergraduate year may apply. A combined MD/Ph.D. is also available.

STUDENT LIFE

SUNY Stony Brook is located on the North Shore of Long Island, about an hour's train ride from New York City. The suburban location has both benefits and drawbacks. Students can enjoy all the amenities of the nation's largest and most exciting city without living in the midst of the corresponding bedlam. Nearby beaches, bike trails, and parks provide low-key recreational opportunities. But housing is expensive.

Although on-campus housing is available, some might not find it completely satisfactory; in some cases, even married students end up sharing apartments with other couples. Also, since clinical teaching sites are widespread and public transportation is limited, upperclassmen may find that the benefits of affordable university housing are outweighed by frustrating commutes to the hospital. Regardless of where they choose to live, new matriculants should begin looking for housing early and should seriously consider bringing their cars.

In addition to off-campus diversions, the HSC and the undergraduate divisions provide numerous educational, cultural, social, and recreational activities. On-campus movies, concerts, and plays are offered on a regular basis, and the Sports Complex provides students with a place to compete on intramural teams and stay in shape.

ADMISSIONS

As a state-supported school, SUNY Stony Brook gives first priority to New York residents. Because of the small number of available spaces for nonresidents, those accepted from out of state generally have exceptional qualifications. All applications should submit their AMCAS applications as early in the admissions cycle as possible. On the basis of the AMCAS and supplemental applications, the Admissions Committee invites promising candidates to interview. Although Stony Brook will consider requests for off-campus interviews, they do not encourage them. For the best chance of acceptance, make every possible effort to travel to the campus if you are invited to an interview.

Although the school requires only sixty hours of undergraduate coursework, few students are admitted without a bachelor's degree. The Admissions Committee's final decisions are based on the GPA, MCAT scores, letters of recommendation, the interview, extracurricular activities, work experience, personal qualities, and the motivation and suitability for the study of medicine.

Special Programs for Members of Underrepresented Minorities: Students from minority groups traditionally underrepresented in medicine are encouraged to apply.

Transfer Policy: Applications for transfer from students who are in good standing at accredited U.S. med schools are considered on a space-available basis.

FINANCIAL AID

Most financial aid is awarded solely on the basis of need. New York residents can take advantage of several state scholarship and loan programs. To secure funding from some of these programs, students must agree to practice in medically-underserved areas of the state.

ADMISSIONS FACTS

Demographics

% men	59
% women	41
% minorities	10

Deadline & Notification Dates

AMCAS	yes
Regular application	11/15
Regular notification	10/15–until filled
Early Decision application	06/15–08/01
Early Decision notification	10/01

In State / Out of State

Applied: 2610 (In State), 1149 (Out of State)
Interviewed: N/A
Matriculated: 98 (In State), 2 (Out of State)

FIRST YEAR STATISTICS

Average GPA

Science	N/A	Nonscience	N/A

Average MCAT

Biology	N/A	Physical Science	N/A
Verbal	N/A	Essay	N/A

FINANCIAL FACTS

Tuition and Fees

In-state	$8,580	On-campus housing	N/A
Out-of-state	$17,230	Off-campus housing	N/A

Financial Aid

% receiving some aid	none
Merit scholarships	no
Average debt	N/A

TUITION OVERVIEW

Out-of-state: $17,230
In-state: $8,580

School's Tuition / National Average

SUNY Health Science Center at Syracuse College of Medicine

Admissions Committee
155 Elizabeth Blackwell Street, Syracuse, NY 13210
(315) 464-4570

OVERVIEW

SUNY Syracuse is ranked among the nation's best comprehensive med schools. Some of its reputation stems from innovative aspects of its curriculum. In addition to the standard pathway, SUNY Syracuse offers the Clinical Campus at Birmingham. This option provides juniors and seniors with the same basic body of knowledge and experiences as the standard track offers, but fosters close working relationships with community physicians and emphasizes ambulatory care. The Clinical Campus's geriatric/gerontology clerkship was the first of its kind at any U.S. med school.

ACADEMICS

All students spend their first two years at the Health Sciences Center in Syracuse. Freshmen begin their medical education with a study of the normal structures and functions of the human organism. The second term of the first year features continued study of the sciences through more interdisciplinary courses and self-directed, individually-paced learning. Clinical correlations are emphasized throughout the year.

In the second year, students shift their focus from the normal to the abnormal. In their investigation of the pathological basis of disease, students continue to study biological principles, but also explore psychosocial aspects of health. To facilitate the transition into the third-year clerkships, SUNY Syracuse's sophomore year curriculum includes Introduction to Clinical Medicine (ICM). In this course, students are taught patient communication, examination, and evaluation skills. Sophomores complete a preceptorship in family medicine at the end of the year.

The main goals of both the standard and the Clinical Campus third- and fourth-year curricular tracks are fundamentally the same. Students learn to apply their basic science knowledge to clinical problems and hone their patient care skills through extensive exposure to ill patients. In the standard program, students complete a required core of clerkships during their last two years. In addition to rotations in the major disciplines, students spend time in otolaryngology, radiology, anesthesiology, orthopedic surgery, neuroscience, ophthalmology, preventative medicine, and urology. To augment these requirements, students choose electives that suit their individual interests.

The Clinical Campus option begins with a two-week program in acute care. Teaching takes place in affiliated hospitals, clinics, community agencies, physicians' offices, and other local health care facilities. Primary care, ambulatory surgery, and geriatrics/gerontology clerkships are among the features that set the Clinical Campus program apart from the standard curriculum.

Although the preparation of skilled clinicians is SUNY Syracuse's top priority, it also has a strong commitment to training academicians and biomedical investigators. The school offers a combined MD/Ph.D. program, but it also provides students with a less intense option: the Medical Student Research Program (MSRP). In this program, students spend 36 weeks (over the course of three years) conducting research. Upon completion of the project, MSRP students must write a publishable research thesis. Summer research projects and research electives are also available for non-MSRP students.

Grading and Promotion Policy: Honors/Pass/Fail.

Additional Degree Programs: MD/Ph.D.; MD/MBA.

STUDENT LIFE

Students have the chance to put their newly acquired skills into action through service projects sponsored by a number of student medical organizations, including chapters of the American Medical Student Association, the American Medical Women's Association, the Medical Society of New York, and Geri-Action (a club for those interested in geriatric medicine). A lecture and dinner series called MASH (Medicine and Staying Human) provides a forum to discuss ethical and professional issues.

Students who need a break from academia can head to the Campus Activities Building (CAB). Aerobics classes, intramural teams, an Olympic-sized swimming pool, Nautilus equipment, squash and racquetball courts, and a sauna help students channel stress and keep fit.

The city, too, offers diversions. Within walking distance of the campus is the Civic Center, home of the ballet, opera, and symphony. The Everson Museum of Art, theaters, and the zoo are also just a few blocks away. Syracuse's surrounding area provides year-round recreation—ski areas, Lake Ontario, and the Adirondack Forest Preserve are nearby.

The Health Science Center provides on-campus housing in the Residence Living Complex—a high-rise that offers dorm-style rooms, studio apartments, and one-bedroom units. The complex is located across the street from the University Hospital and next to the CAB.

ADMISSIONS

Since it's state-supported, SUNY Syracuse gives New York residents top priority in admissions. Only a small percentage of students come from out of state, and successful nonresidents generally have exceptional qualifications. Because the school operates on a rolling admissions basis, candidates should apply as early in the admissions cycle as possible. Upon receipt of the AMCAS application, the school requests supplemental material from all candidates. The most highly qualified of those are invited to interview. The interview day usually includes two or more meetings with school representatives and a tour of the med school facilities.

About one-fourth of interviewed candidates are ultimately admitted. Selection factors include science and nonscience GPAs, MCAT scores, the interview, letters of recommendation, interpersonal skills, extracurricular activities, work experience, character, and motivation.

Special Programs for Members of Underrepresented Minorities: SUNY Syracuse recently implemented Project 90, a program to recruit and retain underrepresented minority and disadvantaged students. Among the features of Project 90 are a prematriculation summer program and an extended curricular track.

Transfer Policy: Applicants in good standing at U.S. or foreign med schools are considered for transfer.

FINANCIAL AID

Most financial aid is awarded on the basis of documented need, and assistance is largely in the form of loans. Despite the school's relatively low in-state tuition, the average student ends up borrowing more than $40,000. Special New York state scholarship and loan forgiveness programs may help reduce debt, but some programs carry a service obligation.

ADMISSIONS FACTS

Demographics

% men	56
% women	44
% minorities	12

Deadline & Notification Dates

AMCAS	yes
Regular application	11/01
Regular notification	10/15–until filled
Early Decision application	06/15–8/01
Early Decision notification	10/01

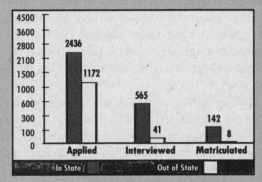

FIRST YEAR STATISTICS

Average GPA

Science	N/A	Nonscience	N/A

Average MCAT

Biology	N/A	Physical Science	N/A
Verbal	N/A	Essay	N/A

FINANCIAL FACTS

Tuition and Fees

In-state	$8,665	On-campus housing	N/A
Out-of-state	$17,315	Off-campus housing	N/A

Financial Aid

% receiving some aid	N/A
Merit scholarships	N/A
Average debt	N/A

TUITION OVERVIEW

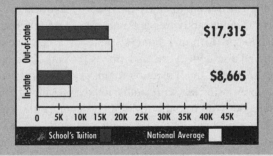

Bowman Gray School of Medicine of Wake Forest University

Office of Admissions
Medical Center Boulevard, Winston-Salem, NC 27157-1090
(919) 716-4264

OVERVIEW

The Bowman Gray School of Medicine (BGSM) is, as its dean suggests, a "school on the move." Recently ranked thirty-fifth in total funding by the National Institutes of Health, BGSM is continuing its efforts to become recognized as a research leader. But research is not this small North Carolina school's only priority. Says the Dean, "Our recently developed emphases on programs to serve the very young and the elderly; our emphasis on programs on prevention of disease; and our thrust into the field of nutrition as it relates to chronic disease can only enhance our national position." The students we surveyed think their school is doing a good job of achieving its complementary aims—BGSM's research efforts and clinical training were both rated as top-notch.

ACADEMICS

BGSM offers two curricular tracks for the preclinical years. While neither is completely classical, the standard path primarily uses traditional lectures and labs to guide students through a discipline-based study of the basic sciences and an investigation of fundamental clinical skills. The Parallel Curriculum, established in 1987, is a problem-based learning track. Under this option, students work in small groups to identify and explore basic science and clinical issues through case studies. According to school officials, "the emphasis [of the Parallel Curriculum] is on independent, self-directed learning to develop sound clinical reasoning and problem-solving skills."

In the standard curriculum, the first two years are divided into four segments. In Unit I, freshmen study normal human structures and functions through courses in biochemistry, embryology, gross anatomy, and microscopic anatomy. The second unit builds on this knowledge base with a continuation of the study of the basic sciences and the introduction of behavioral, social, and ethical perspectives. Included in this semester is an Introduction to Clinical Diagnosis course which helps students apply their scientific knowledge to clinical problems.

Unit III is a multidisciplinary Introduction to Clinical Medicine (ICM). ICM provides an integrated study of pathology, physiology, and pharmacology, and serves to emphasize the clinical relevance of the sciences. The fourth unit includes an Introduction to Clinical Clerkships course and instruction in patient interviewing, examination, and diagnosis skills. According to the students we surveyed, the combination of ICM and Introduction to Clinical Clerkships provides solid clinical exposure and facilitates the transition to the third and fourth years.

Students in both curricular tracks meet for Units V and VI, the clinical period. The third year is composed of required clerkships and rotations in Neurology, Anesthesiology, Radiology, and Family Medicine augment those in the traditional disciplines. Although much of the fourth year is free for electives, seniors must complete a clerkship in Community Medicine and advanced experiences in Medicine, Obstetrics/Gynecology, Pediatrics, and Surgery.

Students rate the quality of teaching as excellent and say that their professors are available to help them outside the classroom. Facilities also receive outstanding marks, with the school's hospitals and affiliates garnering the highest praise.

Grading and Promotion Policy: Students are evaluated on a numerical scale that corresponds to grades of High Honors/Honors/Pass/Low Pass/Fail (e.g., a course grade of Pass would earn 2 points). Parts I and II of the USMLE are required.

Additional Degree Programs: MD/MBA; MD/MS in Epidemiology.

STUDENT LIFE

Although students admit that they work hard, they also say they have time to enjoy fairly active extracurricular lives. Campus activities are available, if not abundant. The Student Life and Fitness Center is a new facility designed for both work and play. Twenty-four hour quiet areas and small meeting rooms give students space to keep up with classwork, and a lounge provides a place to hang out with friends. To build up stamina to survive the rigors of med school, students can work out in on-site aerobics classes and Nautilus rooms. Saunas help melt away stress.

Additional recreational and social opportunities can be found just a few miles away at the main campus of BGSM's parent institution, Wake Forest University. Winston-Salem also offers its share of diversions. Students looking for culture can head to museums, the symphony, or plays, concerts, recitals, and dance productions at the North Carolina School of the Arts. The outdoor set can take advantage of the area's temperate climate; students can swim, play tennis, picnic, ride horses, or just relax at nearby Tanglewood and Hanes Parks. Although students don't really love Winston-Salem, they don't hate it either. The area around the campus is reportedly safe, and housing is more than adequate. Public transportation is a sore spot, however; students warn that it can be rather difficult to function at BGSM without a car.

ADMISSIONS

Although BGSM admissions officials say they show no preference to state residents, about 60 percent of students come from North Carolina. Admission is very selective; at present BGSM admits fewer than two percent of its applicants. To increase your chance of getting in, the Admissions Office advises that you take the Spring MCAT, apply as early as possible, and "use the personal comment section of the secondary application to address specific interests in the school, programs, or area." Only well-qualified candidates are asked to submit the supplemental application, and only the best of those are asked to interview; traditionally between 10 and 15 percent of candidates are interviewed.

The Admissions Office lists as its primary selection factors the science and nonscience GPA, the interview, and MCAT scores. It also considers essays, extracurricular activities, exposure to the medical field, volunteer work, and letters of recommendation.

Special Programs for Members of Underrepresented Minorities: BGSM's minority affairs division coordinates recruitment and support services for members of underrepresented minorities. Among these are a postbaccalaureate development program, a summer prematriculation session, academic advising, tutoring, peer counseling, and review sessions for Parts I and II of the USMLE.

Transfer Policy: Applicants in good standing at U.S. or Canadian medical schools who have good reasons for wanting to transfer are considered.

FINANCIAL AID

BGSM is an affordable private school; tuition is relatively low and the cost of living in Winston-Salem is reasonable. In addition to need-based scholarships and loans, the school offers up to seven full-tuition merit scholarships to North Carolina residents.

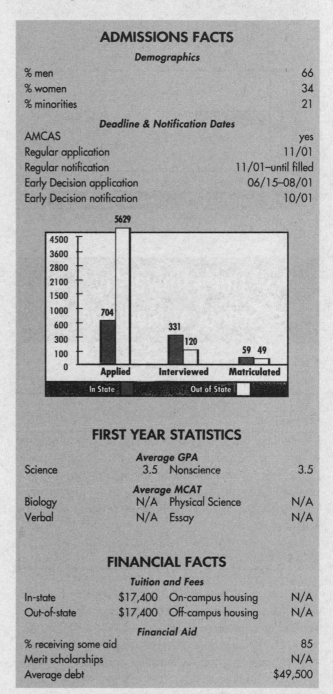

ADMISSIONS FACTS

Demographics

% men	66
% women	34
% minorities	21

Deadline & Notification Dates

AMCAS	yes
Regular application	11/01
Regular notification	11/01–until filled
Early Decision application	06/15–08/01
Early Decision notification	10/01

[Bar chart showing Applied, Interviewed, Matriculated by In State and Out of State]

	In State	Out of State
Applied	704	5629
Interviewed	331	120
Matriculated	59	49

FIRST YEAR STATISTICS

Average GPA

Science	3.5	Nonscience	3.5

Average MCAT

Biology	N/A	Physical Science	N/A
Verbal	N/A	Essay	N/A

FINANCIAL FACTS

Tuition and Fees

In-state	$17,400	On-campus housing	N/A
Out-of-state	$17,400	Off-campus housing	N/A

Financial Aid

% receiving some aid	85
Merit scholarships	N/A
Average debt	$49,500

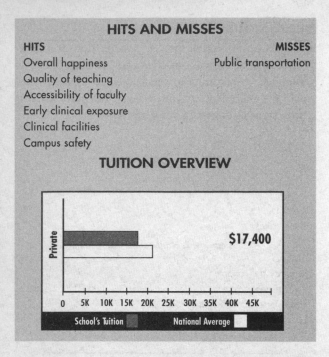

HITS AND MISSES

HITS

Overall happiness
Quality of teaching
Accessibility of faculty
Early clinical exposure
Clinical facilities
Campus safety

MISSES

Public transportation

TUITION OVERVIEW

Private

$17,400

0   5K   10K   15K   20K   25K   30K   35K   40K   45K

School's Tuition ▓   National Average ☐

Duke University School of Medicine

Committee on Admissions, Medical Center,
P.O. Box 3710, Durham, NC 27710
(919) 684-2985

OVERVIEW

The number one reason students cite for choosing Duke is "prestige." Considering the school's reputation as one of the best med schools in the nation, this isn't too surprising. All in all, students say they're not disappointed with their choice; the overwhelming majority are happy at Duke.

ACADEMICS

Duke's curriculum is unusual, and it has been that way for a long time. The current curriculum, in which students spend only one year in basic science classes before beginning clinical rotations, was established in 1966, well before many other schools jumped on the curriculum-revision bandwagon. Students seem to like the setup. As one enthusiast says, "The best part of Duke is that you spend only one year in class!"

Duke describes the purpose of the first year: "Rather than mastering an encyclopedic array of facts, the purpose is to acquire familiarity with the major principles of each subject." In addition to science courses, students are required to take a no-credit course, Clinical Arts, that correlates basic science principles to clinical applications. Even so, first-year students say they would like more exposure to patients during the basic science year.

The second year stresses the clinical context of basic science principles. For the first seven weeks, students take Introduction to Clinical Diagnosis. They then move on to eight-week rotations in internal medicine, surgery, obstetrics and gynecology, pediatrics, psychiatry, and either an eight-week rotation in family medicine or four weeks each in family medicine and neurology. The third and fourth years provide a lot of elective time, allowing students to better direct their own course of study and build a foundation for lifelong medical education.

Students report that the quality of teaching and the accessibility of the faculty are outstanding. Says one, "The professors are very helpful and energetic." Duke is known as a research-oriented school, and students were almost unanimous in giving the school's research efforts the highest possible rating (only Johns Hopkins students topped Duke in this category). Some feel that emphasis on academic medicine overshadows clinical concerns, however, especially in family medicine. Complains one, "There is way too [much stress] on research and not clinical work." Another adds, "[Duke] tends to push people into specialties and discourage those interested in primary care." Overall, students rate the school's classroom, laboratory, library, and clinical facilities as excellent; lower marks go to the computer facilities, with which students are only moderately satisfied.

Grading and Promotion Policies: Honors/Pass/Fail or Satisfactory/Unsatisfactory.

Additional Degree Programs: The Medical Scientist Training Program is funded by the NIH, takes six to seven years and culminates in a combined MD/Ph.D. Other special degree programs include the Medical Historian Program, the Medicine and Public Policy Program, the MD/JD Program, and the MD/MPH Program.

STUDENT LIFE

Students are surprisingly noncompetitive. Although relatively few students participate in organized study groups, students agree that their classmates are committed to helping others, in and out of med school. Most first-year students agree that people even have a relatively active social life. Says one, "Duke is fun and not very stressful." Another adds, "This place is great. [It is a] very supportive environment (faculty and students). I would not go anywhere else."

While students don't think much of Durham, the attractiveness of Duke's campus more than makes up for it for most. Duke offers two different apartment-complex type housing facilities, but students greatly prefer the off-campus offerings. Students say public transportation is not particularly accessible, but they do find it safe. This is especially important since parking, one student says, "is a nightmare."

ADMISSIONS

There is no residence requirement, but some special consideration is given to North Carolina residents. "Good study habits, intelligence, character, and integrity are essential qualifications for admission," says Duke's catalogue. Of course, like all other med schools, Duke also puts strong emphasis on your academic record, particularly your GPA and MCAT. Interviews are also an important consideration.

Special Programs for Members of Underrepresented Minorities: Duke awards seven full Dean's Tuition Scholarships to "academically excellent" minority students each year. Preference for these grants is given to state residents.

Transfer Policy: Transfers are not accepted except in unusual circumstances.

FINANCIAL AID

Admissions decisions are made without regard to financial need, so financial aid packets are mailed to all students who interview regardless of economic situation. Financial aid awards are made in the form of grants and loans, and, with the exception of merit and research scholarships, are based on the GAPSFAS needs analysis. North Carolina residents are currently granted up to $10,000 to meet financial need. If need is in excess of this amount, students must obtain a Stafford Loan of $5,000. Need beyond $15,000 is met through a combination of grants and loans. For nonresidents, there is no initial grant, but everything else is the same.

ADMISSIONS FACTS

Demographics

% men	62
% women	38
% minorities	10

Deadline & Notification Dates

AMCAS	yes
Regular application	10/15
Regular notification	02/01–until filled
Early Decision application	No EDP
Early Decision notification	N/A

FIRST YEAR STATISTICS

Average GPA

Science	N/A	Nonscience	N/A

Average MCAT

Biology	N/A	Physical Science	N/A
Verbal	N/A	Essay	N/A

FINANCIAL FACTS

Tuition and Fees

In-state	$20,831	On-campus housing	$3,668*
Out-of-state	$20,831	Off-campus housing	N/A
		(*meals not included)	

Financial Aid

% receiving some aid	75
Merit scholarships	yes
Average debt	N/A

HITS AND MISSES

HITS	MISSES
Teaching	On-campus housing
Accessible faculty	Durham
Teaching facilities	Computer labs

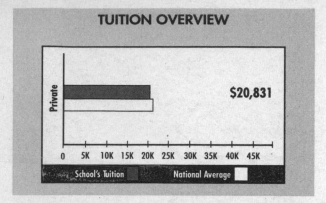

TUITION OVERVIEW

Private

$20,831

0 5K 10K 15K 20K 25K 30K 35K 40K 45K

School's Tuition ▮   National Average ☐

East Carolina University School of Medicine

Office of Admissions, Greenville, NC 27858-4354
(919) 551-2202

OVERVIEW

A state-supported institution, East Carolina University School of Medicine places strong emphasis on providing and improving health care for the residents of North Carolina. The curriculum is oriented toward training highly-skilled clinicians, especially in primary care disciplines. Clinical correlations and experiences with practicing physicians help East Carolina students focus on patients from the first year of med school.

ACADEMICS

Although elements of East Carolina's curriculum are classical—notably its structure—students get more early clinical exposure than their peers at many other med schools. Through investigation of the basic, clinical, and behavioral sciences and hands-on patient contact, students learn to integrate the various aspects of medicine.

In the first year, students build a foundation of scientific knowledge through courses that include anatomy, biochemistry, physiology, microbiology, and genetics. They also explore humanistic and psychosocial aspects of health and health care. To keep the ultimate goal of their education in focus, students begin to consider the clinical applications of scientific principles and have the chance to experience medical practice first-hand in a family medicine preceptorship.

The mix of basic, clinical, and behavioral sciences continues into the second year, but there is increased attention to abnormal human structures and functions. Courses in pathology and pharmacology focus on the disease process and the ways in which physicians can intervene therapeutically. The clinical orientation intensifies in the Introduction to Medicine sequence. During this time, students learn how to take medical histories, conduct examinations, and form diagnoses. A second preceptorship in family medicine is required.

Juniors build on the experiences of their first two years by completing clerkships in obstetrics/gynecology, pediatrics, psychology, family medicine, internal medicine, and surgery. For the final year, students devise an individualized plan of study that incorporates both required and elective experiences. Clinical teaching takes place at the Pitt County Memorial Hospital and inpatient and outpatient affiliates.

Students give the faculty high marks. One fourth year comments, "Far and away, ECU's greatest strength is the faculty. They work us hard but they are kind and humane at the same time." Students also support one another, reports one respondent, which enabled her to attend to a personal crisis and keep up with her school responsibilities. Finally, students are lukewarm about ECU's facilities; one student singled out the "uncomfortable" classrooms for criticism.

Grading and Promotion Policy: East Carolina uses a letter grading system. Students are required to take Parts I and II of the USMLE.

Additional Degree Programs: None.

ADMISSIONS

East Carolina shows strong preference for residents of North Carolina; in fact, no out-of-state candidates were accepted into the entering class of 1992. All students apply through AMCAS, but only state residents may participate in the Early Decision Program. Candidates who show exceptional promise are invited to Greenville for a pair of interviews with members of the Admissions Committee.

Among the criteria the committee uses in making its final evaluation of candidates are MCAT scores, GPA, letters of recommendation, the interview, academic and nonacademic achievements, and personal qualities.

Special Programs for Members of Underrepresented Minorities: East Carolina encourages members of underrepresented minorities, especially those from North Carolina, to apply. The Academic Support and Counseling Center coordinates services to help enrolled students succeed in med school.

Transfer Policy: Applications for transfer are considered on a space-available basis. Very few transfers have been granted in recent years.

FINANCIAL AID

Although most financial aid is awarded on the basis of need, there are some merit scholarships available.

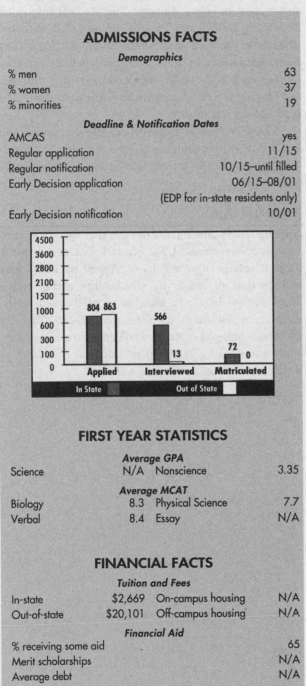

ADMISSIONS FACTS

Demographics

% men	63
% women	37
% minorities	19

Deadline & Notification Dates

AMCAS	yes
Regular application	11/15
Regular notification	10/15–until filled
Early Decision application	06/15–08/01
	(EDP for in-state residents only)
Early Decision notification	10/01

Applied: In State 804, Out of State 863
Interviewed: In State 566, Out of State 13
Matriculated: In State 72, Out of State 0

FIRST YEAR STATISTICS

Average GPA

Science	N/A	Nonscience	3.35

Average MCAT

Biology	8.3	Physical Science	7.7
Verbal	8.4	Essay	N/A

FINANCIAL FACTS

Tuition and Fees

In-state	$2,669	On-campus housing	N/A
Out-of-state	$20,101	Off-campus housing	N/A

Financial Aid

% receiving some aid	65
Merit scholarships	N/A
Average debt	N/A

TUITION OVERVIEW

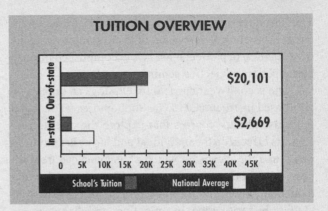

Out-of-state: $20,101
In-state: $2,669

School's Tuition — National Average

University of North Carolina at Chapel Hill School of Medicine

Admissions Office, CB #7000 MacNider Hall
Chapel Hill, NC 27599-7000
(919) 962-8331

OVERVIEW

Recognized as one of the top research-oriented med schools, the UNC School of Medicine emphasizes problem-solving, communication skills, and self-directed learning in its curriculum. Part of the University Medical Center, the school shares resources with the schools of Dentistry, Nursing, Pharmacy, and Public Health. The UNC Hospitals, Biological Sciences Center, Cancer Research Center, and statewide area health education centers are the primary sites for clinical instruction.

ACADEMICS

UNC allows for academic flexibility in all four years. Although structured along fairly classical lines, the curriculum emphasizes integration between the basic and clinical sciences and reserves considerable time throughout the four years for students to pursue individual interests.

Preclinical coursework is coordinated by a committee made up of basic science and clinical faculty. This cooperative approach leads to multidisciplinary, organ-system instruction in much of the first two years. As freshmen, students gain an understanding of the scientific concepts that form the foundation for medicine and investigate social and behavioral aspects of medicine.

The Introduction to Medicine course helps freshmen focus on the clinical relevance of their studies. In-depth investigation in particular areas is accomplished through participation in elective seminars.

The second-year curriculum employs an organ system-based instructional mode. Sophomores take several multidisciplinary courses that explore the disease process, its effects on the individual and his or her environment, and the means by which physicians can treat illness. Also in this period, students begin to acquire fundamental patient-interaction and assessment skills, including history-taking, examination, and diagnosis. As in the first year, elective seminars allow students to pursue their own interests.

The third and fourth years are primarily devoted to required and elective clinical experiences. To augment the skills they learned in the basic science years and to learn to function as part of the health care team, juniors must complete clerkships in the major disciplines. The fourth year provides students with the opportunity to expand on their clinical skills, to pursue further study in the basic, clinical, and behavioral sciences, and to participate in research projects. Although students are required to do a family medicine preceptorship and to complete an acting internship, they may use the majority of the year to participate in electives and free electives. In addition, all seniors must spend a portion of the year in primary care settings.

Grading and Promotion Policy: Honors/Pass/Fail.

Additional Degree Programs: MS/MD, MD/Ph.D., MD/MPH.

ADMISSIONS

UNC shows a strong preference for residents of North Carolina and encourages only exceptionally well-qualified nonresidents to apply. Resident and nonresident candidates with outstanding credentials may participate in the Early Decision Program.

All students must apply through AMCAS. Although North Carolina residents may take the new-format MCAT as late as September, nonresidents must take the April administration. On the basis of the completed application, the Admissions Committee invites promising candidates to submit supplemental applications and to interview at the Chapel Hill campus.

In making its final selections, the Admissions Committee considers the interview, academic record, MCAT scores, letters of recommendation, motivation, maturity, leadership potential, extracurricular and scholastic achievements, and personal qualities. Although undergraduate major is not a factor, the level and breadth of coursework and proficiency in the natural sciences are considered important.

Special Programs for Members of Underrepresented Minorities: UNC has an active program to recruit and support minority students. The Medical Education Development Program exposes premed and accepted students to the med school curriculum and faculty and helps educationally disadvantaged students develop learning and study skills. Academic advising, tutoring, and summer review classes are available to students who need special attention.

Transfer Policy: Transfers are rarely accepted, but applications from students in good standing at accredited U.S. institutions are considered on a space-available basis.

FINANCIAL AID

Although it is among the least expensive U.S. med schools for residents, UNC offers financial aid in the form of scholarships and loans. Award packages may include state or university scholarships and/or subsidized student loans. In addition to need-based funds, there are a few merit scholarships. Resident minority and disadvantaged students who demonstrate need may apply for Board of Governors' Medical Scholarships which include full tuition and a stipend.

ADMISSIONS FACTS

Demographics

% men	56
% women	44
% minorities	13

Deadline & Notification Dates

AMCAS	yes
Regular application	11/15
Regular notification	10/15–until filled
Early Decision application	06/15–08/01
Early Decision notification	10/01

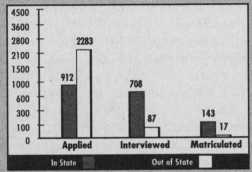

FIRST YEAR STATISTICS

Average GPA

Science	N/A	Nonscience	N/A

Average MCAT

Biology	N/A	Physical Science	N/A
Verbal	N/A	Essay	N/A

FINANCIAL FACTS

Tuition and Fees

In-state	$2,564	On-campus housing	N/A
Out-of-state	$19,998	Off-campus housing	N/A

Financial Aid

% receiving some aid	54
Merit scholarships	N/A
Average debt	N/A

TUITION OVERVIEW

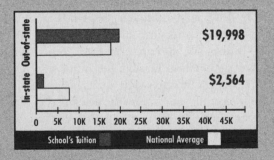

University of North Dakota School of Medicine

Office of Admissions, 501 North Columbia Road, Grand Forks, ND 58203
(701) 777-4221

OVERVIEW

University of North Dakota School of Medicine's primary mission is to provide primary care to the residents of North Dakota. Because of the population patterns of the state, there is a strong emphasis on rural family practice. The main campus, where students spend the majority of their first two years, is in Grand Forks. There are additional locations for clinical training in Fargo, Bismarck, and Minot.

ACADEMICS

UND employs a five-phase curriculum that expands on the traditional basic science/clinical division by providing three transitional periods. During the preclinical years, problem-based, small-group learning is used in required Focal Problems courses. In Focal Problems, basic science principles are correlated with clinical problems through the use of case studies and class discussion. Students give this program high marks; comments one, "The Focal Problems course is very innovative and interesting. Paper patients allow us to integrate what we're learning in the classroom." Additional early clinical exposure comes just before the clerkships, when students are assigned a three-week preceptorship in rural North Dakota. Students want more hands-on preclinical experience, though; they report being only moderately satisfied with the patient contact in the first two years. During the junior and senior years, students complete required and elective clerkships. To help ease the transition from med school to residency, UND offers a unique Introduction to Graduate Training program.

In general, students rate the quality of teaching at UND as good, but they are even more impressed with how much individual attention and support their professors give them. Says one, "The faculty here is wonderful. They're concerned about students and are very helpful in dealing with individual problems. Students are given every chance to succeed."

Students are not so enthusiastic about the school's facilities, however. While students rate the library and labs as satisfactory, they say the classrooms and computer labs need major improvement. According to one student, help is on the way: "The school is in the midst of renovating its medical school facilities so rooms that are in poor condition will soon be replaced."

STUDENT LIFE

With classes of around fifty-seven students, UND is relatively small. Students like the personal atmosphere a small class affords. "Professors treat us like individuals rather than numbers," reports one second-year student. Another adds, "I know all my fellow students on a first-name basis." Despite generally good relations with classmates, UND students report that they spend a lot of time preparing for class and, as a result, don't have much of a social life. They also complain that there aren't a lot of school clubs and activities. In fact, of the schools we surveyed, UND students gave themselves one of the lowest ratings in extracurricular involvement.

A variety of on-campus and off-campus housing options are available. Students rate both arrangements satisfactory, but show a slight preference for living off campus. The town gets mixed reviews. Says one fan, "Grand Forks is a clean, crime-free, relatively inexpensive town to live in. The people here are very friendly." But another complains, "This has got to be the flattest place on earth! Also, it's cold here—minus 50 degrees Fahrenheit over Christmas!" Whatever their feelings about the amenities of the town, students agree that "the medical community of Grand Forks is behind the school 100 percent."

ADMISSIONS

UND's primary mission is to educate students from North Dakota, so there is a strong preference for state residents. Up to four spaces in each year's class are reserved for students from western states without medical schools (through the WICHE program); in addition, some Minnesota residents may be considered. Native American students, regardless of state of residence, are encouraged to apply through the INMED program. Other nonresidents are discouraged from applying.

UND does not participate in AMCAS and applications may be obtained through the Admissions Office. To be considered for admission, students must submit an official transcript; scores from the new MCAT; four letters of recommendation, one of which must be written by a peer; and the written application. The written application includes a one-page autobiographical statement. Promising candidates are invited to an on-campus interview which is conducted by the entire Admissions Committee. The Committee is composed of administrators, medical faculty, and student representatives. A minimum of a 3.0 GPA is expected if a candidate is to be considered competitive.

Special Programs for Members of Underrepresented Minorities: UND focuses its minority recruiting programs on Native American students through the Indians Into Medicine (INMED) program. The purpose of this program, run in conjunction with South Dakota's medical school, is to educate Native American students who are interested in practicing in the Indian Health Service.

Transfer Policy: Although UND does not normally accept transfers, requests will be considered in very unusual cases.

FINANCIAL AID

Financial aid is available in the form of loans and scholarships. Currently, about 85 percent of students receive assistance. Assistance is based on need or a combination of scholastic achievement and need.

FIRST YEAR STATISTICS

Average GPA

Science	3.53	Nonscience	3.55

Average MCAT

Biology	8.9	Physical Science	8.6
Verbal	8.7	Essay	N/A

FINANCIAL FACTS

Tuition and Fees

In-state	$8,778	On-campus housing	N/A
Out-of-state	$22,656	Off-campus housing	N/A

Financial Aid

% receiving some aid	85
Merit scholarships	no
Average debt	N/A

HITS AND MISSES

HITS	MISSES
Focal Problems course	Classrooms
Faculty accessibility	Computer labs
Campus safety	Diversity
Cost of living	Extracurricular involvement

TUITION OVERVIEW

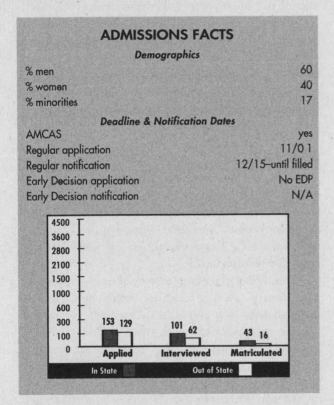

$22,656

$8,778

| School's Tuition | National Average |

ADMISSIONS FACTS

Demographics

% men	60
% women	40
% minorities	17

Deadline & Notification Dates

AMCAS	yes
Regular application	11/01
Regular notification	12/15–until filled
Early Decision application	No EDP
Early Decision notification	N/A

	Applied	Interviewed	Matriculated
In State	153	101	43
Out of State	129	62	16

Case Western Reserve University School of Medicine

Associate Dean of Admissions
10900 Euclid Ave., Cleveland, OH 44106-4920
(216) 368-3450

OVERVIEW

Case Western is nationally recognized as a top research school, and the students we surveyed are proud of its cutting-edge biomedical investigation. But students are also quick to add that Case isn't unidimensional—students find a wealth of clinical opportunities and a "humanitarian" approach to educating physicians.

ACADEMICS

What most impresses the first- and second-year students we surveyed is the extent to which their study of the basic sciences is integrated with clinical problems. Teacher-directed departmental and interdisciplinary courses are augmented by small group, problem-based learning. Clinical applications aren't limited to "paper patients," however; from the very beginning, students get hands-on experience. Explains one freshman, "Case [provides] early exposure to patient care. Every first-year student is assigned a maternity patient. The student tracks the patient and, eventually, the baby until the end of the second year."

Experiences like this prepare students for second-year ambulatory care preceptorships in which they learn physical examination and diagnosis skills from practicing physicians. Not surprisingly, students give Case extremely high marks on early clinical exposure and feel well prepared for the third-year clerkships.

The Flexible Program is another feature of the curriculum that students say attracted them to Case. Through the Flexible Program, students in all four years may choose electives from course or clinical offerings, or even design their own. Says one student, "I like that I can take an active part in shaping my medical education." The fourth year is entirely elective.

So, Case offers a lot of innovative programs, but how's the teaching? According to students, it, too, is excellent. Professors are also said to be supportive and accessible outside the classroom. Considering the level of enthusiasm for nearly everything else at Case, students' lukewarm praise of the school's facilities stands out. Although classroom, science, and clinical facilities are given high marks, students say that computer labs and the library could be better. Academic advising, which is rated only "fair," is the subject of criticism.

Grading and Promotion Policy: In the first two years, Pass/Fail. Thereafter, Honors/Pass/Fail. Students must pass USMLE Parts I and II.

Additional Degree Programs: A combined baccalaureate/MD is offered in conjunction with the undergraduate division. Case also offers the MD/Ph.D. and a fully-funded Medical Scientist Training Program, which also grants the MD/Ph.D.

STUDENT LIFE

Students say that Case is not at all cutthroat. "The atmosphere at Case is cooperative," reports one sophomore. It is also fairly social, and students are involved in a variety of school and community organizations. One student explains, "Student groups are very active here, especially the American Medical Student Association. Activities include everything from teaching about AIDS in local schools and doing blood pressure screenings to making public affairs television broadcasts."

Although the university offers residence halls, students say they prefer to find their own places off campus. Commuting without a car is something of a hassle, though because public transportation is not particularly accessible. Although the area around Case offers plenty of cultural and recreational opportunities, students express some concerns about its safety.

ADMISSIONS

Traditionally, between 50 and 60 percent of students come from the state of Ohio. Grades and MCAT scores are considered, but they are not the sole factors on which the Admissions Committee bases its decisions. Although the MCAT is not required, it is waived only in unusual circumstances.

Case actively seeks to admit a student body with a wide variety of experiences and encourages nontraditional students to apply. In fact, Case has a special program for nontraditional students who lack the scientific background to enter medical school. The six-year program includes two years of undergraduate premed courses before the beginning of the medical curriculum.

Special Programs for Members of Underrepresented Minorities: The Office of Minority Programs coordinates Case's efforts to recruit underrepresented minority students. A prematriculation summer session is among its offerings.

Transfer Policy: Transfers are not normally accepted, but exceptions may be made in unusual circumstances.

FINANCIAL AID

The school administers both its own and governmental scholarship and loan programs. Awards are made on the basis of need as determined by the GAPSFAS analysis.

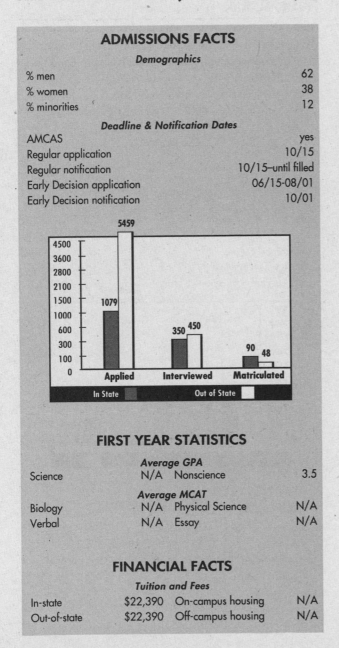

ADMISSIONS FACTS

Demographics

% men	62
% women	38
% minorities	12

Deadline & Notification Dates

AMCAS	yes
Regular application	10/15
Regular notification	10/15–until filled
Early Decision application	06/15-08/01
Early Decision notification	10/01

5459

	In State	Out of State
Applied	1079	5459
Interviewed	350	450
Matriculated	90	48

FIRST YEAR STATISTICS

Average GPA

Science	N/A	Nonscience	3.5

Average MCAT

Biology	N/A	Physical Science	N/A
Verbal	N/A	Essay	N/A

FINANCIAL FACTS

Tuition and Fees

In-state	$22,390	On-campus housing	N/A
Out-of-state	$22,390	Off-campus housing	N/A

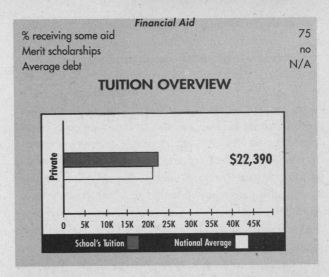

% receiving some aid	75
Merit scholarships	no
Average debt	N/A

TUITION OVERVIEW

$22,390

School's Tuition   National Average

University of Cincinnati College of Medicine

Office of Admissions Room E-251, MSB, ML #552,
231 Bethesda Avenue, Cincinnati, OH 45267-0552
(513) 558-7314

OVERVIEW

UC has intriguing opportunities for clinical exposure early on, with electives that allow you to participate in community health care.

ACADEMICS

Although UC divides its curriculum into the traditional two-year basic science and clinical segments, there is considerable integration in the preclinical years. In addition to investigating the scientific basis for medicine, first- and second-year students are required to take an Introduction to Clinical Practice course. The third year consists of required clinical rotations, including a primary care clerkship that must be completed in a regional, ambulatory care setting. Required and elective rotations make up the fourth year.

Clinical exposure in the basic science years is provided through the Introduction to Clinical Practice course and electives. Introduction to Clinical Practice correlates scientific principles with clinical aspects of medicine and lays the foundation for third- and fourth-year clerkships; medically relevant legal, ethical, and social issues are also discussed. Contact with patients begins the first semester, when students learn and practice interviewing and history-taking skills. In the spring semester, students spend one afternoon per week in an ambulatory care setting. During the second year, students learn physical examination and diagnosis skills from a physician preceptor. Students may also choose to enroll in electives in family care or homeless health care. In the family care option, students monitor a woman's pregnancy, observe her delivery and participate in postnatal care. Students who choose the homeless health care elective attend to a homeless family's medical, social, and emotional needs. Research opportunities are also available during the school year and in the summer.

Grading and Promotion Policy: Honors/Pass/Fail in the basic science years. Honors/High Pass/Pass/Fail in the clinical years. Students must pass Parts I and II of the USMLE.

Additional Degree Programs: MD/Ph.D.

STUDENT LIFE

Although UC's workload is heavy, the Office of Student Services provides academic support through counseling, tutoring, and a Learning Effectiveness Program. Out of the classroom, the medical school and the undergraduate university offer a wide range of activities—from parachuting clubs to singing groups to, if you feel up to it, a Medical Student Talent Show. Students also have full use of the university's athletic facilities. There is a limited number of on-campus apartments, but most students choose to live off campus. Many students comment that Cincinnati is a very conservative city.

ADMISSIONS

UC gives priority to Ohio residents, but a significant proportion of students come from out of state. All interested nonresidents are encouraged to apply. In making its decisions, "The Admissions Committee is interested in students with diverse backgrounds, interests, and talents. Personal characteristics and learning skills are as important as demonstrated academic performance. There should be evidence of commitment, not only to acquiring an adequate knowledge base, but also to developing learning and problem-solving skills which will sustain the individual beyond medical school." The MCAT, in its new format, is required of all applicants.

Special Programs for Members of Underrepresented Minorities: UC encourages individuals from underrepresented minority groups to apply. A Summer Prematriculation Program (SPP) is available for students with disadvantaged educational backgrounds. In the summer session, students enroll in one of the major courses from the first year and learn time management and study skills. Enrollment in the SPP is open to any accepted student.

Transfer Policy: UC considers transfers into the second or third year. Transfer students must be in good standing at a U.S. medical school.

FINANCIAL AID

About 67 percent of UC students receive financial aid, with the majority of assistance coming from low-interest loans. Some scholarship awards are based solely on academic merit.

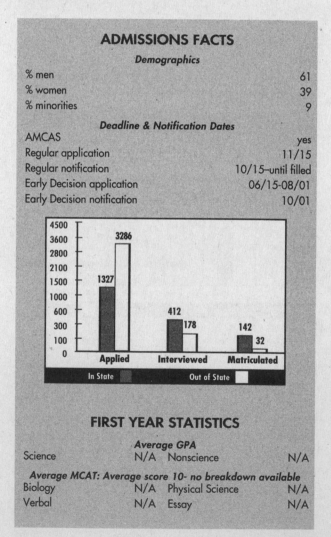

ADMISSIONS FACTS

Demographics

% men	61
% women	39
% minorities	9

Deadline & Notification Dates

AMCAS	yes
Regular application	11/15
Regular notification	10/15–until filled
Early Decision application	06/15-08/01
Early Decision notification	10/01

	In State	Out of State
Applied	1327	3286
Interviewed	412	178
Matriculated	142	32

FIRST YEAR STATISTICS

Average GPA

Science	N/A	Nonscience	N/A

Average MCAT: Average score 10- no breakdown available

Biology	N/A	Physical Science	N/A
Verbal	N/A	Essay	N/A

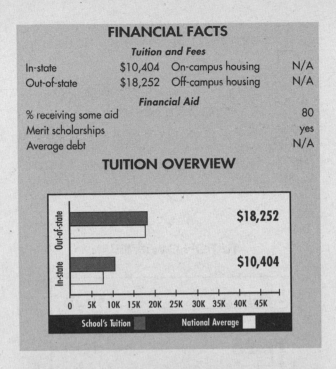

FINANCIAL FACTS

Tuition and Fees

In-state	$10,404	On-campus housing	N/A
Out-of-state	$18,252	Off-campus housing	N/A

Financial Aid

% receiving some aid	80
Merit scholarships	yes
Average debt	N/A

TUITION OVERVIEW

Out-of-state: $18,252

In-state: $10,404

☐ School's Tuition ☐ National Average

Medical College of Ohio

Admissions Office, P.O. Box 10008, Toledo, OH 43699-0008
(419) 381-4229

OVERVIEW

As a state-supported institution, MCO recognizes its responsibility to serve the medical needs of the state. About half the school's graduates go into a primary care specialty, and around 40 percent remain in Ohio to practice.

ACADEMICS

MCO's curriculum is divided into preclinical and clinical segments. For the first seven quarters, students concentrate mainly on the basic sciences. During this time, they also explore psychosocial aspects of medicine through behavioral science courses and take an Introduction to Clinical Medicine course (ICM).

Overall, students are pleased with the amount of early clinical exposure they get through ICM. In the early stages of the course, students learn how to take a patient history and how to conduct a physical exam. They also use clinical case studies to integrate basic science principles with clinical problems. As ICM progresses, students continue to refine their decision-

making and patient-interaction skills and explore ethical issues in medicine. These experiences prepare students for the third-year clerkships, some of which must be done in Area Health Education Centers. The fourth year is largely elective.

Most students are very pleased with the quality of teaching, but some complain that basic science instruction calls for too much memorization and not enough critical thinking. Professors are very accessible, though. Says one first-year student, "They never hesitate to help you outside of class." Students are also pleased with MCO's facilities, giving especially positive reviews of the basic science classrooms and labs.

Grading and Promotion Policy: Honors/High Pass/Pass/Fail. Students must take Parts I and II of the USMLE.

Additional Degree Programs: MCO offers a combined BS/MD program with Bowling Green and University of Toledo. An MD/Ph.D. is also available.

STUDENT LIFE

Overall, MCO students are very happy. Despite a fairly competitive atmosphere, students say they like their classmates and enjoy socializing with them. The school offers plenty of clubs and activities, including a Student-to-Student program, in which med students present health seminars to local schoolchildren.

The campus, which is located in a residential area in South Toledo, gets rave reviews, but students are somewhat less enthusiastic about the city itself. Although some respondents complain that Toledo is fairly industrial, others say it offers numerous cultural and recreational opportunities, including an art museum, a top-rated zoo, and—as *M*A*S*H* fans will no doubt remember—a minor league baseball team, the Toledo Mud Hens. There are no university residence halls, but students say off-campus housing opportunities are very good.

ADMISSIONS

Preference in admissions is given to residents of Ohio, but nonresidents with superior qualifications are sometimes accepted. Candidates applying through the regular admissions process are strongly encouraged to submit their applications as early as possible. Only Ohio residents are permitted to apply through the Early Decision Program.

The Admissions Committee considers a number of factors in making its final decisions, including the interview, GPA, MCAT scores, personal qualities, and motivation for studying medicine.

Special Programs for Members of Underrepresented Minorities: MCO strongly encourages members of underrepresented minorities to apply. The school's Minority Affairs Office coordinates recruitment efforts that include a prematriculation summer session.

Transfer Policy: MCO does not accept transfers.

FINANCIAL AID

Financial aid is awarded on the basis of need as determined by the ACT analysis.

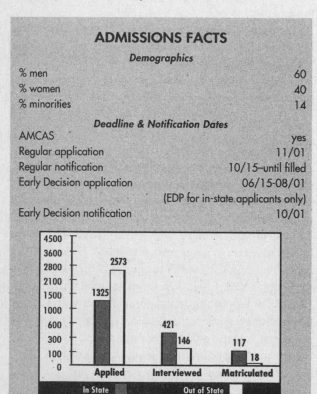

ADMISSIONS FACTS

Demographics

% men	60
% women	40
% minorities	14

Deadline & Notification Dates

AMCAS	yes
Regular application	11/01
Regular notification	10/15–until filled
Early Decision application	06/15-08/01
	(EDP for in-state applicants only)
Early Decision notification	10/01

Applied: In State 1325, Out of State 2573
Interviewed: In State 421, Out of State 146
Matriculated: In State 117, Out of State 18

FIRST YEAR STATISTICS

Average GPA

Science	3.28	Overall	3.36

Average MCAT

Biology	9.18	Physical Science	8.86
Verbal	8.70	Essay	N/A

FINANCIAL FACTS

Tuition and Fees

In-state	$9,621	On-campus housing	N/A
Out-of-state	$12,873	Off-campus housing	N/A

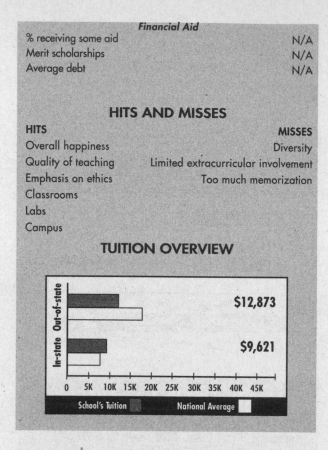

Financial Aid

% receiving some aid	N/A
Merit scholarships	N/A
Average debt	N/A

HITS AND MISSES

HITS	MISSES
Overall happiness	Diversity
Quality of teaching	Limited extracurricular involvement
Emphasis on ethics	Too much memorization
Classrooms	
Labs	
Campus	

TUITION OVERVIEW

Out-of-state: $12,873
In-state: $9,621

School's Tuition | National Average

Northeastern Ohio Universities College of Medicine

Admissions Office
College of Medicine, P.O. Box 95, Rootstown, OH 44272-0095
(216) 325-2511

OVERVIEW

Northeastern Ohio Universities College of Medicine (NEOUCOM) was established in the early 1970s to fulfill a clearly defined mission: "to graduate well-qualified doctors, capable of entering any field of specialization while being oriented to principles and practices of primary care, especially family medicine." The school is doing a good job of satisfying this goal; about half of its graduates enter primary care residencies and a large percentage stay in Ohio to practice.

If you're a high school student committed to medicine and you're not afraid of a lot of hard work, NEOUCOM is certainly worth looking into. On the other hand, if you're a college or post-grad applicant, don't get your hopes up. Although a handful of NEOUCOM students are accepted into a traditional four-year program, the vast majority are admitted through a combined, six-year BS/MD program.

ACADEMICS

Students admitted through the BS/MD program spend twenty-seven intense months in undergraduate studies at Kent State, University of Akron, or Youngstown State. According to an admissions official, NEOUCOM seeks to create a link with the med school from the beginning of the curriculum; there is a summer orientation for new students and a fall "Trying Medicine on for Size" seminar. After the initial undergraduate sequence, all students move to the medical campus in Rootstown for the first year of the medical curriculum. Joining them are students admitted to the traditional four-year path.

In the freshman medical year, students spend the majority of their time studying the basic sciences. Because of the large amount of time devoted to clinical experiences in the sophomore year, the first year is pretty intense. Students spend about thirty-three hours per week in class, primarily in lectures and labs. A Behavioral Science segment augments science courses and lends psychological, social, and ethical perspectives.

Sophomores continue their study of the sciences through courses that include Pharmacology and Systemic Pathology, but there is considerable integration among disciplines and emphasis on the clinical relevance of scientific principles. The year-long Introduction to Clinical Medicine (ICM) provides students with opportunities to apply their growing biological knowledge to clinical problems and to learn fundamental patient communication, examination, and evaluation skills. NEOUCOM's approach to instruction in this transitional year allows for extensive clinical exposure and patient contact; students spend three days per week in family practice centers and two in classrooms and labs.

After a short vacation, students enter the third-year clerkships at affiliated hospitals in either the Akron, Canton, or Youngstown area. In accordance with its mission to train generalists, NEOUCOM augments clerkships in the traditional disciplines with a rotation in family medicine and a one-month Primary Care Preceptorship. In the final year, students must complete at least twenty-four weeks of electives and a four-week Human Values in Medicine course.

Grading and Promotion Policy: Honors/Satisfactory/Unsatisfactory/Conditional Unsatisfactory. Students must take Parts I and II of the USMLE.

Additional Degree Programs: MD/Ph.D.

STUDENT LIFE

Because of the intensity of the six-year program and the multiple campuses in both the undergraduate and medical portions of the curriculum, NEOUCOM students have a rather unconventional med school experience. BS/MD students have the choice of attending one of three northeastern Ohio State Universities. While all of the schools are relatively large, the University of Akron is the biggest, with a total student body of just under 30,000. Each school offers a wealth of student organizations, extracurricular activities, and housing arrangements, and each is within about thirty-five miles of the Rootstown campus.

Rootstown itself is a small town located about fifteen miles east of Akron. On the med school campus are recreation and exercise centers; student lounges; a picnic area; and tennis, basketball, and volleyball courts. Canton, Youngstown, Akron, and Cleveland are within easy driving distance for students looking for the amenities of a larger city.

ADMISSIONS

Since NEOUCOM is state-supported, strong preference is given to Ohio residents. Only a handful of exceptionally well-qualified out-of-state candidates are admitted. There are three separate paths for admission: through the BS/MD program; through the four-year MD program, and through Clinical Advanced Standing—a fancy name for the school's transfer program.

Most students are admitted to the six-year curriculum, and the competition is fierce. To be eligible for admission, high school applicants must have taken four years of math and science and rank in the top 10 percent of their class. Since a sincere commitment to medicine is so vital in this intense program, candidates are strongly encouraged to gain experience in the medical field through volunteer or paid work. Successful candidates, according to the admissions office, show exceptional maturity and are motivated and self-disciplined. The average accepted student has a high school GPA of 3.9 (on a 4.0 scale), and an average of 29 on the ACT or 1200 on the SAT.

Depending on the number of students who drop out during the initial two years of the BS/MD program, some spots become available for the four-year medical curriculum. Traditionally, between ten and twenty students—fewer than one percent of the total applicant pool—are admitted through the AMCAS application process. The primary selection factors for four-year candidates are, in order of importance: science GPA, MCAT scores (from the new test), nonscience GPA, letters of recommendation, the interview, exposure to the medical field, volunteer work, extracurricular activities, and essays. Because of the limited number of openings in the first-year class, the associate director of admissions encourages all students who apply through AMCAS to take part in the Early Decision Program. EDP applicants may be either residents or nonresidents, but must possess exceptional qualifications.

Special Programs for Members of Underrepresented Minorities: NEOUCOM's minority affairs division coordinates programs to recruit, retain, and graduate underrepresented minority students. Among its special offerings are community outreach programs, peer counseling, academic advising, and tutoring. Minority students receive some special consideration in admissions.

Transfer Policy: Applications for transfer into the second and, occasionally, the third, medical school years, are considered on a case-by-case basis when space becomes available through attrition. Ohio residents in good standing at accredited med schools are given preference.

FINANCIAL AID:

BS/MD students save a considerable amount of money by completing both their undergraduate and medical degrees in six years instead of the traditional eight. As a result, they owe significantly less than their counterparts at other schools; total debt for all six years is approximately $50,000. Financial assistance is available through loan, grant, and scholarship programs. While most aid is awarded on the basis of need, NEOUCOM offers some merit scholarships. In exchange for a promise of future service, students interested in practicing in medically-underserved areas of Ohio may be eligible for state tuition remission programs.

ADMISSIONS FACTS

Demographics

% men	56
% women	44
% minorities	42

Deadline & Notification Dates

AMCAS	yes
Regular application	11/01
Regular notification	10/15-until filled
Early Decision application	06/15-08/01
Early Decision notification	10/01

FIRST YEAR STATISTICS

Average GPA

Science	N/A	Nonscience	N/A

Average MCAT

Biology	N/A	Physical Science	N/A
Verbal	N/A	Essay	N/A

FINANCIAL FACTS

Tuition and Fees

In-state	$9,954	On-campus housing	N/A
Out-of-state	$19,209	Off-campus housing	$9,800

Financial Aid

% receiving some aid	75
Merit scholarships	yes
Average debt	$50,000

TUITION OVERVIEW

Ohio State University College of Medicine

Admissions Committee, 270-A Meiling Hall,
370 West Ninth Ave., Columbus, OH 43210-1238
(614) 292-7137

OVERVIEW

OSU is more than just one of the nation's top comprehensive schools. Certainly, the students we surveyed say the school deserves its reputation and give the school high marks in nearly every category. But the school's best feature, according to the students who go there, is the flexibility of its basic science curriculum. This, and the vision OSU has of the doctor as a whole person, combine to make most OSU students very happy.

ACADEMICS

Although OSU splits its curriculum along the usual basic science and clinical lines, its program is innovative. Students may select one of three instructional formats for the preclinical years: the Lecture/Discussion Program, Independent Study, or a Problem-based Learning Pathway.

While the Lecture/Discussion program is the most traditional of the options, interdisciplinary courses, clinical correlations, and significant integration of technology in the basic sciences are among its progressive features. The Independent Study program—which about 20 to 25 percent of students select—allows students to direct their own course of study with faculty support, but minimal structure. The Problem-based Learning Pathway features a case study, discussion-oriented teaching method with strong emphasis on clinical application of basic scientific principles.

OSU integrates a Medical Humanities Program into all three options. Psychosocial aspects of medicine are presented and discussed, and there is considerable emphasis on health care delivery systems and physician responsibility. The humanities program is extremely popular and students are especially pleased with the emphasis it places on medical ethics.

Clinical exposure in the basic science years comes through patient-oriented courses, a required community project, and a preceptorship in an ambulatory setting. To facilitate the transition between the basic science and clinical periods, third-year students are required to start the year with a general clerkship. Although first- and second-year students are satisfied with the amount of early patient contact they have, most students say they would like more exposure.

Students are much more enthusiastic about the quality of basic science and clinical teaching. Professors are rated outstanding, and students are especially pleased with the emphasis the faculty places on the "caring, compassionate side of the physician." A strong clinical orientation does not preclude biomedical investigation, though; students rate the school's research efforts as outstanding. Facilities, too, receive excellent reviews, with the most enthusiastic accolades for OSU's varied clinical settings.

Grading and Promotion Policy: Satisfactory/Unsatisfactory.

Additional Degree Programs: MD/Ph.D. OSU also offers the Medical Scientist Training Program.

STUDENT LIFE

Although our survey shows that OSU students study comparatively more than do their counterparts at other schools, many are quick to point out that there's life outside the classroom. And there's plenty to do. Medical students have access to the considerable amenities of the university. Students can even practice for their Wednesday-afternoon-off future on the school's golf course.

Students are happy with both their campus and Columbus, though many voice concerns about safety. Although the university offers some housing, most students say it's marginal and prefer to find their own accommodations.

ADMISSIONS

OSU shows preference to residents of Ohio. Although out-of-state applicants will not be accepted until all qualified Ohioans are admitted, nonresidents are welcome to apply. In making final selections, the Admissions Office considers the academic record, MCAT scores, letters of recommendation, essays, personal qualities, and the interview.

Special Programs for Members of Underrepresented Minorities: The Office of Minority Affairs coordinates OSU's efforts to recruit, educate, and graduate underrepresented minority students. A variety of early intervention programs are geared toward motivating talented secondary school and undergraduate students who are interested in medicine. OSU also offers a postbaccalaureate premedical program for students who wish to improve their skills before applying to med school and a prematriculation summer session for students who wish to get a head start on the basic sciences.

Transfer Policy: Under exceptional circumstances, OSU considers transfers into the third year.

FINANCIAL AID

Most assistance is based on financial need, but a limited number of merit scholarships are available. The Financial Aid Office encourages applicants to apply for assistance as early as possible, even before acceptance.

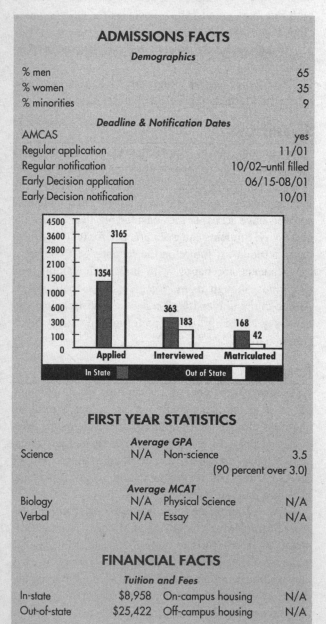

ADMISSIONS FACTS

Demographics

% men	65
% women	35
% minorities	9

Deadline & Notification Dates

AMCAS	yes
Regular application	11/01
Regular notification	10/02–until filled
Early Decision application	06/15-08/01
Early Decision notification	10/01

In State / Out of State

FIRST YEAR STATISTICS

Average GPA

Science	N/A	Non-science	3.5
		(90 percent over 3.0)	

Average MCAT

Biology	N/A	Physical Science	N/A
Verbal	N/A	Essay	N/A

FINANCIAL FACTS

Tuition and Fees

In-state	$8,958	On-campus housing	N/A
Out-of-state	$25,422	Off-campus housing	N/A

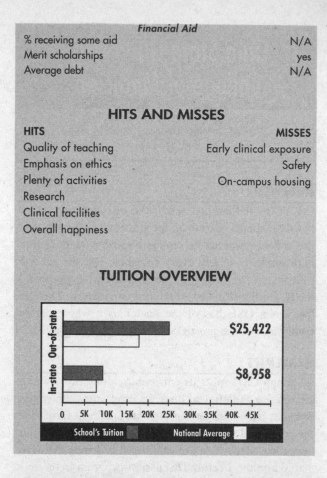

Financial Aid

% receiving some aid	N/A
Merit scholarships	yes
Average debt	N/A

HITS AND MISSES

HITS	MISSES
Quality of teaching	Early clinical exposure
Emphasis on ethics	Safety
Plenty of activities	On-campus housing
Research	
Clinical facilities	
Overall happiness	

TUITION OVERVIEW

$25,422

$8,958

School's Tuition / National Average

Wright State University School of Medicine

Office of Student Affairs/Adm., P.O. Box 1751, Dayton, OH 45401
(513) 873-2934

OVERVIEW

If you're committed to primary care, you might want to look at Wright State. This relatively small southwestern Ohio institution has the highest percentage of graduates entering residencies in family practice of any U.S. med school. To develop the kind of doctor "that considers the individual, not just the immediate diagnosis, disease, or injury," Wright State employs a patient-centered curriculum with early hands-on clinical experience. A strong emphasis on ambulatory care and a wide variety of teaching sites, including hospitals, clinics, and private physicians' offices, give students a strong grounding in community medicine.

ACADEMICS

Wright State's curriculum includes time for students to pursue their own interests during the basic science years. Freshmen and sophomores may take two-week electives at the end of each of the five initial quarters, giving them the chance to enhance their basic science knowledge, to practice their developing clinical skills, or to participate in research activities. Summer experiences, including an Undergraduate Fellowship in Family Practice, are also available.

The formal coursework in the first two years centers around the basic sciences, but Wright State puts considerable emphasis on clinical correlations. Through their studies, freshmen and sophomores learn to recognize and understand the normal and abnormal structures and functions of the human body. Complementing science instruction is a strong emphasis on the humanistic aspects of medicine. In the Medicine in Society course, students discuss ethical issues in medical treatment and gain an understanding of the responsibilities of a physician.

Patient contact begins in the first week and continues throughout the four years. The freshman- and sophomore-year Introduction to Clinical Medicine (ICM) course provides a graduated series of patient care and interaction experiences. In ICM, students learn to communicate with patients, take a thorough medical history, and conduct a comprehensive physical exam. Innovative instructional methods, including small group conferences, independent study, and computer-assisted learning, complement the traditional lectures and labs of the preclinical years.

Third-year students complete clerkships in the major disciplines and in family practice. Clinical teaching is conducted at twenty-eight different locations, including seven major affiliated hospitals. During rotations, juniors take histories, conduct examinations, evaluate lab results, learn procedures, and assist the medical team in treatment of patients. Requirements continue in the final year when all students do clerkships in emergency medicine, orthopedics, and neurology. The remainder of the senior year is free for electives.

Grading and Promotion Policy: Wright State uses two grading systems: A–F and Honors/Pass/Fail.

Additional Degree Programs: MD/Ph.D.

STUDENT LIFE

Since most Wright State students are interested in practicing family medicine, it should come as no surprise that they are involved in a number of service projects directed at improving community health. In one popular program, "Student to Student," med students discuss health topics like teenage pregnancy, AIDS, and substance abuse with children and adolescents.

Outside of med school and University activities, students looking for a break from their studies can tap the resources of Dayton. Art museums, a ballet company, and the Philharmonic Orchestra are part of the city's cultural center. The Oregon Historic District, a quaint downtown spot peppered with pubs, shops, and restaurants, is popular not only with Wright State students, but also with those from the Dayton area's twenty-six other colleges and universities. Numerous city parks, rivers, and lakes offer peaceful settings for recreation and relaxation.

The cost of living is relatively low in Dayton—almost 20 percent below the national average. Many students live in the Oregon District or in other neighborhoods close to the school. The average cost of an off-campus efficiency apartment, according to the school's promotional materials, is under $300 per month.

ADMISSIONS

Wright State shows a strong preference for Ohio residents, but up to 15 percent of students may come from out of state. Because the school has a rolling admissions policy, candidates are encouraged to apply as early as possible.

Most of the admissions directors we surveyed for this book listed the science GPA, MCAT scores, or the interview as the most important selection factor. Although these credentials are near the top of Wright State's list, admissions officials rank volunteer activities and exposure to the medical profession as the top considerations. Other major evaluation criteria, in descending order of importance, are science GPA, MCAT scores (from the new test), nonscience GPA, the interview, letters of recommendation, and essays. Personal qualities are also considered; an admissions official reports, "The admissions committee looks for evidence of intellectual ability, maturity, motivation, ability to interact with people, dedication to human concerns, ability to learn independently and potential for medical service in an underserved area."

Special Programs for Members of Underrepresented Minorities: Wright State is among the nation's leaders in underrepresented minority admissions, retention, and graduation. Strong recruitment and support efforts, coordinated by a minority affairs division, are behind this success. Among the school's special offerings are community outreach programs, summer sessions for high school students, weekend immersion programs for college students, a prematriculation summer session, academic advising, tutoring, and peer counseling. Qualified minority students also receive special consideration in the admissions process.

Transfer Policy: Applications for transfer into the third-year class are considered on a space-available basis. Applicants must be in good standing at an LCME-accredited med school.

FINANCIAL AID

Although the school offers a few merit scholarships, most financial aid is based on need. Loans are the primary source of assistance, and Wright State students have the debt levels to prove it. In 1993, the average student owed nearly $70,000 at graduation.

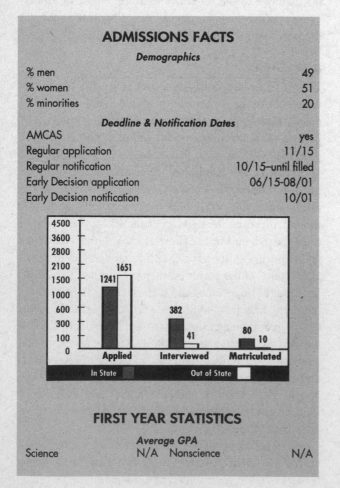

ADMISSIONS FACTS
Demographics

% men	49
% women	51
% minorities	20

Deadline & Notification Dates

AMCAS	yes
Regular application	11/15
Regular notification	10/15–until filled
Early Decision application	06/15-08/01
Early Decision notification	10/01

FIRST YEAR STATISTICS
Average GPA

Science	N/A	Nonscience	N/A

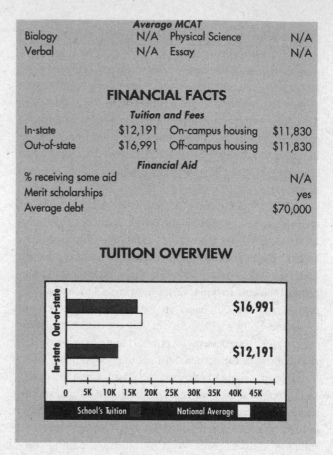

Average MCAT

Biology	N/A	Physical Science	N/A
Verbal	N/A	Essay	N/A

FINANCIAL FACTS
Tuition and Fees

In-state	$12,191	On-campus housing	$11,830
Out-of-state	$16,991	Off-campus housing	$11,830

Financial Aid

% receiving some aid	N/A
Merit scholarships	yes
Average debt	$70,000

TUITION OVERVIEW

$16,991

$12,191

School's Tuition	National Average

University of Oklahoma College of Medicine

Director of Student Affairs, P.O. Box 26901, Oklahoma City, OK 73190
(405) 271-2331

OVERVIEW

The University of Oklahoma College of Medicine's mission is to provide access both to "progressive research and progressive patient care." The school also places great emphasis on primary care and on training physicians to serve the health care needs of Oklahoma residents. Of the most recent graduating class, about half of the students chose internships in primary care and about half of all graduates completed their residencies within the state.

ACADEMICS

Oklahoma's curriculum is divided into two-year preclinical and clinical units, but the school emphasizes clinical correlations in the basic science years. All students begin their training at the Oklahoma City campus, but about 25 percent move to the College of Medicine's Tulsa campus for their clinical work.

In the first of the preclinical years, students develop an understanding of normal human structures and functions through a study of the basic, behavioral, and clinical sciences. To help students integrate the scientific principles with patient problems, Oklahoma requires freshmen to spend one afternoon a week in Introduction to Clinical Care. In this course, students assist local physicians and clinical faculty with patient care.

The second-year curriculum continues to integrate basic, behavioral, and clinical sciences, but the focus shifts to the disease process, its effects on the individual and society, and therapeutic agents to treat illness. Major sophomore courses include microbiology/immunology, pathology, lab medicine, pharmacology, and Introduction to Clinical Medicine (ICM). In ICM, students build on the patient interaction skills they developed as freshmen, learn to take thorough medical histories, conduct physical examinations, and make rudimentary physical diagnoses. This full-year course and a last semester review facilitate the transition to the clinical period.

Major clerkships in medicine, surgery, pediatrics, psychiatry, obstetrics, and family medicine and a selective rotation in a subspecialty are required of all juniors. In addition, third-year students complete introductory experiences in dermatology, neurology, and otorhinolaryngology. In December of the junior year, the entire class participates in a two-week mini-course that focuses on ethical issues and medical jurisprudence.

The fourth year is a mix of required and elective experiences. All seniors complete externships in pediatrics and psychiatry, do a clerkship in gynecology, and participate in an ambulatory care experience. They must also complete a rural preceptorship in a community of fewer than 10,000 people. Beyond these requirements, students complete five months of electives.

Oklahoma is also making an effort to increase the research activities of its students. An MD/Ph.D. program, which provides full scholarship support to its participants, is available for students who are interested in careers in biomedical investigation or academic medicine. For those seeking less of a long-term commitment, the school offers an Honors Research Program through which twenty summer scholarships are available.

Grading and Promotion Policy: A letter grading system is used. Students must take Parts I and II of the USMLE.

Additional Degree Programs: MD/Ph.D.

ADMISSIONS

Although Oklahoma shows strong preference for state residents, up to 15 percent of students can come from out of state. Still, nonresidents must be exceptionally well qualified to be competitive. For the 1992 entering class, for example, only between 1 and 2 percent of out-of-state candidates were admitted.

All candidates apply through AMCAS and are required to complete supplemental applications. Since the deadline date for supplemental materials is the beginning of November, candidates should try to submit their AMCAS applications well before the October 15 deadline. On the basis of the completed application, promising candidates are invited to interview with student, faculty, and local physician members of the Admissions Board.

Final admissions decisions are made on the basis of the interview, GPA, MCAT scores, letters of recommendation, leadership abilities, empathy, and other personal characteristics.

Special Programs for Members of Underrepresented Minorities: The College of Medicine is committed to increasing the number of underrepresented minority physicians in Oklahoma and strongly encourages qualified minority students to apply.

Transfer Policy: Applications for transfer into the third year are considered on a space-available basis. Candidates must be in good standing at accredited medical schools.

FINANCIAL AID

In addition to federal loan and scholarship programs, Oklahoma offers a number of state and institutional financial aid opportunities. Among these are the Regents' Scholarships Fee Waiver program, which provides assistance to underrepresented minority students and the Rural Medical Education Loan and Scholarship fund, which aids students who wish to practice in rural communities.

FINANCIAL FACTS

Tuition and Fees

In-state	$6,874	On-campus housing	N/A
Out-of-state	$16,534	Off-campus housing	N/A

Financial Aid

% receiving some aid	94
Merit scholarships	N/A
Average debt	N/A

TUITION OVERVIEW

$16,534

$6,874

School's Tuition   National Average

ADMISSIONS FACTS

Demographics

% men	58
% women	42
% minorities	11

Deadline & Notification Dates

AMCAS	yes
Regular application	10/15
Regular notification	12/01–until filled
Early Decision application	No EDP program
Early Decision notification	N/A

In State   Out of State

FIRST YEAR STATISTICS

Average GPA

Science	N/A	Nonscience	3.55

Average MCAT

Biology	N/A	Physical Science	N/A
Verbal	N/A	Essay	N/A

Oregon Health Sciences University School of Medicine

Office of Education and Student Affairs
3181 SW Sam Jackson Park Road, Portland, OR 97201
(503) 494-4499

OVERVIEW

Although the Oregon Health Sciences University School of Medicine has a strong commitment to training highly skilled physicians, its clinical orientation doesn't preclude research activities. A "vigorous research program" is supported primarily by funding from the National Institutes of Health, and a combined MD/Ph.D. degree is available in a large number of basic science disciplines. Recognized as a leader among comprehensive schools, OHSU is not content to rest on its laurels; a completely revamped curriculum has just been implemented.

ACADEMICS

The new curriculum reflects trends in both medical education and health care delivery. Major changes include more small group learning; increased integration of the basic and clinical sciences; a mandatory six-week primary care rotation; and transitional courses after the second and fourth years.

The first two years are now divided into units that are comprised of interdisciplinary courses. Freshmen study the body's normal structures and functions and begin to investigate the disease process and its effects on the body. In the second year, students continue their study of the sciences, but there is an increased emphasis on clinical correlations and psychosocial, economic, and ethical issues.

A Principles of Clinical Medicine course spans the basic science years. In this course, students learn patient-interaction skills, examine behavioral science topics, consider ethical scenarios, and study epidemiology and statistics. Throughout the preclinical years, students spend one afternoon a week in the office of a physician preceptor. Three afternoons a week are reserved for self-directed learning, study, and free time.

The third and fourth years are devoted to clinical clerkships and electives. Juniors and seniors complete rotations at the university hospitals and clinics and in area affiliates. Electives may be taken in both basic and clinical sciences.

Although all students are encouraged to participate in research activities during vacation or elective time, those who are interested in extensive scientific investigation and/or academic medicine may choose to pursue a combined MD/Ph.D.

Grading and Promotion Policy: Honors/Acceptable/Marginal/Fail. Students must pass Parts I and II of the USMLE.

Additional Degree Programs: MD/Ph.D.

STUDENT LIFE

The School of Medicine is part of the Oregon Health Sciences University, which also includes Schools of Nursing and Dentistry, three research units, and four patient care units. Students from all disciplines share the Student Activities Building. This facility houses a gym; a weight training room; tennis, squash and racquetball courts; and a pool. Instruction in a variety of sports is available, and aerobics classes are held on site. For those who prefer organized sports, intramural basketball and volleyball teams offer a chance to compete with classmates throughout the year.

In addition to the activities afforded by the university, students can take advantage of the recreational, cultural, and entertainment opportunities of one of the Northwest's largest and most popular cities. Close to Portland's business district, OHSU is located on a large site in Sam Jackson Park, overlooking the city. A limited number of housing units are available on campus, but the university maintains a list of off-campus apartments for those who'd rather make their own living arrangements.

ADMISSIONS

OHSU gives first priority to state residents, but nonresident applicants who are members of underrepresented minorities; who are from Wyoming, Alaska, or Montana; or who apply to the combined MD/Ph.D. program are also given special consideration. Very few out-of-state applicants who don't fit into one of these categories are admitted.

The Admissions Committee makes an initial evaluation of each candidate's AMCAS application to decide whether to solicit supplementary material; approximately half of the total applicant pool is eliminated in this first step. On the basis of the complete application, the Committee invites the most promising candidates to campus for a pair of one-on-one interviews and a luncheon with current students.

After the interview, the committee makes its final decisions. According to OHSU's literature, primary selection factors include: the interview; the overall academic record; MCAT scores; letters of recommendation; "an understanding and appreciation of health care issues and/or biomedical research" (be prepared for interview questions about these topics); interest in primary care or practice in medically underserved areas; motivation; maturity; interpersonal skills; and problem-solving ability.

Special Programs for Members of Underrepresented Minorities: OHSU actively encourages members of underrepresented minorities to apply and gives qualified minority students—even nonresidents—special consideration in the admissions process. The Office of Multicultural Affairs develops and coordinates "programs and services that reflect the diversity of cultures and support academic development for minority students."

Transfer Policy: Only Oregon residents and their spouses are eligible to transfer to OHSU. Even then, applicants are accepted only if a space becomes available. No transfers have been accepted in recent years.

FINANCIAL AID

OHSU coordinates a variety of financial aid programs for students who can't meet costs. Most financial aid is awarded on the basis of need as determined by the College Scholarship Service analysis.

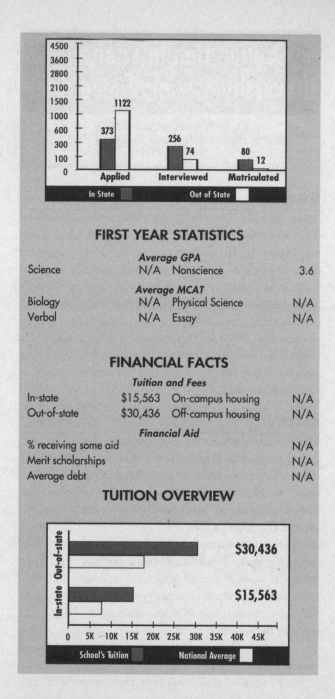

FIRST YEAR STATISTICS

	Average GPA		
Science	N/A	Nonscience	3.6
	Average MCAT		
Biology	N/A	Physical Science	N/A
Verbal	N/A	Essay	N/A

FINANCIAL FACTS

	Tuition and Fees		
In-state	$15,563	On-campus housing	N/A
Out-of-state	$30,436	Off-campus housing	N/A
	Financial Aid		
% receiving some aid			N/A
Merit scholarships			N/A
Average debt			N/A

TUITION OVERVIEW

ADMISSIONS FACTS

Demographics

% men	57
% women	43
% minorities	5

Deadline & Notification Dates

AMCAS	yes
Regular application	10/15
Regular notification	11/1–until filled
Early Decision application	No EDP program
Early Decision notification	N/A

Hahnemann University School of Medicine

Medical School Admissions
Mail Stop 442, Broad and Vine Streets, Philadelphia, PA 19102-1192
(215) 762-7600

OVERVIEW

If you're looking for a school where students are in accord about what their med school experience is and should be like, then Hahnemann may not be for you. Some students we surveyed love their school, while others think it has a lot of room for improvement. But all agree on one thing—Hahnemann is in the process of sweeping changes, and things are getting better.

ACADEMICS

Although Hahnemann's curriculum is not completely traditional, there is little clinical exposure until the spring semester of the sophomore year. The first year and a half is primarily devoted to the basic sciences, but there is some emphasis on the behavioral sciences and clinical problem-solving. In the second half of the sophomore year, students apply their basic science knowledge to clinical situations and learn to interact with patients in the Introduction to Clinical Medicine course. The third and part of the fourth year are devoted to clinical clerkships, including a required rotation in ambulatory care. The balance of the last year is spent in electives.

Students are only moderately satisfied with the curriculum in the first two years. Specifically, they complain that there are too many unnecessary reading assignments and not enough emphasis on the clinical relevance of scientific principles. But one student says, "The school is changing for the better, with earlier clinical exposure and a more problem-based curriculum."

The faculty, on the other hand, gets high marks. Professors are described as "friendly" and "supportive," and students agree that the quality of teaching is very good. The administration does not fare nearly so well. "The overall level of organization of the school is poor," complains one student. "The students rarely know about events that involve them because nobody tells them." But a classmate is more optimistic: "Under Hahnemann's new president, things appear to be improving."

Physical changes are also on the horizon. Says one student, "Major renovations are currently underway, so the library, facilities, and campus will be great in a few years." According to students, improvements are long overdue. Criticism for all but the clinical facilities—which are rated as superior—is widespread.

Grading and Promotion Policy: Honors/High Pass/ Satisfactory/Marginally Unsatisfactory/Unsatisfactory.

Additional Degree Programs: MD/Ph.D. Hahnemann also participates in early assurance programs with several undergraduate institutions.

STUDENT LIFE

Is the atmosphere competitive at Hahnemann? That depends on who you ask. Some students say it's absolutely cutthroat, but others say their classmates are not at all competitive. Most responses fall somewhere in between. This lack of consensus extends to answers to our questions about students' social life. About 30 percent say their classmates play hard; an almost equal percentage say students keep their noses in their books. It's fairly obvious that either these folks don't know the same people or they have different social expectations. Either way, extracurricular life at Hahnemann appears to be what you make of it, and a prematriculation visit is a good idea for anyone seriously considering the school.

One thing students agree on is that the area around the campus isn't a great place to be at night. Students suggest that new matriculants pass on university housing because better opportunities—and safer neighborhoods—can be found off campus. Public transportation is accessible, but again, safety is a big concern.

ADMISSIONS

Hahnemann gives preference to Pennsylvania residents, but welcomes applications from nonresidents. Especially encouraged to apply from out of state are nontraditional and underrepresented minority students. In making its decisions, the Admissions Committee considers the interview, academic performance, MCAT scores (from the new format test), letters of recommendation, essays, extracurricular activities, and personal qualities.

Special Programs for Members of Underrepresented Minorities: A minority affairs office coordinates Hahnemann's efforts to recruit and educate members of underrepresented minorities. Among special programs are a prematriculation summer session, academic tutoring, and counseling.

Transfer Policy: Hahnemann considers transfers into the second or third year on a space-available basis.

FINANCIAL AID

The financial aid office coordinates university, governmental, and private aid programs. Much of the available assistance is made on the basis of need as determined by the GAPSFAS analysis.

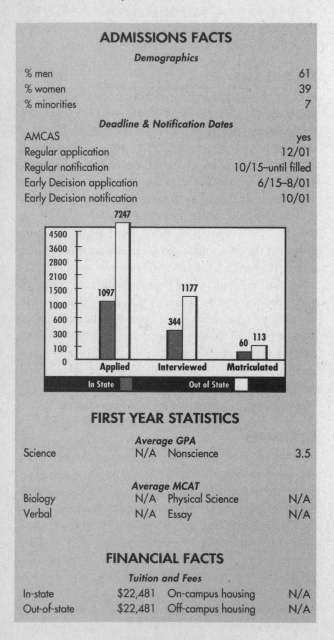

ADMISSIONS FACTS

Demographics

% men	61
% women	39
% minorities	7

Deadline & Notification Dates

AMCAS	yes
Regular application	12/01
Regular notification	10/15–until filled
Early Decision application	6/15–8/01
Early Decision notification	10/01

In State / Out of State chart:

	Applied	Interviewed	Matriculated
In State	1097	344	60
Out of State	7247	1177	113

FIRST YEAR STATISTICS

Average GPA

Science	N/A	Nonscience	3.5

Average MCAT

Biology	N/A	Physical Science	N/A
Verbal	N/A	Essay	N/A

FINANCIAL FACTS

Tuition and Fees

In-state	$22,481	On-campus housing	N/A
Out-of-state	$22,481	Off-campus housing	N/A

Financial Aid

% receiving some aid	N/A
Merit scholarships	yes
Average debt	N/A

HITS AND MISSES

HITS	MISSES
Faculty accessibility	Basic science teaching facilities
Clinical facilities	Library
New administration	Computer labs
Quality of teaching	Philadelphia
	On-campus housing
	Safety

TUITION OVERVIEW

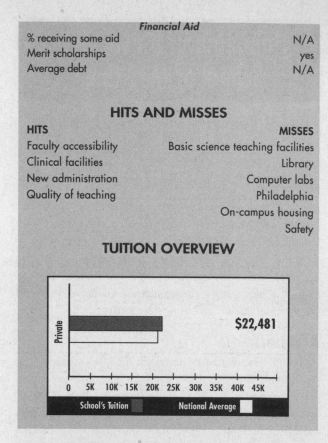

$22,481

School's Tuition ▮ National Average ▯

Jefferson Medical College of Thomas Jefferson University

Associate Dean for Admissions
1025 Walnut Street, Philadelphia, PA 19107
(215) 955-6983

OVERVIEW

Evidently, the top honors Jefferson received in a recent ranking of comprehensive med schools paid off during applications season: over a thousand more students applied to Jefferson in 1993 than did in 1992. But a stellar reputation isn't the only thing that draws would-be doctors to this Philadelphia school; a progressive curriculum, a strong clinical orientation, and a growing, well-respected research program are all part of the package.

ACADEMICS

Jefferson's curriculum is structured around the traditional two-year preclinical and clinical units, but includes progressive features. In the first year, students take departmental and interdisciplinary courses in the basic sciences to gain an understanding of normal human physiology and function. Anatomy, biochemistry, molecular biology, biostatistics, histology, and neurosciences are among the science requirements. Freshmen also investigate ethical, social, and behavioral aspects of medicine and take the initial segment of a two-year Introduction to Clinical Medicine (ICM) course. Throughout the preclinical phase, ICM allows students to apply their developing scientific knowledge to patient problems and to learn fundamental patient-interaction, history-taking, examination, and diagnosis skills.

In the second year, students focus on abnormal structures and functions through course work in microbiology, immunology, pathology, and pharmacology. ICM continues and students explore biopsychosocial issues in a Medicine and Society course. In each of the first two years, students have the opportunity to pursue their particular interests through elective credits.

The clinical period is divided into two phases. In the initial phase, students complete clerkships in family medicine, surgery, internal medicine, pediatrics, psychiatry, and obstetrics/gynecology. Phase II requirements include experiences in anesthesiology, orthopedic surgery, urology, neurology/neurosurgery, ophthalmology, otolaryngology, oncology/radiation, and rehabilitation medicine. Advanced basic science work, inpatient and outpatient subinternships, and electives round out the final period of the curriculum.

Grading and Promotion Policy: In the first two years, Jefferson uses a numerical grading system. In the last two years, students are graded on a High Honors/Above Expected Competence/Expected Competence/Marginal Competence/Fail system. Students must pass Parts I and II of the USMLE.

Additional Degree Programs: Jefferson offers combined BS/MD programs in conjunction with Penn State University and the University of Delaware. MD/MA and MD/Ph.D. programs are also available.

ADMISSIONS

Jefferson is a private school and, though approximately half of its students are traditionally from Pennsylvania, it gives no preference to state residents. Highly-qualified applicants for whom Jefferson is the first choice may apply through the Early Decision Program. Regardless of the method of application, candidates are encouraged to take the MCAT in the spring of the year prior to the year of intended matriculation.

The Admissions Committee makes its final decisions on the basis of the AMCAS and supplemental applications and the personal interview. The most important selection factors, according to the associate dean of admissions, are the science GPA, MCAT scores, and the interview. Letters of recommendation, extracurricular activities, exposure to the medical profession, and volunteer activities are also considered important. Essays are not considered. Children of alumni and of faculty have received special consideration in past years.

Special Programs for Members of Underrepresented Minorities: Jefferson's minority affairs division coordinates programs for members of underrepresented minorities. Among its offerings are a prematriculation summer session, a decelerated program for the basic science years, academic advising, and peer counseling. Qualified applicants who belong to a minority group traditionally underrepresented in medicine may also receive special consideration for admission.

Transfer Policy: Applications for transfer from students in good standing at accredited med schools are considered on a space-available basis if there is a compelling need for the transfer.

FINANCIAL AID:

Financial aid is awarded primarily on the basis of need as determined by the GAPSFAS analysis. Students who demonstrate need beyond what can be met through federal loan sources are generally assisted through a combination of grant and loan funds.

ADMISSIONS FACTS

Demographics

% men	65
% women	35
% minorities	7

Deadline & Notification Dates

AMCAS	yes
Regular application	11/15
Regular notification	11/15–until filled
Early Decision application	6/15–8/01
Early Decision notification	10/01

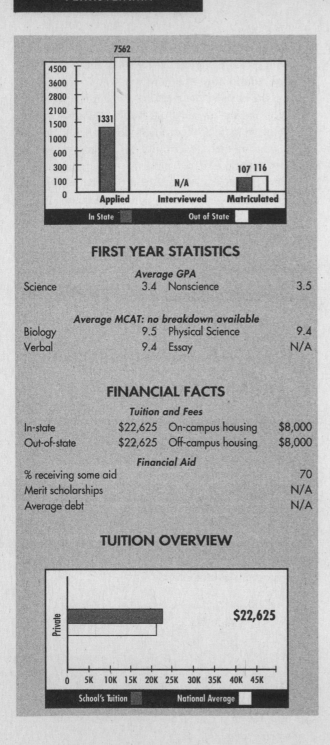

FIRST YEAR STATISTICS

Average GPA

Science	3.4	Nonscience	3.5

Average MCAT: no breakdown available

Biology	9.5	Physical Science	9.4
Verbal	9.4	Essay	N/A

FINANCIAL FACTS

Tuition and Fees

In-state	$22,625	On-campus housing	$8,000
Out-of-state	$22,625	Off-campus housing	$8,000

Financial Aid

% receiving some aid	70
Merit scholarships	N/A
Average debt	N/A

TUITION OVERVIEW

Medical College of Pennsylvania

Admissions Office, 2900 Queen Lane, Philadelphia, PA 19219
(215) 991-8202

OVERVIEW

Although students rave about a "dynamic, well-rounded curriculum" and "brand new, state-of-the-art facilities," what really sets MCP apart from the other schools we surveyed is its treatment of women. According to students, the school's "commitment to supporting women in medicine" is more than just lip service. Some of the features that add to the MCP's female-friendly atmosphere are a faculty that's one-third female—a much higher proportion than at most schools—and a mentor program that allows students to focus on women's issues in medicine.

ACADEMICS

MCP offers a progressive curriculum with nontraditional programs in both the preclinical and clinical years. Instruction in the basic sciences, which is given in the first two years, is marked by alternative teaching methods and a strong clinical emphasis. In addition to lecture classes, MCP uses small-group discussion sections, computerized learning models, and standardized patients. Some students choose an alternative, problem-based learning track, the Program for Integrated Learning (PIL).

In the PIL, small groups of students use case studies to learn scientific principles as they apply to clinical problems. Clinical exposure isn't limited to paper patients, though; PIL students learn physical examination and diagnostic skills through an Introduction to the Patient section and participate in a ten-week primary care preceptorship. Participants report that the program is excellent.

Students in the regular program are also enthusiastic. They like the patient contact they have in the clinical skills introduction that augments the basic sciences. They are also proud of MCP's "tradition of humanistic medicine" and the emphasis on ethics it affords. Although students say that "some lecturers are poor," they are pleased with the overall quality of teaching and applaud the "amount of energy" the teachers bring to the classroom. The administration is awarded high marks both for its "responsiveness to students" and its "commitment to improving medical education."

Progress can also be seen in the physical plant at MCP. Students love the new education and research building. Especially popular features are the technologically advanced lecture halls and "a clinical learning lab that simulates doctors' offices."

Grading and Promotion Policy: Honors/Pass/Fail. Passing grade on USMLE Part I is required for graduation, and score must be recorded for USMLE Part II.

Additional Degree Programs: MD/Ph.D.

STUDENT LIFE

Students enjoy MCP's "supportive, noncompetitive atmosphere" but say they don't have much time for a social life. For those who need a break from their studies, MCP offers a variety of clubs and activities, including a school newspaper and an annual skit night. Students who want to stay in shape can work out in the new on-site fitness center or take advantage of a free membership at the local YMCA. Or, if they prefer organized sports, they can join MCP teams that compete with students from other area med schools.

Students say the worst aspect of MCP is its location. Although they concede that "Philadelphia has some great parks and bike trails," students dislike the city and express concern about the safety of its public transportation system. There is no university housing at the Philadelphia campus, but, if students choose to do clerkships at one of the school's affiliated hospitals (located in other parts of the state), housing and partial board is provided at no cost.

ADMISSIONS

MCP states no preference for residents of Pennsylvania. An unusual offering of MCP's admissions office is a "counseling interview" for students who are interested in applying to med school or who have applied once and have been rejected. This is not the admissions interview; the focus is to help students clarify their objectives and improve their applications.

All applicants receive the supplemental application form, and promising candidates—usually about 10 percent of the total applicant pool—are invited to an admissions interview. Among the final selection factors are the interview, academic record, MCAT scores, letters of recommendation, and personal qualities. Since MCP has a rolling admissions policy, students should apply as early in the cycle as possible.

Special Programs for Members of Underrepresented Minorities: MCP encourages underrepresented and other nontraditional students to apply. The school's minority affairs office coordinates recruitment and retention efforts.

Transfer Policy: Transfers into the second and third year are considered on a space-available basis.

FINANCIAL AID

Loans and most scholarships are awarded on the basis of need as determined by the GAPSFAS analysis. In addition, there are several half-tuition merit scholarships available. Approximately 85 percent of students receive assistance.

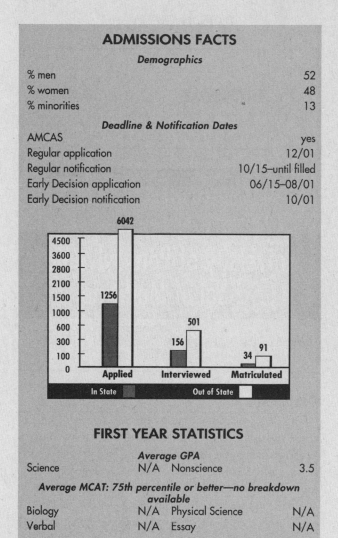

ADMISSIONS FACTS

Demographics

% men	52
% women	48
% minorities	13

Deadline & Notification Dates

AMCAS	yes
Regular application	12/01
Regular notification	10/15—until filled
Early Decision application	06/15–08/01
Early Decision notification	10/01

In State / Out of State

Applied: 1256 / 6042
Interviewed: 156 / 501
Matriculated: 34 / 91

FIRST YEAR STATISTICS

Average GPA

Science	N/A	Nonscience	3.5

Average MCAT: 75th percentile or better—no breakdown available

Biology	N/A	Physical Science	N/A
Verbal	N/A	Essay	N/A

FINANCIAL FACTS

Tuition and Fees

In-state	$20,010	On-campus housing	none
Out-of-state	$20,010	Off-campus housing	N/A

Financial Aid

% receiving some aid	N/A
Merit scholarships	N/A
Average debt	N/A

HITS AND MISSES

HITS	MISSES
Treatment of female students	Philadelphia
Facilities	No on-campus housing
Overall happiness	
Problem-based learning track	
Supportive atmosphere	

TUITION OVERVIEW

Private $20,010

0 5K 10K 15K 20K 25K 30K 35K 40K 45K

School's Tuition ▨   National Average ▢

University of Pennsylvania School of Medicine

Director of Admissions
Edward J. Stemmler Hall, Suite 100, Philadelphia, PA 19104-6056
(215) 898-8001

OVERVIEW

Penn is recognized as one of the top ten research-oriented med schools, and the students we surveyed say it deserves its reputation. Aside from its location in a fairly scary part of Philadelphia, students love nearly everything about their school. Especially popular among our respondents are excellent teaching, extensive clinical exposure, outstanding hospitals, and top-notch research efforts.

ACADEMICS

With only a little over a year and a half devoted to preclinical coursework, Penn's curriculum provides students with earlier entry into clinical clerkships than that of most other schools. The program is divided into three phases. Coursework in Stage I is a mixture of departmental and interdisciplinary courses that cover basic scientific principles, behavioral and social aspects of medicine, and introductory clinical skills. Although the bulk of the time is spent on normal structures and function, toward the end of the year students begin to investigate the effects of disease. Stage II begins in the second year and serves as a bridge to the Stage III clerkships. Courses structured around organ systems stress integration between the basic and clinical sciences. The continuation of the Introduction to Clinical Medicine course begun in Stage I helps students refine their history-taking, examination, and diagnosis skills. In March of the sophomore year, students enter Stage III—the clerkship and elective phase.

Students like Penn's innovative approach and are enthusiastic about the extensive clinical exposure it provides in all four years. They also applaud the opportunities available to them through the Penn Medical Scholars Program. Through this program, students can pursue combined degrees or take a year off for research or independent study. Some combined programs are fully funded, and there are stipends available for research activities.

Praise for Penn's "excellent education" extends to its faculty, as well. High marks go to professors both for their teaching acumen and their approachability. Says one freshman, "The faculty is extremely caring and supportive. They put much less emphasis on memorizing and more on reasoning . . . than [teachers] at most schools." Basic science and clinical teaching facilities, the library, and computer labs are rated as outstanding.

Grading and Promotion Policy: Honors/Pass/Fail in the basic sciences; Honors/High, Pass/Pass/Fail in clinical years.

Additional Degree Programs: MD/Ph.D., MD/MBA, MD/JD. Penn also offers a funded Medical Scientist Training Program.

STUDENT LIFE

Students say that Penn is not particularly competitive and that their classmates are "friendly" and "cooperative." Reports one freshman, "The [atmosphere] of the place is one in which people help one another even when the stresses of medical education become too much." Although respondents say they work hard, they also have active social lives. Penn offers plenty of extracurricular activities on and around campus, and students are very involved in school and community organizations.

Despite Philadelphia's array of recreational and cultural offerings and its relatively close proximity to other metropolitan areas, beaches, and mountains, over half of the students we surveyed dislike the city. Most of this ill-will stems from crime problems around the campus; in fact, more than 90 percent feel the area is unsafe. Though university housing is available, students prefer to make their own arrangements off campus, preferably in more secure neighborhoods.

ADMISSIONS

Some preference is given to residents of Pennsylvania, but any student with outstanding qualifications is encouraged to apply. All candidates are asked to submit supplementary applications, but only those whose credentials are highly competitive are invited to interview.

Among the factors the Admissions Committee considers in its final selections are the interview, the competitiveness of the undergraduate school, GPA, MCAT scores (from the revised test), letters of recommendation, extracurricular activities, volunteerism, exposure to the medical profession, and personal qualities.

Special Programs for Members of Underrepresented Minorities: Penn has had an Office for Minority Affairs since 1968. This office coordinates efforts to recruit underrepresented minority candidates, acts as an advocate during the admissions process, and provides counseling and support services to enrolled students.

Transfer Policy: Transfers are generally accepted only into the third-year class, and then only if space becomes available through attrition. Special consideration is given to students with compelling reasons for the transfer.

FINANCIAL AID

Financial aid is based solely on need as determined by the GAPSFAS analysis.

ADMISSIONS FACTS

Demographics

% men	55
% women	45
% minorities	15

Deadline & Notification Dates

AMCAS	yes
Regular application	11/01
Regular notification	11/15–until filled
Early Decision application	No EDP program
Early Decision notification	N/A

FIRST YEAR STATISTICS

Average GPA

Science	N/A	Nonscience	3.6

Average MCAT: Mean MCAT scores in the 10-11 range— no breakdown available

Biology	N/A	Physical Science	N/A
Verbal	N/A	Essay	N/A

FINANCIAL FACTS

Tuition and Fees

In-state	$24,359	On-campus housing	N/A
Out-of-state	$24,359	Off-campus housing	N/A

Financial Aid

% receiving some aid	Over 75
Merit scholarships	no
Average debt	$52,000

HITS AND MISSES

HITS	MISSES
Noncompetitive atmosphere	Campus safety
Students involved outside of class	On-campus housing
Quality of teaching	Public transportation
Research efforts	
Overall facilities	
Early clinical exposure	
Overall happiness	

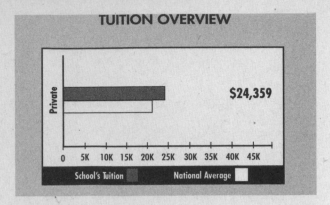

TUITION OVERVIEW

Private

$24,359

0 5K 10K 15K 20K 25K 30K 35K 40K 45K

School's Tuition ▣   National Average ☐

Pennsylvania State University College of Medicine

Office of Student Affairs, P.O. Box 850, Hershey, PA 17033
(717) 531-8755

OVERVIEW

Like many other schools, Penn State is in the process of reevaluating and revising its curriculum. There is precedence for innovation at the College of Medicine, which was the first medical school in the country to add separate departments of family and community medicine, humanities, and behavioral science, a trend more and more schools are following. Through the inclusion of these nontraditional divisions, students get a perspective in their education that med students at other schools don't have. Comments one second-year student, "The inclusion of humanities [and other nontraditional] courses allows for discussion of those issues within medicine beyond the purely scientific."

ACADEMICS

Penn State's current revision includes the addition of a separate, problem-based learning track for first- and second-year students. This new approach is designed to encourage students to direct their own course of study and to lay the foundations for lifelong learning. In 1992, the track was implemented on an experimental basis for second-year students. Under this option, small groups of students meet with faculty tutors two to three times a week for a series of seven-week study blocks. Clinical problems are used as a means to learn and correlate the basic science information usually conveyed in lectures.

One student who took advantage of the new alternative enthusiastically reports, "It is much better than last year's didactic curriculum (which I enjoyed anyway). It is an exciting, motivating, and personal growth-stimulating program. A hybrid between didactic and clinical curricula." The problem-based learning track will be available for both classes in 1994.

"The Department of Family and Community Medicine strives to provide medical students with a basic introduction to important aspects of primary care,...the fundamentals of patient-interviewing and ambulatory care....," says the Admissions Office. Although they are required to take the Physician-Patient Interaction course in the first semester and the three-part Physical Diagnosis course throughout the remainder of the basic science years, students say they'd like to have more clinical exposure before the third-year clerkships. According to admissions, summer electives in between the first and second year are available for students who want additional patient experiences before entering the clerkship phase.

All students are required to complete a research project at some time during the four years. Perhaps because of this mandate, the College of Medicine's research efforts receive consistently high marks. Students are not quite so enthusiastic about the faculty's efforts in the classroom. Although teaching is rated as generally good, some students say the quality can be spotty. Comments one student, "Teaching sometimes leaves a lot to be desired." Faculty accessibility and attention to medical ethics received positive reviews.

Overall, students are happy with the facilities. They voice complaints, however, about the library and computer labs, which they rate as moderately satisfactory. Science labs and clinical facilities were rated as very good. Problems with the physical environment will be taken care of soon, though. One student reports, "There are major construction projects going on in both clinical and student areas."

Grading Policy: Honors/High Pass/Pass/Fail. Parts I and II of the USMLE must be taken. A passing grade on Part I is required for graduation.

Additional Degree Programs: MD/Ph.D.

STUDENT LIFE

Students report that their classmates are fairly competitive and that they spend much more time studying than they do socializing. This perception might be accounted for, in part, by the fact that Penn State students say their classmates aren't the type of people they like to hang out with. Of the schools we surveyed, Penn State was at the bottom of the list in this category.

Although students complain that there aren't too many clubs or activities to get involved in, they find the campus attractive and are generally positive about the town of Hershey. On-campus and off-campus housing both received excellent ratings, as did the safety of the campus and surrounding area.

ADMISSIONS

Admissions officials say the school gives no preference to Pennsylvania residents. They rate as the most important selection factors the science GPA, MCAT scores (from the new format test), nonscience GPA, letters of recommendation, and the interview. Also considered, in order of importance are essays, exposure to medicine, volunteer activities, and extracurricular activities.

Special Programs for Members of Underrepresented Minorities: Students rate their school as being only moderately diverse, but Penn State is beginning to make inroads. Efforts to recruit and retain minority students include special consideration for admission, academic advising, and tutoring. Any student, regardless of minority status, has access to advising and tutoring programs.

Transfer Policy: Transfers are considered if there are family-related reasons behind the move.

FINANCIAL AID

The College of Medicine's relatively high cost is a source of unhappiness for many. "Although this is a state school, the tuition is as high as it is at private medical schools," complains one student. Financial need is determined by the GAPSFAS analysis service, and the admissions office reports that approximately 85 percent of students receive some assistance. Scholarships based solely on merit are available.

ADMISSIONS FACTS

Demographics

% men	49
% women	51
% minorities	22

Deadline & Notification Dates

AMCAS	yes
Regular application	11/15
Regular notification	10/01-until filled
Early Decision application	06/15-08/01

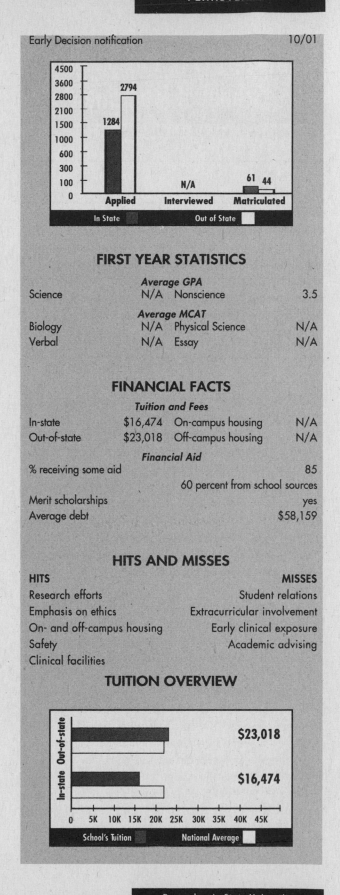

Early Decision notification   10/01

FIRST YEAR STATISTICS

Average GPA

Science	N/A	Nonscience	3.5

Average MCAT

Biology	N/A	Physical Science	N/A
Verbal	N/A	Essay	N/A

FINANCIAL FACTS

Tuition and Fees

In-state	$16,474	On-campus housing	N/A
Out-of-state	$23,018	Off-campus housing	N/A

Financial Aid

% receiving some aid	85
	60 percent from school sources
Merit scholarships	yes
Average debt	$58,159

HITS AND MISSES

HITS	MISSES
Research efforts	Student relations
Emphasis on ethics	Extracurricular involvement
On- and off-campus housing	Early clinical exposure
Safety	Academic advising
Clinical facilities	

TUITION OVERVIEW

$23,018

$16,474

University of Pittsburgh School of Medicine

Office of Admissions, 518 Scaife Hall, Pittsburgh, PA 15261
(412) 648-9891

OVERVIEW

Pitt has recently implemented a new basic science curriculum which, according to the admissions office, "uses problem-based learning, primarily small group sessions, self-directed learning, a central governing body, early exposure to patients, and system-based (not discipline-based) organization and courses." Students couldn't be happier about the change.

ACADEMICS

The second-year students we surveyed belong to the last class who experienced the old curriculum, and they were vociferous in their complaints about long class hours, little clinical exposure, and the anonymity of large lecture classes. First-year students, beneficiaries of the new teaching methods, have nothing but praise for their experience thus far. Reports one, "Our new curriculum is really very good. We have less class time and more small groups and free time." Another adds, "Classes are divided between problem-based learning sessions and lectures. The school has implemented an ambulatory care program that gives students great clinical experience in the first year. The school is very much oriented to patient-doctor care."

Until the new curriculum was instituted, older students say, Pitt was "adequate" in the basic sciences, but well-known as an outstanding research and clinical school. One student raves, "The second two years are phenomenal! You can't find a better clinical program anywhere. Pitt is on the cutting edge of medical advances." Adds another, "The third and fourth years give students the chance to interact with excellent faculty. Also, if students show their own initiative, there are opportunities for excellent outside research."

Although overall students gave relatively lukewarm reviews of the quality of teaching, there was a preponderance of older students in our sample. First-year students in the new curriculum rated both teaching and the accessibility of the faculty as very good, signs that what one student termed "a palpable feeling of rapid growth

and improvement" has extended not only to the curriculum, but to the classroom as well.

Currently, students rate science and classroom facilities as good, but they, too, are getting better. One student reports, "We are getting a new lounge and remodeling teaching labs." Reviews of the school's study facilities are mixed: students praise the computer labs, but say the library is only satisfactory. There was a consensus on the clinical facilities, however, with students agreeing that they are excellent. Since Pitt is the only medical school in Pittsburgh, students note that they have the resources of eight area hospitals all to themselves.

Grading and Promotion Policy: Honors/Pass/Fail. Students must take the USMLE Parts I and II.

Additional Degree Programs: MD/Ph.D. (affiliated with Carnegie Mellon University).

STUDENT LIFE

Although students report that Pitt is both rigorous and competitive, they get involved in the many extracurricular activities available both on and off campus. Says one student, "The students are among the most active in extracurricular and community projects that I have seen anywhere." Many do object, however, to the lack of space for relaxation. Says one, "My biggest gripe is the lack of nonacademic facilities like a decent gymnasium and a comfortable student lounge."

Student complaints extend to the lack of university housing and the unattractiveness of the campus. They are, however, enthusiastic about Pittsburgh. One student comments, "Pittsburgh is an ideal city in which to get a medical education. It has outstanding cultural and recreational offerings; however, housing is affordable and available, cost of living is very low, crime is low, and the overall environment is pleasant and easygoing—an ideal antidote to the stresses of medical school." Not everyone agrees with this student's assessment of the incidence of crime; Pitt's campus rates relatively low for safety.

ADMISSIONS

Pitt gives preference to residents of Pennsylvania. Applicants with outstanding academic qualification, women, members of underrepresented minorities, alumni children, and students interested in primary care are especially encouraged to apply from out of state.

The admissions office ranks as the most important selection factors the science GPA, the interview (beware, students report that Pitt's interviews can resemble a trivia quiz), MCAT scores (from the new format), letters of recommendation, and the nonscience GPA. Volunteer activities, exposure to the medical profession, extracurricular activities, and essays are also considered important.

Special Programs for Members of Underrepresented Minorities: Pitt actively seeks to enroll and retain minority students. A minority affairs division coordinates programs that include community outreach programs, a prematriculation summer session, academic advising, and peer counseling. Majority students who have been out of college a long time before matriculation are encouraged to participate in the summer session.

Transfer Policy: Pitt currently considers transfers into the third year only.

FINANCIAL AID

The Financial Aid Office uses the GAPSFAS needs analysis service to determine the amount of assistance students are eligible for. Although it is a state school, Pitt's tuition is relatively high, and some students complain that it can be hard to find attractive loans. Complains one student, "Except for the higher interest government loan programs, there is not much accessibility to good financial aid." Pitt awards some scholarships solely on the basis of merit.

ADMISSIONS FACTS

Demographics

% men	61
% women	39
% minorities	12

Deadline & Notification Dates

AMCAS	yes
Regular application	11/01
Regular notification	10/15–until filled
Early Decision application	06/15–08/01
Early Decision notification	10/01

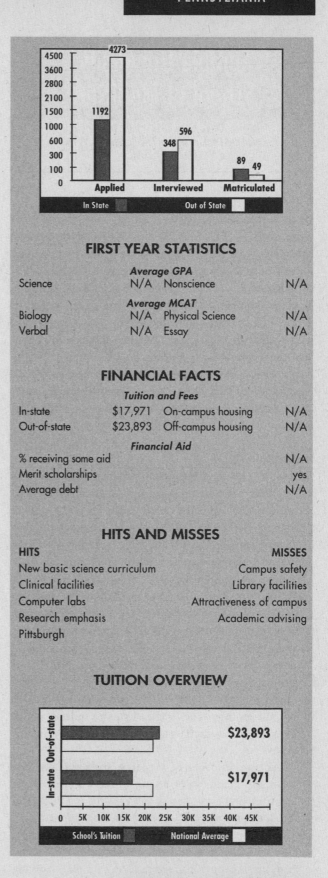

	In State	Out of State
Applied	1192	4273
Interviewed	348	596
Matriculated	89	49

FIRST YEAR STATISTICS

Average GPA

Science	N/A	Nonscience	N/A

Average MCAT

Biology	N/A	Physical Science	N/A
Verbal	N/A	Essay	N/A

FINANCIAL FACTS

Tuition and Fees

In-state	$17,971	On-campus housing	N/A
Out-of-state	$23,893	Off-campus housing	N/A

Financial Aid

% receiving some aid	N/A
Merit scholarships	yes
Average debt	N/A

HITS AND MISSES

HITS	MISSES
New basic science curriculum	Campus safety
Clinical facilities	Library facilities
Computer labs	Attractiveness of campus
Research emphasis	Academic advising
Pittsburgh	

TUITION OVERVIEW

Out-of-state: $23,893
In-state: $17,971

School's Tuition	National Average

Temple University School of Medicine

Admissions Office, Suite 305, Student Faculty Center,
Broad and Ontario Streets, Philadelphia, PA 19130
(214) 221-3656

OVERVIEW

Open Temple's admissions bulletin, and the first thing you'll read is, "This year, Temple University School of Medicine and about 180 students will select each other for that most stimulating rite of passage known as medical education." Turn the page and peruse the Message from the Dean. He writes, Temple "is a school of and for people. It is a place where people care about each other: faculty and students alike." Where's the gloating about how selective and prestigious an institution it is, the boast of state-of-the art research and clinical facilities? All that comes later. What comes first, in Temple's catalogue—and in its educational philosophy—is the student.

ACADEMICS

Although Temple has recently made curricular advancements that incorporate more small-group and problem-based learning, what really sets the school apart, students report, is the teaching. The rave reviews of the faculty would fill many pages, but the following comment is representative of what students have to say: "Teaching at Temple is A+. . . . I have never had such great teachers. They are motivated, fun, creative, go well beyond their basic duties, and will spend hours helping students." Praise for the faculty's willingness to go the extra mile is widespread. Asserts one student, "The faculty are not only accessible, *they find you* if you're having trouble." Another explains, "Faculty members help [us] study in the late evening hours in individual settings. They really listen to student's concerns and work to teach us how to be the best physicians possible."

Teaching students how to become great doctors, says Temple, begins with students playing an active role in acquiring and assimilating information, an important goal of the curriculum. "Temple's medical curriculum," says the admissions bulletin, "will keep you on the go. But with independent study and small-group instruction making inroads on lecture hours, and problem-solving

vying with memorization as the learning mode of choice, you'll be running in fewer circles. . . . Your medical education will make sense with respect to your professional future, for you'll be acquiring the most valuable of professional skills—the ability to master new knowledge on your own."

Students like the variety of learning styles and appreciate the level of integration between the basic and clinical sciences. Reports one first-year student, "The first semester is established in a manner that allows the student to view all aspects of medicine...incorporat[ing] a great deal of clinical correlation even in the first year." The first-semester Gross Anatomy course, which employs nontraditional teaching styles with "very few" lectures, is a particular favorite.

As enthusiastic as they are about their teaching and curriculum, Temple students don't have a lot of nice things to say about most of their facilities. While clinical facilities get high marks, classrooms, labs, and computing facilities receive lukewarm reviews. The library, students complain, "is very poor."

Grading and Promotion Policy: Honors/High Pass/Pass/Conditional Fail. Letter grades are sometimes used. Passing grades on USMLE Parts I and II are required.

Additional Degree Programs: MD/Ph.D.

STUDENT LIFE

"It seems to me Temple has done a good job in bringing in a very heterogeneous class," says one second-year student. Her classmates agree; Temple receives high marks on racial and ethnic diversity. One student adds, "There is a diversity of ages and backgrounds represented here as well—Ph.D.s, nurses, ministers, parents, married, and single." By and large, the diverse students get along, describing their classmates as "relaxed" and "easygoing." According to one second-year student, "Cooperation is emphasized over competition."

Students are not nearly so positive when they describe Temple's location. They don't find the campus very attractive and one student reports, "[It's] located in a poverty-stricken and unsafe area of Philadelphia." Safety—or rather, the lack of it—is a major concern for most students, both on the campus and on the city's accessible, but reportedly dangerous, public transportation system.

ADMISSIONS

Temple gives Pennsylvania residents preference in admissions, but out-of-state students are invited to apply either through the regular admissions process or the Early Decision Program. Any student applying Early Decision should have outstanding credentials that include a GPA of 3.5 or above and high MCAT scores. The MCAT is required of all applicants.

About 42 percent of applicants are interviewed. Says the Admissions Office, "This statistic says a lot about [our] admissions philosophy. Yes, standards are high...but [they] are not rigid, and what's more they're not purely quantitative—an applicant's performance during the interview may weigh just as heavily as test scores and grades; and grade progress in college...could tip the scales in an applicant's favor." Temple says it does not give "stress interviews." One student assures prospective applicants, "The interview is very important, but very relaxed. Don't be afraid to let a little of yourself show.... It will be to your benefit."

Transfer Policy: Temple accepts transfers into its second- and third-year classes. The admissions office can provide specific guidelines for this policy.

Special Programs for Members of Underrepresented Minorities: Temple is a leader in minority enrollment and retention, but is committed to continuing to increase the numbers of traditional underrepresented students. Coordinating this effort is the school's Recruitment, Admissions, and Retention (RAR) program. Among its offerings are a prematriculation summer session and academic and personal counseling.

FINANCIAL AID

Approximately 80 percent of Temple students receive financial assistance, primarily in the form of loans. Most awards are made solely on the basis of need. The GAPSFAS analysis is used to determine the amount of aid students are eligible for.

ADMISSIONS FACTS

Demographics

% men	59
% women	41
% minorities	20

Deadline & Notification Dates

AMCAS	yes
Regular application	12/01
Regular notification	10/15–until filled
Early Decision application	06/15–08/01
Early Decision notification	10/01

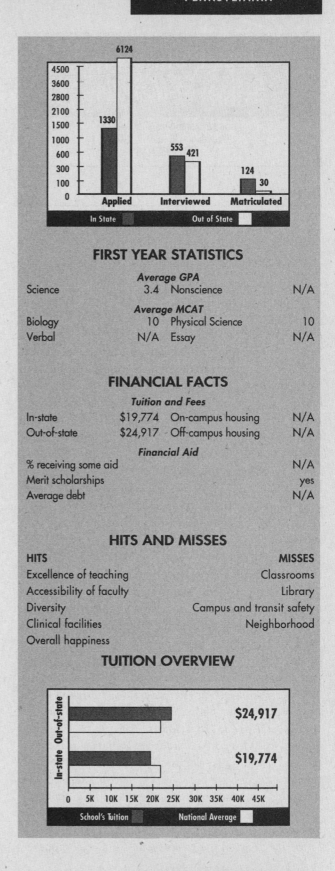

FIRST YEAR STATISTICS

Average GPA

Science	3.4	Nonscience	N/A

Average MCAT

Biology	10	Physical Science	10
Verbal	N/A	Essay	N/A

FINANCIAL FACTS

Tuition and Fees

In-state	$19,774	On-campus housing	N/A
Out-of-state	$24,917	Off-campus housing	N/A

Financial Aid

% receiving some aid	N/A
Merit scholarships	yes
Average debt	N/A

HITS AND MISSES

HITS	MISSES
Excellence of teaching	Classrooms
Accessibility of faculty	Library
Diversity	Campus and transit safety
Clinical facilities	Neighborhood
Overall happiness	

TUITION OVERVIEW

Out-of-state $24,917
In-state $19,774

School's Tuition   National Average

Brown University
School of Medicine

Office of Admissions, Box G-A212
Providence, RI 02912-9706
(401) 863-2149

OVERVIEW

Brown University School of Medicine is among the nation's leading comprehensive med schools. Unfortunately, though, admission to this highly-regarded institution is beyond the reach of most traditional applicants. The student body is comprised almost exclusively of students who are admitted to the school's eight year continuum, the Program in Liberal Medical Education (PMLE), which leads to both the bachelor's degree and the MD. According to the school's literature, the remainder of openings in the first-year class are limited to "students who apply for the MD/Ph.D. Program, those currently attending Brown University who are not enrolled in the eight-year program, and those entering through special programs at institutions with whom the school of medicine has a formal relationship." This last category includes students who are admitted through the Early Identification Program (EIP), the postbaccalaureate program, or the Brown-Dartmouth Program.

EIP is a cooperative venture between the med school and Providence College, Rhode Island College, the University of Rhode Island, and Tougaloo College. EIP seeks to increase opportunities in medicine for Rhode Island residents and for students from racial and ethnic groups currently underrepresented in medicine. Students are accepted into the EIP during their sophomore undergraduate year, participate in selected med school activities during the remainder of college, and enter med school after receiving the bachelor's degree.

The postbaccalaureate program is designed to admit students who participate in postgraduate premed studies at Brown, Bryn Mawr College, or Columbia University. Most of the students admitted to the med school through this program fit one of more of the following categories: are 25 years of age or older, became interested in medicine after completing college, engaged in activities other than formal education between college and applying to med school, are Rhode Island residents, or are members of underrepresented minority groups.

The Brown-Dartmouth program is jointly sponsored by the Brown University and Dartmouth med schools. Under this option, students spend their first two years at Dartmouth's campus in Hanover, New Hampshire. The clinical period is completed at Brown and the medical degree is awarded by Brown.

ACADEMICS

Students enrolled in the eight-year continuum (PMLE) spend much of the first four years pursuing areas of academic interest within the context of a broad liberal arts education. PMLE participants and those admitted through other programs then take part in the four-year medical curriculum.

In the first year, students study normal human structures and functions, are introduced to pathology, and explore social and psychological aspects of medicine. From the first semester, freshmen also learn fundamental history-taking skills.

In the second year, the study of the disease process intensifies through courses that include pathophysiology, systemic pathology, and organ system pharmacology. To help sophomores understand mental health and the effects of illness on human behavior, Brown requires an introduction to psychiatry. A physical diagnosis segment helps students apply their scientific knowledge to clinical problems and provides opportunities to refine patient interaction skills.

The third and fourth years are viewed as a continuum of required and elective experiences. Forty-eight weeks are devoted to clinical clerkships in the major disciplines, a community health rotation, and an ambulatory care experience. Students are allowed to tailor the remainder of the clinical period to their own interests.

Grading and Promotion Policy: Honors/Pass/Fail.
Additional Degree Programs: MD/Ph.D.

ADMISSIONS

Although Brown gives special consideration to Rhode Island residents in some of its admissions programs, it is a private school and welcomes applications from any interested party. In all of its programs, competition is extremely keen. Applicants are evaluated on a number of scholastic, extracurricular, and personal criteria.

Students apply to the PMLE program directly from high school. According to Brown's literature, "The PMLE seeks highly qualified and strongly motivated high school students who are committed to a career in medicine and who also wish to pursue another area of academic interest to an advanced level of scholarship." Competition for the PMLE (which constitutes most of the first-year medical class) is fierce; of the approximately 1,300 candidates who apply each year, only about seventy are admitted.

Those who attend one of the schools involved in the EIP apply during their sophomore year. Rhode Island residents and members of underrepresented minorities have the advantage in this process. Although EIP students are conditionally admitted to the med school before their junior undergraduate year, final acceptance is contingent upon successful completion of the bachelor's degree. Generally, two candidates from each participating school are accepted.

The postbaccalaureate program, another avenue for admission, is intended to give nontraditional students access to medical education. In this program, the pre-med advisor at each of the participating schools nominates candidates for admission. Nominees then apply directly to Brown; at least two spots in the first-year class are reserved for postbaccalaureate students from each school.

A few students each are also admitted through the MD/Ph.D. program and through the Brown Avenue for Admission. MD/Ph.D. applicants must take the MCAT or the GRE. If the candidate chooses the GRE, he or she must take both the general and subject tests. Brown undergrads or grad students should contact the med school for more information on the Brown Avenue.

The final way to apply to Brown is through the Brown-Dartmouth program. Interested candidates should apply through Dartmouth and are evaluated by a committee composed of representatives of both med schools.

Special Programs for Members of Underrepresented Minorities: Brown's Office of Minority Affairs coordinates programs to identify, recruit, educate, and graduate members of underrepresented minority groups. Among the OMA's offerings are academic advising, counseling, skills workshops, an alumni network program, and summer research opportunities for undergrads.

Transfer Policy: Applications for transfer into the third year are considered on a space-available basis. Any student in good standing at a U.S. or Canadian med school and Rhode Island residents attending accredited U.S., Canadian, or foreign med schools are eligible to apply.

FINANCIAL AID

Financial aid is awarded primarily on the basis of documented need. Once students obtain the federal loans for which they qualify, they become eligible for institutional scholarships, grants, and loans.

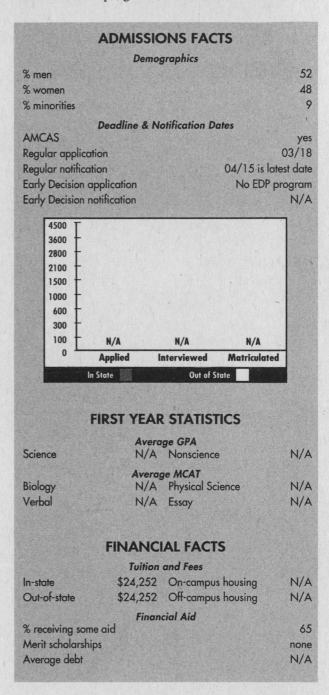

ADMISSIONS FACTS

Demographics

% men	52
% women	48
% minorities	9

Deadline & Notification Dates

AMCAS	yes
Regular application	03/18
Regular notification	04/15 is latest date
Early Decision application	No EDP program
Early Decision notification	N/A

FIRST YEAR STATISTICS

Average GPA

Science	N/A	Nonscience	N/A

Average MCAT

Biology	N/A	Physical Science	N/A
Verbal	N/A	Essay	N/A

FINANCIAL FACTS

Tuition and Fees

In-state	$24,252	On-campus housing	N/A
Out-of-state	$24,252	Off-campus housing	N/A

Financial Aid

% receiving some aid	65
Merit scholarships	none
Average debt	N/A

TUITION OVERVIEW

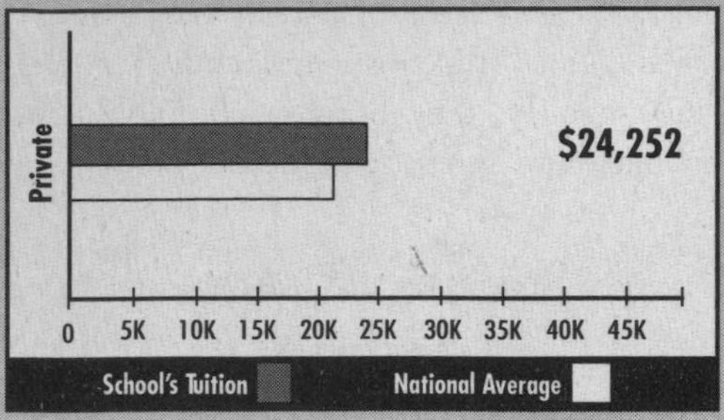
Private
$24,252
0
5K
10K
15K
20K
25K
30K
35K
40K
45K
School's Tuition
National Average

Medical University of South Carolina College of Medicine

Office of Enrollment Services
171 Ashley Avenue, Charleston, SC 29425-2970
(803) 792-3281

OVERVIEW

Do you think you can take a lot of competition as long as you're in beautiful Charleston? Even if the student body is not so diverse? Well, so do a lot of other people. On the whole, students say they're happy at MUSC, citing strong teaching, an accessible faculty, and a gorgeous setting as the school's best features. What they're not thrilled about is a "very competitive" student body that some say makes the atmosphere "extremely stressful."

ACADEMICS

MUSC's curriculum is divided into the usual preclinical and clinical segments. The primary goals of the first two years are for students to learn the basic science concepts underlying medicine, develop problem-solving strategies, investigate behavioral and social aspects of health care, and acquire patient-interaction skills. Freshmen and sophomores take a mix of departmental and interdisciplinary science courses, most of which include clinical correlations. Although lectures are the main mode of instruction, most classes incorporate small-group conferences. In these sessions, students use case studies to integrate scientific principles with clinical problems.

In the first segment of the two-year Introduction to Clinical Medicine course (ICM), students explore psychological and cultural issues in health care and begin to learn interviewing skills. Patient contact intensifies during the subsequent semesters of ICM, preparing students for the third- and fourth-year clerkships. Although most freshmen and sophomores are pleased with the amount of early clinical exposure they get through ICM, some first-years say they'd like fewer presentations and more hands-on experience. According to school officials, there's good news for these clinically-oriented students; starting in 1994, MUSC will offer an alternate curriculum for between eighteen and twenty-four students. Under this option, students will study the basic sciences in

small-groups, using case studies as the primary mode of instruction.

Students give their professors high marks both for the quality of teaching and for their willingness to help students outside of class. Praise extends to the school's facilities, as well, with the best reviews reserved for the computer labs and clinical facilities.

Grading and Promotion Policy: There are two grading systems, one a four-point numerical scale and the other Honors/Pass/Fail. Students must pass Part I of the USMLE.

Additional Degree Programs: MD/Ph.D.

STUDENT LIFE

The atmosphere at MUSC is pretty intense. Students spend more time studying and less time socializing than their counterparts at most other schools we surveyed. For those who need a break, though, the Student Programs staff organizes social, recreational, and cultural activities both on and off campus.

MUSC's location in the heart of Charleston is very popular; students like the city's charming, historical neighborhoods and the recreational opportunities afforded by its seaside location. Although there are no university residence halls, off-campus housing opportunities are plentiful, and the Student Affairs office maintains a list of available apartments.

ADMISSIONS

Residents of South Carolina are given preference, but nonresidents with outstanding credentials are sometimes admitted. All applicants are reviewed on the basis of the AMCAS application, and candidates with good qualifications are asked to submit a supplementary application. Initially, candidates are evaluated on the basis of their total MCAT scores and their cumulative GPAs. If applicants pass the initial screening, they are invited to interview.

An admissions official at MUSC described for us the interview and final selection process: "[Interviews] are friendly and informative for the candidates and include opportunities to tour the university and medical facilities, visit with faculty and students, discuss questions and meet with support organizations to iron out personal, academic, and financial concerns. After the campus visit, committee members (students and faculty from the basic science and clinical areas) weigh many factors in their efforts to identify the best potential physicians. Academic records and scores on the MCAT are used to determine an applicant's intellectual capacity to handle the academic workload, while personal attributes such as integrity, motivation, compassion, maturity, and character are evaluated from the interview, letters of support, and applicant activities."

MUSC also offers an Early Assurance Program (EAP). In this program, talented South Carolina residents may apply to med school as early as the summer after their freshman year, giving them the freedom pursue a broad-based undergraduate education. EAP applicants should have a GPA of about 3.5 and should score approximately 1200 on the SAT in order to be considered competitive.

Special Programs for Members of Underrepresented Minorities: Students give MUSC extremely low marks for diversity, but the school says it's dedicated to increasing minority representation. The Office of Minority Affairs coordinates efforts to recruit minority students. Programs include summer sessions for college students, MCAT review classes, a prematriculation summer session, academic advising, tutoring, peer counseling, and review for Parts I and II of the USMLE. MUSC, in conjunction with the College of Charleston, also offers a one-year PREP program that is designed to improve the chances for med school admissions of competitive, but academically underprepared, South Carolina applicants.

Transfer Policy: MUSC's policy for accepting transfers varies from year to year and is dependent on available space; students interested in transferring should contact the admissions office to discuss their individual cases.

FINANCIAL AID

The Scholarship Board—made up of administrators, professors, students and members of the medical community—administers all need- and merit-based institutional funds. In addition to these scholarships, MUSC offers governmental, private, and institutional loans.

ADMISSIONS FACTS

Demographics

% men	62
% women	38
% minorities	13

Deadline & Notification Dates

AMCAS	yes
Regular application	12/01
Regular notification	10/15–until filled
Early Decision application	06/15–08/01
Early Decision notification	10/01

Bar chart: In State vs Out of State
- Applied: In State 495, Out of State 1918
- Interviewed: In State 270, Out of State 79
- Matriculated: In State 121, Out of State 20

FIRST YEAR STATISTICS

Average GPA

Science	N/A	Nonscience	3.46

Average MCAT

Biology	N/A	Physical Science	N/A
Verbal	N/A	Essay	N/A

FINANCIAL FACTS

Tuition and Fees

In-state	$5,760	On-campus housing	none
Out-of-state*	$15,490	Off-campus housing	$10,524

*Fees are substantially higher for out-of-state students.

Financial Aid

% receiving some aid	N/A
Merit scholarships	yes
Average debt	$44,000

HITS AND MISSES

HITS	MISSES
Overall happiness	Competitive atmosphere
Quality of teaching	Heavy workload
Faculty accessibility	Not much social life
Computer facilities	Diversity
Charleston	

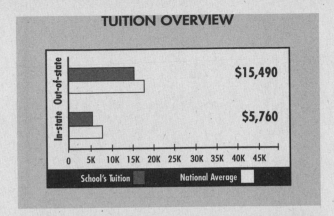

TUITION OVERVIEW

$15,490

$5,760

0 5K 10K 15K 20K 25K 30K 35K 40K 45K

School's Tuition ▨   National Average ☐

University of South Carolina School of Medicine

Associate Dean for Student Programs, Columbia, SC 29208
(803) 733-3325

OVERVIEW

You'll get early exposure to clinical patient issues, but this, as well as most of the other academic issues here, is very traditional. The mission of the University of South Carolina School of Medicine (USC) is "to improve the health of the people of the state...through medical education, research, and the delivery of health care." Located in Columbia, the state capital, USC is a young school with a fairly traditional curriculum.

Students spend their first two years studying the basic sciences at the med school complex, just a few miles away from the main university campus. During the clinical period, juniors and seniors complete rotations at Richland Medical Park and other hospitals and clinics. Although most students choose to do their clerkships in the Columbia area, the school's recent affiliation with the Greenville Hospital system makes it possible to do clinical work in upstate South Carolina, about one hundred miles from the main campus.

ACADEMICS

In the first two years, students focus most of their efforts on developing the scientific knowledge base necessary for the practice of medicine. Freshmen concentrate on the body's normal structures and functions and sophomores turn their attention to the disease process and

therapeutic principles. Throughout the first two years, clinical correlations help to integrate basic science principles with actual patient problems. Students also develop an understanding of the psychological, social, and economic determinants and effects of disease through interdisciplinary courses. Although traditional lectures and labs are the primary modes of instruction, some courses include small-group sessions.

Freshmen and sophomores get early clinical exposure to patient care issues and skills in a family medicine course and in Introduction to Clinical Practice (ICP). The two-year ICP continuum "permits an increased emphasis on small-group interaction among faculty members and students, clinical problem-solving, self-instruction, independent learning, and improved correlation of basic science and clinical science [material]." The first segment of ICP concentrates on the physician's relationships with patients and the community. Among the requirements in the first year is a community health project.

In the continuation of ICP, sophomores focus on the disease process, refine the history-taking skills they developed in the previous year, learn to conduct a physical examination, and use their accumulated knowledge to make physical diagnoses. In addition to attending lectures, demonstrations, and practical exercises, sophomores work alongside faculty preceptors.

Hands-on patient contact intensifies during the third year, when students complete clerkships in medicine, surgery, obstetrics/gynecology, psychiatry, pediatrics, and family medicine. Advanced rotations in surgery and medicine and a four-week rotation in neurology are required in the fourth year, but there is significant time left over for selectives and free electives. "To promote scholarship and independent learning," USC requires each student to complete an original research paper during the clinical phase.

Grading and Promotion Policy: The primary grading system is A–F, though some courses use a Satisfactory/Unsatisfactory system. Students must pass Parts I and II of the USMLE.

Additional Degree Programs: MS/MD; MD/Ph.D.

STUDENT LIFE

USC students participate in social, recreational, and community service activities through specialty clubs and local chapters of major medical student associations. The student lounge area of the Basic Science building provides a place to relax and socialize, and a physical fitness center in the Dorn Veterans' Hospital Auditorium houses exercise equipment for between-class workouts. More extensive athletic facilities, a large student union, an intramural sports program, and a large number of organizations and events can be found on the nearby main university campus.

Although the university offers a limited number of on-campus apartments, most students prefer to make their own living arrangements.

ADMISSIONS

Since USC is a state-supported institution, residents of South Carolina are given strong preference. The school rejects all but a handful of out-of-state candidates, so nonresidents should seriously evaluate their qualifications before applying.

All students must apply to USC through AMCAS. On the basis of an initial review of the AMCAS material, the Admissions Committee, which is comprised of med school and university faculty members, med students, and local physicians, requests supplemental information from well-qualified candidates. Once the committee reviews the complete application, it invites promising candidates to interview on campus. In the 1991–92 admissions season, a little over one-fifth of applicants were interviewed.

The Admissions Committee bases its final decisions on quantitative and qualitative factors. Among the important considerations are the GPA, MCAT scores, the interview, letters of recommendation, and motivation and suitability for medical practice.

Special Programs for Members of Underrepresented Minorities: "Obtaining a fair representation of minority medical students" is one of USC's stated goals.

Transfer Policy: Applications for transfer into the second or third year are considered on a space-available basis. Students must be in good standing at accredited med schools.

FINANCIAL AID

Although both in-state and out-of-state tuition rates are lower than the national averages, financial aid in the form of loans, grants, and scholarships is available. The school also offers a few merit awards and coordinates some service obligation programs.

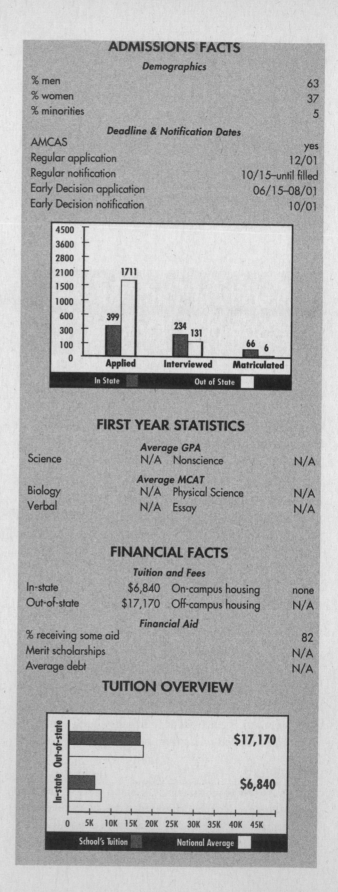

ADMISSIONS FACTS

Demographics

% men	63
% women	37
% minorities	5

Deadline & Notification Dates

AMCAS	yes
Regular application	12/01
Regular notification	10/15–until filled
Early Decision application	06/15–08/01
Early Decision notification	10/01

Bar chart:
Applied — In State 399, Out of State 1711
Interviewed — In State 234, Out of State 131
Matriculated — In State 66, Out of State 6

FIRST YEAR STATISTICS

Average GPA

Science	N/A	Nonscience	N/A

Average MCAT

Biology	N/A	Physical Science	N/A
Verbal	N/A	Essay	N/A

FINANCIAL FACTS

Tuition and Fees

In-state	$6,840	On-campus housing	none
Out-of-state	$17,170	Off-campus housing	N/A

Financial Aid

% receiving some aid	82
Merit scholarships	N/A
Average debt	N/A

TUITION OVERVIEW

Out-of-state: $17,170
In-state: $6,840

School's Tuition / National Average

University of South Dakota School of Medicine

Office of Student Affairs, Room 105,
414 E. Clark Street, Vermillion, South Dakota 57069-2390
(605) 677-5234

OVERVIEW

USD is committed to preparing students to serve the needs of the residents of South Dakota. Accordingly, the curriculum emphasizes primary care and rural practice. Currently, USD students spend their basic science years in Vermillion—a town of about ten thousand—and do their clinical training in Sioux Falls, Rapid City, and Yanktown. The students we surveyed dislike this setup and complain about Vermillion and its isolation from hospital settings. There may be good news for prospective applicants, though; according to our respondents, there is talk of making Sioux Falls the site of all four years of instruction.

ACADEMICS

Aside from their vehement criticism of the physical location of basic science instruction, students are pleased with the preclinical experience. During the first two years, students study the scientific basis of medicine and take an Introduction to Clinical Medicine (ICM) continuum. Through ICM, freshmen and sophomores learn communication, examination, and evaluation skills. Patient contact is centered in affiliated hospitals outside of Vermillion and in the offices of community physicians.

Students say they are relatively pleased with the clinical exposure they get in the first two years, but they are frustrated by the town's lack of a hospital and their limited access to clinicians. This situation changes for the better during the third and fourth years when students complete core clerkships and electives; hospitals and clinics in Sioux Falls, Yanktown, and Rapid City are the main teaching sites. An "ambulatory clinic-based curriculum" is offered as an alternative to traditional clinical clerkships.

Despite their complaints about other features of USD, students in all four years are impressed with their professors, both in and out of the classroom. Says one freshman, "The faculty has a genuine commitment to helping students learn." Another adds, "A small school means the professors know you as people, not social security numbers, and interactions are more personal."

Facilities do not fare as well. Students say classrooms, the library, and the computer labs at the Vermillion campus have a lot of room for improvement. They are much more positive about the affiliated hospitals, though, rating clinical facilities as very good.

Grading and Promotion Policy: A through F
Additional Degree Programs: MD/Ph.D.

STUDENT LIFE

Students say they're fairly close to their classmates and like to hang out together. Explains one freshman, "Having a class of our size (50 students) gives us the potential to pull together and support each other." This feeling of cooperation predominates; only a handful of students say USD's atmosphere is competitive. It's a good thing students like to spend time with one another—in the first two years, there's not much else to do.

Since Vermillion is a very small town, there are "not many entertainment opportunities" and the med school offers few clubs and activities of its own. Housing, too, is a major source of frustration. Off-campus apartments are not widely available, and one freshman complains, "[University-owned] married housing resembles a slum." In short, one student says, "The situation is terrible."

The good news is that if you can survive the first two years, things get much better. Students are as happy with Sioux Falls as they are unhappy with Vermillion.

ADMISSIONS

As a state school, USD gives preference to residents of South Dakota. Nonresidents especially encouraged to apply are candidates with close ties to the state and Native American students.

The Director of Admissions ranks as the primary selection factors the science GPA, MCAT scores, the interview, the nonscience GPA, and compatibility with the school's mission to provide primary care for the residents of South Dakota. Also considered important are letters of recommendation, exposure to the medical profession, volunteer activities, extracurricular activities, and essays.

Special Programs for Members of Underrepresented Minorities: Students give USD extremely low marks for diversity, but add that the composition of the student body reflects the homogeneity of the state. The school's efforts to recruit underrepresented minority students, especially Native Americans, are ongoing. Special programs designed to promote diversity include summer sessions for college students, a prematriculation summer session for accepted students, review classes for Part I of the USMLE, and academic advising. In addition, a satellite office of the INMED program at the University of North Dakota has staff available to counsel Native American applicants.

Transfer Policy: Transfers into the second or third year are considered if the applicant is in good standing at an LCME accredited med school. Preference is given to South Dakota residents and students with significant ties to the state.

FINANCIAL AID

Although there are some merit scholarships, most of USD's aid is awarded on the basis of need. Students interested in practicing in underserved communities may also benefit from state programs that offer tuition remission for service in rural areas.

FIRST YEAR STATISTICS

Average GPA
Science	3.60	Nonscience	3.67

Average MCAT
Biology	N/A	Physical Science	N/A
Verbal	N/A	Essay	N/A

FINANCIAL FACTS

Tuition and Fees
In-state	$10,338	On-campus housing	$12,500*
Out-of-state	$19,205	Off-campus housing	$12,500*
			(*10 months)

Financial Aid
% receiving some aid	88
Merit scholarships	yes
Average debt	$44,000

HITS AND MISSES

HITS	MISSES
Quality of teaching	Vermillion
Accessibility of faculty	Extracurricular involvement
Noncompetitive atmosphere	Diversity
Small class size	Basic science facilities
	Library
	Computer labs

TUITION OVERVIEW

Out-of-state $19,205
In-state $10,338

School's Tuition | National Average

ADMISSIONS FACTS

Demographics
% men	48
% women	52
% minorities	0

Deadline & Notification Dates
AMCAS	yes
Regular application	11/15
Regular notification	12/23–until filled
Early Decision application	None
Early Decision notification	None

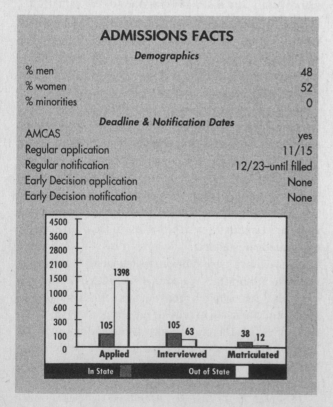

In State | Out of State

East Tennessee State Univ.: James H. Quillen College of Medicine

Associate Dean for Admissions
P.O. Box 70580, Johnson City, TN 37614-0580
(615) 929-6219

OVERVIEW

East Tennessee State University's James H. Quillen School of Medicine (ETSU) is among the nation's youngest and smallest med schools. Fully accredited in the early 1980s, this northeastern Tennessee school is committed to serving the health care needs of the state. What's great about its youth is that the curriculum is adjusted to include many of the innovations in the medical education system that other schools are only now beginning to incorporate. The main mission of ETSU is to train primary care physicians, and there is significant emphasis on preparing students to practice in rural areas. Evidence of this focus is the school's Interdisciplinary Rural Primary Care (IRPC) curricular track.

ACADEMICS

Up to one fourth of ETSU students may participate in the IRPC track. Under this option, students have earlier patient contact, work with primary care preceptors in the preclinical years, have more extensive exposure to community medicine, and complete most of their third year in a rural setting. IRPC students spend much of the first two years with their regular-track classmates.

During the first year, students study the basic sciences. Most courses are arranged by discipline, and lectures, case studies, small-group discussions, demonstrations, and lab exercises are the main methods of instruction. Freshmen begin their science education with courses in gross anatomy, biochemistry, cell and tissue biology, neurobiology, and physiology. Nonscience courses, including the first two segments of Introduction to Clinical Medicine (ICM) lend psychological, social, economic, and ethical perspectives. The year-long Freshman Grand Rounds course employs clinical case studies and bedside teaching to help students apply their developing knowledge to actual patient problems.

During the second year, students continue their investigation of the basic sciences, but the focus is on the disease process and its effects on the human body. By the second semester, students spend most of their time exploring the doctor-patient relationship and learning basic clinical skills. Through the continuation of ICM and other clinical courses, students learn to take a thorough history, conduct a physical examination, present their findings, and make rudimentary diagnoses.

After completing the sophomore year, students enter the clinical phase of the curriculum. Required eight-week rotations in internal medicine, surgery, psychiatry, obstetrics/gynecology, family medicine and pediatrics, and a short course in clinical pharmacology comprise the junior year. Although the fourth year is largely elective, seniors must complete senior clerkships in internal medicine and surgery. Clinical teaching takes place in five affiliated teaching hospitals, three ambulatory facilities, and a rural training site.

Grading and Promotion Policy: A–F. Students must pass Parts I and II of the USMLE.

Additional Degree Programs: The med school offers a combined BS/MD with the undergraduate colleges of the university. An MD/Ph.D. program is also available.

STUDENT LIFE

Because the med school is located on ETSU's main campus, students are involved in both school and university cultural, athletic, recreational, and social activities. The Campus Activities Board coordinates most university events: movies, concerts, and plays are among typical offerings. Student organizations provide a social and service outlet. Volunteerism is encouraged, and many find time to lend a hand in special projects.

Athletics are big at ETSU, whether that means cheering on intercollegiate teams or battling on the field in intramural sports. The university's location in the "heart of beautiful Appalachian country" is ideal for backpackers, canoers, skiers, and water sports enthusiasts.

Graduate housing is limited, but the school helps students find apartments off campus. Those interested in living on campus are encouraged to apply for housing as early as possible after acceptance.

ADMISSIONS

ETSU gives strong preference to state residents. Less than one percent of nonresident applicants were accepted in the 1991–92 admission season, so out-of-state students should carefully consider their chances of acceptance before applying.

ETSU makes an initial evaluation of each candidate on the basis of the AMCAS application. Only well-qualified applicants are asked to submit supplementary information. Those who survive a second cut are asked to interview. Candidates who are invited to campus usually have a pair of meetings with members of the Admissions Committee. A discussion of financial aid, lunch, a tour, and an opportunity to speak with enrolled students round out the interview day.

The interview is an important selection factor. Other considerations include the academic record, MCAT scores, letters of recommendation, extracurricular activities, research, work experience, and motivation to study and practice medicine. An interest in primary care, especially in rural regions, is also helpful.

Special Programs for Members of Underrepresented Minorities: ETSU actively encourages members of underrepresented minorities to apply. As part of its recruitment efforts, the school offers a summer reinforcement and enrichment program to minority premed students.

Transfer Policy: Applications for transfer into the second and third years are considered if the student is in good standing at an accredited med school. Preference is given to Tennessee residents and to veterans of the U.S. military.

FINANCIAL AID

Financial aid is awarded primarily on the basis of need. Most assistance is in the form of long-term loans.

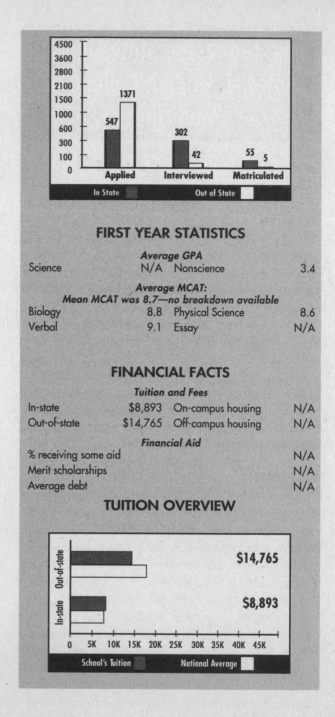

FIRST YEAR STATISTICS

Average GPA

Science	N/A	Nonscience	3.4

Average MCAT:
Mean MCAT was 8.7—no breakdown available

Biology	8.8	Physical Science	8.6
Verbal	9.1	Essay	N/A

FINANCIAL FACTS

Tuition and Fees

In-state	$8,893	On-campus housing	N/A
Out-of-state	$14,765	Off-campus housing	N/A

Financial Aid

% receiving some aid	N/A
Merit scholarships	N/A
Average debt	N/A

TUITION OVERVIEW

ADMISSIONS FACTS

Demographics

% men	52
% women	48
% minorities	15

Deadline & Notification Dates

AMCAS	yes
Regular application	12/01
Regular notification	10/15–until filled
Early Decision application	06/15–08/01
Early Decision notification	10/01

Meharry Medical College School of Medicine

Director of Admissions
1005 D.B. Todd, Jr. Boulevard, Nashville, TN 37208
(615) 327-6223

OVERVIEW

One of three predominantly black U.S. med schools, Meharry has graduated a large percentage of the nation's black physicians and has a long history of responding to the medical concerns of minorities and the disadvantaged. If you're dedicated to improving health care for the underserved and are interested in a school with a close student body and a strong sense of community, Meharry students say you might want to look at their school.

ACADEMICS

Meharry's curriculum is divided into traditional preclinical and clinical units. Most of the first two years is devoted to departmental science classes. In addition, students take a two-part, interdisciplinary behavioral science course that emphasizes psychological, social, and economic aspects of health care and introduces medical interviewing techniques. Sophomores expand on their patient-interaction skills during an Introduction to Clinical Medicine (ICM) segment. Lectures are the main method of instruction in the basic science year, but some courses include labs, demonstrations, and small-group conferences. Although the curriculum makes an effort to integrate scientific principles with clinical problems, students say that these correlations and the ICM experiences don't provide enough clinical exposure in the first two years. For extensive hands-on patient contact, students have to wait until the third- and fourth-year clerkships or participate in an elective Family Medicine Preceptorship during the summer break.

Students say the learning environment makes up for deficiencies in the curriculum. "Professors have faith in you," says one student. Adds another, "There is a strong support network at Meharry. The faculty, staff, and students stress the importance of providing a family-like atmosphere." Although some respondents say that the quality of teaching can be uneven from course to course, professors get extremely high marks for their willing-

ness to help students cope with academic demands. There is praise also for the academic advising system. Says one sophomore, "I think it's really important to have guidance through medical school. Meharry has given me that." Overall, students say the school's facilities are good.

Grading and Promotion Policy: A–F. Students must pass Part I of the USMLE.

Additional Degree Programs: MD/Ph.D.

STUDENT LIFE

Student relations are among the best of those at any school we surveyed. "At Meharry, I feel like I belong," says one satisfied freshman, and a lot of her classmates echo her sentiment. The atmosphere is more supportive than competitive, and students say their classmates are genuinely committed to helping others. Evidence of this is the large proportion—nearly 80 percent—who say they participate in organized study groups. Involvement in service projects is also very high.

When they're not studying or giving back to the community, Meharry students say they have fairly active social lives. Since Meharry, Fisk University, and Tennessee State are within a few blocks of each other, the three schools form an educational center and provide social and cultural activities for students at all three schools. Opinions on Nashville are widely divergent; though some say they hate the country-music capital, others say it's a great place to live.

ADMISSIONS

Special consideration in admissions is given to underrepresented minority students and students from disadvantaged backgrounds, but Meharry seeks a diverse student body. All qualified applicants are invited to apply.

On the basis of the AMCAS application, Meharry sends supplementary applications to all qualified candidates. Those who show promise are then invited to interview. Final decisions are made on the basis of "acceptable scholastic records, satisfactory scores on the MCAT, favorable recommendations...and...evidence [that candidates will become] successful medical students and practitioners."

Special Programs for Members of Underrepresented Minorities: Since it is a predominantly black medical school, Meharry welcomes applications from all members of underrepresented minorities and from students with disadvantaged backgrounds. Among programs which assist all students are the Special Medical Program, which allows students to take additional time to complete the basic science curriculum, and the Early Entry Program, which begins the summer before the first year. The Early Entry Program's main focus is to assess students' skill levels and to set up support systems for those who may experience academic difficulties.

Transfer Policy: Meharry does not accept transfers.

FINANCIAL AID

Financial aid is awarded primarily on the basis of need as determined by the GAPSFAS analysis. Academic merit is also a consideration for some scholarships.

ADMISSIONS FACTS

Demographics

% men	47
% women	53
% minorities	90

Deadline & Notification Dates

AMCAS	yes
Regular application	12/15
Regular notification	10/15-until filled
Early Decision application	06/15-08/01
Early Decision notification	10/01

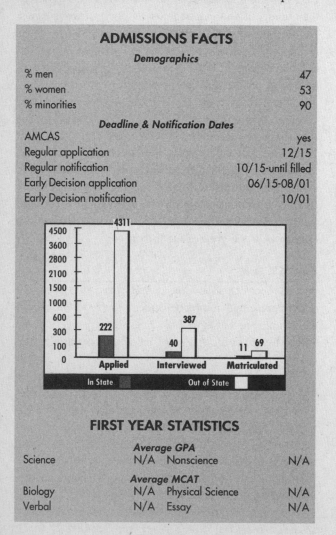

FIRST YEAR STATISTICS

	Average GPA		
Science	N/A	Nonscience	N/A
	Average MCAT		
Biology	N/A	Physical Science	N/A
Verbal	N/A	Essay	N/A

FINANCIAL FACTS

Tuition and Fees

In-state	$17,016	On-campus housing	none
Out-of-state	$17,016	Off-campus housing	N/A
	Financial Aid		
% receiving some aid			N/A
Merit scholarships			N/A
Average debt			N/A

HITS AND MISSES

HITS	MISSES
Social scene	Overall quality of teaching
Student relations	Heavy workload
Accessibility of faculty	Early clinical exposure
Academic advising	Location
Emphasis on ethics	Safety
Study groups	
Extracurricular activities	

TUITION OVERVIEW

$17,016

| School's Tuition | National Average |

University of Tennessee, Memphis, College of Medicine

Admissions Office, 800 Madison Avenue, Memphis, TN 38163
(901) 528-5559

OVERVIEW

The College of Medicine is part of the University of Tennessee, Memphis Health Science Center. Sharing the campus with the medical school are the Colleges of Allied Health Sciences, Dentistry, Pharmacy, Nursing, and Graduate Health Sciences. The primary mission of the HSC is to provide and improve health care for the citizens of Tennessee.

ACADEMICS

Tennessee's curriculum is divided into the traditional two-year basic science and clinical units. All students spend the preclinical period at the university's campus in Memphis. During the clinical phase, juniors and seniors can choose to complete up to half of their required and elective clerkships in the school's facilities in Knoxville or Chattanooga.

In the first year, students concentrate on the normal structures and functions of the human body. Basic science coursework includes gross anatomy, molecular and cellular biology, biochemistry, physiology, neuroanatomy, and histology. In addition to developing scientific foundations, students investigate psychological and social issues and begin to explore preventative medicine.

The focus on the basic sciences continues in the second year, but the emphasis is on the abnormal. Students spend much of their time investigating the disease process, its effects on the body, and therapeutic intervention strategies. Concurrently, sophomores take an Introduction to Clinical Medicine. In this course, students learn the fundamental patient-interaction skills of history-taking and physical examination. Through direct patient contact and class discussions, sophomores begin to apply scientific principles to clinical problems, effecting a transition to the clerkship stage.

The third and fourth years are devoted to clinical clerkships and electives. Juniors complete rotations in medicine, surgery, obstetrics/gynecology, psychiatry, pediatrics, and family medicine. Although a portion of the senior year is elective, all students must complete one-month clerkships in neurology, ambulatory medicine, and the surgical subspecialties. Subinternships in medicine and one of the other major disciplines are also required.

Grading and Promotion Policy: A–F. Students must pass USMLE Parts I and II.

Additional Degree Programs: MD/Ph.D., MD/MS.

ADMISSIONS

Tennessee gives first priority to state residents and accepts applications only from residents of eight other states: Mississippi, Arkansas, Missouri, Kentucky, Virginia, North Carolina, Georgia, and Alabama. The school makes exceptions for children of alumni, who may apply regardless of their state of residence. Students applying from out of state should be aware that very few nonresidents are accepted; of the two hundred or so who applied in 1992, only six were admitted. Since Tennessee does not participate in AMCAS, interested students should obtain applications directly from the admissions office. For the best chance for admission, apply as early as possible.

The Admissions Committee evaluates both quantitative and qualitative criteria when selecting each year's class. The most important factors include the academic record, including the depth and breadth of undergraduate coursework, MCAT scores, letters of recommendation, the interview, extracurricular activities, motivation for studying medicine, and personal qualities.

Special Programs for Members of Underrepresented Minorities: Tennessee has an active program to recruit, retain, and graduate underrepresented minority students. The Student Tracking System (STS) offers a range of services and support for students from the time of application to the time of graduation.

Transfer Policy: Applicants are considered for transfer into the third year. To be eligible, students must be Tennessee residents or the children of alumni and must have passed Part I of the USMLE.

FINANCIAL AID

Most financial aid is awarded on the basis of need as determined by the College Scholarship Service analysis. In addition to standard assistance programs, the College of Medicine offers a few full-tuition scholarships to students who show outstanding academic promise and awards grants to students who agree to practice in medically underserved areas.

ADMISSIONS FACTS

Demographics

% men	65
% women	35
% minorities	10

Deadline & Notification Dates

AMCAS	yes
Regular application	11/15
Regular notification	10/15–4/15
Early Decision application	No EDP program
Early Decision notification	N/A

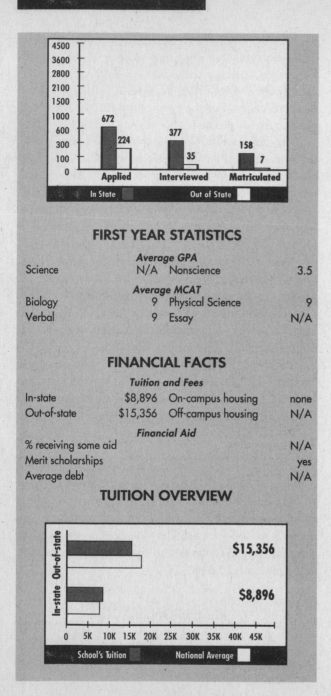

FIRST YEAR STATISTICS

Average GPA

Science	N/A	Nonscience	3.5

Average MCAT

Biology	9	Physical Science	9
Verbal	9	Essay	N/A

FINANCIAL FACTS

Tuition and Fees

In-state	$8,896	On-campus housing	none
Out-of-state	$15,356	Off-campus housing	N/A

Financial Aid

% receiving some aid	N/A
Merit scholarships	yes
Average debt	N/A

TUITION OVERVIEW

$15,356

$8,896

Vanderbilt University School of Medicine

Office of Admissions, 209 Light Hall, Nashville, TN 37232-0685
(615) 322-2145

OVERVIEW

Vanderbilt University School of Medicine ranks among the top research-oriented med schools. A major part of its mission, school officials say, is a commitment "to the education of physicians who are firmly grounded in basic medical science; who can recognize, treat, and prevent diseases and disorders in their patients; who can obtain, evaluate, and apply the results of scientific research; and who can translate their proficiency into effective humanitarian service." Evidently, students feel they made the right choice in entrusting this Nashville institution with their medical future; Vanderbilt's attrition rate is just 2 percent—well below the national average.

ACADEMICS

Vanderbilt's curriculum has two major facets: required core courses and electives. In all four years, students may choose from a wide range of elective experiences, including seminars, lectures, and clinical clerkships. Since Vanderbilt is interested in continuing its reputation for investigative excellence, students are also encouraged to pursue research activities during elective and vacation time. To further augment the formal course of study, Vanderbilt invites members of the medical community to present weekly lectures that address topics of school-wide interest.

During the first two, preclinical years, students study the basic sciences, investigate nontechnical aspects of medicine, learn the fundamentals of patient interaction, and explore the research process. Much of the first year's instruction centers around the structures and functions of the human body, and strong emphasis is placed on the clinical relevance of the basic sciences. To lend a human perspective, the curriculum includes a course in behavioral science. An innovative feature of Vanderbilt's first year is the required Introduction to Biomedical Research. Through this program, each freshman is paired with a faculty preceptor, under whose tuelage the student formulates a research project, conducts experiments, and presents findings.

In the second year, students continue their study of the basic sciences, but shift their focus from the normal to the abnormal. The disease process, diagnostic procedures, and therapeutic intervention are among the topics presented. Because the second year is intended to facilitate the transition from the basic sciences to the third-year clerkships, sophomores also spend a considerable amount of time developing basic clinical skills such as history-taking, physical examination, and physical diagnosis. Lectures, small group conferences, demonstrations, and direct patient contact are among the methods of instruction.

The clinical years include both required and elective experiences. Mandatory rotations in medicine, obstetrics/gynecology, pediatrics, surgery, psychiatry, and neurology are usually completed in the third year, leaving the majority of the fourth year free for electives. The senior year is divided into four-week academic units; in addition to basic science and clinical electives, all seniors must complete three units of clinical selectives, one in ambulatory care and two in inpatient settings.

Grading and Promotion Policy: A, B+, B, B-, C, F.
Additional Degree Programs: MD/Ph.D.

STUDENT LIFE

The School of Medicine's status as a part of a major university and its location in Tennessee's state capital make it easy for almost everyone to find plenty to do. At the Sarratt Student Center, students can take in a free movie, stroll through the art gallery, study, take part in school organizations, or just hang out with friends. A Black Cultural Center and a Women's Center further serve the needs and interests of African-American and female students. The school's athletic facilities, which include a swimming pool, courts, playing fields, exercise rooms, and a rock-climbing wall, provide ways to work off tension. A full range of sports instruction, from tennis to tae kwon do, gives novice athletes a chance to get in shape.

Although Nashville is renowned as the country music capital of the world, students who need a break from the Ivory Tower find that the city has a lot more to offer than the Grand Old Opry. Nashville has recently experienced significant cultural growth. The Tennessee Performing Arts Center hosts music, theater, and dance performances and the Nashville Symphony Orchestra

gives indoor and outdoor concerts. Of course, Music City, USA provides plenty of opportunities to listen to live bands—not all of them country.

Outdoor enthusiasts might enjoy heading to the area's rivers, lakes, and streams for leisurely float trips, whitewater rafting, kayaking, sailing, and fishing. Those who'd rather stay on the sidelines can cheer on Vanderbilt's Southern Conference Collegiate teams or take in a minor league baseball or hockey game.

University housing for single and married students is available, and the school maintains lists of off-campus rental units. Shuttle and escort services help students get around safely.

ADMISSIONS

Vanderbilt is a private institution, and it has no preference for state residents. Since the school has a rolling admissions cycle, those who are seriously interested should apply as early as possible. On the basis of the AMCAS application, the Admissions Committee asks highly qualified candidates to submit additional material and come to campus for an interview. Although regional interviews are offered, our research shows that it is in applicants' best interests to attend an on-site meeting.

Admission to Vanderbilt is extremely competitive; the entering class in 1992 represented just over two percent of the total applicant pool. In making its final decisions, the Admissions Office evaluates the candidate on a number of factors, including the interview, the science and nonscience GPA, MCAT scores (from the new test), letters of recommendation, and essays. The candidate's life outside the classroom is also considered important; extracurricular activities, work experiences, volunteerism, and research experiences are reviewed.

Special Programs for Members of Underrepresented Minorities: Vanderbilt's minority affairs office coordinates programs to recruit and support members of underrepresented minorities.

Transfer Policy: Because of its low attrition rate, Vanderbilt rarely accepts transfers.

eMail: Gottergs@Ctrvax.Vanderbilt.Edu

FINANCIAL AID

In addition to scholarship, loan, and grant funds that are awarded on the basis of documented need, Vanderbilt offers several honors scholarships that are partially or fully merit based.

ADMISSIONS FACTS

Demographics

% men	63
% women	37
% minorities	7

Deadline & Notification Dates

AMCAS	yes
Regular application	10/15
Regular notification	10/15–until filled
Early Decision application	10/15–08/01
Early Decision notification	10/01

Bar chart:

5710

	In State	Out of State
Applied	309	5710
Interviewed	57	647
Matriculated	17	84

In State   Out of State

FIRST YEAR STATISTICS

Average GPA

Science	N/A	Nonscience	N/A

Average MCAT

Biology	N/A	Physical Science	N/A
Verbal	N/A	Essay	N/A

FINANCIAL FACTS

Tuition and Fees

In-state	$19,510	On-campus housing	N/A
Out-of-state	$19,510	Off-campus housing	N/A

Financial Aid

% receiving some aid	N/A
Merit scholarships	yes
Average debt	$57,203

TUITION OVERVIEW

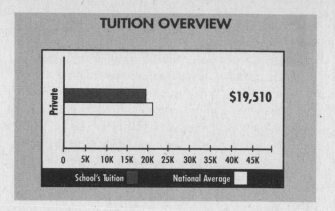

$19,510

School's Tuition   National Average

Baylor College of Medicine

Office of Admissions, One Baylor Plaza, Houston, TX 77030
(713) 798-4841

OVERVIEW

The students we surveyed are happy with just about everything about Baylor, putting it in the top ten in nearly every category. Teaching, facilities, research, clinical exposure, and, yes, even social life were rated outstanding. One student explains this phenomenon better than we could ever hope to: "The majority of students...are so happy to be here, it's more like a commune than a medical school."

ACADEMICS

Baylor has recently overhauled its curriculum. Instead of the traditional two-year preclinical period, students spend just seventeen months in the basic sciences. The remaining twenty-nine months are devoted to clinical clerkships, a few required courses, and considerable elective time.

The preclinical period extends from August of the first year to December of the second. During this time, basic science lectures and labs are supplemented by small group discussion sessions and intermittent clinical correlations. Some courses are taught interdepartmentally. In the beginning of the second year, students integrate scientific principles with clinical applications through Introduction to the Clinical Specialties and Introduction to Patients. In these courses, students work with patients to learn medical interviewing and examination skills. These courses provide a transition to the clinical phase.

Students rate their clinical preparation as outstanding. Because of the increased length of the clinical phase, Baylor requires rotations, like orthopedics and plastic surgery, that other schools do not. Students believe this breadth of exposure better prepares them for residency. Students are nearly unanimous in awarding Baylor's hospital and clinical affiliates the highest possible rating, giving their school top honors in this category.

Despite the strong clinical emphasis, Baylor students give the school's research efforts high marks. They are not alone in this assessment—the school was recently rated among the nation's top twenty research-oriented schools. Teaching is also top-notch, say Baylor students; they add, however, that many prestigious faculty members don't do much teaching.

Although students say the library, which the med school shares with UT–Houston, suffers from bad hours, poor organization, and congestion, other facilities are considered satisfactory.

Grading and Promotion Policy: In the basic sciences: Honors/Pass/Marginal Pass/Fail. In the clinical period: Honors/High Pass/Pass/Marginal Pass/Fail.

Additional Degree Programs: MD/Ph.D. Baylor also offers a National Institute of Health–funded Medical Scientist Training Program.

STUDENT LIFE

Only one school we surveyed has students who are happier than those at Baylor. And considering that Baylor students rate their classmates as competitive, verging on cutthroat, this is a bit of a surprise. Evidently, intensity in the classroom doesn't get in the way of friendship; students say they have active social lives and like hanging out with their classmates.

Baylor has a variety of clubs and organizations, and students enjoy the opportunities afforded by its location in one of Texas's largest cities. They give Houston high ratings, but say getting around is something of a problem. Public transportation is not particularly accessible and the parking situation at and around the Medical Center is notorious. Living within walking distance is the best solution. Baylor reports that about 10 percent of students live in university residence halls. While university housing gets pretty good reviews, students say they prefer to try their luck off campus.

ADMISSIONS

Although Baylor states no preference for state residents, Texans make up about 70 percent of the class. For the best chance for admission, applicants should apply as early as possible. The mean GPA for recent classes was 3.6 and the average MCAT score for each area was around 10. The Admissions Office warns that students with GPAs lower than 3.0 have little chance for acceptance. Although Baylor encourages applicants with a diversity of academic backgrounds, the intensity of the basic science curriculum makes a strong grounding in the sciences especially important.

In making its selections, the Admissions Committee considers the academic record, including science and nonscience GPAs and the level and breadth of coursework; MCAT scores (from the revised MCAT); motivation and suitability for studying medicine; extra-curricular activities; and the interview. Interview sessions last two days; in addition to the actual interview, students are invited to tour the campus, attend classes, and speak with medical students.

Special Programs for Members of Underrepresented Minorities: Baylor encourages applications from underrepresented minority students. Among special programs the med school offers is an Honors Premedical Academy, a joint effort with Rice University. In this summer program, selected minority college students take science classes and participate in research and clinical experience.

Transfer Policy: Transfers into the clinical portion of the program are considered. Students must have a good reason for the transfer and must be in good standing at the school they are transferring from.

FINANCIAL AID

Texas residents pay the same tuition as they would at one of the UT schools, which may account for the large number of Texans at Baylor. Financial aid is available through grants, scholarships, and loans. Most awards are made on the basis of need and consist of long-term loans.

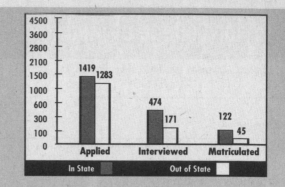

	In State	Out of State
Applied	1419	1283
Interviewed	474	171
Matriculated	122	45

FIRST YEAR STATISTICS

Average GPA

Science	N/A	Nonscience	3.6

Average MCAT

Biology	N/A	Physical Science	N/A
Verbal	N/A	Essay	N/A

FINANCIAL FACTS

Tuition and Fees

In-state	$8,109	On-campus housing	N/A
Out-of-state	$21,209	Off-campus housing	N/A

Financial Aid

% receiving some aid	N/A
Merit scholarships	yes
Average debt	N/A

HITS AND MISSES

HITS	MISSES
Clinical facilities	Prestigious faculty who don't teach
Overall happiness	Very competitive environment
Students like each other	Accessible public transportation
Quality of teaching	
Research efforts	

ADMISSIONS FACTS

Demographics

% men	63
% women	37
% minorities	8

Deadline & Notification Dates

AMCAS	yes
Regular application	11/01
Regular notification	10/15–until filled
Early Decision application	06/15–08/01
Early Decision notification	10/01

TUITION OVERVIEW

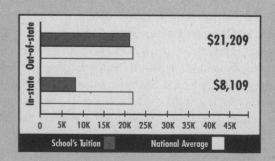

	School's Tuition	National Average
Out-of-state	$21,209	
In-state	$8,109	

University of Texas: Southwestern Medical Center at Dallas Southwestern Medical School

Office of the Registrar
5323 Harry Hines Boulevard, Dallas, TX 75235-9096
(214) 688-2670

OVERVIEW

Rated among the best research-oriented med schools, the University of Texas Southwestern Medical Center at Dallas (UTSMS) "is dedicated to the education of physicians who are thoroughly grounded in the scientific basis of modern medicine, who are inspired to maintain lifelong medical scholarship, and who will care for patients in a responsible and compassionate manner." While the majority of graduates eventually practice medicine, those who want to enter careers in research find that UTSMS gives them plenty of opportunities to pursue their goals through summer projects or in combined MD/Ph.D. programs.

ACADEMICS

Although UTSMS says it has maintained a classical four-year curriculum, it is not completely traditional. Many courses are taught by multidisciplinary faculty, and small-group conferences, problem-based learning, clinical correlations, labs, and demonstrations complement lectures.

The purpose of the first two years is to give students a firm grounding in the basic sciences and to develop fundamental clinical problem-solving and interaction skills. Freshmen begin their medical education with courses that deal with the normal structures and functions of the human body on a molecular and cellular level. The second semester focuses on physiology, the neurosciences, and ethical issues. Human reproduction and endocrinology round out the first year.

Sophomores study the disease process, its effect on the body, and therapeutic intervention strategies. Although students continue to study the biological basis of medicine, year-long courses in pathology and clinical medicine help integrate the basic and clinical sciences.

The first contact with patients comes early in the second semester as sophomores learn history-taking and physical examination skills. Lectures, seminars, visits to outpatient clinics, and direct patient contact are among the primary learning methods.

Hands-on experiences with patients intensify during the third year. In the course of ten months, juniors complete rotations in the major disciplines and in family medicine. Requirements, including a clerkship in neurology and a subinternship in internal medicine, extend into the fourth year. Seniors must also take clinical selectives and choose free electives. A one-month didactic course that covers legal, ethical, and other issues relevant to postgraduate training is also mandatory.

Grading and Promotion Policy: Letter grades are used in required courses. Pass/Fail is used for electives.

Additional Degree Programs: For outstanding students interested in academic medicine, UTSMS offers a funded Medical Scientist Training Program that leads to a combined MD/Ph.D. A regular MD/Ph.D. program is also available.

STUDENT LIFE

The Skillern Student Union is the hub of UTSMS's extracurricular activities. Convenient to lecture halls, this building houses exercise facilities, a lounge, and space for socializing. The University Activities Office, also located in the student union, offers a variety of recreational pursuits designed to reduce the stress of med school. Intramural sports and nonmedical classes provide a break from studying, and special events like the annual Oktoberfest and Spring Fling celebrations give students a chance to play as hard as they work. Those who need a change of scenery can pick up discounted tickets to some of Dallas's popular cultural, entertainment, and sports events.

UTSMS offers no on-campus apartments, but there is housing available nearby. Since Dallas has little in the way of public transportation, students may be well-advised to bring their cars. Parking at the medical center is limited, however.

ADMISSIONS

Since it is a state-supported school, UTSMS gives first priority to residents of Texas. Up to 10 percent of each year's class can come from out of state, but nonresidents should have qualifications that put them in the top one-third of the entering class.

Like the other Texas Schools, UTSMS does not participate in AMCAS. Rather, candidates must apply through the University of Texas's central processing office in Austin. For the class entering in 1992, UTSMS was the most selective of the UT schools, just edging out Houston. (The other two schools that belong to the system are located in Galveston and San Antonio.)

The Admissions Committee is composed of basic science and clinical faculty members, practicing physicians from the community, and current med students (though student representatives don't participate in interviews). The committee's final decisions are made primarily on the basis of GPAs, MCAT scores, the interview, letters of recommendation, and personal characteristics. Extracurricular activities, the level and breadth of coursework, and work experience are also considered important.

Special Programs for Members of Underrepresented Minorities: UTSMS encourages qualified members of underrepresented minorities to apply, particularly those who reside in Texas.

Transfer Policy: Transfers are currently accepted only in exceptional circumstances. Any student who wishes to transfer should contact the Admissions Office to discuss his or her case.

FINANCIAL AID

At under $7,000 a year, UTSMS—like the rest of the Texas schools—is a good buy for state residents. Financial aid, awarded primarily on the basis of need, is available in the form of scholarships, grants, and loans.

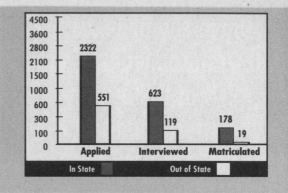

FIRST YEAR STATISTICS

	Average GPA		
Science	N/A	Nonscience	N/A
	Average MCAT		
Biology	N/A	Physical Science	N/A
Verbal	N/A	Essay	N/A

FINANCIAL FACTS

	Tuition and Fees		
In-state	$7,084	On-campus housing	N/A
Out-of-state	$20,184	Off-campus housing	N/A
	Financial Aid		
% receiving some aid			N/A
Merit scholarships			N/A
Average debt			N/A

TUITION OVERVIEW

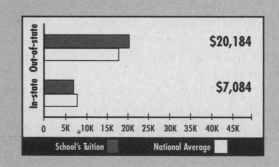

ADMISSIONS FACTS

Demographics

% men	64
% women	36
% minorities	16

Deadline & Notification Dates

AMCAS	yes
Regular application	10/15
Regular notification	01/15–until filled
Early Decision application	No EDP program
Early Decision notification	N/A

University of Texas: Medical Branch at Galveston School of Medicine

Office of Admissions
G.210, Ashbel Smith Building, Galveston, TX 77550-1317
(409) 772-3517

OVERVIEW

A medical school on the coast of Texas has terrific clinical facilities but a somewhat aloof administration. Does this sound like your kind of paradise? Consider UTMB. The medical school at the University of Texas Medical Branch at Galveston (UTMB) is one of the four med schools in the state system. Although there are a number of similarities among the schools, the curricula are different, and each school has its own unique atmosphere.

ACADEMICS

Although UTMB divides its curriculum along the usual basic science and clinical lines, it updates the preclinical years with an increased emphasis on interdisciplinary courses, preventative medicine, and early patient care. The third and fourth year are occupied with clinical rotations, electives, and a course on medical jurisprudence.

UTMB students are pleased with the amount of clinical exposure they get during the Basic Science Core. Patient contact begins first semester and intensifies throughout the remainder of the two years. Clinical training begins through Introduction to Patient Evaluation. In this two-year course, students learn the fundamentals of physical examination and rudimentary diagnostic skills. Small group instruction, simulated patients, and case studies are among the methods of instruction. Introduction to Clinical Medicine, taken after completion of the basic sciences, eases the transition into third-year clerkships.

Students report that the quality of teaching is very good and that faculty members go out of their way to ensure students' success. The administration does not fare so well, however. Complains one student, "Deans need to prioritize student concerns...They are practically worthless around here."

Clinical facilities are rated outstanding and, since the school is reportedly in the process of renovating some of its older clinics, they are expected to get even better. Library and computer labs also receive excellent reviews. All other facilities are rated very good.

Grading and Promotion Policy: A–F. Students are required to pass Parts I and II of the USMLE.

Additional Degree Programs: MD/Ph.D., MD with Research Honors.

STUDENT LIFE

The letter grading system leads to a fairly competitive atmosphere, but most students say their classmates aren't "cutthroat." If the pressure is on, students can work off steam in the campus athletic facility, which also sponsors intramural sports. UTMB students are enthusiastic about the campus and like its setting near the water. They are not as positive about Galveston, however.

Overall, students say they lead relatively active lives outside the classrooms. An unusual feature of UTMB's social scene is its medical fraternities; these organizations, some of which are coeducational, provide housing and social opportunities for their members.

ADMISSIONS

A minimum of 90 percent of students must be residents of Texas. Although out-of-state students with outstanding credentials are welcome to apply, they will be admitted only if there is space left after every qualified Texan is admitted.

Application to UTMB is made through the University of Texas Medical and Dental Application Center in Austin. On the basis of the initial application, promising students will be invited to interview. The interview, grades, MCAT scores, letters of recommendation, activities, and personal qualities are considered important in the selection process.

Special Programs for Members of Underrepresented Minorities: UTMB students rate the school as fairly diverse, but, as is true at many of the schools we surveyed, a number of students express resentment about the special programs available to underrepresented minorities. "[There is] reverse discrimination against whites. Blacks and other minorities are accorded special privileges," is a representative comment. The Office of Special Programs coordinates efforts to recruit minority students.

Transfer Policy: UTMB considers transfers from LCME approved schools. Transfers are permitted into the third and fourth year only.

FINANCIAL AID

Most assistance is based on need. Although there is some scholarship money available, most awards are in the form of long-term loans. Several scholarships are available for minority students. About 45 percent of students receive financial assistance.

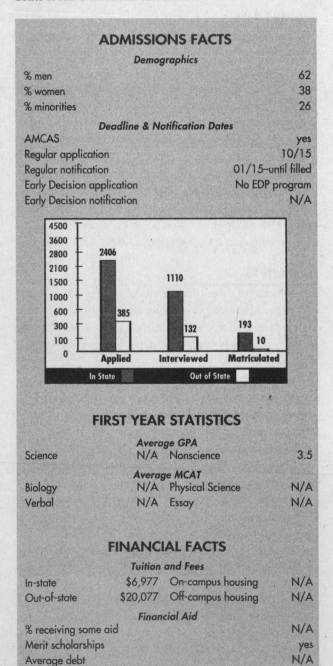

ADMISSIONS FACTS

Demographics

% men	62
% women	38
% minorities	26

Deadline & Notification Dates

AMCAS	yes
Regular application	10/15
Regular notification	01/15–until filled
Early Decision application	No EDP program
Early Decision notification	N/A

In State / Out of State bar chart:
Applied: 2406 / 385
Interviewed: 1110 / 132
Matriculated: 193 / 10

FIRST YEAR STATISTICS

Average GPA

Science	N/A	Nonscience	3.5

Average MCAT

Biology	N/A	Physical Science	N/A
Verbal	N/A	Essay	N/A

FINANCIAL FACTS

Tuition and Fees

In-state	$6,977	On-campus housing	N/A
Out-of-state	$20,077	Off-campus housing	N/A

Financial Aid

% receiving some aid	N/A
Merit scholarships	yes
Average debt	N/A

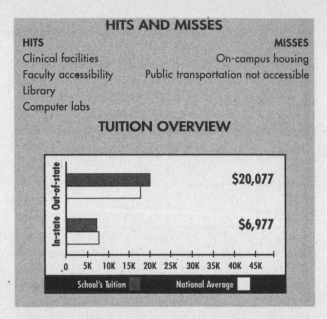

HITS AND MISSES

HITS	MISSES
Clinical facilities	On-campus housing
Faculty accessibility	Public transportation not accessible
Library	
Computer labs	

TUITION OVERVIEW

Out-of-state: $20,077
In-state: $6,977

School's Tuition / National Average

University of Texas: Medical School at Houston

Office of Admissions, Rm. G-024, P.O. Box 20708, Houston, TX 77225
(713) 792-4711

OVERVIEW

Can a bad parking situation really influence the way students feel about their whole med school experience? If the responses of the UT Houston students we surveyed are any indication, the answer is a resounding yes. Nearly every comment we got included a vehement condemnation of the school's parking policies. A few even said that if they had to do it over again, they'd find a school where they didn't have to take a bus from the place they left their car. Fortunately, most students— even those with transportation woes—say UT Houston has a lot of other things going for it.

ACADEMICS

UT Houston's curriculum is fairly traditional. The primary focus of the first two years is on the basic sciences, with instruction progressing from anatomy and molecular and cell biology to normal and abnormal organ systems. Throughout the two years, students also explore social, behavioral, and ethical aspects of medicine. An Introduction to Clinical Medicine course (ICM) introduces students to interviewing, history-taking, and physical examination skills.

Despite the exposure provided through ICM, students say they don't get enough contact with patients in the basic science years. "We are not exposed to clinical experiences early enough," complains one third-year student. But a first-year student tempers his criticism, "Clinical experience is limited . . . but we have good clinical correlation lectures where they bring patients to class to apply what we're learning." During the third and fourth years, students complete required clerkships in a variety of disciplines and design an elective course of study that suits their interests.

The majority of respondents say that the quality of teaching is very good, but some say that professors' research orientation sometimes gets in the way of their instruction. Almost all students agree that the faculty is accessible. The feeling does not extend to the administration, though. Says one sophomore, "[It] is very political and does not consider how students are affected by decisions." Affiliated hospitals and computer labs are the standouts among the school's facilities.

Grading and Promotion Policy: UT Houston uses a version of an Honors/Pass/Fail grading system.

Additional Degree Programs MD/MPH, MD/Ph.D.

STUDENT LIFE

Competition at UT Houston is low, and student relations are among the best of the schools we surveyed. Says one sophomore, "People are generally good, caring folks with their heads and hearts in the right places." Others comment on "the caring environment" and the "supportive student body." This atmosphere of goodwill lends itself to an lively social scene. A wide variety of school clubs and activities augment the nightlife and other recreational opportunities afforded by the school's urban location. Although there are a few dissenters, most respondents say they like Houston.

In comments about housing, the parking problem is, again, a sore spot. UT offers apartments a short distance from the school, but students say the benefits of living there are mitigated by the recent removal of a shuttle between the complex and the Med Center. Because of this, both on- and off-campus students face the commuting hassle. As one sophomore puts it, "You have a choice of either parking in a nearby public garage and paying out the butt for it, or paying a fortune to park miles from campus and waiting forty-five minutes for a bus."

ADMISSIONS

Preference in admissions is given to Texas residents and very few out-of-state candidates are accepted. Like the other University of Texas schools, UT Houston does not participate in AMCAS.

Among the most important selection factors are the GPA, MCAT scores, depth and breadth of coursework, letters of recommendation, and the interview. If you are invited to interview, and UT Houston is at the top of your list, tell your interviewer; the school gives special consideration to students who have specific—and valid—reasons for wanting to attend.

Special Programs for Members of Underrepresented Minorities: The Admissions Office encourages all members of underrepresented minorities to apply.

Transfer Policy: UT Houston does not accept transfers.

FINANCIAL AID

Financial aid is awarded primarily on the basis of academic ability.

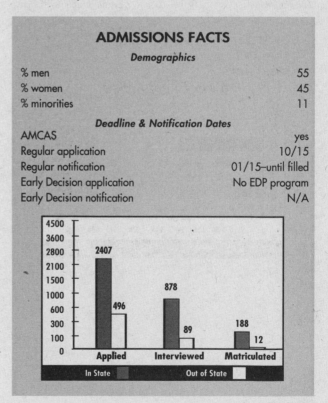

ADMISSIONS FACTS

Demographics

% men	55
% women	45
% minorities	11

Deadline & Notification Dates

AMCAS	yes
Regular application	10/15
Regular notification	01/15–until filled
Early Decision application	No EDP program
Early Decision notification	N/A

In State / Out of State

Applied: 2407 / 496
Interviewed: 878 / 89
Matriculated: 188 / 12

FIRST YEAR STATISTICS

Average GPA

Science	N/A	Nonscience	3.41

Average MCAT

Biology	N/A	Physical Science	N/A
Verbal	N/A	Essay	N/A

FINANCIAL FACTS

Tuition and Fees

In-state	$6,800	On-campus housing	N/A
Out-of-state	$19,900	Off-campus housing	N/A

Financial Aid

% receiving some aid	60
Merit scholarships	yes
Average debt	N/A

HITS AND MISSES

HITS	MISSES
Student relations	Parking
Social activity	Early clinical exposure
Accessibility of faculty	On-campus housing
Clinical facilities	Public transportation
Computer labs	
Research emphasis	

TUITION OVERVIEW

Out-of-state	$19,900
In-state	$6,800

0 5K 10K 15K 20K 25K 30K 35K 40K 45K

School's Tuition ▪ National Average ☐

University of Texas: Health Science Center at San Antonio Medical School

Medical School Admissions Office
7703 Floyd Curl Drive, San Antonio, TX 78284-7701
(210) 567-2665

OVERVIEW

The Medical School at San Antonio is part of the University of Texas system of medical schools. Other schools in the system are located in Dallas, Houston, and Galveston. While it has an original curriculum, it also has some less-than-stellar teaching formats, so UTSA leaves its students with mixed feelings. Although the students we surveyed are not wildly enthusiastic about UTSA, neither are they very critical—most ratings fell into the median range.

ACADEMICS

UTSA's curriculum is somewhat unusual, especially in the second year. In the first year, students learn basic scientific principles, investigate the psychosocial aspects of medicine, and train in physical examination skills. Second-year instruction centers on clinical introductions to each of the major clerkship areas. These introductions provide a transition to the third-year rotations. Fourth-year students continue clerkships through electives and investigate legal, ethical, and social issues as they apply to medicine.

Although both the structure and the content of the preclinical years are nontraditional, teaching methods are not. Large lecture formats are a frustration for many students and class attendance is reportedly poor. Complains one student, "Too many hours...are spent listening to a person talking. Some originality needs to be used in presenting material." Students rate the overall quality of teaching as good, but report that professors are only moderately accessible outside of class.

Academic support services pick up some of the slack by providing tutoring and counseling. Says one student, "They do their best to help you learn to do your best." Students are generally positive about UTSA's facilities with highest marks going to the library.

Grading and Promotion Policy: A–F.
Additional Degree Programs: none.

STUDENT LIFE

A little over 70 percent of the students we surveyed say they're happy at UTSA, a relatively low percentage in comparison to the other schools we surveyed. Although students report that they like to spend time with their classmates, a heavy workload, especially in the first two years, hampers their social lives and extracurricular involvement.

There is no on-campus housing, but students find off-campus offerings satisfactory. The medical school shares San Antonio with several other colleges and universities. The city, with its student orientation and its bicultural atmosphere, is popular.

ADMISSIONS

Ninety percent of students must be Texas residents, so nonresidents are encouraged to apply only if their credentials are outstanding. According to the Admissions Office, about 50 percent of successful applicants have GPAs above 3.5 and fewer than five percent are below 3.0.

Application to UTSA is made through the University of Texas Medical and Dental Application Center in Austin. On the basis of the initial application, UTSA decides which candidates to interview. Grades, breadth of coursework, MCAT scores, letters of recommendation, activities, and personal qualities are considered in making this initial determination. Final decisions are made after the interview.

Special Programs for Members of Underrepresented Minorities: The Office of Special Programs coordinates efforts to recruit and serve underrepresented minority students. Among its offerings are peer counseling, tutoring, and a mentor program.

Transfer Policy: Transfers are not considered.
eMail: livaudais@uthscsa.edu

FINANCIAL AID

Students may apply for financial aid only after they have been accepted. Approximately 90 percent of students who apply for financial aid receive some assistance. Most awards are made primarily in the form of long-term federal loans.

ADMISSIONS FACTS

Demographics

% men	62
% women	38
% minorities	11

Deadline & Notification Dates

AMCAS	yes
Regular application	10/15
Regular notification	01/15–until filled
Early Decision application	No EDP program
Early Decision notification	N/A

FIRST YEAR STATISTICS

Average GPA

Science	N/A	Nonscience	3.58

Average MCAT

Biology	N/A	Physical Science	N/A
Verbal	N/A	Essay	N/A

FINANCIAL FACTS

Tuition and Fees

In-state	$6,907	On-campus housing	none
Out-of-state	$20,007	Off-campus housing	N/A

Financial Aid

% receiving some aid	N/A
Merit scholarships	no
Average debt	N/A

HITS AND MISSES

HITS	MISSES
Library	Faculty accessibility
Diversity	No on-campus housing
Classrooms	No time for social life
Location	Too many lectures in first year

TUITION OVERVIEW

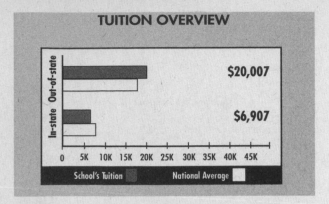

Out-of-state **$20,007**

In-state **$6,907**

0 5K 10K 15K 20K 25K 30K 35K 40K 45K

School's Tuition ▪   National Average ▫

Texas A & M University College of Medicine

Associate Dean of Admissions, College Station, TX 77843-1114
(409) 845-7744

OVERVIEW

Texas A&M College of Medicine is part of the University's Health Science Center and is affiliated with the Olin E. Teague Veterans' Center, Scott and White Hospital and Clinic, the Darnall Army Community Hospital, and two Veterans' Administration Hospitals. Says the admissions bulletin, "This remarkable configuration of a research-oriented state university, a comprehensive private sector health care provider, two of the largest federal health service agencies in the region, and the largest armored military installation in the free world integrates the strengths and resources of each institution." Through this unusual combination of hospitals, Texas A&M's small student body is exposed to an incredibly large and diverse patient base—each year, a total of over 1.5 million patients are treated at the school's affiliates.

ACADEMICS

Students spend the preclinical period on the university's College Station campus before moving on to the clinical phase at the hospitals in and around the town of Temple. In the basic science years, the curriculum emphasizes clinical correlations and the development of patient-interaction skills. First-year students concentrate on the scientific basis of medicine and explore the social, psychological, and ethical aspects of medicine in behavioral science and medical humanities segments. Freshmen also begin to focus on the doctor-patient relationship and develop rudimentary clinical skills.

During the sophomore year, students build on their knowledge of the clinical sciences. Courses in pathology, microbiology, and pharmacology explore the disease process, its effect on the human body, and strategies for therapeutic intervention. Sophomores also spend a half-day per week learning interviewing, examination, and diagnostic skills under the direction of practicing physicians. Introductions to major clinical areas—pediatrics, obstetrics/gynecology, medicine, and psychiatry—and a primary care preceptorship facilitate the transition to the third year.

During the junior year, students spend most of their time completing clerkships in the major disciplines and family medicine. Juniors must also take courses that introduce diagnostic instruments. Although much of the senior year is free for electives, students work for six weeks each in neurology and in an alcohol and drug dependence program. Didactic experiences in medical jurisprudence, epidemiology, public health, biostatistics, and medical humanities are also mandatory.

Grading and Promotion Policy: A–F.
Additional Degree Programs: MD/Ph.D.

STUDENT LIFE

Texas A&M's small class size fosters a cooperative atmosphere in which classmates join together in a variety of co- and extracurricular pursuits. Students are actively involved in projects that benefit the community, and each class chooses to support different area service organizations. Still, there's time to play. Yearly events like the Cadaver Ball, a Chili Cook-off, and the med school talent show give students a chance to socialize and strut their nonacademic stuff. During the first two years at College Station, the med school community also has access to the sports, recreational, and cultural activities of the University. Those looking for a break from the campus can explore the Bryan–College Station area's many parks or can practice their tennis and golf swings at nearby recreational facilities.

On-campus housing is limited in College Station, but the University's Off-Campus Center provides assistance in locating apartments. A Texas A&M transit system helps students get around. For their clinical work, juniors and seniors live in Temple, a small but growing town of about 50,000. The University subsidizes a number of one- and two-bedroom apartments in Temple.

ADMISSIONS

As a state-supported school, Texas A&M gives strong preference to Texas residents. Although up to 10 percent of students can come from out of state, traditionally only a couple of nonresidents are accepted each year.

Like the other Texas schools, Texas A&M does not participate in AMCAS. To apply, request materials from your premed office or directly from the school. Although applications are accepted until November 1, it is in your best interest to take the spring MCAT and apply as early in the admissions cycle as possible.

Among the most important selection factors are the academic record, MCAT scores (from the new test), the interview, and letters of recommendation. According to the Admissions Office, "interpersonal skills, integrity, leadership, initiative, and breadth of interests" are among the personal characteristics successful applicants display.

Special Programs for Members of Underrepresented Minorities: Texas A&M "actively identifies and recruits" members of underrepresented minorities. The Health Careers Opportunities Program-Bridge to Medicine is one example of the school's efforts. In this program, minority college students take an intensive academic session to prepare for the MCAT. The school's Hispanic Center for Excellence offers a summer prematriculation program to facilitate the transition to the first year.

Transfer Policy: Students interested in transferring to Texas A&M should contact the Admissions Office to find out about the current policies.

FINANCIAL AID

Financial aid is awarded primarily on the basis of academic need. Although the Financial Aid Office coordinates some grant and scholarship programs, most assistance is in the form of long-term loans.

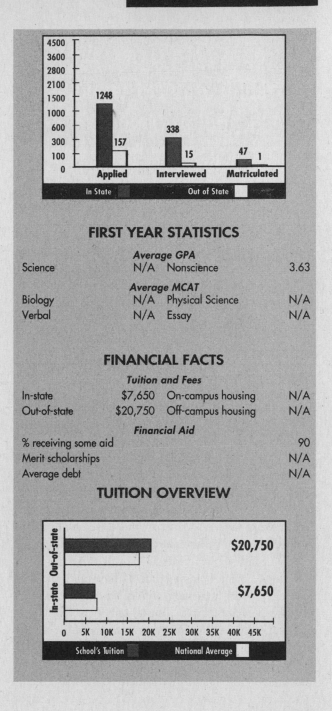

FIRST YEAR STATISTICS

Average GPA		
Science	N/A	Nonscience	3.63

Average MCAT		
Biology	N/A	Physical Science	N/A
Verbal	N/A	Essay	N/A

FINANCIAL FACTS

Tuition and Fees

In-state	$7,650	On-campus housing	N/A
Out-of-state	$20,750	Off-campus housing	N/A

Financial Aid

% receiving some aid	90
Merit scholarships	N/A
Average debt	N/A

TUITION OVERVIEW

$20,750

$7,650

School's Tuition   National Average

ADMISSIONS FACTS

Demographics

% men	60
% women	40
% minorities	7

Deadline & Notification Dates

AMCAS	yes
Regular application	11/01
Regular notification	11/15–until filled
Early Decision application	No EDP program
Early Decision notification	N/A

Texas Tech University Health Sciences Center School of Medicine

Office of Admissions, Lubbock, TX 79430
(806) 743-3005

OVERVIEW

Texas Tech is dedicated to providing health care to residents of west Texas. Students spend their basic science years at Lubbock and receive clinical training in Lubbock, Amarillo, and El Paso. According to those we surveyed, the best thing about this regional med school is the faculty.

ACADEMICS

Texas Tech's curriculum is fairly traditional. The first two years are devoted primarily to the basic sciences, and the third and fourth consist of required clerkships and electives. Topics in preventative medicine, psychiatry, and ethics are also presented in the preclinical phase. Clinical orientation begins during the second year through Introduction to Patient Assessment. This course integrates pathophysiology with physical diagnosis, but students say there aren't enough hands-on experiences with patients. Most of those we surveyed are dissatisfied with the amount of clinical exposure in the first two basic science years.

Despite the problems students have with the curriculum, they're extremely enthusiastic about the faculty. Respondents say the overall quality of teaching is excellent, and they're nearly unanimous in giving the faculty the highest possible rating for accessibility. Professors are described as "friendly" and "relaxed," and students say teachers go out of their way to make themselves available outside of class. Teaching sites, especially the affiliated hospitals, receive high marks. Students say the other facilities, too, are very good, but some complain that the library is sometimes crowded with other Health Professions students and that "the hours are somewhat restrictive."

Grading and Promotion Policy: Texas Tech uses a numerical grading system.

Additional Degree Programs: MD/Ph.D.

STUDENT LIFE

Texas Tech's atmosphere is "relaxed," and students say there isn't much overt competition. During their stay at the Lubbock campus, students have the opportunity to participate in a number of school clubs and organizations. The politically-minded can wage a campaign to be one of the med school representatives to the Health Sciences Center Student Senate or one of the officers of the Medical School Government. Students can explore their future professional roles with a variety of organizations; Texas Tech hosts chapters of most state and national medical organizations and boasts a number of special-interest clubs. For those interested in fitness, the school offers exercise equipment; aerobics classes; squash, tennis, and basketball courts; an Olympic-sized pool; intramural sports; and a Recreational Sports program that coordinates climbing, skiing, and rafting trips. Despite the variety of diversions available to them, students say their heavy workload hampers social interaction with their classmates. The location in Lubbock also limits off-campus social activity. Though most preclinical students agree with the one who says it's a "safe town with lots of sunshine and clear blue skies," many complain that "it's not very exciting." Since there are no university residence halls, students live off-campus and commute, mainly by car.

ADMISSIONS

Texas Tech gives preference to state residents and residents of neighboring counties in Oklahoma and New Mexico. Nonresidents with outstanding qualifications are welcome to apply, but should be aware that out-of-state candidates are admitted only when there are insufficient numbers of qualified candidates from Texas and its border states. Like the other schools in the state, Texas Tech doesn't participate in AMCAS; applications may be obtained directly from the Admissions Office. Candidates who show promise on the basis of the application are invited to the Lubbock campus for interviews.

According to the Director of Admissions, science and nonscience GPAs, MCAT scores, and the interview are the primary selection factors. Also important are letters of recommendation, extracurricular activities, exposure to the medical profession, and volunteer activities.

Special Programs for Members of Underrepresented Minorities: Texas Tech encourages underrepresented minority students to apply and offers a few special services to recruit and support such individuals. Among the school's offerings are summer sessions for college students, academic advising, and tutoring. Students with disadvantaged backgrounds may also be eligible for a decelerated program for the basic science years.

Transfer Policy: Transfers into the third year are considered on a space-available basis. Transfer candidates must be Texas residents and must have passed Part I of the USMLE.

FINANCIAL AID

The tuition at Texas Tech is the same as it is at the University of Texas system schools. Financial aid, based primarily on need, is available.

FINANCIAL FACTS

Tuition and Fees

In-state	$7,414	On-campus housing	N/A
Out-of-state	$20,514	Off-campus housing	$6,618
			(includes food)

Financial Aid

% receiving some aid	65
Merit scholarships	yes
Average debt	N/A

HITS AND MISSES

HITS	MISSES
Overall happiness	Early clinical exposure
Quality of teaching	Lubbock
Faculty accessibility	Extracurricular involvement
Clinical facilities	Public transportation
Safety	

TUITION OVERVIEW

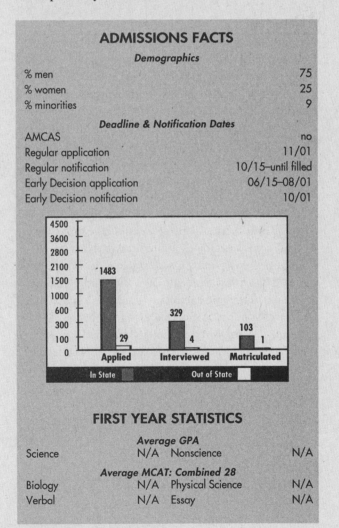

ADMISSIONS FACTS

Demographics

% men	75
% women	25
% minorities	9

Deadline & Notification Dates

AMCAS	no
Regular application	11/01
Regular notification	10/15–until filled
Early Decision application	06/15–08/01
Early Decision notification	10/01

FIRST YEAR STATISTICS

Average GPA

Science	N/A	Nonscience	N/A

Average MCAT: Combined 28

Biology	N/A	Physical Science	N/A
Verbal	N/A	Essay	N/A

University of Utah School of Medicine

Office of Admissions, 50 North Medical Drive, Salt Lake City, UT 84132
(801) 581-7498

OVERVIEW

The question to ask yourself is, "Can I function in an almost entirely white, Mormon, conservative environment?" Many of the students we surveyed chose Utah because of its cost—it's one of the least expensive schools in the country. While some students (like the Yogi Berra sound-alike who makes the statement, "It's the best bargain for the price") are satisfied with their choice, others say they're disappointed by mediocre teaching, a homogeneous student body, and a lack of significant clinical exposure during the basic science years.

ACADEMICS

Although Utah has recently revised its curriculum to provide more interdisciplinary courses and an introduction to clinical fundamentals in the basic science years, students report that too much of their time is spent in lectures. Complains one student, "Class time could be cut by half... Lots of people leave anyway, because it's such a waste of time." There is also frustration about unnecessary assignments; over three quarters of the students we surveyed say it is not very important to do all the reading in order to do well in their classes. One student comments, "A good undergrad background and a few hours with some old tests is plenty...to pass most classes." Utah's faculty receives mixed reviews. While students rate their teachers as only satisfactory in the classroom, they do appreciate professors' efforts to make themselves available outside of class.

Clinical exposure begins during the second year, when students are taught history-taking and physical examination skills. While second-year students are less critical than their first-year classmates, a significant percent of the preclinical students we surveyed say they are dissatisfied with the amount of hands-on experience they have had. Research efforts, clinical facilities, the library, and computer facilities get high marks.

STUDENT LIFE

Utah's student population is predominantly white, Mormon, and married. If you don't fit that profile, warns one student who says she is none of the above, you may find Utah "very isolating." But another student says the school does the best it can with a bad situation: "The lack of diversity is a reflection of the relatively heterogeneous state population and is *not* a product of school policy."

Despite their complaints, though, Utah students are relatively happy. Perhaps because of the similarities in their backgrounds, most students report that classmates get along well. The location in Salt Lake City is popular, as is the close proximity to top-notch ski resorts and Utah's many national parks.

ADMISSIONS

At least 75 percent of students in each class must be Utah residents and a portion of the remaining spaces is reserved for residents of Wyoming and Idaho. Special consideration is also given to students from western states without medical schools, underrepresented minority student, and students with close ties to the states. For the best chance for admission from out of state, nonresidents should apply Early Decision.

Utah sends supplementary applications to students who show promise on the basis of their academic records, letters of evaluation, MCAT scores and personal qualities. After supplemental applications are reviewed, some candidates are invited to interview.

Special Programs for Members of Underrepresented Minorities: Students give the school extremely low marks for ethnic and racial diversity, a situation the Office of Minority Affairs is trying to change. Special programs for minority applicants and students include special consideration for admissions and financial aid, a prematriculation summer session, and academic support services.

Transfer Policy: Utah's transfer policy varies from year to year. Call the school to discuss your individual case.

FINANCIAL AID

Utah's tuition is well under the average for state medical schools. There is some financial assistance available, however. All awards are made solely on the basis of need.

ADMISSIONS FACTS

Demographics

% men	22
% women	78
% minorities	6

Deadline & Notification Dates

AMCAS	yes
Regular application	10/15
Regular notification	11/01–until filled
Early Decision application	06/15–08/01
Early Decision notification	10/01

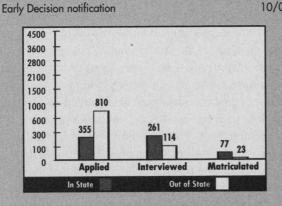

TUITION OVERVIEW

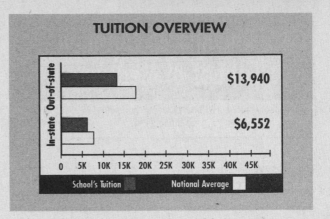

$13,940

$6,552

FIRST YEAR STATISTICS

Average GPA

Science	N/A	Nonscience	N/A

Average MCAT

Biology	N/A	Physical Science	N/A
Verbal	N/A	Essay	N/A

FINANCIAL FACTS

Tuition and Fees

In-state	$6,552	On-campus housing	N/A
Out-of-state	$13,940	Off-campus housing	N/A

Financial Aid

% receiving some aid	N/A
Merit scholarships	N/A
Average debt	N/A

HITS AND MISSES

HITS	MISSES
Hot research areas	Homogeneous student body
Research efforts	Too much lecture time
Clinical facilities	So-so teaching
Library	Not enough early clinical exposure
Computer labs	Unnecessary reading assignments
Cost	
Location Safety	

University of Vermont College of Medicine

Admissions Office, E-109 Given Building, Burlington, VT 05405-0068
(802) 656-2154

OVERVIEW

University of Vermont School of Medicine (UVM) has a reputation for producing top-notch clinicians, especially in rural family practice. Most students say this "strong doctor-patient orientation" is the main reason they chose Vermont. But, they are quick to add, UVM's "friendly, supportive atmosphere" and the beauty of its surroundings sure don't hurt.

ACADEMICS

UVM's curriculum is innovative. Rather than employing the traditional two-year split, Vermont arranges its curriculum into three phases. The first of these, the Basic Science Core, lasts for the first year and a half. The second phase, the Clinical Core, begins in January of the second year, allowing students to begin clerkships a full semester before students at most other schools. The third phase, the Senior Selective Program (actually something of a misnomer), begins in the middle of the third year and lasts for the final year and a half.

Students believe that the unique structure of the curriculum is responsible, in large part, for UVM's reputation for training quality doctors. Even in the Basic Science Core, students are taught clinical fundamentals such as physical diagnosis and communication skills. Because of this exposure and the earlier than normal entry into clerkships, says one fourth-year student, "students are better prepared clinically than they are at most schools." Overall, students' ratings of UVM's excellence in early clinical exposure placed the school in the top five for this category.

Students also applaud UVM's faculty. Both quality of teaching and accessibility are rated outstanding. Comments one first-year student, "I'm very encouraged by the supportive, upbeat, caring attitude of the professors and faculty." Facilities do not fare as well; students particularly dislike their library and computer labs. Clinical facilities, located not only in Burlington but also in Maine and upstate New York, are considered

very good, however. Although students, praise of classroom and science labs is tepid at best, improvement may be in sight.

Grading and Promotion Policy: Honors/Pass/Fail. The USMLE is optional.

Additional Degree Programs: MD/Ph.D.

STUDENT LIFE

Although UVM is not racially diverse, nontraditional students are well-represented. Approximately forty-two percent (relatively high for a med school) of students are age 25 or older and only about twenty-eight percent enter the medical school straight out of college. Women are in the majority. Students report that this heterogeneity, combined with the University's applied policy of non-discrimination, results in fair treatment of students regardless of race, gender, or sexual preference. It's worth noting that UVM is the only school in our survey at which a gay student comments on the treatment of homosexuals. She reports, "I have found that the [gay] community in Burlington is very strong and visible. [T]he med school is generally a safe place for gay men and lesbians"

Whether or not it is because of the reported "high level of maturity" of the student body or because of the calming effects of the gorgeous scenery around the campus, almost every respondent to our survey reports that UVM has a "relaxed, non-competitive atmosphere." Students are socially active and—because of the multitude of recreational activities afforded by the school's location—enjoy "experienc[ing] the great outdoors together." Overall, students rate the quality of life at UVM as outstanding.

ADMISSIONS

Since UVM is a state school, it gives top priority in admissions to residents of Vermont. Still, approximately 50 percent of the student body comes from out of state. If you do apply from out of state, you should be aware that your chance for admission is slim; in the 1993–94 admissions season, just over two percent of out-of-state applicants were accepted.

According to the Admissions Office, science and nonscience GPAs, MCAT scores, and the interview are the top selection factors. Extracurricular activities, exposure to the medical profession, volunteerism, and personal qualities are also evaluated.

Transfer Policy: Because of UVM's unusual curriculum, transfers are usually not accepted; however, students who wish to transfer due to unusual circumstances are invited to contact the Admissions Office for specific guidelines.

Special Programs for Members of Underrepresented Minorities: Students rate Vermont extremely low on diversity, but some students say it's not really the school's fault. Says one such student, "This is not due to discrimination. Rather, Vermont is not diverse, so I believe there is not a strong community for attracting minorities." Whatever the cause, the Admissions Office says it recognizes and is addressing the problem: "The UVM College of Medicine is eager to recruit minority students for admission.... Increased cultural diversity in the academic community is a goal strongly espoused by the university."

FINANCIAL AID

Financial aid awards are based solely on need as determined by the College Scholarship Service. Since scholarship funds are limited, assistance comes primarily in the form of loans.

ADMISSIONS FACTS

Demographics

% men	52
% women	48
% minorities	10

Deadline & Notification Dates

AMCAS	yes
Regular application	11/01
Regular notification	12/10–until filled
Early Decision application	06/15–08/01
Early Decision notification	10/01

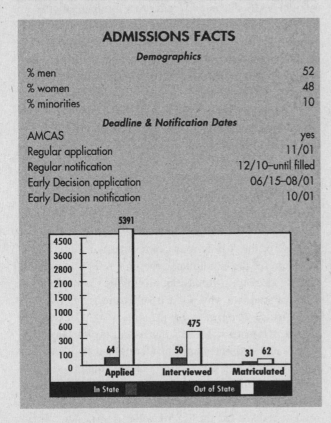

FIRST YEAR STATISTICS

	Average GPA		
Science	N/A	Nonscience	3.3
	Average MCAT		
Biology	N/A	Physical Science	N/A
Verbal	N/A	Essay	N/A

FINANCIAL FACTS

Tuition and Fees

In-state	$14,180	On-campus housing	$5,900
Out-of-state*	$26,350	Off-campus housing	$5,900

*Maine residents pay $16,740 as part of an interstate agreement.

Financial Aid

% receiving some aid	83
Merit scholarships	yes
Average debt	$70,000

HITS AND MISSES

HITS	MISSES
Early clinical exposure	Diversity
Quality of teaching	Computer labs
Accessibility of faculty	Library
Outdoor recreation	
Surrounding area	
Overall happiness	

TUITION OVERVIEW

Out-of-state $26,350
In-state $14,180

0 5K 10K 15K 20K 25K 30K 35K 40K 45K

School's Tuition ■   National Average □

Eastern Virginia Medical School

Office of Admissions, 700 Olney Road, Norfolk, VA 23507-1696
(804) 446-5812

OVERVIEW

If you are becoming a doctor to help people through one-on-one contact, the Eastern Virginia Medical School of the Medical College of Hampton Roads (EVMS) may be your school. Patient care comes first at EVMS. "I chose this school for the emphasis on primary care and the ability to get good clinical experience," explains one third-year student. As a state med school, EVMS's primary mission is to train physicians who will provide health care to the residents of Eastern Virginia. Since it serves an entire region of the state, students are exposed to diverse patients and clinical experiences. Says the Admissions Office, "Because of EVMS's affiliation with more than thirty different health care institutions, our graduates know what it is like to practice medicine in a wide variety of clinical settings."

ACADEMICS

Students are enthusiastic about both the variety and the amount of hands-on training they get at EVMS, even in their preclinical years. Some basic science courses are problem-based and are conducted in small groups with basic science and clinical faculty members working as co-facilitators. During the first two years students also learn history-taking and physical diagnosis skills and work with community physicians in required preceptorships. The last two years are spent in required and elective clinical clerkships.

Overall, EVMS students rate their faculty and administration as caring and accessible. Says one second-year student, "[The] faculty and administration are very student-oriented. We have input in almost all academic decisions that affect us." There is some frustration, however, about unevenness in the quality of teaching, especially in the basic science years. While many faculty members "go beyond the call of duty to make sure students understand material," others aren't so diligent. One embittered student complains: "The Ph.D.s are, by and large, frustrated MD want-to-bes who have

no interest in actually teaching us, but rather in breaking our spirit."

Except for the clinical facilities, which receive high marks for diversity and quality, students are fairly tepid in their praise of the school's facilities. Lowest ratings go to the library and classrooms, which students rate as satisfactory, while students are somewhat more positive about science and computer labs.

Grading Policy: Pass/Fail/High Pass/Honors.

Additional Degree Programs: Combined baccalaureate/MD.

STUDENT LIFE

Students at EVMS work hard, but find time to participate in a wide array of community and school activities. The school offers some on-campus housing, but students find it less than ideal and strongly prefer to live off campus. Although respondents say they're not crazy about the town of Norfolk, there are opportunities to get away from it all; one student reminds prospective applicants, "Norfolk is keenly situated close to the beach."

ADMISSIONS

While EVMS shows preference to Virginia residents, up to 60 percent can come from out of state. Especially encouraged to apply as nonresidents are students with outstanding academic qualifications, members of underrepresented minorities, women, and students interested in primary care.

The admissions office ranks the science GPA, MCAT scores (from the new test), nonscience GPA, letters of recommendation, and the interview as the most important selection factors. Exposure to the medical profession, volunteer activities, extracurricular activities and essays are also considered. Interviews are conducted by a panel consisting of a clinician, a basic scientist, and a medical student. One of the panel is a member of the Admissions Committee and will act as an advocate for the candidate in the final selection process. One-third of the Admissions Committee is made up of medical students who possess full voting rights.

Special Programs for Members of Underrepresented Minorities: EVMS has a minority affairs division that coordinates special recruitment and retention activities. Among these programs are summer sessions for college students, an MCAT review, a prematriculation summer session, academic advising, tutoring, and a review session for the USMLE Part I. All students are invited to participate in appropriate programs.

Transfer Policy: EVMS considers transfers from accredited medical schools if the applicant is a U.S. citizen or a permanent resident of the U.S.

FINANCIAL AID

EVMS uses the GAPSFAS needs analysis to determine eligibility for financial assistance. Virginia residents with need are eligible to receive a state Tuition Assistance grant. About 84 percent of students receive financial aid.

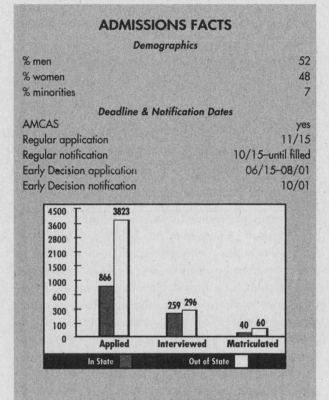

ADMISSIONS FACTS

Demographics

% men	52
% women	48
% minorities	7

Deadline & Notification Dates

AMCAS	yes
Regular application	11/15
Regular notification	10/15–until filled
Early Decision application	06/15–08/01
Early Decision notification	10/01

In State / Out of State
Applied: 866 / 3823
Interviewed: 259 / 296
Matriculated: 40 / 60

FIRST YEAR STATISTICS

Average GPA

Science	N/A	Nonscience	3.32

Average MCAT

Biology	9	Physical Science	9
Verbal	9	Essay	N/A

FINANCIAL FACTS

Tuition and Fees

In-state	$14,319	On-campus housing	N/A
Out-of-state	$23,819	Off-campus housing	N/A

Financial Aid

% receiving some aid	90
Merit scholarships	yes
Average debt	$65,000

HITS AND MISSES

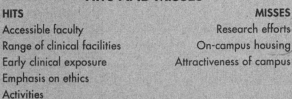

HITS	MISSES
Accessible faculty	Research efforts
Range of clinical facilities	On-campus housing
Early clinical exposure	Attractiveness of campus
Emphasis on ethics	
Activities	

TUITION OVERVIEW

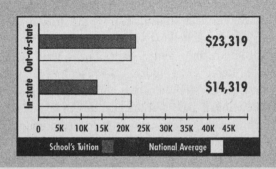

Out-of-state: $23,319
In-state: $14,319

School's Tuition / National Average

Virginia Commonwealth University, Medical College of Virginia

Medical School Admissions,
MCV Station, Box 565, Richmond, VA 23298-0565
(804) 786-9629

OVERVIEW

Among the strengths of MCV's medical program, the Admissions Office says, "are a basic science curriculum which provides students with a strong foundation in the sciences and their clinical application" and "a clinical experience that is among the most varied in the nation." The students are happy with these features, as well as with the people who teach.

ACADEMICS

Although MCV offers the traditional two-year split of basic science and clinical preparation, the school makes considerable effort to correlate the two aspects of training. For the majority of the preclinical period, MCV uses an interdisciplinary approach to teach the basic sciences. A committee made up of faculty members from different departments plans and implements elements of the curriculum, and a faculty member coordinates each course. Students like the set-up. One explains, "Our coordinators make sure the classes run smoothly and act as our advocates in certain class matters." Students, too, play an active role in evaluating and improving the curriculum. Says one: "We have student representatives who relay class comments to our course directors. We also have a challenge system on all exams in case of mistakes in questions or poorly written questions."

The enthusiasm students feel for the structure of the curriculum also extends to the quality of teaching and accessibility of the faculty, both of which are rated as superior. Reports one student, "The faculty is outstanding; they are excellent teachers and caring people."

The clinical aspect of the curriculum begins in the first year, when students are assigned to a primary care physician's office for a week. This experience and the emphasis on clinical correlations of basic science courses are behind the rave reviews students give early clinical exposure. Comments one, "Clinical medicine doesn't get any better than here at MCV; we will see *everything* before we are graduated." Despite the overall feeling of satisfaction, however, according to some students, there is "perhaps an over-bias toward primary care." An unusual feature of MCV's curriculum is the requirement that students complete a research project at some time during the four years; research can be conducted in either a basic science or a clinical field.

In contrast to the praise they give MCV's varied clinical outlets, students have few good things to say about the school's basic science and library facilities. A common complaint is a lack of study space, especially in the library. Improvement may be in sight, though. One second year student reports, "Although the facilities are lacking today, a great deal of new building is in the works. In five to ten years MCV will be ahead of the game." Unfortunately, it will be too late for current classes.

Grading and Promotion Policy: Honors/High Pass/Pass/Marginal/Fail. USMLE Parts I and II are required for graduation.

Additional Degree Programs: MD/Ph.D.; MD/MPH.

Student Life

The admissions office writes, MCV's "many non-traditional students...add diversity and maturity to the class. Competition among students is de-emphasized and most students feel they function in a cooperative, caring, and non-competitive manner with classmates." The administration seems to have its finger on the pulse of the student body, because our survey found that students agree with this statement. Elaborates one second year: "The students work together—it's not a cutthroat place, which is a major reason why I chose to come here. Of course, we have our share of study geeks—but on the whole, our class is very social and involved in many outside activities." One older student expressed some reservations, however, complaining: "Because of demographics, the activities are designed for young, unattached students. Students who are older, married, or who have kids are sorely neglected."

Students are also ambivalent about Richmond. While many appreciate the amenities of the state capital and applaud the low cost of living, most express reservations about the safety of the town and the campus. Students also had harsh words about the dorms. Objects one, "On-campus housing is poorly represented in brochures." Students are enthusiastic, however, about the affordability and quality of off-campus offerings.

Admissions

MCV gives preference to Virginia residents, but between 20 and 25 percent of the student body can come from out of state. Any qualified candidate is invited to apply, but to be competitive, non residents should have GPAs and MCAT scores at or above the school average. In addition to offering the regular admissions program, the School of Medicine has guaranteed admissions programs with both Virginia Commonwealth University and George Mason University.

The MCV Admissions Office reports that the science and nonscience GPAs, MCAT scores, and the interview are the most important selection factors. Also considered, in descending order of importance, are essays, exposure to the medical profession, letters of recommendation, extracurricular activities, and volunteer activities.

Special Programs for Members of Underrepresented Minorities: MCV's Heath Care Opportunities Program (HCOP) coordinates recruitment of minority students. Among HCOP's offerings are summer outreach programs for high school and college students and a prematriculation summer session. Academic advising, tutoring, and peer counseling are also available. Minority students receive some special consideration for admission.

Transfer Policy: Transfers into the third year are considered if the applicant is transferring from an accredited U.S. medical school.

FINANCIAL AID

Approximately 60 percent of students receive some financial assistance. In addition to need-based loans and grants, MCV offers some merit scholarships. A limited number of Commonwealth of Virginia Medical Scholarships are also available. Recipients of these scholarships agree to practice family medicine in an underserved area of Virginia. Students provide one year of service for every year of support. The current amount is $10,000/year.

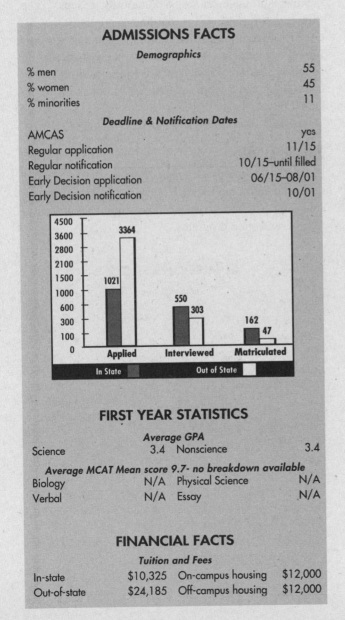

ADMISSIONS FACTS

Demographics

% men	55
% women	45
% minorities	11

Deadline & Notification Dates

AMCAS	yes
Regular application	11/15
Regular notification	10/15–until filled
Early Decision application	06/15–08/01
Early Decision notification	10/01

In State / Out of State

Applied: 1021 / 3364
Interviewed: 550 / 303
Matriculated: 162 / 47

FIRST YEAR STATISTICS

Average GPA

Science	3.4	Nonscience	3.4

Average MCAT Mean score 9.7- no breakdown available

Biology	N/A	Physical Science	N/A
Verbal	N/A	Essay	N/A

FINANCIAL FACTS

Tuition and Fees

In-state	$10,325	On-campus housing	$12,000
Out-of-state	$24,185	Off-campus housing	$12,000

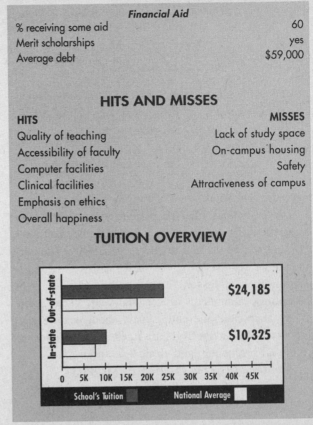

Financial Aid

% receiving some aid	60
Merit scholarships	yes
Average debt	$59,000

HITS AND MISSES

HITS	MISSES
Quality of teaching	Lack of study space
Accessibility of faculty	On-campus housing
Computer facilities	Safety
Clinical facilities	Attractiveness of campus
Emphasis on ethics	
Overall happiness	

TUITION OVERVIEW

$24,185

$10,325

0 5K 10K 15K 20K 25K 30K 35K 40K 45K

School's Tuition / National Average

University of Virginia School of Medicine

Medical School Admissions Office, Box 235, Charlottesville, VA 22908
(804) 924-5571

OVERVIEW

UVA has a lot going for it. Students say the quality of teaching is great, the facilities are first-rate, and Charlottesville is a beautiful setting in which to spend four years. However, they wish they had more clinical experience during the first two years.

ACADEMICS

The med school Dean writes, "At the University of Virginia, we believe that art and science should be blended in medicine." UVA's curriculum makes a serious effort to accomplish this goal. Although the main aim of the first two years is to "confer scientific knowledge", students also explore behavioral science and ethical aspects of medicine and have hands-on experiences with patients. In the Introduction to Clinical Medicine course in the second year, small groups of students use case studies to apply basic scientific principles to clinical problems.

A one-month community medicine preceptorship in the spring semester of the second year facilitates the transition to the clinical clerkships. In addition to completing rotations in the major disciplines, juniors are required to participate in seminars and lectures that integrate the basic sciences with what they're seeing in the hospitals. The fourth year is entirely elective.

UVA students like the patient contact they have during the basic science period, but wish they had more exposure before the end of the second year. They are much more enthusiastic about their faculty, though, applauding their professors' efforts both in and out of the classrooms. Comments one second-year, "The faculty is very accessible and enthusiastic about dealing with students." Research efforts are rated as outstanding, as are the lab, computer, and clinical facilities.

Additional Degree Programs: MD/Ph.D.

Grading policy: A–F. Students must take Parts I and II of the USMLE.

STUDENT LIFE

Although some respondents view their fellow students as competitive, most describe them as friendly and helpful people who are involved in life outside medicine. A few students complain that Charlottesville lacks big-city amenities.

On-campus housing for both single and married students is available and, according to students, satisfactory, but most of those we surveyed prefer to make their own living arrangements. The school housing office provides information about both university and off-campus housing.

ADMISSIONS

UVA gives preference to residents of Virginia, but as many as 35 percent of students can come from out of state. Candidates should apply as early as possible, preferably with the April MCAT scores in hand. Because the school operates on a rolling admissions basis, those who file applications late in the season have little chance of being admitted.

Although UVA's Admissions Office declined to rank the importance of selection factors, they offered

this statement, "The University of Virginia is interested in applicants who are not only highly qualified academically, but who also provide evidence of their eagerness to serve others. We expect successful applicants to be extensively involved in their communities in some altruistic fashion, and to have had significant exposure to the health care field. Strong GPAs and MCAT scores alone are not enough to gain admission."

Transfer Policy: UVA considers transfers into the third year on a space-available basis. Preference is given to Virginia residents.

Special Programs for Members of Underrepresented Minorities: UVA is committed to recruiting members of underrepresented minority groups. The Minority Affairs division coordinates programs that include community outreach programs, summer sessions for college students, MCAT review, a prematriculation summer session, academic advising, tutoring, peer counseling, and review sessions for Parts I and II of the USMLE.

eMail: BAB76@VIRGINIA.EDU

FINANCIAL AID

Financial aid awards are generally made on the basis of need as determined by the College Scholarship Service analysis. Assistance is available through university, federal, and state programs.

ADMISSIONS FACTS

Demographics

% men	57
% women	43
% minorities	23

Deadline & Notification Dates

AMCAS	yes
Regular application	11/01
Regular notification	10/15–until filled
Early Decision application	06/15–08/01
Early Decision notification	10/01

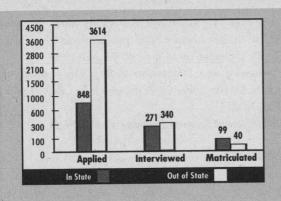

FIRST YEAR STATISTICS

Average GPA

Science	N/A	Nonscience	3.56

Average MCAT: Mean score in the 85th percentile— no breakdown available

Biology	N/A	Physical Science	N/A
Verbal	N/A	Essay	N/A

FINANCIAL FACTS

Tuition and Fees

In-state	$9,006	On-campus housing	$9,910
Out-of-state	$20,174	Off-campus housing	$9,910

Financial Aid

% receiving some aid	80
Merit scholarships	yes
Average debt	$38,000

HITS AND MISSES

HITS	MISSES
Clinical facilities	Competitive facilities
Computer labs	Early patient contact
Research efforts	Unnecessary reading assignments
Charlottesville	
Faculty accessibility	

TUITION OVERVIEW

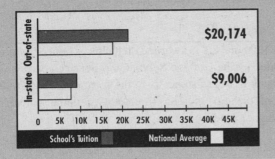

University of Washington School of Medicine

Admissions Office, SM-22 Health Sciences, T-545, Seattle, WA 98195
(206) 543-7212

OVERVIEW

The University of Washington enjoys a reputation as a leader among U.S. med schools. Among its strengths are its rural medicine, ethics, community care, substance abuse, and preventative medicine programs and its record in biomedical investigation. Unfortunately for non-Washingtonians, the school accepts few out-of-state applicants, making admittance to this excellent institution a long shot for all but the most highly qualified candidates.

ACADEMICS

Although most Washington students spend all four years at the Seattle campus, nonresidents admitted through the WAMI program (which gives special consideration to residents of Alaska, Montana, and Idaho) are "expected to spend the first year at the university site in their home state." In addition, about twenty students complete their freshman year at Washington State University in Pullman. Regardless of the location of their first year, however, Washington students can expect a progressive, integrative approach to medical education.

The first two years of Washington's curriculum focus on the basic sciences and their clinical relevance. This period includes three basic phases: the pre-organ system courses, which are predominately departmental; multidisciplinary organ system courses; and an introduction to clinical medicine and health care delivery systems. In addition to the required coursework in the basic, clinical, and behavioral sciences, students have considerable time to pursue their individual interests through electives.

After completing the basic science years, students embark on a series of clinical experiences. Again, the curriculum is divided into three categories: prescribed clerkships in the major disciplines; clinical selectives, which must be taken in family medicine, rehabilitation medicine/chronic care, and emergency care/trauma; and electives. Clinical teaching takes place at the university hospital and other sites in Seattle and the Pacific North-

west region. All Washington students must also complete an independent study project that gives them in-depth exposure to an area of their choice.

Grading and Promotion Policy: Honors/Satisfactory/Not Satisfactory. Students must pass Parts I and II of the USMLE.

Additional Degree Programs: MD/Ph.D.

ADMISSIONS

Strong preference in admission is given to residents of Washington, Alaska, Montana, and Idaho (WAMI). Qualified underrepresented minority applicants who are not residents of these states are also given consideration. Since fewer than one percent of candidates who do not fit into one of these categories were accepted into the entering class of 1992, such candidates should carefully consider the quality of their credentials before taking the time to apply.

According to the Admissions Office, "Candidates... are considered comparatively on the basis of academic performance, motivation, maturity, personal integrity, and demonstrated humanitarian qualities. A knowledge of, and exposure to, the needs of individuals and society and an awareness of health care delivery systems are desired." Except in extremely rare cases, candidates must take the new-format MCAT to be considered for admission.

Special Programs for Members of Underrepresented Minorities: Washington has an active minority affairs program that coordinates recruiting and support services for underrepresented minority students. Among its offerings are summer programs for undergrads, a prematriculation summer session for enrolled students, academic advising, tutoring, and counseling.

Transfer Policy: Although students may contact the Admissions Office to discuss their reasons for wanting to transfer, they should be aware that Washington very rarely accepts transfer students.

FINANCIAL AID

All financial aid is awarded on the basis of need as determined by the College Scholarship Service analysis. Although most assistance is in the form of federal student loans, the university has limited institutional scholarship and loan funds available.

ADMISSIONS FACTS

Demographics

% men	54
% women	46
% minorities	10

Deadline & Notification Dates

AMCAS	yes
Regular application	11/01
Regular notification	11/01—05/05
Early Decision application	No EDP program
Early Decision notification	N/A

Chart values:
- Applied: In State 846, Out of State 2524
- Interviewed: In State 525, Out of State 94
- Matriculated: In State 150, Out of State 15

In State / Out of State

FIRST YEAR STATISTICS

Average GPA

Science	N/A	Nonscience	3.58

Average MCAT

Biology	10.3	Physical Science	10.0
Verbal	9.9	Essay	N/A

FINANCIAL FACTS

Tuition and Fees

In-state	$7,458	On-campus housing	N/A
Out-of-state	$18,933	Off-campus housing	N/A

Financial Aid

% receiving some aid	N/A
Merit scholarships	N/A
Average debt	N/A

TUITION OVERVIEW

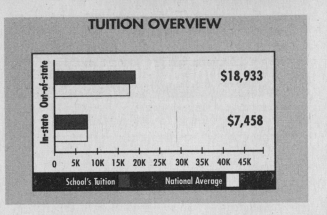

Out-of-state $18,933
In-state $7,458

School's Tuition   National Average

Marshall University School of Medicine

Office of Admissions, 1542 Spring Valley Drive, Huntington, WV 25755
(304) 696-7312 or (800) 544-8514

OVERVIEW

"A sense of commitment to the state, the community, and the student." "Tremendous clinical experience." "A warm, supportive, and intimate setting." "A dedicated faculty devoted to teaching." These are the things Marshall students say make them happy with their choice of this small, West Virginia school. Another part of this feeling of well-being stems from the school's serious commitment to its stated goals. Fully accredited in the late 1970s, Marshall University School of Medicine is primarily concerned with serving the health care needs of West Virginia residents, particularly those who live in medically-underserved regions of the state. In accordance with its mission, Marshall's approach to medical education is clinically-oriented and the school produces an unusually high number of primary care physicians—generally about two-thirds of each year's graduating class.

ACADEMICS

Marshall's curriculum is divided into traditional preclinical and clinical units, but the patient-centered philosophy of the school ensures that students have contact with patients from the first semester.

During the freshman year, students focus much of their attention on acquiring the scientific knowledge that is the basis for medicine. In addition to the traditional study of the basic sciences, though, students investigate psychosocial aspects of medicine and begin to develop patient-interaction skills.

The combined emphasis on basic, behavioral, and clinical sciences continues in the second year as students explore the disease process, its physical manifestations, and therapeutic measures to control illness. Courses in community medicine and physical diagnosis augment science courses and a year-long Introduction to Clinical Medicine provides a transition to the clinical years.

Third-year students have the option to participate in the standard curriculum or to choose an alternative track, the Rural Physicians Associate Program (RPAP).

In the standard curriculum, juniors complete clerkships in the major disciplines and in family practice. RPAP gives students interested in primary care the chance to work alongside a physician practicing in a small community.

Although seniors must complete four-week rotations in surgery, medicine, and emergency medicine, the balance of the final year is free for electives. Clinical training sites are varied: a Veterans' Administration Medical Center, rural clinics, community hospitals, and private physicians' offices are among the primary settings.

Students say their relationship with professors is outstanding. Some attribute this rapport to the intimate atmosphere. Says one fourth-year, "Small classes give students the opportunity for one-to-one interaction with teaching faculty. Others credit the staff's "phenomenal accessibility" and teachers' "eagerness to share their knowledge, experience, and philosophy."

The opportunity afforded students to have meaningful contact with patients during the preclinical period is also a major strength at Marshall; students give early clinical exposure top marks. "Successful programs introduce students to clinical situations in the first year, " says one student. "These experiences keep you motivated and focused on the objective of medical school." Ethical considerations in medicine are also emphasized, contributing, students say, to the general patient-centered philosophy of the med school.

Students are generally satisfied with Marshall's academic facilities, though most say the library and some classrooms could be improved. Clinical teaching sites are rated as outstanding.

Grading and Promotion Policy: A letter-grading system is used. Students are required to take Parts I and II of the USMLE.

Additional Degree Programs: MS/MD.

STUDENT LIFE

Despite Marshall's letter-grading system, students report that competition is low. Our respondents give much of the credit for this cooperative environment to the school's size: "Class size adds to a certain feeling of family," says one representative student. Another adds, "The family-type atmosphere at Marshall contrasts with the 'I don't care' attitudes of other schools."

Students report that social and extracurricular activity is moderate. Two reasons for this, according to several respondents, are the med school's distance from the undergraduate campus and the heavy workload. One student explains: "The medical education building is located about fifteen minutes from the main campus and downtown Huntington, so it's a bit out-of-the-way. I'm sure there are plenty of campus activities going on, but we don't have access to such things. We never leave this building!" For those students who can make the time and effort to get away from their studies, Marshall offers a number of cultural, recreational, and social programs and events. The town of Huntington and the nearby cities of Pittsburgh and Cincinnati support a diversity of activities.

Although Huntington isn't a booming metropolis, most students are satisfied with Marshall's location and find that housing offerings near the med school are good. Public transportation is reported to be both accessible and safe.

ADMISSIONS

Since it is a state-supported school, Marshall gives strong preference to West Virginia residents. However, a limited number of positions in each year's class are reserved for residents of states that border West Virginia and for candidates with strong ties to the state. Other candidates currently have little chance for admissions and should carefully consider their qualifications before taking the time to apply. Only state residents may participate in the Early Decision Program.

According to Marshall's literature, admissions decisions are based primarily on the evaluation of the academic record, MCAT scores, the interview, and letters of recommendation. Personal qualities, including judgment, responsibility, altruism, integrity, and sensitivity are also considered important.

Special Programs for Members of Underrepresented Minorities: Although students criticize Marshall for its current lack of ethnic and cultural diversity, the school is interested in attracting a student body more representative of the population. The Admissions Office encourages members of underrepresented minorities to apply.

Transfer Policy: Applications for transfer into the third year are considered on a space-available basis if the student meets the residency requirements for regular admission.

FINANCIAL AID

Financial aid is awarded primarily on the basis of need. Most assistance is in the form of long-term federal loans.

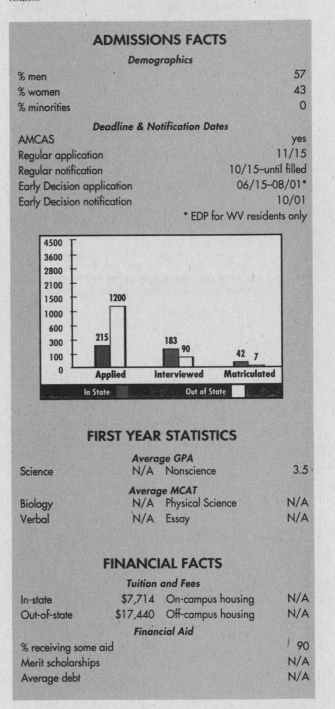

ADMISSIONS FACTS

Demographics

% men	57
% women	43
% minorities	0

Deadline & Notification Dates

AMCAS	yes
Regular application	11/15
Regular notification	10/15–until filled
Early Decision application	06/15–08/01*
Early Decision notification	10/01

* EDP for WV residents only

Chart (In State / Out of State):
- Applied: 215 / 1200
- Interviewed: 183 / 90
- Matriculated: 42 / 7

FIRST YEAR STATISTICS

Average GPA

Science	N/A	Nonscience	3.5

Average MCAT

Biology	N/A	Physical Science	N/A
Verbal	N/A	Essay	N/A

FINANCIAL FACTS

Tuition and Fees

In-state	$7,714	On-campus housing	N/A
Out-of-state	$17,440	Off-campus housing	N/A

Financial Aid

% receiving some aid	90
Merit scholarships	N/A
Average debt	N/A

HITS AND MISSES

HITS	MISSES
Faculty accessibility	Few extracurricular activities
Early clinical exposure	Library
Emphasis on ethics	Diversity
Overall happiness	Research emphasis
Cooperative atmosphere	Racial diversity
Clinical facilities	Classrooms
Classmates	On-campus housing
Campus safety	

TUITION OVERVIEW

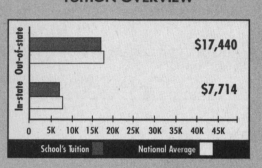

$17,440

$7,714

| 0 5K 10K 15K 20K 25K 30K 35K 40K 45K |

School's Tuition ▨ National Average ☐

West Virginia University School of Medicine

Office of Admissions and Records
Health Sciences Center, P.O. Box 9815, Morgantown, WV 26506
(304) 293-3521

OVERVIEW

Okay, West Virginia University School of Medicine isn't a research giant, but it more than makes up for this in other areas. Without exception, students have great things to say about the accessibility and caring of their faculty. According to WVU, "In the basic sciences, there is one faculty member for every two students. At the clinical level, there are two faculty for every student." Students appreciate the extra attention this ratio affords. They're so happy with the curriculum and each other, it's amazing they found time to refer to anything else.

ACADEMICS

WVU has a relatively traditional curriculum, with the first two years devoted to basic sciences and the last two spent doing clinical rotations. But a recently instituted change in the curriculum requires all medical students to spend a portion of their clinical period learning primary care in one of several rural facilities. Programs like this lead students to laud their school for the emphasis that it puts on the "art" of being a doctor. Explains one, "WVU is known for putting out physicians with excellent clinical skills and quite a bit more hands-on experience than many other schools in the East." Some add, however, that this clinical emphasis has its price—students are only mildly enthusiastic about the school's research efforts. Says one third-year student, "Overall, this school gives excellent exposure to clinical medicine with less exposure to academics and research."

The faculty? According to one student, "The teachers are so caring that they can give you inspiration to go on and on, even when it is cold, ugly, and you haven't slept in awhile." Another adds, "This survey does not adequately reflect the quality of teaching at this school, the concern afforded the student, and the sincerity to produce excellent doctors. I am very impressed with the education."

Students are also impressed by the clinical facilities. Boasts one, "[WVU has] a small town atmosphere with big city facilities. We take pride in this." Reviews of the science teaching facilities are not as glowing, however. Classrooms, labs, and the library all received relatively low marks.

Grading and Promotion Policy: Honors/Pass/Fail. USMLE Parts I and II are required.

Additional Degree Programs: For students who are interested in research and academic medicine, WVU offers a combined MD/Ph.D. program.

STUDENT LIFE

WVU students have good things to say about each other. Says one, "I think it's important that this school has students that are well-rounded, socially aware, very motivated, bright, and caring." Students report that their classmates are committed to helping each other, which, according to one student, makes med school a little more pleasant. "WVU has a very uncompetitive atmosphere—takes off a lot of stress." In fact, several students comment that they selected WVU, in part, because of the student body. Says one, "I chose to attend this school because I was very impressed in the friendliness and confidence of the medical students here. They didn't look as harassed or beaten down as they did at most of the other schools I interviewed at."

It's a good thing student relations are so good, because students dislike WVU's location and are displeased with its lack of amenities. Explains one student, "Morgantown is a depressing town lacking theater, coffee shops, and the social awareness one would find in bigger cities. It has a harsh winter and if it weren't for the excellent education I receive here, I'd be gone in a flash." Students also criticize the quality of an-and off-campus housing.

ADMISSIONS

Admissions writes, "Top priority is given to qualified West Virginia residents; second priority is given to applicants who have a combination of close ties to West Virginia and highly competitive credentials." Up to 15 percent of students can come from out of state. Out-of-state students with good qualifications who are members of underrepresented minorities are also encouraged to apply. Only state residents may apply through the Early Decision Program.

The Admissions Office ranks the science GPA, the nonscience GPA, and the interview as the most important selection factors. Other considerations, in descending order of importance, are extracurricular activities, MCAT scores (from the new format test), letters of recommendation, essays, exposure to the medical profession, and volunteer activities. Over one-fourth of the Admissions Committee is comprised of third- and fourth-year medical students with full privileges and responsibilities.

Special Programs for Members of Underrepresented Minorities: Students gave WVU low marks for diversity. According to the Admissions Office, only 3 percent of the first-year class is African-American, and it keeps track of statistics for no other minority group. The school is working to increase representation, however. Among the special programs used to recruit, enroll, and retain underrepresented minority students are academic advising, tutoring, an MCAT review, peer counseling, special consideration for admission, summer sessions for college students, and a Health Career Opportunities Program. These programs are also open to "persons disadvantaged economically, culturally, socially (including geographically isolated)."

Transfer Policy: In evaluating transfers, WVU considers "hardship, curriculum compatibility, and academic equivalence."

FINANCIAL AID

Students have few complaints about the tuition. In fact, many are pleased with how little they pay for a quality medical education. One student's comment, "I feel that, for the money, WVU Medical School is a very good choice for any student" represents the views of many we surveyed.

ADMISSIONS FACTS

Demographics

% men	49
% women	51
% minorities	3

Deadline & Notification Dates

AMCAS	yes
Regular application	11/15
Regular notification	10/15–until filled
Early Decision application	06/15–08/01*
Early Decision notification	10/01

*EDP for WV residents only

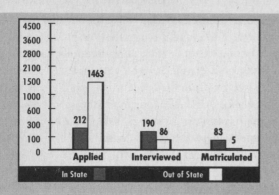

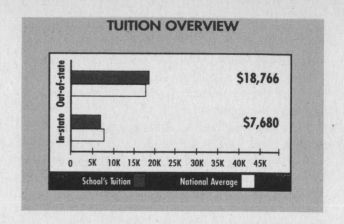

TUITION OVERVIEW

FIRST YEAR STATISTICS

Average GPA

Science	N/A	Nonscience	3.55

Average MCAT

Biology	8.8	Physical Science	8.5
Verbal	8.6	Essay	N/A

FINANCIAL FACTS

Tuition and Fees

In-state	$7,680	On-campus housing	N/A
Out-of-state	$18,766	Off-campus housing	N/A

Financial Aid

% receiving some aid	N/A
Merit scholarships	yes
Average debt	$46,300

HITS AND MISSES

HITS	MISSES
Caring and accessible faculty	Research emphasis
Classmates	Racial diversity
Clinical facilities	Classrooms
Campus safety	Library
Clinical exposure	Campus activities not plentiful
	On-campus housing

Medical College of Wisconsin

Office of Admissions,
8701 Watertown Plank Road, Milwaukee, WI 53226
(414) 257-8246

OVERVIEW

Solid teaching, outstanding clinical facilities, and a vital research effort combine to make Medical College of Wisconsin students confident that they're getting a quality medical education. But what makes these students among the happiest future MDs we surveyed? The school's cooperative atmosphere, large proportion of non-traditional students, and location in a vibrant, attractive college town are behind our respondents' assertion that MCW is a fine place in which to spend four years.

ACADEMICS

MCW's curriculum is divided into the traditional two-year preclinical and clinical units. In addition to the regular preclinical path, students may choose to enter an Alternate Studies Program (ASP) after the first semester. According to one fourth-year student we surveyed, this option allows students "who study better independently or want to take an extra year to complete their first two years" to determine their own course of study for the basic sciences

In the regular path, first-year students concentrate on acquiring the scientific knowledge necessary for the study of medicine. In addition to completing basic science courses, students begin a Clinical Medicine and Practice course that extends into the second year.

The main course in the sophomore year is Pathophysiology of Disease, an interdisciplinary course that is organized around organ systems. The second-year portion of Clinical Medicine and Practice prepares students for the last two years as students investigate clinical problems and learn physical examination and evaluation skills. At present, students aren't wild about the major division of the basic science and clinical portions of the curriculum, but they say things will improve very soon. "There is presently much effort involved in changing the basic science years so that more practical clinical information is taught and more frequent clinical exposure is gained," says one third-year. The new curriculum is scheduled to be implemented in the fall of 1994.

In the third and fourth years, students complete a variety of required clerkships. Among the requirements in the senior year is an eight-week preceptorship with a practicing physician. About 16 weeks of the fourth year are free for electives.

The quality of teaching at MCW gets generally good marks. "Professors take teaching seriously and are sincerely interested in the students," says one appreciative second-year. Members of the faculty also get high marks for their investigative activities, and our respondents say there are plenty of opportunities for students to get involved in research efforts.

Students at MCW tell us support outside the classroom and lab is available and accessible. Study skills workshops and stress reduction classes are provided for those having difficulties coping with the demands of med school.

Grading and Promotion Policy: Letter and numerical grades are used. Students must take Parts I and II of the USMLE.

Additional Degree Programs: A Medical Scholars Program, sponsored by the undergraduate and med school divisions, results in a combined baccalaureate/MD. Other combined programs are MD/Ph.D. and MS/Ph.D.

STUDENT LIFE

"The appeal of MCW is the relaxed atmosphere of the medical school," says one student we surveyed. His classmates agree. Although some say that students are competitive, they hasten to point out that they aren't at all cutthroat. A representative second-year explains, "Unlike other schools where one may compete against fellow students, here one competes against the material. The student body here is very cooperative and always willing to help each other out." But this spirit of cooperation isn't the only remarkable thing about MCW's student body. According to those we surveyed, there is also widespread appreciation for the "variety of life experiences the average student has." This is not a school dominated by recent college grads; older students, many of whom are involved in the Alternate Studies Program, make up a considerable portion of each year's class. Diversity may have its price, however. Although students say that MCW has a variety of clubs and activities in which to become involved, most of our respondents say they're not particularly active in extracurricular pursuits and don't spend a lot of time hanging out with their classmates.

Despite their ambivalence about their social lives, students are nearly unanimous in giving their city the highest possible ratings for both livability and safety. The capital of Wisconsin and a booming college town, Madison is immensely popular with students. Cultural, recreational, educational, and social opportunities are available both on- and off-campus, and a wider array of diversions is available in nearby Milwaukee and Chicago. Housing is varied and relatively reasonable, and safe, accessible public transportation makes it easy to get around.

ADMISSIONS

MCW gives preference to residents of Wisconsin, but some out-of-state applicants are accepted each year. Nonresidents are encouraged to apply if they have outstanding academic qualifications and/or are interested in the MD/Ph.D. program. Candidates may apply through the regular admissions process or through Early Decision. Since the Admissions Committee does not fill the entire class until the final application deadline, students applying through the regular admissions process gain no significant advantage by submitting their applications early.

When the Admissions Committee receives the AMCAS application, a supplemental application is mailed to the candidate. Once an individual's application is complete, the Committee gives the candidate an initial rating, which is determined by a numerical formula based on science GPA, nonscience GPA, and MCAT scores. The application is then evaluated by a committee and given an adjusted rating. Based on this number, promising candidates are invited to interview, after which students are accepted, placed on a wait list, or rejected. In addition to evaluating the interview, the academic record, and MCAT scores, the Admissions Committee considers letters of recommendation, essays, extracurricular activities, and work experience.

Special Programs for Members of Underrepresented Minorities: MCW is committed to increasing the number of underrepresented minority physicians. Minority students from in and out of state are encouraged to apply.

Transfer Policy: Applications from Wisconsin residents are considered for transfer into the second and third years.

FINANCIAL AID

All financial aid is awarded on the basis of documented need. Because grant funds are limited, most assistance is in the form of long-term loans.

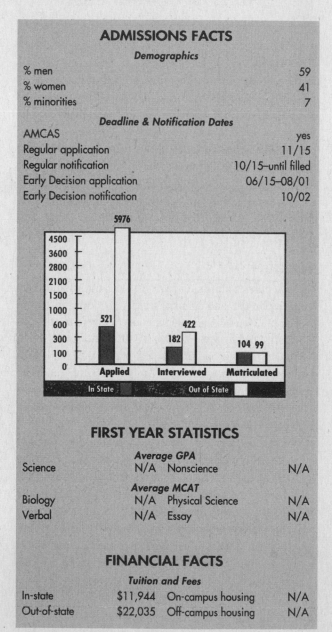

ADMISSIONS FACTS

Demographics

% men	59
% women	41
% minorities	7

Deadline & Notification Dates

AMCAS	yes
Regular application	11/15
Regular notification	10/15–until filled
Early Decision application	06/15–08/01
Early Decision notification	10/02

FIRST YEAR STATISTICS

Average GPA

Science	N/A	Nonscience	N/A

Average MCAT

Biology	N/A	Physical Science	N/A
Verbal	N/A	Essay	N/A

FINANCIAL FACTS

Tuition and Fees

In-state	$11,944	On-campus housing	N/A
Out-of-state	$22,035	Off-campus housing	N/A

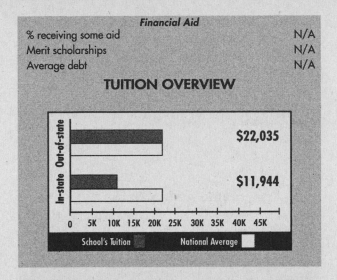

Financial Aid

% receiving some aid	N/A
Merit scholarships	N/A
Average debt	N/A

TUITION OVERVIEW

Out-of-state: $22,035
In-state: $11,944

0 5K 10K 15K 20K 25K 30K 35K 40K 45K

School's Tuition   National Average

University of Wisconsin Medical School

Admissions Committee, Medical Sciences Center, Room 1205
1300 University Avenue, Madison, WI 53706
(608) 263-4925

OVERVIEW

The Medical School is a part of the University of Wisconsin Center for Health Sciences. This means you have access to large undergraduate facilities at the Madison campus. Most clinical teaching is done in the six University of Wisconsin hospitals, but the school has a number of other affiliated sites throughout the state.

ACADEMICS

UWMS's curriculum is divided into the traditional two-year preclinical and clinical units. In addition to the regular preclinical path, students may choose to enter an Alternate Studies Program (ASP) after the first semester. This option allows students to determine their own courses of study for the basic sciences.

In the regular path, first-year students concentrate on acquiring the scientific knowledge necessary for the study of medicine. In addition to basic science courses, students begin a Clinical Medicine and Practice course that extends into the second year.

The main course in the sophomore year is Pathophysiology of Disease, an interdisciplinary course that is organized around organ systems. In the second-year por-

tion of Clinical Medicine and Practice, which prepares students for the last two years, students investigate clinical problems and learn physical examination and evaluation skills.

In the third and fourth years, students complete a variety of required clerkships. Among the requirements in the senior year is an eight-week preceptorship with a practicing physician. About sixteen weeks of the fourth year are free for electives.

Grading and Promotion Policy: Letter and numerical grades are used. Students must take Parts I and II of the USMLE.

Additional Degree Programs: A Medical Scholars Program, sponsored by the undergraduate and med school divisions, results in a combined baccalaureate/MD. Other combined programs are MD/Ph.D. and MS/Ph.D.

STUDENT LIFE

Because the med school is located on the University of Wisconsin campus in Madison, students have access to the facilities of the large undergraduate school. On-campus housing is available, but most students prefer to live off campus. "Madison is a medium-sized city organized around three lakes, which provide many opportunities for outdoor recreation. But be warned: the winters are long and very cold!

ADMISSIONS

UW gives preference to residents of Wisconsin, but some out-of-state applicants are accepted each year. Nonresident students are encouraged to apply if they have outstanding academic qualifications and/or are interested in the MD/Ph.D. program. Students may apply through the regular admissions process or through Early Decision. Since the Admissions Committee does not fill the entire class until the final application deadline, students applying through the regular admissions process gain no significant advantage by submitting their applications early.

When the Admissions Committee receives the AMCAS application, a supplemental application is mailed to the candidate. Once an individual's application is complete, the committee gives the candidate an initial rating, which is determined by a numerical formula based on science GPA, nonscience GPA, and MCAT scores. The application is then evaluated by a committee and given an adjusted rating. Based on this number, promising candidates are invited to interview, after which students are accepted, placed on a wait list, or rejected. In addition to the interview, the academic record, and MCAT scores, the Admissions Committee considers letters of recommendation, essays, extracurricular activities, and work experience.

Special Programs for Members of Underrepresented Minorities: UW is committed to increasing the number of underrepresented minority physicians. Minority students from in and out of state are encouraged to apply.

Transfer Policy: Applications from Wisconsin residents are considered for transfer into the second and third years.

FINANCIAL AID

All financial aid is awarded on the basis of documented need. Because grant funds are limited, most assistance is in the form of long-term loans.

ADMISSIONS FACTS

Demographics

% men	59
% women	41
% minorities	14

Deadline & Notification Dates

AMCAS	yes
Regular application	11/01
Regular notification	11/15–varies
Early Decision application	06/15–08/01*
Early Decision notification	10/01
	*EDP for WI residents only

FIRST YEAR STATISTICS

Average GPA

Science	N/A	Nonscience	N/A

Average MCAT

Biology	N/A	Physical Science	N/A
Verbal	N/A	Essay	N/A

FINANCIAL FACTS

Tuition and Fees

In-state	$12,138	On-campus housing	N/A
Out-of-state	$17,581	Off-campus housing	N/A

Financial Aid

% receiving some aid	N/A
Merit scholarships	N/A
Average debt	N/A

HITS AND MISSES

HITS	MISSES
Overall happiness	Classrooms
Research effort	Computer facilities
Clinical facilities	
Madison	
Campus safety	
Accessible and safe public transportation	

TUITION OVERVIEW

Med School Admission Goes Electronic

Medical school admission is finally moving onto the "information superhighway." Here are a couple of ways to use your computer to best effect.

Looking For Med Schools On-line

First off, *we've* put up a lot of information about medical schools and med school admissions through our on-line services on the Internet, America Online, eWorld, and the Microsoft Network.

The Internet is the most interesting of all on-line information services, because the med schools themselves have posted information there. You can connect to the Net through an *Internet service provider* or through America Online, CompuServe, or Prodigy (if you've never played with the Internet, you'll find these last three companies the easiest way). Once you're on the Internet, you can reach the schools directly.

Note that the Internet changes every day—content is added or deleted, and sites change their look and feel regularly. Addresses (known as URLs) change; some sites disappear completely. All of the URLs that we have provided here were accurate and functioning at the time of publication, but the best way to find schools is through our own World Wide Web (also known as the Web, this is the graphical interface to the Internet) page. (For those without a speedy PC, we have a text-only gopher server, too.) We've set up a search engine, and posted some of the information in this book, so you can access virtually every med school Internet site by just clicking. We've also posted useful (we hope) career and internship advice, info about all of our books and software, an extensive phone list of useful numbers, and hotlinks to our favorite educational sites on the Internet.

Our boards on America Online and eWorld offer more information, and a very different look and feel. One of the most popular features of these boards is our Student Message areas, where you can create your own topic folders and post questions for other students and for our own on-line admissions and testing experts. We also schedule live on-line forums where you can get answers in real time to your questions about admission, testing, and just about anything else to do with med school direct from our experts and special guests. By the time you read this, we will have launched our newest on-line board on the Microsoft Network, set to debut with the release of Windows 95.

To reach The Princeton Review at any of these sites, or to eMail us, use the following addresses:

- *eMail*: info@review.com
- *World Wide Web*: http://www.review.com
- *America Online*: keyword "student"
- *eWorld*: shortcut "test prep"
- *Gopher*: bloggs.review.com
- *Microsoft Network*: eMail us for the address

Applying To Med School Via Electronic Application

Once you've gathered all the information that you need about the schools and have decided where to apply, you may not need to leave your computer keyboard. Just a handful of years ago electronic applications were *never* going to happen. Today, med schools are scrambling to make electronic versions of their applications available.

We included Windows software with this book (you'll need Windows *3.x* and 4 meg of memory) that's a good first step. It should help you to create a tight, clean application with a lot less work. Med App allows you to enter all the information for the AMCAS application (which is used by almost every med school included in this book), and then print out the information onto the application form itself. For obvious reasons, you'll need the AMCAS application (202/828-0600) to use this software.

To run Med App, simply insert the enclosed disk into the floppy drive and select **File** from the menu bar. Then select **Run** and type **A:\medapp**. (You can also copy Med App onto your hard drive. To do this, use the file manager to set up a new directory on your hard drive, and copy everything on the A: drive to it.) You can then create an icon in Windows by selecting **File** from the menu bar and selecting **New**.

Using Med App

In order to use the Med App, there are a few things that you'll need to know.

General

- You'll find an example of a completed Med App on the diskette, with the filename *Example.Med*
- Always print each sheet on plain 8.5 x 11 paper first to check spacing and alignment.
- **Do not** use parentheses in the **Telephone Number** field; parentheses are already on the form.

Personal Comments

- The best way to enter the Personal Comments is to copy and paste (**ctrl+c**, **ctrl+v**) them from within your own word processor.
- The Personal Comments section of the Med App program will not wrap around because the AMCAS, pre-printed form is 92 characters wide (i.e. wider than the standard word processor). Without line breaks, your text will type as one long line. You must press the **Enter/Return** key after 92 characters on a line. When using your word processor, save the file as **Text with Line Breaks** before copying and pasting. This will bring the file into the personal comments section correctly. You must then widen the text to the 92 character width.

- Your Med App information will be stored in two files, the .med file and the .ini file. When you do a **Save As**, you save to the .med file. When you are asked if you want to save the current information after you select **Exit**, you should answer **Yes**. This **Yes** will save your information to the .ini file. The .ini file allows your information to be called up when you enter the program. Therefore, **always answer Yes** to the question regarding saving the current information as default. If you allow someone else to copy your disk, you should remove the .med files and the .ini file. Otherwise, the other person will have access to your information.

Academic Record

- There are 95 course entries possible.
- Course 54 (first course, page 4) must have college name and location.
- To leave a line blank between courses and/or schools, you must skip one screen and leave it blank.
- Leaving the Course Name blank will cause a blank line to be printed.
- If you select SS for term after a blank line, you must change the term of the blank line.
- Once you type a school and a location you do not have to type it again until you change schools.

Printing Options

- You can print directly onto the AMCAS form by inserting it into the 11 x 17 tray of a laser printer and using the Med App print facilities.
- You can fold the AMCAS form and print using the 8.5 x 11 print facilities in the Med App program.
- You can print your information onto plain paper and have a print shop copy your information onto your AMCAS form by copier or scanner/copier.

In order to most effectively print your application information onto your application form, you will more than likely need to use the printing adjustments. The printing adjustments are located under the Print menu selection as "Adjust Printing Parameters." These adjustments will allow you to move the text to the correct location on the form. These printing adjustments are necessary because various brands of printers have different margins by default. The program was designed to work best with a Hewlett Packard compatible printer. This should allow the text to fall very close to the correct location even before the printing adjustments are made.

If you're not using a standard printer, you can use the following steps to accurately print your information.

1. Enter all of your application information.
2. Print the application information onto plain white paper.
3. Lay one of the printed pages on the appropriate page of the application form.
4. Align the text on the printed page with the application form. (Move the printed page until your name is in the correct location and your family information is correct, etc., all the way down the page, by looking through the printed page and seeing the application form lines and boxes.)
5. Use a ruler to measure the alignment adjustments needed; just measure the distance between the top left corner of the application form and the top and left margins of the print out.
6. Enter these distances into the appropriate field on the "Adjust Printing Parameters" dialog box in fractions of an inch. (i.e. 1/4 = .25") If the edge of your printed document needs to be moved up or to the left, the number that you enter will be negative. If your printed document needs to be moved down or to the right, the number that you enter will be positive.
7. Now, print on plain white paper to verify your measurements. If your measurements were good and the alignment is now correct, you are ready to print that page of your application onto your pre-printed application form.

The best option that we have found for printing is to print on the form using the 8.5 x 11 option. This way, you can print each page individually after checking with plain paper printouts. Check with plain paper printouts by overlaying the printouts on the AMCAS form and measuring any type location differences. These differences can be used in the printer adjustments section of the program. The form should proceed through the printer folded over with no problem. Also, you might want to tape the transcript inventory to a plain page, as it is smaller than a full size page and could twist when printing.

The Med App Software supports almost all standard printers. However, if you are attempting to use a printer in 600 dpi mode, the font may be very small. Simply set the printer you are using to the 300 dpi mode and the Med App will print just fine. Most 600 dpi printers have a 300 dpi mode.

....

If you have any questions about the printing process (or anything else), please call our help line at (212) 874-8600.

Index

Index

T

U

V

W

Y

State Index

North Carolina

North Dakota

Ohio

Oklahoma

Oregon

Pennsylvania

Rhode Island

South Carolina

South Dakota

NOTES

NOTES

NOTES

NOTES

About the Author

Andrea Nagy graduated from Washington University in St. Louis and is a former director of The Princeton Review in Chicago. She currently resides in the Chicago area where she is pursuing a graduate degree in Educational Psychology.

CULTURESCOPE

The
Princeton Review
Guide to an Informed Mind

Has this ever happened to you?

You're at a party. An attractive person who you have been dying to meet comes over and says, "Man, does that woman have a Joan of Arc complex, or what?" and you, in a tone that is most suave, say "Uh," while your mind races wildly, *"Joan of Arc, OK, France, uh...damn,"* as the aforementioned attractive person smiles weakly and heads for the punch bowl.

No? How about this?

Your boss finally learns your name and says, "Ah, good to have you aboard. Do you like Renaissance painting?" You reply with an emphatic "Yes! I do!" to which she returns, "What's your favorite fresco?" You start stammering, glassy-eyed, your big moment passing you by as visions of soda pop dance through your brain.

CULTURESCOPE can help.

If you have gaps of knowledge big enough to drive a eighteen-wheeler through, The Princeton Review has the thing for you. It's called CULTURESCOPE. It's a book that can make people think you've read enough books to fill a semi, even if you haven't.

CULTURESCOPE covers everything: history, science, math, art, sports, geography, popular culture—it's all in there, and it's fun, because along with all of the great information there are quizzes, resource lists, fun statistics, wacky charts, and lots of pretty pictures.

It's coming soon to a bookstore near you.

You won't go away empty-headed.

THE
PRINCETON
REVIEW